More advance praise for *Becoming American under Fire:*

"In *Becoming American under Fire*, Christian G. Samito brings his legal and historical training effectively to bear on the complex struggles of Irish American and African American soldiers as they sought to craft and claim meaningful citizenship in the Civil War–era United States. Rich with detail, deeply researched, and carefully argued, this is an important contribution to the literature of the period."
—ELIZABETH D. LEONARD, author of *Men of Color to Arms: Black Soldiers, Indian Wars, and the Quest for Equality*

"Historians are increasingly recognizing the importance of citizenship as a concept, and Christian G. Samito wisely takes a bottom-up approach, recognizing the agency of those displaced groups agitating for inclusion. *Becoming American under Fire* is a very good book on an important and timely topic."
—CHRISTOPHER WALDREP, Jamie and Phyllis Pasker Professor of History, San Francisco State University, author of *Roots of Disorder and The Many Faces of Judge Lynch*

"*Becoming American under Fire* makes an important contribution to the history of American citizenship. Christian G. Samito demonstrates that the Civil War military service of Irish and African Americans led them to make demands for full inclusion and it created a moral indebtedness on the part of the native-born white population that made opposing those demands difficult. No other book illuminates this subject as well as this one does. No one else has related the progress of this development so well to the experience of the Civil War."
—LAWRENCE F. KOHL, University of Alabama, author of *The Politics of Individualism*

Becoming American under Fire

Becoming American under Fire

IRISH AMERICANS, AFRICAN AMERICANS, AND THE POLITICS OF CITIZENSHIP DURING THE CIVIL WAR ERA

Christian G. Samito

Cornell University Press
Ithaca and London

First published 2009 by Cornell University Press
Printed in the United States of America

Library of Congress Cataloging-in-Publication Data

Samito, Christian G.
   Becoming American under fire : Irish Americans, African
Americans and the politics of citizenship during the Civil War era /
Christian G. Samito.
        p. cm.
   Includes bibliographical references and index.
   ISBN 978-0-8014-4846-1 (cloth : alk. paper)
  1. United States—History—Civil War, 1861–1865—
Participation, Irish American.   2. United States—History—Civil
War, 1861–1865—Participation, African American.   3. Irish
American soldiers—History—19th century.   4. African American
soldiers—History—19th century.   5. Irish Americans—Legal
status, laws, etc.—History—19th century.   6. African
Americans—Legal status, laws, etc.—History—19th century.
7. Citizenship—United States—History—19th century.
8. United States—Politics and government—1861–1865.
I. Title.

E540.I6S25 2009
973.7'415—dc22   2009023335

Cornell University Press strives to use environmentally responsible
suppliers and materials to the fullest extent possible in the publishing of its books. Such materials include vegetable-based, low-VOC
inks and acid-free papers that are recycled, totally chlorine-free, or
partly composed of nonwood fibers. For further information, visit
our website at www.cornellpress.cornell.edu.

Cloth printing   10 9 8 7 6 5 4 3 2 1

To my parents, for their constant love and support

Contents

Acknowledgments

I thank the many people who helped me in the course of writing this book. At Boston College, David Quigley, Alan Rogers, James O'Toole, and Thomas H. O'Connor continue to be true mentors who provided me with valuable suggestions as well as their friendship. Tyler Anbinder, William A. Blair, Lorien Foote, Elizabeth Leonard, James McPherson, Kerby Miller, Donald Yacovone, and the anonymous readers for Cornell University Press and *Civil War History* provided me with helpful comments and encouragement about the portions of my work that they read. I especially appreciate Lorien's and Elizabeth's friendship and enthusiasm for my work. I also benefited from the comments of Thomas J. Brown, Aaron Sheehan-Dean, Andrew Slap, and Michael Smith as we participated at various conferences. Michael McGandy shared my enthusiasm for this book and has proven to be an outstanding editor.

Ben Maryniak kindly provided me with typescript copies of letters in his possession, and Mike Ruddy sent me a portion of John Savage's *Fenian Heroes and Martyrs*. The Abraham Lincoln Presidential Library in Springfield, Illinois, the American Social History Project, and the Library of Congress and National Archives in Washington, D.C., have been extremely helpful in providing me with illustrations and documents. As they have done for years, the Interlibrary Loan Staff at Boston College's O'Neill Library obtained for me all sorts of primary sources regardless of their obscurity.

I am grateful for funding provided to me by Boston College, the Mark De-Wolfe Howe Fund, and the Irish American Cultural Institute. Chapter 4 was originally published as "The Intersection between Military Justice and Equal

Rights: Mutinies, Courts-martial, and Black Civil War Soldiers," *Civil War History*, 53, no. 2 (June 2007), 170–202. It is reprinted here with the permission of The Kent State University Press.

Finally, I would like to express my deepest thanks to all of my friends for their support and fellowship and my parents and family for their love.

Becoming American under Fire

INTRODUCTION

Attorney General Edward Bates grew frustrated as he contemplated, in late 1862, what constituted citizenship in the United States. Despite the Supreme Court's exclusionary *Dred Scott v. Sandford* ruling in 1857, Secretary of the Treasury Salmon Chase asked Bates for his official opinion as to whether the United States could recognize black men as citizens, making them eligible to command American ships, after a federal revenue cutter detained a schooner captained by a black man. Bates examined legal treatises and court rulings to find an explanation of what it meant to be a citizen of the United States in the first place, but his search proved exasperating and fruitless: "I find no such definition, no authoritative establishment of the meaning of the phrase," the attorney general admitted. Bates concluded that "eighty years of practical enjoyment of citizenship, under the Constitution, have not sufficed to teach us either the exact meaning of the word, or the constituent elements of the thing we prize so highly."[1]

Today, we feel as surprised as Bates likely did that national citizenship existed as such a vague concept prior to the Civil War. At that time national citizenship largely functioned to determine whether one owed allegiance and certain obligations to the United States in exchange for its protection but left to the states the definition of most of the rights and privileges now attached to it. The rights and privileges one enjoyed depended on a complicated network of factors, including whether one was a naturalized or native-born citizen, where one lived, and one's race, slave status, gender, political office, job, position within a family, and membership in different associations.[2]

We hold a dramatically different understanding of citizenship today. American citizenship is now primarily national in character. Furthermore, as T. H. Marshall described in a definition that scholars continue to track in an American context, the modern Western ideal of citizenship contains three elements of rights bundled together: civil rights, political rights, and socioeconomic rights. Civil rights are "the rights necessary for individual freedom—liberty of the person, freedom of speech, thought and faith, the right to own property and to conclude valid contracts, and the right to justice," which itself comprised "the right to defend and assert all one's rights on terms of equality with others and by due process of law." Political rights include "the right to participate in the exercise of political power, as a member of a body invested with political authority or as an elector of the members of such a body." Socioeconomic rights "range from the right to a modicum of economic welfare and security to the right to share in the social heritage and to live the life of a civilised being according to the standards prevailing in the society."[3]

Citizenship has several interrelated sides: it acts as a political creation and a legal concept, and it also operates on a social and cultural level. Citizenship proclaims that a self-governing society exists and it defines inclusion and exclusion in that community. Citizenship helps to distribute power, articulate rights and duties, and create an intersection between political participation by the people and formal governmental structures. Additionally, citizenship offers an identity that individuals can embrace and that often becomes essential to their personal perceptions, and it helps to forge a collective civic identity and culture as well. Citizenship affects real lives in official ways, such as helping to define the rights individuals enjoy and duties they owe to their country, but also in terms of personal identity and allegiance.[4]

The modern American vision of national citizenship began to develop as a result of the tumult of the Civil War. Events leading up to and occurring during the 1860s challenged Americans to think about national citizenship in definite terms for the first time and the concept emerged dramatically transformed. During the 1860s, a distinctly American citizenship crystallized into a form that eventually integrated national rights and duties along with notions of loyalty and the embrace of American ideals. Following the Civil War, the rapid nationalization of citizenship, its heightened importance, and its association with claims to rights represent a major break with prior history. This book explores how, amid the tempest of war, statesmen, soldiers, and ordinary people forged a more robust definition of citizenship. What one legal scholar identified as the "moral, political, and constitutional crisis" of antebellum America resolved after Americans undertook the most comprehensive reconsideration of the government, society, and laws of the United States since the constitutional convention in 1787. As New York Republican Daniel Morris announced in 1864 to his fellow congressmen, they faced a "moment of greater responsibility than has devolved upon a like body since the year 1776."[5]

In official terms, the most obvious manifestation of legal changes came in the form of constitutional amendments that emancipated the slaves (the

Thirteenth), defined American citizens as all persons born or naturalized in the United States and ensured that they were entitled to "equal protection of the laws" and "due process of law" (the Fourteenth), and granted black men voting rights (the Fifteenth). Each of these amendments also empowered Congress to enforce them with "appropriate legislation." Congress augmented these amendments with the first national civil rights statutes in American history and, in 1870, creation of the Department of Justice to help enforce them. The Civil Rights Act of 1866 defined for the first time some rights associated with national citizenship and, along with the Enforcement acts of 1870–72, conferred on federal courts jurisdiction to enforce these rights. The Civil Rights Act of 1875 went even further, desegregating public accommodations and outlawing racial discrimination in inns, public conveyances, and theaters, before the Supreme Court nullified it in 1883. Additionally, the Fourteenth Amendment sanctified the idea that the same rights and protections enjoyed by native-born Americans applied to naturalized citizens in the United States. The Act of July 27, 1868, extended this concept when naturalized citizens traveled abroad. By upholding the right of individuals to expatriate and choose a new allegiance without the assent of their native country, the Act of July 27, 1868, also affirmed the voluntary and consensual nature of citizenship.[6]

These statutes and amendments went beyond engraving the Union's battlefield victory onto the law. Reconstruction legislation and constitutional revision strengthened the American nation-state by establishing the primacy of national citizenship, defining the body of national citizens and marking out some of the rights associated with that status. Moreover, the Fifteenth Amendment linked voting, which comprised not just a political act but one also signifying inclusion in the community, to national citizenship for men. The Civil War amendments and associated legislation created a new order not only by recognizing nearly 4.5 million blacks as national citizens, and freedmen as voters, within years of the *Dred Scott* case, but also by removing many rights from their traditional keepers (the states) and associating them with national citizenship. While states could continue to determine local variations under which civil and political rights could be enjoyed based on categories such as age, sex, and education, they could do so only so long as their legislation did not conflict with federal law.

Attorney General Bates thus stood at the vanguard of a broader cultural and legal shift when in 1862 he held that free native-born blacks *were* U.S. citizens. Bates extracted race and held birth and allegiance as the paramount sources of American citizenship. Citing the Constitution's supremacy clause, Bates further held, "Every citizen of the United States is a component member of the nation, with rights and duties, under the Constitution and laws of the United States, which cannot be destroyed or abridged by the laws of any particular State." Other people concurred in this stronger conception of the nation, as well as the meaning of citizenship in it. German American political philosopher Francis Lieber argued that the United States formed, "and ought to form, a Nation," and he called for the American people "to provide constitutionally for a national expression on the necessity of the integrity of our country, on allegiance, the treasonable character of elevating so-called State sovereignty above the National Government, and for the extinction of the Dred Scott principle."[7]

To accomplish what Bates, Lieber, and others contemplated, Americans had to define national citizenship and imbue it with priority over state citizenship, wrestling with and revising long-held doctrines of federalism along the way. Similar to the way in which emancipation demanded discussion of what freedom actually encompassed, the task would remain incomplete if national citizens were designated without a determination of what this meant in practical terms. As the *Philadelphia American* argued in support of the Fourteenth Amendment, "If there be one lesson written in bloody letters by the [Civil] War, it is that the national citizenship must be paramount to that of the State," while in October 1866 Presbyterian minister Samuel T. Spear asked, "Ought not the word [citizen] to have the same meaning throughout the whole country?"[8]

The military served as a primary site of this rethinking of what citizenship meant in terms of identity and allegiance, rights, status, and protection. The Union armed forces mobilized Americans from different classes, ethnicities, races, and states in unprecedented ways, on a national scale. Wartime experiences cut across people's different backgrounds and created stronger links between the federal government and the people. Politics pervaded the armed forces during the Civil War, turning the military into an institution that raised political consciousness within soldiers and sailors in the ranks. After the war, the experiences and leadership of veterans stood at the center of the clarification of American citizenship that took place. The federal military operated as a nation-building tool not only by reconstituting the country but by unleashing forces that helped to shape the emergence of a stronger concept of national citizenship.

Two groups, African Americans and Irish Americans, greatly influenced the more modern understanding of citizenship that emerged out of the crucible of war. The identity component of African American and Irish American citizenship changed during the 1860s. These changes, and the expectations they created, merged with and influenced a broader movement to redefine the legal meaning and political practices of American citizenship. Veterans and civilians of both groups articulated demands for change on the basis of service to the Union and asserted views on how the federal victory should affect what it meant to be an American citizen. Through separate but simultaneous efforts, African Americans and Irish Americans in the 1860s helped solidify three principles in the law: the primacy of a national citizenship that incorporated certain rights; the concept that individuals had the right to change their birth citizenship and allegiance; and the doctrine that all citizens, whether by birth of naturalization, stood equal in rights and protections regardless of race or prior status as a slave or alien.

American constitutionalism encompasses more than legislation and judicial interpretation, it also relies on the acceptance of official pronouncements by the people. The people hold power to challenge official practice and to move it into conformity with their vision, often by use of moral suasion and the ballot (for example, see the Republican Party's growth in response to *Dred Scott*). Episodes of public disagreement can resolve to create new accords on constitutional issues. Public deliberation thus makes up a critical, nongovernmental aspect of constitutional development. Because popular sovereignty forms the bedrock of American constitutionalism, the issues of who comprise "the people," how they may act, what they believe, and what rights they enjoy, remain fundamental. Moreover, citizenship as an identity often comes into being as a result of both political practices and personal experiences. These circumstances render the popular constitutionalism of African Americans and Irish Americans in the 1860s all the more important. Members of both groups not only helped to change citizenship as a legal concept, they *acted* as citizens in the process.[9]

Participation in the Civil War dramatically increased the political awareness of African Americans and Irish Americans. Members of both groups fought in America's prior conflicts, but the unprecedented numbers in which they served during the Civil War allowed them to assert, more powerfully than ever before, their American identity and vision of how they should fit into the United States. Even where their specific goals differed, members of both groups used the long-held understanding in America that military service particularly entitled and schooled individuals to be citizens. Both Irish Americans and African Americans sought to bring to fruition George B. Loring's ideal, announced at the 1866 dedication of a Massachusetts town's monument to its fallen Civil War soldiers (including an ex-slave who died in the black Fifth Massachusetts Cavalry's training camp): "To do service on the battle field today, and to perform the part of an educated American citizen tomorrow, is the highest ideal of a citizen soldier."[10]

African Americans and Irish Americans challenged racial and ethnic views, and contested legal assumptions, in order to participate in the recrafting of American citizenship. Both groups weighed in with their expectations and supported the emerging, nationalized view of citizenship in this process. Military service allowed African Americans to argue that loyalty trumped race, and Irish Americans to argue that loyalty trumped ethnicity, as a mark of citizenship. Blacks used the contrast between their allegiance and the treason committed by white Confederates, for example, to demand and obtain recognition of their status as national citizens, a more expansive definition of the rights and protections associated with that status, and the vote for men (all in the law, if not always actual practice), while the Fourteenth Amendment allowed the states to disfranchise white ex-Confederates due to their breach of allegiance (and, some Southern states did so). Moreover, Irish Americans and African Americans joined other proponents of legal change by invoking the patriots of 1776, who validated their own actions by claiming to offer a true interpretation of British constitutionalism in the face of its perceived betrayal by Parliament and the crown.[11]

For blacks, military service shattered the old order, helped end slavery, and fueled expectations for inclusion and broadened citizenship rights. Frederick Douglass recognized that a racial point of no return had been crossed during the Civil War, arguing in mid-1863 that arming blacks not only guaranteed a war of emancipation but confirmed for them national citizenship: "Once let the black man get upon his person the brass letters U.S.; let him get an eagle on his button, and a musket on his shoulder, and bullets in his pocket, and there is no power on the earth or under the earth which can deny that he has earned the right of citizenship in the United States."[12]

Fighting under the American flag caused many former slaves to recognize, probably for the first time, an allegiance to the United States. Black soldiers further situated themselves as citizens by opposing discrimination and policies that failed to acknowledge their equality and by actively asserting their interpretation of legal meanings and practices. Unexpected wartime experiences, such as the surprising level of due process enjoyed by black defendants tried by general courts-martial, helped inform the African American definition of citizenship. During and after the war, blacks demanded more than simple emancipation in name, they called for broad changes so as to secure for themselves an enduring freedom and real meaning behind the legal title of national citizen. Blacks used a vigorous national and statewide convention movement, including across the South almost immediately on the close of the war, to force whites to acknowledge their new citizenship status. Black organizations helped shape the contours of that status and foster legal change by lobbying legislators, showing that blacks could rationally engage with constitutional questions, and challenging all Americans, white and black, Republican and Democrat, to live up to the egalitarianism of the Declaration of Independence.[13]

Irish Americans argued for different objectives, although their expectations and tactics sometimes paralleled those of African Americans in unintentional ways. Instead of fighting in the Irish revolutionary movement, many Irish in America struck their blow for Ireland by protecting what they perceived as the global bastion of republicanism, the United States. Through the war, and as a part of the transatlantic upheavals of the mid nineteenth century, a sense of American allegiance strengthened within many Irish Americans, even in the face of continuing devotion to Irish nationalism. As African Americans did, Irish Americans not only relied on their support for the Union to situate themselves within the American people, they linked themselves with the Founding generation by virtue of their defense of the Constitution. In contrast to the political position of African Americans, many Irish Americans remained loyal to the Democratic Party during the war and sought restoration of the Union as it was before the war. Nonetheless, events during the 1860s also energized certain radical currents within this ethnic community, and led many of its members to support a more broadly defined national citizenship that included both naturalized and native-born Americans on equal status.

Regardless of party affiliation, Irish Americans forced a rethinking of who could be part of "the people" by arguing that the choice to embrace American principles formed the basis of citizenship as much as native birth. Irish Americans took up Massachusetts governor John A. Andrew's August 1862 assurance that, "whether born upon our soil or in other lands and wandering here, you are citizens of this united government, equally sharing in the heritage of freedom. Its opportunities and blessings belong to you all." The demands of Irish Americans, with their Civil War veterans in the lead, caused the United States to resolve important differences in treatment between native-born and naturalized citizens. Taking place against the backdrop of the Fourteenth Amendment's ratification debates, this pressure compelled the United States to link the right to change one's allegiance to the inalienable rights described in the Declaration of Independence, pursuant to a statute still in force today. Moreover, American diplomatic pressure, generated by Irish American activism, obliged Britain to abandon its long-established doctrine of perpetual allegiance, which held that one could never disclaim birth allegiance, not even by swearing an oath of loyalty to another country. Irish Americans in this way not only influenced foreign policy, they stood at the vanguard of a movement that expanded the right of human mobility, choice, and freedom.[14]

In this book, I look at changes in how Irish Americans and African Americans felt about belonging to the American people, and the rights to which they felt entitled. I also consider the native-born white population's idea of whether these groups should be included in the American people, and the rights to which they were entitled. Finally, I examine how this dialogue resulted in a newly defined concept of citizenship embodied in the laws and the Constitution of the United States. I have not written a comparative history of the African Americans and Irish Americans during the 1860s, even though this study operates that way in places. Instead, this book tells the complicated story of how two separate groups, acting in pursuit of different goals yet operating at the same time and incited by military participation in the same event, helped to change American citizenship in practice and as a legal doctrine.

While other groups also influenced the development of American citizenship during the 1860s, the experience of African Americans and Irish Americans proves particularly revealing because both groups stood at the center of the crisis of American citizenship that took place in the 1850s. Both groups were excluded before the war, to differing extents, from the full enjoyment of what we today consider to be citizenship rights. Active participation in defense of the Union spurred both groups to demand inclusion in the American people at a time of fluidity and reform regarding the identity and legal components of citizenship.[15]

While examining these topics reveals unexpected similarities between the histories of both groups during this time period, it also underscores major distinctions. African Americans battled for inclusion as national citizens in the first place, whereas Irish Americans sought to remove distinction based on their status as naturalized ones. In light of continuing race-based strictures against them on a local level, African Americans sought definition of the rights associated with national citizenship. Irish Americans instead focused more simply on ensuring that native-born and naturalized citizens stood as equals in society and before the law, and that, as naturalized citizens, they received the same protection from the U.S. government when abroad.

Sometimes, the experiences and efforts of both groups intersected or at least ran parallel; other times, they were vastly different and even antagonistic. In some areas, the experiences of each group were so different that comparison is not fruitful, and for that reason, the narratives about each group cannot be intertwined in most of the chapters. Irish Americans never were slaves or had to deal with Black Codes or Klan violence against them, for example, and African Americans were generally unconcerned about what it meant to be a naturalized citizen. African American men were overwhelmingly disfranchised until the passage of the Reconstruction Act of March 2, 1867, and ratification of the Fifteenth Amendment in 1870. Irish American men, on the other hand, could and did vote. Enmity marred overall relations between both communities during the Civil War era. Many Irish Americans loathed the thought of African Americans exercising political and other rights and continued to define citizenship along racial lines, while some African American leaders appealed to lingering nativism to urge that their claim for rights had higher priority than that of immigrants.

Yet, while points of divergence and rivalry existed between Irish Americans and African Americans, the fact that striking similarities also existed in their histories during the 1860s has to date largely been lost to history. Irish Americans and African Americans separately claimed that the choice of loyalty to the United States trumped ethnicity or race, respectively. Members of both groups linked themselves to the Revolutionary generation in order to gain credibility, and as paradoxical as it initially appears, employed Irish or African nationalistic language as a tool of assimilation and a demand for acceptance. Both groups claimed their place among "the people" not only by defending the Union, but by challenging the United States, in far-reaching ways, to conform citizenship doctrine to the ideals they felt the Declaration of Independence articulated. Both groups used moral arguments built on their military service, and pragmatic arguments based on the lure of their votes, to persuade native-born whites (blacks used the benefit their ballots could provide the Republican Party to obtain the franchise in the first place). The experiences of Irish Americans and African Americans come together in that their sometimes complementary, but often separate, agendas helped to redefine the legal concept and practical meaning of American citizenship.

Moreover, startling moments of rapprochement between African Americans and Irish Americans show that insurmountable hostility did not wholly define relations between both groups, as some who study "whiteness" argue. African Americans and Irish Americans occasionally found themselves unexpected allies. When the delegates of a convention of Fenians, an organization of Irish nationalists in America, learned in September 1867 that several thousand black men of New Orleans offered to fight for Irish freedom, they swiftly resolved to "accept the services of every man who truly loves liberty, and is willing to fight for Ireland, without distinction of race, color, or nationality." In the end, the Fenians had difficulty mustering even Irish Americans to fight, and the African American volunteers from New Orleans never grasped the green banner. Yet this dialogue between the two groups reveals an unexpected link between at least some of their members: the mutual goal of advancing liberty and promoting republicanism. The era of the Civil War and Reconstruction created a broader consciousness in both groups, and Americans as a whole, of the place the United States held as the worldwide beacon of republican values such as representative self-government and determination of political issues at the ballot box.[16]

Law, society, and politics inextricably mixed during the 1860s and set the development of American citizenship on a path that was not predetermined. Things now taken for granted—black citizenship, for example—could have had a far different history and outcome. The United States that ratified the Civil War amendments in 1865–70 stood in marked contrast to the United States of 1861. Congress in March 1861 approved and sent to the states a proposed thirteenth amendment that would have protected slavery from federal interference in the states. The idea of citizenship and suffrage for blacks had been unpopular within even the wartime Republican Party, despite its support for emancipation. Blacks relied on their military service to hasten their remarkably swift recognition *by the law* as citizens, even if recognition in *practice* was another story. African American arguments for inclusion, as well as the exigencies created by postwar white Southern resistance, led Republicans to make a profound shift during the 1860s to embrace the idea that blacks stood entitled not just to the rights of persons but to those of a broadened concept of citizenship as well.[17]

The crisis that culminated in the Civil War necessitated and enabled this large-scale rethinking of American constitutionalism. Members of the Reconstruction generation came to realize that they could correct the error of slavery while continuing to respect the legitimacy of the Constitution and the basic vision of the Founders. As early as April 21, 1861, abolitionist Wendell Phillips announced to Bostonians that the Civil War would permit Americans to remold the Constitution so as to reclaim the ideals encapsulated in the Declaration of Independence. Phillips added his vision of a future America: "When the smoke of this conflict clears away, the world will see under our banner all tongues, all creeds, all races,—one brotherhood,—and on the banks of the Potomac, the Genius of Liberty, robed in light." In the end, a radicalization of politics and fluidity of party, postwar conditions and white resistance in the South, and a "moral revolution" (at least in the North), transformed marginal abolitionist arguments into bedrock principles enshrined in corrective Civil War constitutional amendments.[18]

Those who advocated reordering society based on a more expansive view of rights argued that the nation could not render hollow the sacrifices at places like Antietam and Gettysburg. As Maryland congressman Henry Winter Davis argued in Philadelphia in September 1863, "Restore the soul to the soulless eyes of the thousands that have fallen martyrs upon the battle-field, and then you can restore the Union as it was." Frederick Douglass and other blacks maintained that constitutional change would fulfill the true principles of the Founders, and many white Republicans agreed. Yet this crossing of the constitutional Rubicon did not mean breaking with the Founders, because Davis and others equated change with reclamation of the Constitution "as it came from the hands of George Washington, and Alexander Hamilton, and James Madison, not the wretched, crippled hump-back that has been presented before our eyes." After identifying the fundamental paradox of the Founding, that a government could be "based in part upon the principle that 'all men are created equal,' and in part upon the principle that a certain portion of mankind have the right to hold a certain other portion in bondage," Massachusetts Republican congressman George S. Boutwell challenged his audience in Weymouth, Massachusetts, as well as the Republic, in a July 4, 1865, speech to decide "whether you will reconstruct the nation upon the eternal principle of the Declaration of Independence, that 'all men are created equal'" or "build upon injustice, upon wrong, upon distinctions of race, of color, or upon caste," so as to "build upon the sand."[19]

In this malleable constitutional moment during and after the war, African Americans and Irish Americans provided some of the most challenging visions of how American citizenship doctrine should be reformed. While social and cultural historians have considered the part African Americans played in the story of how American citizenship changed during the 1860s, the role played by Irish Americans has received less attention. Political and legal scholars mostly have focused elsewhere. Surprisingly, little has been written about the redefinition of American citizenship during the 1860s overall. Mitchell Snay's recent book, *Fenians, Freedmen, and Southern Whites: Race and Nationality in the Era of Reconstruction,* does compare Irish nationalists in the United States, white racists in the South, and Southern black freedpeople during the 1860s and 1870s. Snay thus begins the process of restoring Irish Americans to the history of Reconstruction. Nonetheless, even Snay's fine book largely ignores the impact of service in the Union army on the African American and Irish American communities, how both groups influenced the nationalization and increasing importance of American citizenship during Reconstruction, and how Fenianism brought to the forefront postwar discussions of Irish American citizenship status.[20]

This book engages military, legal, social, political, and diplomatic history and, as a study about changing ideas of American citizenship, it encompasses evidence on a national scale. Additionally, the story of citizenship's evolution during the era of the Civil War and Reconstruction investigates a phase in American political development. Americans considered during this time various, sometimes paradoxical interpretations about nationhood, especially as casualties mounted and as the federal government's power expanded and increasingly required the people's support for wartime measures such as emancipation, taxation, and conscription. According to historian Melinda Lawson, Civil War–era nation-builders articulated a "preeminent national loyalty," revised the relationship individuals had with a formerly distant national government, and sanctified the nation-state so that "by war's end, a 'Union' of states had become a 'nation' of Americans."[21]

Irish Americans and African Americans played a key role in this development. For their own separate reasons, both groups helped to advance the priority of nationalized citizenship. In doing so, Irish Americans broke philosophically from a Democratic Party that continued to place primacy on state authority over citizenship. Moreover, both groups helped to bring about official pronouncements, such as the Fourteenth Amendment and Act of July 27, 1868, which affirmed the national government's power to define and protect American citizens. Members of both groups worked to establish their place as full members in the polity based on their choice to embrace the same republican political values that loyal white, native-born American citizens maintained, even where they continued to celebrate their ethnic and racial identity. The Civil War thus became an important turning point in the discussion over who and what comprised the United States, especially as the meaning of American patriotism, and who could celebrate it, remained contested in the face of continuing nativism and racism.[22]

The nationalization of citizenship and the development of American nationalism mutually reinforced each other in institutional and personal ways. Citizenship involves more than rights claims, it encompasses matters of loyalty and American identity as well. The Civil War afforded Americans an opportunity to join in national life in unprecedented fashion. Irish Americans and African Americans participated in this moment not only in their demand for inclusion in "the people," but as a function of genuinely intensified American identity and patriotism, generated through their experiences in the struggle for the Union.[23]

Similarly, nation-building occurred in official ways during the 1860s, but also through deeply personal individual experiences and choices. Soldiers, families, and communities interacted with the federal government and its armed forces, engaged with issues raised by the war, and considered, sometimes for the first time, the issues of individual allegiance and identity. Few slaves, for example, likely considered before the war whether they owed allegiance to any nation. Meanwhile, even free-born blacks in the North found themselves excluded, by Chief Justice Roger Taney's decision in *Dred Scott,* from national citizenship. The choices involved in determining whether to volunteer for the federal armed forces, or to support the Union in other ways, forced individuals, including African Americans and Irish Americans, to confront and determine the issue of their personal allegiance. Such experiences helped many individuals work out what allegiance they held in the first place, as well as think about what this allegiance meant.

The story of American citizenship is not one of linear progression, and it did not end with the ratification of the Civil War amendments and the passage of associated legislation. Many African Americans and Irish Americans continued to lead challenging lives and struggled to make practical reality conform to these legal changes. Members of the Irish American working class, for example, experienced and participated in the turbulent realities of postwar industrial life and labor strife. African Americans first confronted powerful white supremacist groups, which operated outside the law to oppose the practices of a racially inclusive citizenship, and then the rise of Jim Crow after the Supreme Court slowly whittled away the impact of the Civil War amendments and legislation. Yet, even where initial expansions of citizenship and accompanying rights contracted for blacks beginning in the 1870s, painful but temporary defeat sowed the seeds for long-term success. The theoretical arguments made regarding citizenship during the 1860s, and the changes that took place in practice and in the law in the wake of the Civil War, set valuable precedents with far-reaching effects. These standards and doctrines influenced struggles over citizenship and rights into the twentieth century, when a new corrective moment, catalyzed this time by black service during the Second World War and in Korea, brought constitutional and citizenship doctrine in line with the ideals of the Founders of 1776, as well as those of the 1860s.

Throughout this book, I interchangeably use the term *black* as well as the modern phrase *African American* simply so as to avoid repetition. I use the phrase *Irish Americans* to refer both to Irish-born immigrants in the United States as well as American-born individuals of Irish parentage. I also use the terms *United States* and *America* interchangeably. I have silently added a period to some quotes where they end a sentence and occasionally changed capitalization where appropriate, although I have retained the original spelling.

CHAPTER 1

The Crisis of Citizenship in the 1850s

A crisis of citizenship wracked the United States between the Mexican War and the Civil War. Debate concerning slavery, citizenship for free blacks and immigrants, and the rights applicable to both groups, intensified during the 1850s. These discussions reveal a broader question with which society wrestled in the decade before the Civil War and another one that it tried to avoid: Who comprised the American people and what did citizenship mean?

The idea of citizenship based on voluntary consent emerged during the Revolutionary era, when Americans rejected subjectship and developed the concept that individuals had the right to choose their allegiance. What citizenship meant in practice, however, remained ambiguous. Because national citizenship implicated relations between the state and federal governments, and rights enforceable against either, unsettled questions arising from the doctrine of federalism complicated its definition. Moreover, who "the people" included remained contested and undefined during the first half of the nineteenth century.[1]

Competing impulses in America during the 1850s helped to heighten the crisis of citizenship. The divergence between North and South, accelerated by industrialization and the market revolution, crystallized at a time when the unifying force of the struggles of the early Republic faded into history. Formerly marginal arguments on both sides of the debate over slavery began to take central stage, while social transformations such as industrialization, urbanization, and immigration unevenly affected different sections of the country, exacerbated strains, and generated additional questions and concerns of their own.

Rather than unify the country, victory in the Mexican War complicated these broad forces and brought all of this tumult and uncertainty to a head.

African Americans before the Civil War

As of 1860, fifteen slaveholding states contained approximately 3,954,000 slaves who were considered property to be bought, sold, and treated largely as their masters wished. Another 262,000 free blacks lived in the slaveholding states, but few of the rights whites held applied to them. The North contained 226,000 free blacks by 1860 who, in contrast to bondage in the South, enjoyed at least basic legal rights such as the ability to purchase and sell property, educate themselves, enter into contracts, sue, and assemble in public meetings or conventions. In most Northern states, blacks could testify against whites; in some, black men could vote.[2]

Slavery as a legal institution justified excluding from national citizenship those blacks held in bondage because property could neither have a national identity nor hold membership in society. The existence of free blacks born in America, however, created a problem: they did not have alien status, nor did the tribal allegiance which justified the exclusion of Native Americans from national citizenship apply to them. Free blacks could not be considered property, and they had a claim to national citizenship by birthright when born on U.S. soil. On the other hand, recognizing free blacks as national citizens involved several controversial implications. Questions about federalism, and the role played by federal and state governments in defining rights and privileges, complicated the issue. Moreover, white Americans recognized that an acknowledgment of national citizenship for free native-born blacks could then be used to challenge the treatment of slaves as property, threatening the institution of slavery as well as the national compromise which tolerated its survival. Additionally, many white Americans did not want to extend to blacks rights and privileges equal to the ones they held, and they feared that recognition of national citizenship for free blacks might lead to that result. Even many whites who opposed slavery held racist views of blacks as inferior and unfit for citizenship or equality.[3]

Two options existed so as to resolve the problem of national citizenship for free blacks: total exclusion, despite the moral implications this raised and the contradiction this posed to the concepts of birthright citizenship and citizenship by consent; or, recognition of free blacks as national citizens and confronting the challenges that went along with doing so. Chief Justice Taney of the Supreme Court chose exclusion in his 1857 *Dred Scott* ruling. Taney declared that no blacks, not even free blacks who could vote in the states where they resided, could be U.S. citizens. Additionally, Taney declared that blacks held no rights that whites had to respect. Any rights that blacks possessed were at the whim of state legislatures, and they continued to suffer curtailment of rights in both official (for example, they could not obtain patents) and unofficial ways.[4]

While blacks in the North enjoyed freedom and some rights, they also confronted political, economic, and social strictures that varied across the states, as well as private acts of discrimination that kept most of them at the bottom rung of the socioeconomic ladder. At the time of the Civil War, only Massachusetts, Maine, New Hampshire, Vermont, and Rhode Island permitted black men to vote on the same terms as white men. After black leader Benjamin F. Roberts challenged Boston regulations that required his five-year-old daughter to travel an extra distance in order to attend an all-black school, Massachusetts's Supreme Judicial Court ruled in 1850 that segregated schools did not violate the equal rights secured for blacks by that state's constitution. In 1855, Boston would desegregate its schools. In the 1850s, Illinois, Indiana, Iowa, and Oregon passed measures, enforced to varying degrees, to prevent migration of free blacks into their states and, as of 1860, blacks could not testify against whites in Indiana, Illinois, California, and Oregon. Oregon removed this stricture in 1862 and California did so by 1863. Older and more Northern states tended to provide more rights, while newer states and those closer to the South proved less egalitarian. Attitudes toward blacks varied even within states: racism in Cincinnati contrasted with the tolerance manifested by Ohio's Oberlin College, which began to admit black students in 1835. In upstate New York in the 1840s and 1850s, integrated schools in Syracuse differed from segregated schools in Buffalo and Albany.[5]

Irish Americans before the Civil War

Irish Americans before the Civil War faced neither slavery nor the legal strictures that blacks confronted, and they could become U.S. citizens. Nonetheless, Irish Americans occupied a tenuous position, and the debates about their status that took place during the 1850s illuminate the hotly contested prewar discussion about American citizenship.

Even the meaning of naturalization remained unsettled as of the Civil War. The Constitution remained silent about the definition of American citizenship, much less whether any distinctions attached to those who naturalized (except as to eligibility to hold the presidency and vice presidency). Moreover, for decades before the Civil War, Americans generally embraced expatriation rights, the doctrine that people held a right to opt out of their birth citizenship, emigrate from their native land, and naturalize where they chose. The United States did not vigorously enforce this policy abroad, however, and confusion reigned over the actual rights and protections enjoyed by naturalized American citizens who returned to visit their homeland. Congress refrained from legislating on the issue, and conflicting rulings from the judiciary and State Department further muddled the matter.

Many native-born Protestant Americans questioned whether the Catholic faith and foreign background of Irish immigrants precluded them from becoming Americans. Anti-Catholic prejudice had run through the United States since the colonial days, and the impulse intensified by 1834, when a mob burned down a convent in Charlestown, Massachusetts. Lurid books recounted purported sexual depravity within convents, while polemical works by Reverend Lyman Beecher and Samuel F. B. Morse in 1835 argued that Catholicism jeopardized Protestantism and republicanism in America. Anti-Catholicism even infected the construction of the Washington Monument, as nativists pared from it and sank into the Potomac River a block of stone donated by Catholics.[6]

Nativism strengthened during the 1850s amid debate over Catholic schools, practices, and a growing Catholic demographic presence. Between 1845 and 1851, at the same time debate intensified as to whether blacks could fit into "the people," three quarters of a million Irish flooded into the United States and frightened many native-born Americans with their poverty, foreignness, and the potential of their political influence. By 1855, the Irish-born population in Boston swelled past 50,000 mostly impoverished immigrants. By 1850, 29,963 Irish-born individuals comprised a fifth of Chicago's population, and by 1860, 95,548 Irish-born made up more than 16 percent of Philadelphia's population; they comprised almost 26 percent of Boston's and New York City's populations as well.[7]

Famine Irish immigrants lacked capital or education and needed immediate employment, forcing them to rely heavily on unskilled positions. While this cheap labor pool spurred industrial growth in some cities, Irish American laborers found their wages low and working conditions poor. Many Famine Irish packed into their city's slum district where putrid air and contaminated water fostered disease in epidemic proportions. Hard labor and low quality of life led to great indulgence in alcohol, and groggeries not only provided cheap whiskey, they served as centers of political activity for Irish immigrants courted by the Democratic Party as a source of votes. The poverty of the newcomers exacerbated nativism. By 1855, Massachusetts's nativist governor Henry Gardner successfully called for deportation of alien paupers by arguing it was cheaper to return them to Liverpool than it was to support them.[8]

Life remained difficult even for the many Irish immigrants who only paused in the eastern seaboard cities to regroup before moving elsewhere. Although smaller cities, towns, and rural regions generally showed more welcome to the newcomers, immigrants there still often fared poorly. Just as blacks experienced different attitudes toward them across the country, so also did the Irish. In the Midwest, a demand for labor sometimes trumped prejudice and, in contrast to the Northeast, some less-populated parts of the Midwest even sought to attract foreigners. The Wisconsin State Emigrant Agency opened in New York in 1852 to publicize the state as a land of opportunity. As voting rights came within the purview of the states, the 1848 Wisconsin constitution gave alien men the right to vote once they had declared intent to naturalize. Indiana in 1850 permitted alien men to vote a year after declaring their intent, and Minnesota in 1857 mandated just six months residence before alien men could vote. A more fluid social situation meant that, in the words of historian Lawrence J. McCaffrey, "the Irish in the Midwest were less physically and psychologically ghettoized than in the East," and accordingly, "tended to be more liberal and less para-noid in their religion and politics." Nonetheless, historian Kerby Miller found that, notwithstanding regional variation, Irish immigrants remained clustered in the lowest-paying and least skilled jobs and experienced a disproportion-ately low quality of life whether in large urban centers such as Boston or New York, smaller industrial towns such as Lawrence, Massachusetts, or Pough-keepsie, New York, or mid-sized cities in the Midwest such as Milwaukee, Wisconsin, or South Bend, Indiana. Nativism was pervasive, and even in less-prejudiced Chicago, the *Tribune* scorned Catholicism as a fatal hindrance to becoming fully American.[9]

Know-Nothings and the Crisis of the 1850s

The turbulence of the 1850s led to the development of the Know Nothing Party, which engaged with issues of slavery, race, ethnicity, religion, and Ameri-can identity. In the North, Know Nothings capitalized on a growing antislavery movement after the enactment of the Kansas-Nebraska bill in 1854 radicalized sectional tensions, and by the end of that year, the party claimed more than a million members. While fighting the extension of slavery was important to Know Nothings in the North, the party also embodied the potent nativist im-pulse that existed in America in the 1850s. Many Know Nothings believed that, unlike earlier immigrants, more recent arrivals in America did not wish to assimilate or embrace American values. At its heart, Know Nothingism promoted the ideas that Protestantism defined and embodied American and republican values, Catholicism and immigrants directly threatened these te-nets, Catholics and immigrants wielded disproportionate political power, and political parties had become corrupt, especially because politicians courted im-migrants for their votes. The Know Nothing Party urged restrictions on liquor and slavery, though not necessarily equal rights for blacks. In 1855, Know Nothings controlled both the governorship and legislature of Massachusetts (where every senator and all but three of 378 representatives in its State House was a Know Nothing), Connecticut, Rhode Island, and New Hampshire. Know Nothings captured the governor's office in Pennsylvania and held a majority in that state's House, likely held a majority of Indiana's and Maine's legislatures, and took a third of New York's legislature and a minority flank in Michigan's legislature. By the end of 1855, Know Nothings had elected eight governors, more than a hundred U.S. congressmen, the mayors of Boston, Philadelphia, and Chicago, and filled thousands of local offices.[10]

The Know Nothing Party accomplished a number of its legislative objec-tives, at least at the state level, before it gave way to the Republicans. Massachu-setts's nativist legislature was representative of the social and cultural struggle against immigrants when it sought to keep Catholic children in public schools imbued with Protestant culture: it mandated reading from the Protestant Bible and prohibited the teaching of foreign languages in its public schools. That same legislature approved a constitutional amendment forbidding the use of state funds to assist sectarian schools. In Massachusetts and Maryland, lingering innuendo of sexual lasciviousness by priests led Know Nothing committees to conduct surprise inspections of Catholic convents and schools, scaring both sisters and students alike. Assaulting the church's financial power, Pennsylvania, Connecticut, New York, and Michigan nativists passed legislation requiring title to church property to pass from bishops to lay trustees.[11]

Know Nothings also acted to curtail the political power of recent immigrants. Massachusetts, Connecticut, Rhode Island, and Maine forbade state courts from participating in naturalization procedures in any way, and New Hampshire restricted its state judges, so that naturalization could take place only in the more limited number of federal courts in those states. Moreover, Know Nothings urged a probation period of between five and twenty-one years before immigrants could naturalize. While Congress did not act on such proposals, some states tried to accomplish the same effect. The 1855 Massachusetts legislature approved an amendment to that state's constitution mandating a twenty-one-year period before any male naturalized citizen could vote, as well as complete prohibition from office for Catholics or immigrants. Technicalities caused by the amendment's wording required the 1856 legislature to revise it, but the already waning power of the Know Nothings resulted in a reduction of the period from twenty-one to fourteen years. Moreover, because the Massachusetts constitution required a two-thirds vote in two consecutive legislatures before a proposed amendment could be sent to the people for ratification, the provision banning Catholics or immigrants from holding office failed. In the end, the 1858 legislature, more Republican than Know Nothing, approved an amendment requiring a two-year period before naturalized male citizens could vote or hold office. An 1859 statewide election ratified the measure by a vote of 21,119 to 15,398.[12]

The issue of slavery divided the party on a national level. Know Nothings in the North generally elected antislavery U.S. senators and opposed admission of additional slave states. Several Northern state legislatures dominated by the party also enacted "personal liberty laws," designed to hamper enforcement of the 1850 Fugitive Slave Act. On the other hand, antislavery sentiment did not translate into a platform of equal rights for blacks. Know Nothings rarely discussed rights even for free blacks, much less a more inclusive concept of citizenship that could incorporate them. Northern Know Nothings sought exclusion of immigrants and an end to slavery's expansion but do not seem to have considered a more defined description of national citizenship as a way to achieve either goal. Instead, Know Nothings continued to look to the states to determine the rights enjoyed by immigrants and blacks.[13]

Irish American antipathy toward abolitionism enflamed Know Nothings in the North, and helped define their relations with blacks. The conditions in Ireland from which many of them fled hardened Irish American attitudes toward African Americans. After describing a state of affairs in Ireland that "swept millions...into the poorhouse, the ocean, and the grave," Irish-born priest

Daniel W. Cahill argued in 1861 that "the negro slaves of America are far happier than the poor Irish" and asked, "Who will therefore deny that the poor Irish cottier, at this moment in Ireland, with his life and death fairly in the hands and at the mercy of the cruel Landlord, is not in a worse condition and is really a more degraded slave, than the negroes of North America?"[14]

More immediate to their lives, the prospect of millions of freed slaves migrating north alarmed Irish American workers who viewed free African Americans as a threat to their jobs and tenuous social position. This tension created a virulent antiblack racism among Irish Americans. In turn, some blacks referred to Irish immigrants as "white niggers," who displaced free African Americans from the job market in Northern cities. Adding to the mix, some abolitionists embraced nativism after taking notice of the Irish American community's proslavery stance, and this mutually reinforced antagonism among the parties. As early as 1839, Boston's Irish Catholic newspaper, the *Pilot,* identified abolitionists as "bigoted and persecuting religionists...[desiring] the extermination of Catholics by fire and sword." Abolitionist characterizations of the Constitution, such as William Lloyd Garrison's declaration that it signified a "covenant with death and an agreement with hell," horrified Irish Americans who honored the founding charter and rights it protected. From the other side, John Mitchel, an Irish-born apologist for the South, repulsed some native-born Americans who initially sympathized with the plight of the Irish when he announced in 1854, "We deny that it is a crime, or a wrong, or even a peccadillo, to hold slaves, or to buy slaves, to sell slaves, to keep slaves to their work by flogging or other needful coercion...and as for being a particular in the wrongs, we, for our part, wish we had a good plantation, well stocked with healthy Negroes in Alabama."[15]

On the other hand, even where many of them held nativist sentiments, some abolitionists and blacks rejected the Know Nothing Party on ideological grounds, or viewed debate about immigrants as a diversion from combating slavery. Black abolitionist William J. Watkins in 1855 stated that Know Nothingism "burrows amid the murky shadows of the grossest ignorance," while that same year, George W. Julian, a former Free-Soil congressman who would return to Congress in 1861 as a Republican, deemed Know Nothingism as "radically vicious in spirit" because it "tramples down the doctrine of human brotherhood," and "judges men by the accidents of their condition instead of striving to find a common lot for all with a common access to the blessings of life." *Frederick Douglass' Paper* noted that national aspirations would force Know Nothings in the North to suppress antislavery candidates for fear of offending Southerners and, later that year, it lamented the defeat of the Republican gubernatorial candidate in Massachusetts by a Know Nothing. According to the paper, "We have reason to believe that had the question of Human Freedom been the only and the real issue presented," instead of the "bait" of anti-foreign sentiment, the Republican would have prevailed. Going further, the abolitionist newspaper the *National Era* criticized Know Nothing strictures against the foreign-born as a matter of principle and as a distraction to abolitionism, but also because they drove some antislavery immigrants to vote for the Democratic Party so as to "rebuke" this "proscriptive spirit."[16]

African American and Irish American Reactions to Exclusion

Although little direct dialogue existed between Northern African Americans and Irish Americans in the years between the Mexican and Civil Wars, many members of both groups argued for the integration of their respective communities into the United States. Some Irish Americans and African Americans relied on their histories in America to respond to strictures against them, while others focused their concern on liberating Ireland or creating a separate black nation, respectively, at least in part to promote their calls for respect in the United States. The contentions African American and Irish American leaders articulated in the 1850s, as well as the internal debates that took place within both groups, helped frame the claims they would assert during the 1860s.

Boston-born black historian William Cooper Nell and other African Americans in the mid-nineteenth-century North repeatedly cited black military participation in the American Founding to bolster their claims to inclusion and equal rights. For blacks, the Revolution exemplified a bitter paradox of antebellum American freedom: African Americans participated in it only to find the memory of their service subsumed by continued racial prejudice, and the history of their allegiance ignored by those who defined the United States as a white republic. According to black abolitionist Charles Lenox Remond in 1857, blacks enjoyed "the right of American citizenship" only for as long as "the patriotic services of colored men in the defence of the country were fresh in the minds of the people."[17]

Nell thus sought, in his *Services of Colored Americans, in the Wars of 1776 and 1812* (1851) and *The Colored Patriots of the American Revolution* (1855), to restore the contribution of blacks to the American Founding to the record of the early Republic. Nell argued that the participation of blacks during the Revolution and War of 1812 warranted their equal inclusion in the American people. Antebellum black conventions and petitions frequently cited Nell's research. Black abolitionist William Howard Day, himself the son of a naval veteran of the War of 1812, responded to the 1850 Fugitive Slave Act by organizing an 1852 memorial for black veterans from earlier wars. In front of an audience of five hundred, including eight African American veterans from the War of 1812, Day delivered a searing critique that unequal treatment of blacks exposed the failed potential of the Declaration of Independence.[18]

Some whites used Nell's historical point to strengthen their arguments that blacks could be citizens. Supreme Court Justice Benjamin Curtis analyzed black rights during the early history of the Republic to bolster his dissent refuting Chief Justice Roger Taney's *Dred Scott* opinion, and in 1861, abolitionist William Lloyd Garrison published *The Loyalty and Devotion of Colored Americans in the Revolution and War of 1812*. Meanwhile, Nell organized a March 5,

1858, commemoration of the Boston Massacre at Faneuil Hall, near the spot of the incident. There, black and white abolitionists spoke out against *Dred Scott,* and the ceremony offered tangible displays of black military participation in American history, such as Crispus Attucks's powder horn, and elderly Brazillai Lew, a veteran of Bunker Hill.[19]

Irish Americans similarly turned to history to affirm their inclusion in American society, while they wrestled at the same time with their own loyalty to Ireland and the United States. William James MacNeven, an Irish-born physician who arrived in New York on July 4, 1805, explored this paradox in his book, *Pieces of Irish History* (1807). MacNeven equated British tyranny against the United States and Ireland, and he argued that resistance by either nation benefited both of them. Subsequent Irish American leaders and editors in the 1840s and 1850s continued to assert this connection to promote assimilation. These spokesmen claimed, in a merger of interests that historian Kerby Miller described as "contrived," that by loving Ireland and struggling for her liberation, Irish Americans helped to protect universal republican principles worldwide and, in the process, deepened their devotion to the United States. Irish nationalists in America, such as Thomas F. Meagher, contended that affection for Ireland was "natural" but also "compatible with all the duties and liabilities the oath of [American] citizenship provides and sanctifies." On the other hand, an editorial in the *Irish American* in June 1850 emphasized the need for Irish immigrants to become "true Americans in heart and soul." In mid-1854, New England intellectual Orestes Brownson, who turned from his Protestant upbringing to convert to Catholicism in 1844, promoted that religion but also urged foreign-born Catholics to slough off characteristics not native to the United States. Brownson urged Irish Americans not to form separate militia companies, presses, or maintain an ethnic culture.[20]

Irish nationalism in America, meanwhile, did not exist simply as a transplant from across the Atlantic. Instead, the Irish nationalist movement in the United States at this time developed in direct response to the alienation many immigrants felt in a foreign land, as well as their sense of loss of their past lives and longing for their Irish heritage. In this transitional period converged their feelings of suffering before immigration, anger at Ireland's increasing squalor, and isolation in America borne of nativism. As Kerby Miller noted, "Ethnic self-consciousness was largely a reaction to *American* disadvantages" but also to "personal sufferings" which, after some "time and distance" had passed, could be translated into nationalist terms. Maintaining their cultural traditions and interest in Irish affairs provided immigrants with a support and social network in the face of the jarring experience of relocating to a new land. Further, the Irish nationalist movement in the United States acted under the assumption that Ireland's humiliation supported American nativism and that elevating Ireland to her place among the nations of the world would generate respect for Irish Americans here. In the late 1850s, the *Irish News* in New York argued that only after Ireland's restoration as a nation would her "children [be] honored or respected," and the *Phoenix* asserted that only then could Irish immigrants face native-born Americans "without being inflamed with feelings of…shame."[21]

A parallel debate took place among Northern blacks. Some African Americans supported separation from white society and the concept of black nationalism, while others advocated integration and emphasized an American identity for blacks. Both these flanks of the black community used different language to argue the same point: that African Americans had the capacity and the right to be treated as equals. Before the war, leaders as diverse as Martin Delaney and Frederick Douglass sought to reclaim African American civilization as a counter to racism and believed that restoring African accomplishments to the rolls of history could puncture the myth of black inferiority on which white prejudice relied. Douglass and integrationists such as Nell focused on blacks' American identity, however, and while they called for self-help within the United States, they also claimed automatic inclusion as part of the American people as a result of their American birth, historical contributions, and civic participation. Other blacks, such as Delaney, responded to exclusion and conditions in America by seeking to form a separate black state and, in that way, expose the economic and moral folly of slavery and prejudice by proving black capacity for production and self-government.[22]

Military Service in the 1850s

The question of whether Irish Americans or free African Americans should serve in the armed forces became particularly prominent during the 1850s. This issue not only foreshadowed events to come during the Civil War, it served as a juncture between the pragmatic realities that loomed as sectional tension, and debate over who could be included within the American people, intensified during that decade. Blacks faced exclusion from the army pursuant to War Department regulations promulgated in 1820 and 1821, and state militias similarly barred their service, although the navy allowed blacks to join in numbers equal to 5 percent of white enlistments. Blacks did not serve in the army during the Mexican War, although about a thousand of them helped man naval vessels during the conflict. Blacks generally opposed that war, viewing any land gained from it as theft from Mexico that helped the slave power.[23]

Northern blacks opposed their exclusion from military service, which comprised a visible and public display of citizenship, and integrationists used the issue to engage further in the debate about American citizenship during the 1850s. In 1852, several resolute blacks, including attorney Robert Morris and abolitionist William J. Watkins, sought a charter to form an African American militia company in Boston. In addressing the Massachusetts legislature's militia committee on February 24, 1853, Watkins actively contested the exclusion of blacks from participating in this form of citizenship rights. "Regard us…as men," Watkins demanded, "who, knowing our rights, dare, at all hazards, to maintain them." Watkins avowed, "We are entitled to ALL the rights and immunities of CITIZENS OF MASSACHUSETTS," as "law-abiding, tax-paying, liberty-loving, NATIVE-BORN, AMERICAN CITIZENS," and he challenged Massachusetts to "carry out the principles of your immortal declaration," which triumphed, Watkins reminded the legislators, in part because of black blood spilled in the Revolution and War of 1812. Despite Massachusetts's progressive reputation on racial issues, however, the committee took no further action on the petition. By 1855, Boston blacks formed the Massasoit Guard without state approval.[24]

Irish Americans, on the other hand, served at all times in the American army, but their participation in the Mexican War complicated their calls for inclusion. Some Protestants argued that Catholicism infected Mexico and made it weak. Irish Americans, meanwhile, asserted that their volunteering to fight in the war evinced loyalty to the United States, notwithstanding their religion. Adding to the mix, some Mexican wartime propaganda questioned the loyalty of Irish Catholics to the United States, or directly asked them how they could fight alongside Protestants in destroying a Catholic country. A band of Catholic American deserters, the San Patricio battalion, provided nativists with a more potent example with which to stain Irish American Catholic soldiers as untrustworthy and disloyal. The members of the battalion deserted for a number of reasons, including harsh disciplinary conditions in the army, the nativist treatment they faced, and the anti-Catholicism they witnessed. Even though not all of its members were Irish Americans, a green flag with the Mexican coat of arms on one side and the figure of St. Patrick on the other, gave the battalion a distinctly Irish American identity.[25]

A few years later, the eagerness displayed by some Irish American militia companies in helping to enforce the Fugitive Slave Act energized the abolitionist-nativist connection, generated further tension between Irish Americans and African Americans, and led some states to curb Irish American militia service. Some ethnic leaders had emphasized enrollment in state militias as a way to integrate into the United States, as well as the highest form of service Irish Americans could provide to their new country. Accordingly, strictures against Irish American militia companies cut exceptionally deep, especially when inspired by nativism and abolitionism. Officials mobilized the militia after the apprehension of runaway slave Anthony Burns in Boston in May 1854, to prevent a mob from blocking Burns's return. Although many native-born militiamen declined to participate, several Irish American units did. A letter in the *Liberator* later protested, "Irishmen, instead of shedding the tear of pity [for Burns], hardened their hearts, and did the business of the oppressor," while another periodical noted, "Where there is base, vile work to be done for slavery, there is your Irish Catholic...ready for business." Eager to limit Irish American participation in civic life anyway, the Know Nothing governors of Massachusetts and Connecticut, Henry J. Gardner and William T. Minor, respectively, disbanded the Irish American militia units in their states. Maine limited the number of immigrants permitted in its militia companies to one-third, and New York disbanded its Irish American Ninth New York State Militia (NYSM) from May 1858 until June 1859 (the Ninth NYSM later served during the Civil War as the core of the Eighty-third New York Infantry).[26]

The controversy over African American and Irish American military service became more pronounced as sectional tension heightened during the 1850s. After John Brown's 1859 raid on Harpers Ferry, Massachusetts's legislature advised repealing the exclusion of blacks from the Bay State's militia but opposition, including from Democratic militia general Benjamin Butler, caused Republican governor Nathaniel P. Banks to veto the measure. Butler and Banks both later commanded black troops during the Civil War, with Butler showing considerably more enthusiasm than the ex-governor. As to Irish Americans, "We hear on all sides the sound of disunion," ethnic leader John C. Tucker cautioned in Massachusetts in 1859. "God forbid that I should live to see the day, but supposing it should come...can Massachusetts...expect that these men, whom she is now about to proscribe, will rush to her assistance? Do you suppose that I would rush to the standard of the State that would put that ignominious mark of political disability and inferiority upon me?"[27]

The actions of Irish Americans themselves in the militia also revealed the uncertain position they held in the antebellum United States. While the native-born debated the level of commitment Irish Americans showed to their new country, persistent loyalty to their native land complicated the issue of allegiance for the Irish in America. Weeks before Confederate forces fired on Fort Sumter, the Irish American Sixty-ninth NYSM celebrated its refusal to parade during an October 1860 visit of the Prince of Wales to the United States. Citing a law that limited the yearly number of parades in which a militia unit had to participate, and ignoring a conflicting law that allowed militia generals to exercise the powers conferred by rank, Colonel Michael Corcoran claimed that his regiment had already satisfied its annual duty. On the evening of March 15, 1861, the uniformed militiamen marched to the festive strains of Irish music into a hall packed with observers and accepted a green silk flag bearing the Irish sunburst in gold.[28]

Thomas F. Meagher delivered the night's keynote address. Deftly using his Irish wit, Meagher turned the meaning of New York's extravagant celebration on its head, noting that the "conqueror can always afford to be munificent to the conquered," and bragging how the prince witnessed the prosperity and freedom of a republic wrested from his ancestors. Meagher acknowledged that Irish Americans had to refrain from the pageant because joining it would have exposed them to charges that they had forgotten the sufferings of their native Ireland. On the other hand, Meagher claimed that Corcoran's refusal to participate would have been a "grievous" breach of military discipline but for (Corcoran's interpretation of) the law. Meagher asserted to his cheering audience that, had the law required Corcoran to do so, he would have paraded the regiment in "submission to the law of the Republic," because acquitting oneself as a "faithful citizen...strengthened...the claims of Ireland to the good will, the advocacy and recognition of America."[29]

While the militiamen wrestled with their dual loyalties, some native-born Americans viewed the Sixty-ninth NYSM's refusal to parade as proof that the Irish in America held a foreign allegiance and could not assimilate or become good citizens of the Republic. In New York City, both Irish Americans and native-born Americans closely followed newspaper coverage of Corcoran's court-martial for disobeying orders, including defenses that relied on Corcoran's Irish heritage. A larger event disrupted the proceedings, however, and led to dismissal of the charges against Corcoran: the shelling of Fort Sumter.[30]

Conclusion

As immigrants and as Catholics, Irish Americans lived under a certain level of exclusion that prewar nativism tried to maintain, institutionalize, and intensify. Even as Know Nothing power changed into Republican power, and the grander anti-immigrant ambitions of the party were thwarted, legal and social challenges to immigrants showed the tenuous status of naturalized citizens.

African Americans confronted even more difficult conditions: slavery in the South and legal strictures and private acts of prejudice in the North. Irish Americans did not face the same legal and social conditions that blacks confronted, and great tension existed between these two groups because they shared the bottom of the socioeconomic scale. Yet, while Irish Americans likely paid little mind to African American discussions, and vice versa, striking echoes nevertheless exist in terms of how both groups reacted to exclusionary forces during the 1850s. Moreover, debates among the native born concerning the rights and status of both groups highlight the contested and undefined nature of national citizenship as the nation reeled toward Civil War.

CHAPTER 2

The Question of Armed Service

As the crisis of citizenship culminated with the Civil War, whether African Americans or Irish Americans would actively participate in the struggle for the Union remained uncertain in light of their prewar experiences and ambiguous allegiances. Yet many Irish Americans and African Americans seized on the opportunity provided them by the Civil War to work toward membership in the broader local and national community, and they entered a new phase in the debate about what American citizenship meant and who could partake in it. Both groups immediately linked any decision to serve in the armed forces with a new location for themselves within the American nation.

Irish American Support of the Union

In contrast to African Americans, few Irish Americans supported the Republican agenda in 1861. Many Irish Americans linked nativism and the Republican Party, which had largely absorbed the Know Nothing Party. Irish Americans overwhelmingly backed Democrat Stephen Douglas during the 1860 presidential election, and Boston's Irish Catholic newspaper, the *Pilot*, argued that no Catholic should vote for Abraham Lincoln because the Republican ranks included many former Know Nothings who advocated "hatred and prejudice and injustice to the Irish." The *Pilot* urged its readers to "remember that every vote cast for a Republican is an endorsement of [Massachusetts's] two year amendment. A naturalized citizen who would vote for a party who proscribes his race, does not deserve the rights of citizenship."[1]

Some Fenians bemoaned involvement in a war that might kill warriors who would otherwise fight for Ireland's liberation. Other Irish Americans in the North lamented the possibility of fighting their ethnic counterparts in the South. Some Irish Americans even expressed sympathy for the South, arguing that "the arrogance and fanaticism" of abolitionists "forced" secession.[2]

For their part, some nativists shunned Irish American offers to participate in words that echo rejection of early African American offers of service. During the summer of 1861, an Illinois recruiter warned that no one should trust Irish Americans to serve as soldiers. Though he later denied making the statement, Quartermaster General S. E. Lefferts of Wisconsin's militia told an Irish American company offering its services, "There are enough young Americans to put down this trouble inside of ninety days and we do not want any red faced foreigners." The company voted to disband.[3]

Yet the reasons why many Irish Americans joined the Union forces reveal much about their growing consciousness of having an American component to their identity, as well as their desire to have a place in the American people. Devotion to the Union and its Constitution inspired many Irish Americans to rally quickly to arms. In November 1860, the *New York Irish American* blamed the "unjustifiable aggressions of Northern Abolitionism" for precipitating disunion, but called on "every good citizen to stand firmly by the Union." Within days of the surrender of Fort Sumter, the ambivalence of many Irish Americans in the North melted, and sympathy for the South crumbled. Thousands of Irish Americans attended a rally at Union Square in New York City on April 20, 1861, beneath buildings bedecked with American flags. Officers from Fort Sumter, including its commander Major Robert Anderson, stood on the speakers' platform, while the colors hauled down from the Fort's flagpole billowed from a perch in the hand of a nearby statue of George Washington. That same day, the *Irish American* reiterated its call for "the adopted children of this glorious nation," to fulfill their duty to the Union, arguing that "our standing in this community, the freedom and equality we proudly claim, are due to no local or sectional concession, but come to us directly from the whole Union, to which our first allegiance is due, under the guarantees of the Constitution which we have sworn to uphold." In June 1861, the Friendly Sons of St. Patrick, a Philadelphia-based Irish American charitable organization, declared that Irish Americans "will yield not in loyalty to the country which they have adopted as their own." In Boston, by November 1861, the *Pilot* argued that the "war of the North is a just one," and viewed it as an opportunity to increase the spirit of patriotism in the general and Irish American community. "This same war has already made us love our country better than ever we did before," maintained the *Pilot,* which predicted, "it will correct the corruption of all our political proceedings." Many Irish Americans hoped that the sight of men from their community enlisting against the Confederate rebellion, standing "together,—no thought over party or sect, / But shoulder to shoulder, as brothers and men," would vanquish nativism.[4]

Similar to the role ministers played in the Northern black community, bishops comprised a corps of leaders for Irish Catholics. Almost immediately,

Catholic bishops in the North displayed their loyalty to the Union. New York's archbishop John Hughes draped an American flag from his cathedral, the bishops of Chicago and Brooklyn had the national symbol hoisted over their residences, and Hughes, Cincinnati's bishop John Purcell, and Bishop Clement Smith of Dubuque, Iowa, all spoke out for the Union. Boston's bishop John Fitzpatrick supported Governor John A. Andrew's immediate initiative of enlisting a regiment of Irish Americans from Massachusetts. The Catholic Church's position of recognizing only lawfully established governments also helped energize Irish American disdain toward a Southern rebellion one early Irish American volunteer identified as standing "against law, order, and constitutional liberty."[5]

England's pro-Confederate stance further antagonized Irish Americans. In late spring 1861, the *Pilot* declared, "When we Irish are side by side with England in any quarrel we *must* be in the wrong. It is the natural instinct of our race to hate the English side, and take the other; and if the southern S[t]ates of America have England for their backer, they must look on it as a thing of fate to have Ireland for their foe."[6]

On the other hand, Irish American willingness to support the Union did not include unbridled enthusiasm for all the changes potentially to be wrought by the war. Some Irish Americans in the North feared distortion of the antebellum Union, and the possibility that the North would impose on the South a relationship similar to the one England imposed on Ireland. One anonymous Irish American advocated action "to subdue the enemies of the Constitution" but cautioned in the summer of 1861 against abandoning the "glorious form of government established by our forefathers in 1787." Writing under the pen name "A Constitutional Unionist," he feared that subjugation of the South would render the region "provincialized," and its population no longer self-reliant to "exercise the duties of citizenship." Another author, from Minnesota, warned that "fanatical" Republicans and "nigger worshippers" sought to alter the nation's political foundation. Both writers sought restoration of the Union, but only on terms as if secession had never occurred.[7]

These views generated paradoxical tensions that persisted through the war and complicated Irish American relations with the Union. In August 1861, the *Pilot* squarely blamed Republicans for bringing about the Civil War. The newspaper stated that Republican insistence on "subjugation of the slave States" and hostility to slavery "endangered the whole fabric of society." In the same edition, the *Pilot* attacked Lincoln for treating Irish Americans "ungratefully and cruelly," and impatiently called for promotions from among that community. Deeming a rumored commission in the federal army for the anti-Catholic Italian revolutionary Giuseppe Garibaldi as an "insult upon the whole Catholic community," the newspaper threatened that the "surest way to stop the war would be to prevail on the whole Irish force to withdraw from the field." Yet, the *Pilot*'s editors still hoped "that by the cooperation of all true lovers of the country, native Americans and adopted Americans, we shall see the majesty of the Government of *our fathers* restored to its former splendor, and the bonds of the Union drawn together." The *Pilot* thus integrated all Americans, native-born and newcomer, through conservative but nationalistic reunion.[8]

In the South, localism and the excitement of participating in the birth of a new country inspired Irish Americans there to support the Confederacy, just as those in the North embraced the Union. Yet, only 84,000 of the 1.2 million Irish immigrants in America as of 1860 resided within the Confederacy, a circumstance which validates generalizing about Irish America based on Northern experiences.[9]

In the end, overlapping and nonexclusive factors motivated Irish American Union enlistees despite their general hostility to the Republican agenda: the wave of patriotism that swept the North after Fort Sumter, devotion to the ideals of the Republic, a desire to conquer nativism, and a view that maintaining the Union assisted Ireland's liberation and ensured the existence of a safe haven for future Irish immigrants. Local loyalties, friendships, and the need for money stood foremost in the minds of other volunteers. The calculation that led to enlistment differed for each man. Recognizing that a variety of factors inspired Irish American volunteers does not detract from the political importance of their service but acknowledges a finer-grained consideration of these individuals who fought for the Union. Ideology, belief in the cause for which they fought, a desire to serve the interests of the United States as well as Ireland, and matters such as personal reputation and financial responsibilities played intersecting roles in encouraging many Irish Americans who volunteered to support the Union.[10]

At the same time many of its members professed a conservative loyalty, Irish America as a community seized on the opportunities for change afforded by the war. Just as African Americans would, in the course of their determining whether to fight for the Union, Irish Americans recognized that military service validated a claim to equal inclusion. Irish Americans almost immediately coupled the question of whether to serve with demands for radical shifts in both society and legal doctrine: the abandonment of nativism, integration of immigrants into the national polity, and an affirmation that American nationalism could incorporate foreign-born newcomers who wished to embrace the Republic.

Irish American Debate about What Service Meant

Irish American soldiers in the field stood at the vanguard of this early wartime conversation about citizenship. Thomas F. Meagher became one of the most prominent voices on the public stage to state that members of his ethnic community had an American identity as well as an Irish one and to promote a concept of American nationalism that incorporated immigrants based on their devotion to the Republic.

Born in Waterford, Ireland, in 1823, Meagher early on established his reputation as an impassioned Irish nationalist. The British banished Meagher to

Van Diemen's Land after he helped lead a failed uprising in 1848. Tasmania could not contain the revolutionary, however, and Meagher escaped to arrive in New York City in late May 1852, where cheering Irish Americans greeted their newest hero. Meagher commenced a lecture tour that took him through New England, the Mid-Atlantic states, and across the Deep South within a year of his arrival in America, gained admission to the New York bar in September 1855, and founded the *Irish News* the following April. Meagher endorsed James Buchanan's candidacy for president, scorned abolitionism as hostile to republican government, and called himself a "Democrat in heart."[11]

As the Civil War loomed, Meagher mirrored the conflicted opinions initially displayed by some Irish Americans. Just prior to the barrage on Fort Sumter, Meagher declared that his "sympathies" were "entirely with the South," but his stance completely changed once hostilities erupted. Meagher joined the Irish American Sixty-ninth NYSM but nonetheless revealed a continuing attentiveness to Irish nationalism, and he hoped that the experience Irish American troops would receive during the war might assist Ireland's future liberation. Meagher's regiment fought at First Bull Run, even though its three-month term of enlistment had expired, and it suffered heavy casualties and lost its colonel, Michael Corcoran, to capture.[12]

The regiment arrived back in New York City on July 27, 1861, and within weeks, began recruiting to fight again as the core of an Irish American brigade that Meagher organized. An Irish revolutionary who had previously focused on the liberation movement for his native land, Meagher now embraced both sides of his identity, at once Irish and American. From his position as one of Irish America's spokesmen, Meagher urged members of his community to defend the Union, and he declared to all Americans how this participation solidified Irish American status within the Republic. Meagher's addresses comprised something more than simple recruiting speeches: they helped define an American identity for Irish in the United States.

On August 29, 1861, tens of thousands of people attended a fair held at Jones's Wood in New York to benefit the widows and children of members of the Sixty-ninth NYSM lost at First Bull Run. There, various stands sold beer, watermelon, and ice cream amid music and dancing. During the keynote oration, Meagher reminded his audience that at the same time they enjoyed the festival's merriment, there existed "little hearts that have grown big and heavy in darkened rooms," while vainly waiting to hear their fathers' footsteps. Meagher offered this sacrifice up on behalf of the entire ethnic community. Those "slain in battle" sealed "their oath of American citizenship with their blood," Meagher declared, and those assembled at the fair claimed "these soldiers as our brothers," who fell in support of the "most encouraging and beneficent" government that "the world has ever known."[13]

Meagher saw glory devolve on all who fell, "wherever they may have been born, at whatever altar they may have worshipped, to whatever school of politics they may have belonged," and he centered attention not on Ireland's liberation but on the Union cause. Meagher resoundingly affirmed the goodness of

American republicanism and the necessity of perpetuating it for the benefit of the entire world. To rousing applause, Meagher appealed for Irish Americans to stand by the Union at any cost. Meagher assured listeners of his Democratic credentials but declared that the president's party became irrelevant in times of crisis because national needs trumped partisanship.[14]

Building to his concluding crescendo, Meagher incorporated a subject sure to arouse the passions of any good Irish American: England. Even here, Meagher used this topic to argue for the primacy of the American struggle. Meagher declared that the same English aristocracy that oppressed Ireland now opposed the United States government, and he vowed that the Confederacy, which enjoyed the "patronage" of such an aristocracy, can "never have the heart and arm of any Irishman who has learned the history of the Stars and Stripes...and who...foresees...the liberty of Ireland." At his oration's zenith, Meagher made his final argument, punctuated by frequent cheering, incorporating Irish Americans into the national polity while inextricably linking the fate of Ireland and the Union. "Every blow that, with the shout of 'Feac an bealac'...clears the way for the Stars and Stripes," Meagher proclaimed to his audience, discouraged the "English aristocracy" and deprived it of allies, "and thus so far avenges and liberates the island of which it has been the persecution." With that being so, Meagher argued, "let us, who hail from Ireland...we, who have taken an oath of loyalty...not to any one isolated State, but to all the States...that built up the powerful and resplendent Union...stand to the last by the Stars and Stripes...the illustrious insignia of the nation that, of all the world, has been the friendliest sanctuary of the Irish race." Deftly weaving through the arguments as to why Irish Americans should fight, Meagher asserted that doing so not only assisted the Irish cause but affirmed their identity as American citizens, even while the meaning of that status remained undefined.[15]

Meagher eagerly took his oratory beyond New York. On September 14, 1861, thousands of people gathered in Bridgeport, Connecticut, to attend a Union rally organized by P. T. Barnum. Placing the Civil War in an international context, Meagher described the United States as bestowing "a glorious future not only to my own native Ireland but to humanity at large," and he emphasized that should the American flame be extinguished, so also would that of republicanism worldwide. Meagher explained that one became an American through the choice of embracing its republican ideals, and he vowed that he would have sustained even a Know Nothing if duly elected (though he did take the opportunity to celebrate the Know Nothing Party's demise). Meagher argued that, regardless of state-imposed strictures, the oaths that Irish Americans gave to the United States created a duty "to the Union." Moreover, according to Meagher, so many Irish lives had mixed into the United States since its founding, and ideological ties so deeply linked Americans and Irish in mutual devotion to the idea of liberty worldwide, that staying out of the war involved turning one's back on both countries.[16]

Meagher delivered a similar speech in Boston a little more than a week later. The event was so popular that some people presented forged tickets in an effort to gain entry, while thousands of others were turned away at the door. Republican Massachusetts governor John A. Andrew introduced Meagher to the cheering crowd and, recognizing the reception he received in what had been a bastion of nativism a few years earlier, Meagher pronounced, "in the centre of the city where this insult to every Irish soldier was conceived, I proclaim it— know nothingism is dead!" Meagher declared that from that point forward "the Irish soldier...shall proudly stand by the side of the native born."[17]

To be sure, in certain instances, Meagher tempered the American focus of his message, perhaps in order to persuade more recent arrivals in the United States. After the carnage of the mid-1862 Peninsula campaign, Meagher spoke at the Seventh Regiment Armory in New York City during a recruiting drive. There, sweltering heat and a cramped space led to a raucous crowd. Along with including his usual American themes, Meagher revealed his dual sense of identity by asking his "countrymen" to stand by his Irish Brigade, "true to the Republic...and true to the memories, the pride and the homes of Ireland," and he spoke not of the American colors but of the green flag borne by Irish heroes. The *New York Times* interpreted the positive reaction of Meagher's audience as proof of their loyalty to the United States, describing how the Irish Americans "adjourned amid the most earnest enthusiasm, evincing as determined patriotism and unswerving loyalty as ever was displayed in a public gathering, and practically demonstrating that the hearts of Irishmen throb with as pure devotion to our flag as ever animated the hearts of a free and noble people."[18]

In contrast to his Seventh Regiment Armory speech, most times, Meagher proclaimed the primacy of the mission in America. In declining an 1862 invitation to celebrate St. Patrick's Day in Chicago, Meagher addressed insinuations that Ireland's plight remained forefront to Irish Americans: "You perceive that...the perils of another land...have been uppermost in my mind," Meagher wrote, before he assured his correspondent, "The country must again be tranquil and united. We, adopted citizens, owe to her our first duty. Upon her destiny depends the fate of Democracy, the world over."[19]

Meagher, who started the war as a pro-Southern Democrat devoted to Irish nationalism, came to articulate how Irish American service earned that community inclusion within the broader nation. By fighting and dying for the Union, Meagher argued, Irish Americans tangibly affirmed their naturalization by showing loyalty to its republican ideals. Moreover, Meagher announced, Irish Americans redeemed the Republic by defeating a nativist impulse that had tarnished America's true values. Meagher consistently asserted that Irish Americans helped restore the United States to her position as a beacon of democracy for the entire world, and gave hope and help to Ireland in the process.

The concepts of equal citizenship, American identity, and inclusion based on military service also appear in private statements from less prominent Irish Americans. Despite coming slightly later than the period on which this chapter focuses, the 1863 letters of Peter Welsh address all three themes in a quintessential way. Welsh's letters shed light on the ideological, as well as the mundane, reasons why Irish Americans joined the Union army. Moreover, the letters reveal Welsh's swift sense of belonging in America and his consciousness of the importance of citizenship, prerequisites if Irish Americans were to press for continued legal change after the war. Welsh's letters help us understand how an Irish American explored privately, in the course of rationalizing his decision to fight for the Union, the dual identity and concept of American citizenship that Meagher articulated publicly.

In contrast to Meagher, Welsh came from the Irish American working class, and he was devoid of political ambition. Born in June 1830 on Prince Edward Island, Welsh settled in the Boston area and married an Irish-born woman in 1857. The young couple moved to New York City, where Peter struggled to earn a living as a carpenter. During the summer of 1862, Peter returned to Boston to help resolve an argument between several family members, but when their wrath turned on him, Peter turned to the bottle. After a drunken spree, Welsh felt so mortified that he enlisted in the Twenty-eighth Massachusetts, and he participated in the Army of the Potomac's battles from South Mountain until he received a mortal wound at Spotsylvania in 1864.[20]

Welsh's unvarnished war letters to a small audience of family members reveal that public pronouncements made by Irish American leaders percolated through the entire ethnic community. Early on in his service, Welsh affirmed his Irish nationalist credentials through his bitter hatred of England, and he argued that helping the United States simultaneously assisted Ireland. Welsh scorned "that acursed harlot of nations England," and claimed that for decades, it sought to divide and destroy the United States because of its republican liberalism and commercial power. Accordingly, Welsh linked the United States, and his own participation in its defense, to the global struggle for liberty, and he argued that the burgeoning influence of the American Republic forced Britain and other nations to treat their own subjects more liberally. Welsh viewed Union victory in the Civil War as indispensable to maintaining the hope of liberty in Europe, and especially in "poor old Erin."[21]

Welsh's wife disagreed with his choice to enlist, and she challenged him to justify further his reasons for volunteering. In response, Welsh placed provocation for the war at the feet of abolitionist fanatics but held that their actions did not justify rebellion. After reminding his wife Margaret that "rebellion without a just cause is a crime of the greatest magnitude," Welsh reiterated the global importance of a Union victory: "People of all nations," Welsh asserted, had a "vital interest" in the outcome of the "first test of a modern free government in the act of sustaining itself against internal enemies," because failure would sound the death knell of republicanism across Europe.[22]

Welsh offered his wife another powerful reason which validated his service: his status as a citizen and American. "This is my country as much as the man that was born on the soil and so it is with every man who comes to this country and becomes a citezen," Welsh proclaimed. Disclaiming any distinction between birthright and naturalized citizenship, Welsh added that he held a deep and vested interest in maintaining the nation's integrity. To discount his wife's anticipated arguments regarding nativism, Welsh reminded her that the United

States provided them, and thousands of others who had experienced misery abroad, with asylum, food, and comfort. "What would be the condition to day of hundreds of thousands of the sons and daughters of poor opressed old erin if they had not a free land like this to emigrate to[?]" In contrast to tyranny in Ireland, Welsh reminded his wife, opportunities existed in America that gave people hope, so that even if starting from the humblest origins, one could aspire to receive all the honors that "a great nation" can bestow.[23]

Welsh embraced it as the duty of all Americans, whether native born or not, to support the Union because of the responsibilities that accrued with citizenship, as well as a moral obligation to help maintain for future generations the best government ever known. While Welsh felt "disgusted with the management of this unfortunate war," and scorned the "imbecility of an incompetent administration and fanatical nigar worshippers," he simultaneously staked his life to the national cause and viewed the war as a divinely ordained agent that could invigorate the United States for the entire world's benefit. As Welsh's assured his skeptical wife, "there is yet something in this land worth fighting for."[24]

Welsh's father-in-law in Ireland remained unconvinced, and the soldier wrote him directly to justify his decision to volunteer. In contrast with British tyranny, Welsh explained, "just laws and a Constitution which guarentees equal rights and privelages to all" governed the United States. Furthermore, Welsh argued, the United States not only served as a land of opportunity for thousands of Irish immigrants, the Irish had helped found the United States and had earlier served in its armed forces. Welsh fought to ensure that the work done, and blood shed, by his predecessors had not been in vain, as well as to preserve this "best and most liberal government in the world" for unborn generations of Irish refugees and oppressed people across the globe. Although Welsh believed that a "party composed almost wholy of native born citizens" agitated the abolition question that precipitated the war, he declared that nothing could negate his interest in its outcome or his duty to participate as a foreign-born citizen.[25]

Besides, Welsh justified to his Irish father-in-law, he was "striking a double blow" by fighting in America, because "while we strike in defence of the rights of Irishmen here we are striking a blow at Irlands enemy and opressor." Privately echoing Meagher's views that England hated the United States because of the threat its growing naval and commercial power posed, and the beacon of republicanism it provided, Welsh viewed preserving the Union as something which weakened Ireland's enemy. Welsh in this way articulated the meaning of his carrying the green regimental flag, the "emblem of Irlands pride and glory" entrusted to him on St. Patrick's Day 1863, in an American army. While displaying devotion to Ireland, Welsh fought for the Union, a compatible duality where Welsh hoped Ireland would someday attain American-style republicanism. Though he inextricably linked his service with striking a blow for Irish liberation, Welsh just as emphatically believed that his enlistment fulfilled a duty of citizenship, and he showed a remarkable sense of his equality and in-clusion within America.[26]

It comes as no surprise that many Irish Americans remembered Ireland's plight, or placed their decision to serve during the Civil War within its military tradition. Moreover, many Irish American volunteers argued that such service helped Ireland, whether as training for a future liberation movement or, more commonly, as a defense of republicanism on a global scale. Irish Americans naturally remained conscious of their ethnic heritage as an inextricable compo-nent of their identity, especially where most of them were either born in Ireland or had parents who were, and many of their leaders possessed Irish nationalist credentials. Yet, at the same time, Irish Americans linked support for the Union with calls for change in their legal, political, and social status. Ethnic leaders and the Irish American press began constructing potent arguments regarding the meaning of Irish American service immediately upon the outbreak of the war. Many Irish American soldiers in the ranks embraced these sentiments as well, as their decision to enlist began a process which accelerated their recogni-tion that they had an American identity along with an Irish one.[27]

African American Service Rebuffed

In contrast to the generally immediate welcome into the armed forces received by Irish Americans, only a slow progression of events led to black inclusion in the army. Strikingly, although their discussions about whether to serve in the war did not engage with each other, African Americans and Irish Americans as-serted some of the same early arguments linking military support for the Union with calls for legal and political change. Black men eagerly sought to partici-pate in the patriotic wave that swept the North after the firing on Fort Sumter, and their efforts to join the military were extensions of prewar claims which sought to transform insecure rights in the North, and enslavement in the South, into a new legal order built on the bedrock of equal rights between races (in contrast to Irish American racism). African Americans in Philadelphia sought to raise two regiments of "Herculean defenders," the "Hannibal Guards" in Pittsburgh offered their services, and for several months, hundreds of Pennsyl-vania blacks drilled for combat. Meanwhile, in the South, long-suffering slaves saw the war as the potential moment of their deliverance. As Elijah Marrs, a Kentucky slave who later joined the Union army, recalled, "ideas of freedom began to steal across my brain" once war broke out.[28]

Most whites, however, rebuffed black initiatives to defend the Union in 1861. The owner of one recruiting center for blacks in Cincinnati felt com-pelled to remove an American flag hanging above his door, while police told the proprietors of another such office, "We want you d—d niggers to keep out of this; this is a white man's war." Police stopped blacks from drilling in New York City and refused to protect them from any racist mob violence that might erupt if they continued to do so. Shortly after the Union disaster at First Bull Run, New York's governor Edwin D. Morgan turned down the offer of three black regiments. Other blacks offered their service directly to the federal government, but they met with similar rejection.[29]

Even Massachusetts shunned its black population's efforts to participate in defending the Union. After the Confederate barrage on Fort Sumter, Boston's blacks thronged into a Baptist church to pledge fifty thousand soldiers for the Union. "If the Government would only take away the disability," Robert Morris elsewhere pleaded, "there was not a man who would not leap for his knapsack and musket, and they would make it intolerable hot for old Virginia." Nonetheless, Massachusetts's legislature declined a petition to remove the whites-only exclusion from state militia laws.[30]

For its part, Congress passed the First Confiscation Act during the special summer session of 1861, authorizing seizure of property used to aid the rebellion and permitting discharge of certain slaves on those grounds. Congress recognized Southern blacks as valuable, but passive, assets of which the Confederacy should be deprived: they did not hold rifles, but they released white men for military service by performing the labor necessary for the South's sustenance. While Republicans sought by the Confiscation Act to nudge the identity of slaves from chattel property to human individuals, blacks were not yet seen as worthy of explicit emancipation or military participation, much less citizenship and inclusion. The First Confiscation Act simply dismissed slaves from the employment of owners deemed to have forfeited their right to the slave's labor as a result of disloyalty to the United States.[31]

White exclusiveness galvanized the separatist impulse in some blacks and, in contrast to the Irish American experience in 1861, early enthusiasm among many blacks gave way to ambiguity. Some African Americans called for their community to remain neutral. One man from Troy, New York, beckoned members of his race to avoid their fathers' experience of serving in combat only to suffer the persistence of slavery and exclusion. Black schoolteacher William H. Parham recounted how the hearts of blacks and whites in Cincinnati beat in indignant unison after the firing on Fort Sumter but vowed that, after subsequent insults, the fight now solely concerned whites. In New York City, blacks considered whether to offer themselves as substitute firemen or a home guard to replace whites who had gone into the army. The plan came to naught after several of them recalled the scorn shown at their earlier offers to serve.[32]

Other blacks anticipated the moment when white Unionists would call on them, and even those who believed that whites would arm blacks only out of grudging necessity saw a moment of opportunity. Just as Irish Americans did, these individuals linked any military service they might provide with an assertion of inclusion and rights claims. Within weeks of the war's outbreak, a vocal proponent of black preparation for service, Philadelphia's Alfred M. Green, sparked a robust debate with those in his community who displayed less enthusiasm. Green called on blacks to set aside "past grievances" in their country's "time of need," and instead, ready themselves to capitalize on an "auspicious moment," as well as participate in the moral contest to crush slavery. A writer identifying himself as "R.H.V." countered Green's call and contended that centuries of labor in bondage already entitled all blacks to citizenship rights and, for men, recognition of manhood. R.H.V. warned that the country stood far from ready to initiate a new era, and he balked at the "sacrifice of thousands of our ablest men to encourage and facilitate the great work of regeneration" for an unreceptive United States. Taking up the prewar debate between black integrationists and separatists, R.H.V. wanted to rely on internal black industry and education, not military strength, to open avenues to wealth, respect, and equality.[33]

R.H.V. challenged Green to respond with a fuller articulation of what he believed blacks could gain from military participation. Green, in turn, argued that war presented an environment conducive to change. Warning against apathy, Green called on blacks to prepare for inevitable service because "no nation" could be emancipated from slavery or prejudice except "by the sword, wielded too by their own strong arms." Green saw war as an energizing force that could focus his people, afford them greater agency in their demands for equality, and eliminate divisions within the black community over colonization and other issues. According to Green, blacks "should all have our shoulders to the wheel in order to enforce...self-reliance, and ourselves striking blows for freedom," grasping "as one man" this "most favorable opportunity" to make themselves "felt as a people" and as "part" of the United States. "If ever colored men plead for rights or fight for liberty," Green counseled, "now of all others is the time. The prejudiced white men, North or South, never will respect us until they are forced to do it by deeds of our own." Green did not suggest that success would come easily, but he recognized the opportune moment for blacks to act and seize not just freedom but inclusion and equality.[34]

The Acts of July 17, 1862

Two separate acts, both given final approval on July 17, 1862, profoundly affected the status of African Americans and Irish Americans by recognizing military service as a vehicle for the rapid naturalization of foreign-born immigrants and opening the door for military participation formerly prohibited to blacks. The legislation also underscored where European immigrants stood in contrast to blacks a year into the war. Neither act helped clarify citizenship as a legal concept, but one statute revealed willingness on the part of American society to fast-track into national citizenship European aliens serving as Union soldiers, while the other bill highlighted unreadiness to accord blacks similar inclusion. Whereas the bill concerning immigrants explicitly linked military service to citizenship, the act as to blacks did no such thing. Instead, the significance, in terms of citizenship doctrine, of the legislation that permitted blacks to serve in the army lay in its potential to create a transformative moment.

At the time, naturalization regulations required five years residence in America before an alien could become a citizen. On January 21, 1862, the Senate resolved that the Committee on the Judiciary should consider a bill to confer citizenship on aliens serving in the armed forces. On January 24, 1862, Connecticut Republican congressman Dwight Loomis introduced a bill to similar effect in the House, and on February 3, 1862, Ohio Republican Benjamin Wade submitted to the Senate a resolution from his state's legislature that urged such a revision to the naturalization laws. During its consideration of the Senate's version of an act to define the compensation of army officers in mid-March 1862, the House Committee on Military Affairs inserted an amendment stating that

> any alien, of the age of twenty-one years and upwards, who has enlisted or shall enlist in the armies of the United States, either the regular or the volunteer forces, and has been or shall be hereafter honorably discharged, may be admitted to become a citizen of the United States, upon his petition, without any previous declaration of his intention to become a citizen of the United States, and that he shall not be required to prove more than one year's residence within the United States previous to his application to become such citizen; and that the court admitting such alien shall, in addition to such proof of residence and good moral character as is now provided by law, be satisfied by competent proof of such person having been honorably discharged from the service of the United States as aforesaid.

The House approved the amendment without debate on June 12, 1862, and the Senate concurred as easily on June 19, 1862. Both bodies continued to deliberate about other provisions in the bill, and ultimately approved it and sent it to the president.[35]

Accelerating the path to citizenship for European immigrants in the Union army generated little congressional discussion. Extensive deliberation about whether even to allow black participation in the war, on the other hand, reached a shrill pitch on both sides of the debate. By the first anniversary of the firing on Fort Sumter, northerners increasingly softened their earlier refusals of black service, and they wanted the federal government to prosecute the war with every available means.[36]

On July 9, 1862, Republican senator James Grimes from Iowa offered an amendment to the militia laws to eliminate any exemption from military service "on account of color or lineage." Democrat senator Willard Saulsbury of Delaware immediately railed against the measure. Saulsbury identified Grimes's proposal as nothing less than an emancipation scheme, and he thundered to his colleagues, "No sooner are we engaged in civil war, notwithstanding the Administration and Congress announced that the object should be simply for the preservation of the Constitution and the restoration of the Union, than an attempt is made on every occasion to change the character of this war, and to elevate the miserable nigger, not only to political rights, but to put him in your Army, and to put him in your Navy; and while this policy is pursued, the Union never will be restored, because you can have no Union without the preservation of the Constitution."[37]

Republican senator John Sherman of Ohio countered Saulsbury, asking whether only the Confederacy should benefit from black labor while "the people of the United States, struggling for national existence, should not employ these blacks for the maintenance of the Government." Admitting that blacks would probably not serve as soldiers, but as "laborers, as servants, as guards, and spies," Sherman declared that "gentlemen from the slave States ought not to feel so sensitive about this matter." Sherman further assured the Senate that "the law of caste is the law of God," and "whites and blacks will always be separate, or where they are brought together, one will be inferior to the other." On the other hand, Sherman reminded his listeners that "blacks are in our country—four millions of them," he recognized an inchoate allegiance by identifying them as "natural friends in subduing this rebellion," and he urged that every resource at the Union's disposal be used to suppress the rebellion. Republican senator Henry Wilson from Massachusetts recalled to the Senate black participation in past American battles during the Revolution and War of 1812. Unionist Party senator Garrett Davis of Kentucky feared that including blacks in any form of military service would humiliate the nation's white men as an admission that "we cannot command white soldiers enough to fight our battles." Davis then warned that the measure might unleash an uncontrollable situation, and he cited slave revolts to argue that the black man was generally "mild and gentle," but "when he becomes excited by a taste of blood he is a demon." Minnesota's Morton Wilkinson rejected Davis's condemnation of black inhumanity by having read by the Senate's secretary Andrew Jackson's proclamation complimenting the service of blacks at New Orleans.[38]

Over the next few days, the Senate continued debating in the same vein whether to authorize blacks to serve as Union laborers or soldiers. The Senate considered additional wrinkles as well: whether to compensate loyal slaveholders for the loss of the services of slaves employed under the bill, as well as New York Republican senator Preston King's point that "when we take a slave to serve the country in this emergency...he should be made free, whether he belongs to a rebel or not." The final bill passed by the Senate on July 15, 1862, included a provision that any slave who served the Union as a laborer or soldier became free, as well as his mother, wife, and children, so long as their owner was disloyal. The next day, the House passed the Senate's bill without amendment or debate, and on July 16, 1862, Lincoln signed into law both the act that offered military service as a quick route to naturalization for foreign-born soldiers, as well as the bill that allowed blacks to serve as Union soldiers. The Senate declared both bills to be law on July 17, 1862.[39]

While the Act of July 17, 1862, did nothing to recognize the citizenship status of blacks, Charles Sumner perceived the revolutionary potential of this law. On July 16, 1862, the Republican senator from Massachusetts proclaimed to his colleagues, "The new levies which are now called for will be placed under the inspiration of an idea which cannot fail...the idea of freedom, and freedom's battle once begun cannot be lost." According to Sumner, "From this day forward the war will be waged with new hopes and new promises. A new power will be enlisted, incalculable in influence, strengthening our armies, weakening the enemy, awakening the sympathies of mankind, and securing the favor of a benevolent God.... The slave everywhere can hope. Beginning to do justice to the oppressed, we shall at last deserve success." Beyond that, military service had explicit links to citizenship and inclusion as part of the American people. Created by the Union's inability to achieve a quick victory, this measure opened the door for groundbreaking shifts in the law and afforded blacks an opportunity to assert an American allegiance denied them by slavery and the legal exclusion of *Dred Scott*.[40]

African American Service, Manhood, and Calls for Citizenship

Arming black troops was not an automatic given, though, and debate continued among whites about whether to actually do so. Proponents contended that arming blacks would help secure the Union, and some advocates additionally argued that military discipline would prepare freedmen for self-sufficiency. Other supporters declared in racist terms that the purported "obedience," "servility," and "ear for music" of blacks would render them useful soldiers. Some whites grudgingly supported arming blacks for the sake of their own self-preservation, admitting that they "would a little rather see a nigers head blowed of then a white mans." Opponents articulated largely racist arguments as to why blacks should not be armed: some feared that black soldiers would commit crimes once in uniform, while the editors of Boston's Irish Catholic newspaper, the *Pilot*, argued that, "*twenty thousand negroes on the march would be smelled ten miles distant.*" The idea of arming blacks proved especially controversial in Border States such as Kentucky, where politicians, editors, and overall public opinion opposed the measure. On the other hand, recruiting for the First Kansas Colored Infantry began in July 1862, and the regiment mustered into service in January 1863. As for the Bluegrass State, by the end of the war, 23,703 black soldiers hailing from Kentucky served, a number second only to the 24,052 African American troops recruited in Louisiana.[41]

Two years after combat began, the fluidity generated by the Civil War permitted Massachusetts governor John A. Andrew to recruit black soldiers for the Fifty-fourth Massachusetts, entrust to them the American and Bay State banners, and review them on May 28, 1863, from the steps of the State House. Even then, some people opposed this policy. New York Democratic governor Horatio Seymour refused to follow Massachusetts's lead, even after a committee of white New Yorkers argued that recruiting black volunteers to fight under the Empire State's flag would save whites from an unpopular draft that Seymour opposed. The federal government followed Massachusetts's suit in earnest, however, arming black regiments that bore the designation United States Colored Infantry (USCI), Cavalry (USCC), Artillery (USCA), or Heavy

Artillery (USCHA). Not until the federal government began recruiting for the United States Colored Troops (USCT) did New Yorkers have the opportunity to raise black regiments.[42]

It also remained to be seen if blacks would enlist in light of earlier rejection of their offers of service. Once recruiting for the Fifty-fourth Massachusetts began, though, the reaction of James Henry Gooding of New Bedford, Massachusetts, was typical: he quickly enlisted and offered an active vision of black participation and its potential fruits. A former cook on a whaling ship, the new soldier unified the separatist and integrationist impulses by challenging fellow blacks to participate in the war and embrace in that way "the only opportunity that will ever be offered them to make themselves a people." Gooding argued that blacks "will have to be the means" of their improvement and exhorted his readers that "there is more dignity in carrying a musket in defence of liberty and right than there is in shaving a man's face, or waiting on somebody's table." For blacks to attain equality, Gooding announced, "they must forego comfort, home, fear, and above all, superstition, and fight for it," deciding to "become something more than hewers of wood and drawers of water." In a revealing jab at the antebellum black convention movement, Gooding challenged African American leaders as well, noting that through military service, blacks had "a chance to obtain what they have 'spouted' for in 'convention assembled.'"[43]

Frederick Douglass agreed, declaring to blacks at a July 6, 1863, Philadelphia rally that "the speediest, and best possible way open to us to manhood, equal rights and elevation, is that we enter this service." Douglass recognized the "revolution" as "tremendous" after the government and army united "in giving us one thunderous welcome to share with them in the honor and glory of suppressing treason and upholding the star-spangled banner." Douglass also acknowledged the nationalizing moment of the Civil War, arguing that regardless of local prejudices, "the State is not more than the nation. The greater includes the lesser. Because the State refuses [to arm blacks], you should all the more readily turn to the United States.... Citizenship in the United States will, in the end, secure your citizenship in the State."[44]

Even emigrationists joined the war effort. Martin Delany accepted a commission as a major in the Union army late in the war, and the Reverend Henry Highland Garnet recruited black troops, blurring the boundaries between Douglass's integrationism and the separatism that they espoused before the war. African American military service supported the agenda of both impulses by demonstrating black ability and power on one hand but also extending the prewar arguments asserted by Nell and others about the value, extent, and identity gained by black participation in American life.[45]

In mid-July 1863, federal troops quelled Draft Riots in New York City, which had turned violently against blacks and resulted in, among other things, Irish American violence against African Americans, lynchings, and the destruction of a black orphanage. At the same time, blacks gathered in Poughkeepsie, New York, to articulate what their community expected in return for its military service for the Union. The Poughkeepsie convention deemed the present war "combat for the sacred rights of Man against the myrmidons of Hell," a struggle between "anarchy, misrule, barbarism, human slavery, despotism and wrong" versus "self-government, true Democracy, just Republicanism, and righteous principles." As all had a duty to struggle for the right, the delegates resolved that "warm lead and cold steel" should be "duly administered by two hundred thousand black doctors" against the South. Yet the same delegates also pressed forward prewar arguments to demand changes if they served. One delegate vowed that blacks would fight only on terms of equality with white soldiers, while another one announced that military service automatically transformed each black enlistee into a "Citizen Soldier of the Union."[46]

The Poughkeepsie delegates cast black soldiers as defenders of the true ideals of 1776 at a hopeful juncture in history for both the United States and the world. Reminding blacks that no one stood ready for liberty who would not fight for it, the convention also claimed for blacks a place among the American people by including "fighting for the land that gave them birth" as one of their "inalienable rights." The delegates proclaimed that the moment had arrived for African Americans to strike "as men and heroes" while Liberty's "benignant eye" gazed upon millions of blacks who held the balance of power in the present struggle. More than 34,000 Northern blacks embraced the convention's message and served in the Union army, a number that comprised about 15 percent of the total 226,000 free blacks in the North, and 7 percent of the total 487,970 free blacks in the United States, as of 1860.[47]

Whites early on took notice of black assertions. By September 1863, Maryland congressman Henry Winter Davis echoed African American statements by identifying blacks as the loyal population of the South, and he rejected the idea that white Union soldiers would shun their assistance, evoking black participation in the Revolution and War of 1812 as evidence. Pushing further, Davis maintained that slaves would take "title to freedom" through military service in a manner far more real than any presidential proclamation could grant them, and he rejected talk of colonizing blacks as a "humiliating and unworthy" idea after these champions of the Republic "fought the battles of liberty, and have aided us to win back our territory."[48]

Linking military service with claims of citizenship, even as that concept remained undefined, merged with one particularly personal issue which also prompted black resolve: their blazing desire to deliver slavery's death blow. The Act of July 17, 1862, freed any black man who labored for or served in the United States armed forces, along with his mother, wife, and children, but only if each one's owner bore arms against the United States or otherwise assisted the Confederacy. In February 1864, the freedom granted by the July 1862 legislation and the Emancipation Proclamation expanded to include black conscripts or volunteers (though not their families) owned by Southern unionists. Congress also provided that in slave states that remained in the Union, the hundred dollar bounty payable to each black conscript would go to loyal owners, as well as compensation in an amount not more than three hundred dollars, as determined by state-level commissions. Not until March 1865 did Congress hold "forever free" the wife and children of any person mustered into the service and, acknowledging the difficulties slavery posed for validating marriage, required only evidence that the soldier and his wife lived together or "associated as husband and wife" at the time of enlistment, regardless of any form or ceremony and whether recognized by law or not.[49]

While legislation slowly evolved to link black military service with freedom, black soldiers knew that in practice they would free individual slaves by pushing forward the Union lines, and that in helping achieve overall Union victory, they assisted in the destruction of slavery as a whole. In training camp with the Fifty-fourth Massachusetts, James Henry Gooding anticipated the symbolic power of uniformed blacks liberating slaves and hoped that all Americans would realize that "a slave can be made a soldier, to fight for his own liberty." White supporters also recognized this powerful motive, as Columbia University's president, Charles King, pointed out to the Twentieth USCI early on: "To you, then, in addition the appeal suitable to every soldier, lies in a higher and holier sense, an appeal as emancipators of your own race, while acting as the defenders and champions of another. You are in arms, not for the freedom and law of the white race alone, but for universal law and freedom."[50]

Conclusion

Irish American soldiers became the vanguard for those of their community who argued that service to the Republic defeated nativism, served as a communion between Irish Americans and native-born Americans, and earned Irish Americans an identity and equal inclusion as American citizens. Irish Americans argued that they established their place as full members within the polity, despite their lack of birthright citizenship, based on their choice to embrace and support the same political values that native-born American citizens held dear.[51]

Moreover, in contrast to Know Nothing contentions that they did not wish to accept American values and political practices, Irish American leaders and soldiers cast their persistent concern for Ireland's liberation as a desire to export American ideals abroad. Irish Americans argued that they not only embraced and wanted to preserve American republicanism here, they wanted to replicate it in Ireland. Irish Americans also associated themselves with the Founding generation by virtue of their defense of the Constitution. In so doing, Irish Americans began to broaden American nationalism, rejecting nativist definitions of it to instead promote the idea that anyone could become an American on embracing common American principles.

Even more striking, more than 178,000 blacks, four-fifths of whom (if not more) had been slaves, served in the Union army. Another 10,000–18,000 blacks served in the Union navy. Approximately 36,000 black soldiers died in the army (disease caused 80 percent of those deaths in contrast to about 60 percent of white Union soldiers' deaths). William J. Watkins's prewar advocacy, claiming for blacks their place as American citizens and soldiers but pronounced in the deliberative calm of a legislative committee room, now thundered across the country in both word and action, and consummated a point of no return in American race relations. Participation in the Civil War helped unify the nationalist/separatist and integrationist wings within the Northern black community, just as it helped blur the boundaries between Irish nationalists and those who advocated sloughing off all characteristics of ethnic culture. Blacks advanced toward equality simply by enlisting in the armed forces, but they also linked Civil War service to demands for major change and began to define and celebrate how it impacted them as individuals and as a community even before the Union's victory. Especially for blacks, military service had profound personal and political meanings that not only hastened the death of slavery but accelerated and helped determine the direction of the transformation of American citizenship.

Both groups quickly linked their support for the Union with an expectation of inclusion and equal standing in the American people, although neither group at this time promoted a more robust definition of what national citizenship meant. On the other hand, arguments for inclusion had been articulated before without permanent success. Whether this service would lead to permanent changes remained yet to be seen.

CHAPTER 3

African Americans in Arms

Minutes after Alexander T. Augusta boarded a train in Baltimore, a white teenager tore off a shoulder strap from his uniform. As Augusta scolded the boy, a man tore off his other strap, and other people menaced the distinguished thirty-eight-year-old doctor as he quietly took his seat. Augusta, educated in Canada and the first black surgeon to serve in the American army, reported the incident to provost guards elsewhere in the car once the group left. Determined that his attackers must be punished, Augusta went with one of the guard to the local provost marshal, who offered that any U.S. officer who claimed his protection would have it, regardless of race, and sent a lieutenant to assist Augusta in capturing the perpetrators.[1]

The lieutenant feared that the culprits would flee if he made his presence too obvious, so he reminded Augusta that the doctor had the same right as any commissioned army officer to take people into custody. As he found and arrested one of the offenders, Augusta realized the extraordinary nature of a black man arresting whites in Baltimore. While he was searching for other perpetrators, a man named Dunn struck Augusta's face. The lieutenant immediately arrested Dunn and several others. Augusta went on to Philadelphia later that night and felt some vindication when he eventually learned that some of his attackers had been tried and imprisoned at Fort McHenry, and that the provost marshal had told the lieutenant that he should have shot Dunn. The continued racism and hostility, as well as the affirmation and respect, present in this episode encapsulated the contradictions experienced by black Civil War soldiers. Augusta directly attacked the language of *Dred Scott* when he asked, in writing about the incident, "What has been gained in this transaction?"

1. Company E, Fourth U.S. Colored Infantry, at Fort Lincoln, District of Columbia.
The regiment was organized in Maryland and composed of slaves
and free blacks. Courtesy Library of Congress.

and then answered, "It has proved that even in *rowdy Baltimore* colored men
have rights that white men are bound to respect." Augusta was later buried in
Arlington National Cemetery.[2]

The black military experience during the Civil War was multifaceted and
complex, and included pervasive racism at the same time that it advanced African American claims to inclusion and equality. Deep-seated racism continued in the Union army, but military service nonetheless provided blacks the
chance to gain self-confidence, and it assisted their conversion from slavery to
freedom, and claim to the rights and privileges of a still-undefined concept of
citizenship. Because military success shored up public support for Republican
policies, including emancipation, blacks also fueled acceptance for an agenda
they supported by helping advance the Union cause.[3]

Wartime experiences affected black troops in deeply personal ways, and
these individual transformations comprise some of the most important fruits
of black military service. As one noncommissioned officer from Louisiana told
his comrades, "I has been a-thinkin' I was an old man; for on de plantation,
I was put down wid de old hands...But since I had come here to de Yankees,
and been made a soldier for de United States, an' got dese beautiful clothes

on, I feels like one young man...An' I feels dis ebenin' dat, if de rebs came down here to dis old Fort Hudson, dat I could jus fight um as brave as any man what is in the Sebenth Regiment."[4]

For tens of thousands of black men who joined the army, experiences in the military also strengthened the identity component of citizenship, heightened their political awareness, and emphasized that participation in the war had the potential to result in stunning legal changes. Especially for slaves, who likely paid little heed to questions of national allegiance while in bondage, serving in the Union military comprised a choice of loyalty. While some blacks may have enlisted for financial reasons, or because federal agents conscripted them, most joined the military for political motives, or eventually came to understand the broader significance and potential of their service. While prejudice in the armed forces persisted throughout the Civil War, serving in them also presented an opportunity for change which blacks eagerly seized, and it afforded them experiences that helped inform their evolving sense of what citizenship entailed as a concept.[5]

Wearing the Union Blue

In and of itself, donning the Union blue comprised a profoundly transformative moment. Colonel Robert Cowden of the Fifty-ninth USCI described slaves with "filthy rags" of crude homespun clothing hanging "slouchily" on their bodies, and who manifested "a cringing manner." Once clothed in a "clean new suit of army blue," Cowden noted in contrast, the former bondmen stood "completely metamorphosed, not only in appearance and dress, but in character and relations also. Yesterday a filthy, repulsive 'nigger,' to-day a neatly-attired man; yesterday a slave, to-day a freeman; yesterday a civilian, to-day a soldier." Another white soldier similarly noted, "Put a United States uniform on his back and the *chattel* is a *man*." Ex-slave Elijah Marrs exulted, "This was the biggest thing that ever happened in my life," because, "I felt like a man with a uniform on and a gun in my hand."[6]

Black soldiers cherished their rifles because, before the war, arms were routinely kept out of their reach. Even when blacks received second-rate uniforms or subpar guns, which they opposed as representing disrespect for their equality, they associated these accoutrements with their change in status. Black soldiers proudly proclaimed their manhood on accepting their equipment, as the chorus of one song popular among them emphasized:

> They look like men, they look like men
> They look like men of war,
> All arm'd and dressed in u-ni-form,
> They look like men of war.[7]

The sight of thousands of black soldiers wearing the eagle and uniform of the U.S. government not only validated African American manhood, it further fueled calls for complete equality. Black noncommissioned officers stood as equal in rank to their white counterparts. Moreover, the service of free blacks and former slaves side by side in regiments and brigades built connections between these formerly largely separated segments of African America. An element of cultural superiority tinged some Northern blacks who saw themselves as elevating less enlightened Southern blacks from slavery's corruption. Life in the army now traversed geography and slave status to create a shared history among blacks of diverse backgrounds.[8]

Ceremonies honoring black regiments before they departed for war operated to contradict the *Dred Scott* exclusion of blacks, and emphasize instead their American identity and allegiance. Frequently, local authorities or fellow African Americans presented an American flag to black regiments and made speeches that proclaimed the important elevation to citizenship and manhood that had taken place, even though blacks still were not American citizens in the eyes of the law. In the North, parades of black regiments down major city streets emphasized newly opened access to public space. Such rituals, similar to those conducted for departing white units, including Irish American regiments, made a visible statement of black equality and agency in shaping the destiny of both the African American community and the United States as a nation. White participation in such ceremonies emphasized the potential at that moment for blacks to earn a measure of acceptance through military service.

While training at Readville, Massachusetts, the men of the Fifty-fourth Massachusetts felt self-respect at their evolution, under public scrutiny, from civilians to soldiers. George E. Stephens recorded that on a sunny May 1, 1863, hundreds of Bostonians "stirred with admiration" as they watched the unit drill "with the regularity and precision of Regulars." On May 18, 1863, Governor John A. Andrew, William Lloyd Garrison, Wendell Phillips, Frederick Douglass, and hundreds of others, including black women who made a flag for the regiment, traveled to Readville to present the Fifty-fourth Massachusetts with its colors. Andrew recognized that, although dozens of Bay State units had carried out similar ceremonies, this moment held unique significance because it occurred for blacks for the first time. "Today," Andrew announced to his multiracial audience, "we recognize the right of every man in this commonwealth to be a MAN and a citizen." According to Andrew, "devoted patriotism and regard for their brethren of their own color," inspired "noble" black soldiers who intended to "strike a blow which, while it shall help to raise aloft their country's flag—*their* country's flag, now, as well as ours—by striking down the foes which oppose it, strikes also the last shackle which binds the limbs of the bondmen in the Rebel States." Acknowledging the dawn of a new legal structure in the United States, Andrew presented the unit with an American flag donated by the women of Boston, a banner of the Commonwealth of Massachusetts given by the black women of Boston, and another insignia with a cross on a blue field and the Latin phrase, In Hoc Signo Vinces ("In this sign, you will conquer," the motto adopted by the Roman Emperor Constantine just before his victory in battle at Milvian Bridge in AD 312).[9]

A mood of excitement and apprehension filled Boston's air on May 28, 1863, as the Fifty-fourth Massachusetts became the first black regiment to parade through a major city. Some officers in the regiment feared that simmering racial tensions might boil over into violence. Governor Andrew even ordered the issue of six rounds of ammunition per man to the regiment, and its rearguard marched with fixed bayonets. As the black soldiers formed at Park Square that morning, white abolitionist Henry I. Bowditch broke a nervous tension within the gathering civilian crowd by shouting, "Three cheers for Col. Shaw." Suddenly, applause rose from the throng, and the rest of the day passed largely in accord with approving sentiments. Merchants closed their businesses as a multiracial crowd gathered along a parade route bedecked with flags, watching as the unit wound through the city's streets behind an escort of black children and a band, led by Irish-born Patrick Gilmore, playing the "John Brown Song." Even Irish American women waved handkerchiefs in greeting, although the offices of Boston's Irish Catholic newspaper, the *Pilot,* remained shuttered.[10]

The Fifty-fourth Massachusetts passed the spot where Crispus Attucks suffered his mortal wound during the Boston Massacre, and William Lloyd Garrison observed the regiment's march from the balcony of Wendell Phillips's house, his hand resting atop a bust of John Brown. Governor Andrew, Senator Henry Wilson, state legislators, and other dignitaries reviewed the regiment from the steps of the State House. After drilling on Boston Common, the Fifty-fourth Massachusetts continued through Boston, with family members charging into the ranks to say final good-byes. One woman traveled from Chicago to bid farewell to her two sons, kissing them while tears streamed down her face. Some onlookers muttered epithets or hissed at the passing regiment, and the day did not end without violence: street toughs beat a son of Frederick Douglass, and policemen narrowly averted an assault on the regiment's rear as the Fifty-fourth reached the wharf to board its transport steamer. Complimentary newspaper reports, however, and a rush to the recruiting office of the Fifty-fifth Massachusetts, indicated the general spirit of the day.[11]

Shortly afterward, a black private of the Fifty-fourth Massachusetts wrote a song revealing the pride and hope he felt at this moment, and it soon became popular in other black units:

> So rally, boys, rally, let us never mind the past;
> We had a hard road to travel, but our day is coming fast;
> For God is for the right, and we have no need to fear;
> The Union must be saved by the colored volunteer.

Casting blacks as the saviors of the country, the soldier's lyrics reveal anticipation to prove African American valor in combat as well as an uplifting faith that, by participating in the preservation of the nation, blacks controlled their own destiny.[12]

Comparable events occurred in Philadelphia. Black artist David Bustill Bowser designed the colors that black civilians presented to the Sixth USCI at its training center at Camp William Penn in the late summer of 1863. The banner featured a female personification of Liberty holding aloft a flag and exhorting a black soldier, armed and uniformed, while a black child applauded in the background. On October 3, 1863, the regiment paraded without incident through Philadelphia on a cloudless day, and its men became the first blacks served by the Union Volunteer Refreshment Saloon. From that day forward, the saloon served both black and white soldiers.[13]

In contrast to the racist violence that ripped through Manhattan during the Draft Riots less than eight months earlier, the Twentieth USCI marched down Broadway behind a band and in front of thousands of cheering spectators on March 5, 1864. In front of the Union League Club, Columbia University's president Charles King saluted the men "as fellow-countrymen" and presented to the regiment a flag donated by the wives and sisters of club members, emblazoned with the symbols of a conquering eagle, a broken yoke, and the armed figure of Liberty. "When you put on the uniform and swear allegiance to the standard of the Union," King reminded his audience, "you stand emancipated, regenerated, and disenthralled—the peer of the proudest soldier in the land." King assured the troops that "prejudice...may still throw obstacles in your way, but that way is upward and onward, and your march in it cannot be stopped, cannot be much delayed, unless by your own want of faith and want of work." The men of the Twentieth USCI then enjoyed food and refreshments before marching down Fifth Avenue, Lexington Avenue, Madison Avenue, and Broadway, to board the steamer that took them to New Orleans.[14]

A black newspaper, the *Christian Recorder,* reported that "some of the same rabble" who committed racist violence during the July 1863 Draft Riots "shed tears of repentance on beholding the Twentieth regiment...in glorious array, onward to the defence of their country, God, and the right." Recounting that white businessmen and twelve hundred "prominent colored men" marched alongside a thousand uniformed black troops, who carried individual flags donated to them by white women, the periodical rhetorically challenged, "Ain't that a victory?" These events do not imply a universal change in white attitude—prejudice against blacks ran so great among some elements in New York City that the Union League earlier chartered a special steamer to ferry hundreds of relatives to the Twentieth USCI's training camp on Riker's Island—but the parade provided a stark contrast to racism and exclusion, and emphasized an American identity for blacks.[15]

Albeit in very partisan tones, white periodicals covered the parade as well. The *New York Herald* implied the threat of race-mixing as "daughters of Fifth Avenue" presented regimental flags to the Twentieth USCI, while the Workingmen's United Political Association feared that armed black troops would someday deploy against white laborers. On the other hand, the *New York Times* described the Twentieth USCI's "splendid appearance" as it marched through the city's "most busy and aristocratic streets," and deemed the parade a "noble vengeance" for blacks who had been hunted down in the Draft

2. The Twentieth United States Colored Infantry receiving their colors on Union Square,
New York City, on March 5, 1864. *Harper's Weekly*, March 19, 1864.
Courtesy Library of Congress.

Riot. The *Tribune* observed how gratifying the ceremonies must have been to
blacks, "near where sundry sable citizens were massacred last summer, for the
crime...of appearing in the color bestowed by the Almighty."[16]

Some black regiments endured violence against them in Northern cities: a
mob assaulted the Second USCI as it passed through Philadelphia in November 1863, and people threw stones at the train on which the regiment traveled.
In other instances, however, black troops noted complimentary attitudes toward them. Sergeant William McCoslin related that, en route to the Army of
the Potomac, his regiment of Illinois blacks arrived to find a "fine breakfast"
waiting for them at the Soldiers' Rest in Chicago, and a "splendid supper"
on reaching Pittsburgh by rail thirty hours later. McCoslin and his regiment
felt "proud of the treatment we have received, being the same, if not better
than some of the white soldiers received." McCoslin reported that even in the
border state of Maryland, "all the citizens" treated the black soldiers "with
some respect."[17]

This process of arming black troops also fueled a nationalist impulse. Black
soldiers enlisted from all parts of the country and, with few exceptions, mustered into service as U.S. troops without a state designation. Speeches delivered
to blacks before they assumed active duty further emphasized that the war had

to do with allegiance to a national Union. While presenting a flag inscribed "Unconditional Loyalty" to the Twenty-sixth USCI, recruited in New York, John Jay (grandson of the man who served as the first Chief Justice and negotiated the 1794 Jay Treaty), declared that the men of the regiment offered their "lives for the defense of our common country and our common freedom. Organized by the National authority, you are henceforth a permanent part of the army of the Republic." In offering the flag to the men, Jay challenged them, "Bring it to us again—tattered, it may be, and stained with the life-blood of your brave soldiers; but bring it, the emblem of a nationality unbroken."[18]

Dignity through Service

Both the idea and the execution of military service encouraged greater self-awareness of black manhood and American identity. The privations of war served as a vehicle for the Northern white upper class to tangibly affirm their manhood and physical abilities. Similarly, blacks of all classes and regions used military service as a badge of their manhood, countering racist conceptions of them as children or as little different from animals. In contrast to competing ideas of blacks as inferior, and the lives many had experienced as slaves up to that point, military service helped to energize a sense of black equality in public and personal ways. This sense percolated not only through soldiers but the civilian black community as well. Soldiers' letters published in newspapers, coverage by war correspondents such as African American Thomas Morris Chester, and the simple oral recounting of wartime experiences by veterans to family and friends all advanced the argument that black military service and bravery earned citizenship and validated manhood.[19]

As USCT regiments gathered in the field, John C. Brock of the Forty-third USCI reported, "What a glorious prospect it is to behold this glorious army of black men as they march with martial tread across the sacred soil of Virginia." Brock understood both the political and personal meanings of military service, noting that black soldiers would look back to say "with exultation" they comprised "one of that noble band," who "toiled for the rights of man, and elevation and liberty of our race." Sergeant George Hatton of the First USCI "felt as though I were in some other country where slavery was never known," as he watched black troops gather at City Point, Virginia, while ex-slave Elijah Marrs recalled that, at his first roll call, "I felt freedom in my bones."[20]

Milton M. Holland, later a Medal of Honor recipient, wrote of his regiment's first engagement in Virginia that "they stood like men, and when ordered to charge, went in with a yell, and came out victorious." The danger of battling Confederates failed to daunt members of a Tennessee regiment, and Henry Prince of the Fourteenth USCI responded to his lieutenant's warning, "Boys, it may be slavery or Death to some of you to day" with the prophetic retort, "Lieutenant, I am ready to die for Liberty," just before a bullet struck him dead.[21]

Black service and valor inspired African American civilians, especially after they witnessed flag presentations or contributed to the well-being of the men. George E. Stephens invited black women to participate in the Fifty-fourth Massachusetts's experience and provide "strong evidence of your patriotism" by organizing sewing circles to support the troops. In the summer of 1863, the black women of New Bern, North Carolina, provided a "splendid battle flag" of rich blue silk for the Thirty-fifth USCI, depicting Liberty resting her right foot on a copperhead snake. The women undoubtedly felt pride in the plate attached to the flagstaff: "Presented to the First Regiment of North Carolina Colored Volunteers by the colored women of Newbern, N.C." By autumn 1863, African American women founded aid societies in Bridgeport, New Haven, Norwich, and Hartford, Connecticut, to assist black troops. In Louisville, Kentucky, the Colored Ladies' Soldiers Aid Society tended to wounded black soldiers and established a school and hospital for the African American community there.[22]

Firsthand encounters with slavery proved educative and motivational for free Northern blacks marching through the South. A member of the Fifty-fourth Massachusetts described some of his shoeless comrades during a hard march through South Carolina, but promised that "when we look at the suffering condition of the poor slaves, we can give it all." For Southern black volunteers, helping to liberate slaves proved an especially bittersweet inspiration, particularly after reports arose that masters sold, whipped, or beat the family members of some enlistees. In March 1864, teams of black soldiers on furlough near St. Louis raided into Howard County, Missouri, to liberate their families. Throughout the South, black soldiers chopped down whipping posts and destroyed slave pens, though instances of violent revenge against actual slaveholders seem rare. Aaron Oates felt emboldened to write directly to Secretary of War Edwin Stanton to ask for the emancipation of his family in Kentucky, reminding Stanton that, "as I am a *Soldier,* willing to loose my life for my Country and the liberty of my fellow man I hope that you will please be So kind as to attend to this." Some white officers affirmed this sense of black self-liberation. After one black enlistee told his captain that he feared for his family's welfare, the officer wrote the slaveholder:

Now all I have to Say is this man is now a Soldier, and is entitled to his family, and *I have promised him that he Shall have them and he Shall,* and you will greatly oblige me, to furnish them with clothing and transportation to the Mo river at Kansas City immediately.

You may Consider this beyond my authority. I Confess it is as an officer, but not as a man, having 100 men with me to execute political Justice where it is necessary.

The delivery of that Negro Woman Martha & her children will insure you the protection and respect of all under my Control. The failure to do so will place the whole matter with me, and I will tell you in the Spirit of Calmness that your *life* or property is but a small Consideration when opposed to the march of freedom.[23]

Movingly, Spotswood Rice of the Sixty-seventh USCI wrote his daughters in September 1864 to let them know that he intended to free them when a planned joint expedition of white and black troops advanced into their area within the month. Rice defiantly wrote his daughters' owner that same day to tell her that his children were his "God given rite," and the longer she tried to keep them, "the longor you will have to burn in hell and the qwicer youll get their." Rice warned his daughters' owner that they were enemies wherever they met and that he had the "powrer and autherity to bring hear away and to execute vengenens on them that holds my Child."[24]

An even more stunning event took place in May 1864 near Wilson's Landing on the James River. The day after the liberation of several female slaves who bore the marks of a "most unmerciful whipping," former owner William H. Clopton found himself under arrest for disloyal activities. As Sergeant George W. Hatton of the First USCI recalled,

> The commanding officer determined to let the women have their revenge, and ordered Mr. C. to be tied to a tree in front of head-quarters, and William Harris, a soldier in our regiment...who used to belong to him, was called upon to undress him and introduce him to the ladies that I mentioned before. Mr. Harris played his part conspicuously, bringing the blood from his loins at every stroke, and not forgetting to remind the gentleman of the days gone by. After giving him some fifteen or twenty well-directed strokes, the ladies, one after another, came up and gave him a like number, to remind him that they were no longer his, but safely housed in Abraham's bosom, and under the protection of the Star Spangled Banner, and guarded by their own patriotic, though once downtrodden race.

Revealing the energy blacks displayed in helping to destroy the hated institution of slavery, the incident also underscores that once blacks served in U.S. uniform, they planned to claim their spot as equals. Successfully helping to deliver family and racial brethren from bondage generated a heightened sense of empowerment in African Americans.[25]

The presence of black troops encouraged newly emancipated slaves to live as free people as the Union lines advanced. John C. Brock of the Forty-third USCI reported that the white inhabitants of Fairfax Court House, Virginia, "looked bewildered" as "they really beheld nearly 10,000 colored soldiers filing by, armed to the teeth, with bayonets bristling in the sun," and "colors flying and the bands playing." Colonel Robert Cowden of the Fifty-ninth USCI, recruited from Tennessee, described how white inhabitants of Memphis, Tennessee, "saw as they peered from their windows or stores, what they had never before seen and had never expected to see,—their own former slaves powerfully and lawfully armed for their overthrow, and led and commanded by those whom they considered their invaders. The sight must have burned into their very souls." These displays also profoundly affected black civilians, such as a former slave and his son-in-law who felt confident enough to arrest and disarm a Confederate veteran who had threatened them, and marched the man ten miles to the First USCI's headquarters.[26]

Inequality in the Ranks

Acknowledging African American expectations of equal treatment, and experiences of respect by some whites, in no way discounts the pervasive racism black soldiers confronted in the Civil War army, and which contradicted some egalitarian facets of including them in the Union's armed forces. While many USCT officers showed sympathy to blacks, and saw themselves not only as helping to prosecute a war but also to elevate a race, others joined the USCT simply to gain an officer's commission. Some of these officers displayed open prejudice at every turn. Other USCT officers held less intense opinions but accepted the notion of black inferiority prevalent at the time and treated their men accordingly. The existence of different perspectives within the USCT officer corps resulted in a wide range of treatment of black soldiers, even where military regulations demanded identical treatment for blacks and whites. Some officers showed fairness and tried to help their men understand military discipline and the rule of law, while others employed severe punishments on subordinates they saw as ignorant by virtue of their race. At its worst, racism among some officers fueled arbitrary abuse of black soldiers and civilians (cruel officers admittedly existed within white regiments as well).[27]

Prejudice regularly manifested itself in the inequitable fatigue duty ordered of black soldiers, borne out of the notion some officers held that blacks should serve primarily as laborers. According to one of the Fifty-fourth Massachusetts's officers, black troops performed fully half of 19,000 soldiers' days work during the siege of Fort Wagner, although white troops outnumbered them ten to one. An inspector at Morganzia, Louisiana, in July 1864 found that, despite orders which prohibited disproportionate fatigue duty for African American troops, blacks performed all the labor at that post while several white regiments did none. Colonel James C. Beecher complained that "so-called 'gentlemen' in uniform" called former slaves turned troops "'d——d Niggers,'" at a time when they were "just learning to be men." Beecher argued that setting black soldiers to "doing for white regiments what those Regiments are entitled to do for themselves...reduces them to the position of slaves again." Within days of Beecher's letter, the commander of the Department of the South, Quincy Gillmore, issued an order prohibiting further use of black troops in its jurisdiction to perform labor for white troops. When Gillmore learned that "improper labors" continued to be imposed on black troops, he insisted that "colored troops will not be required to perform any labor which is not shared by the white troops, but will receive in all respects the same treatment, and be allowed the same opportunities for drill and instruction."[28]

Black soldiers resented unequal treatment in fatigue duty, and the *Christian Recorder* printed angry letters from the field that described poor living conditions. One man in the Thirty-second USCI furiously complained in July 1864 of incompetent and uncaring officers, having to toil day and night on half rations that "white soldiers would not eat," and hauling guns "like horses or mules" for miles under a beating South Carolina summer sun. Yet the contrasting meanings of the black experience during the war are evident in a letter published by the *Christian Recorder* in February 1864. "R.W.W." of the Fifty-fifth Massachusetts reported the men having "been worked almost to death" after arriving on Folly Island, South Carolina, though he also recounted how white soldiers "have come to see that they are bound to treat us as men and soldiers, fighting for the same common cause."[29]

Inequality in pay comprises one of the major examples of discrimination against blacks in the army. The War Department originally intended to pay black soldiers the same as whites, $13 a month with a $3.50 clothing allowance, and higher salaries for noncommissioned officers. Despite his Republican credentials, however, Solicitor William Whiting reviewed the Act of July 17, 1862, which authorized the enlistment of blacks, and held that black soldiers stood entitled to receive only the pay contemplated by the act for black laborers. The relevant provision read, "That all persons who have been or shall be hereafter enrolled in the service of the United States under this act shall receive the pay and rations now allowed by law to soldiers, according to their respective grades: *Provided,* That persons of African descent, who under this law shall be employed, shall receive ten dollars per month and one ration, three dollars of which monthly pay may be in clothing." On June 4, 1863, the federal government changed its policy so that black troops would receive $10 a month in pay, regardless of rank, with $3 deducted for clothing.[30]

Shortly after the men of the Fifty-fourth Massachusetts charged against Fort Wagner and heard of the atrocities committed against blacks during the New York City Draft Riot, both of which occurred in mid-July 1863, they learned of this reduction in their pay. The men became "highly incensed" at their treatment as "drafted ex-slaves," observed George E. Stephens of that regiment, who noted as well as that offering noncommissioned officers seven dollars effectively reduced these burgeoning black leaders to the "level of privates." Observing that no special law need be passed to pay Spaniards or Sandwich Islanders in the U.S. service (or, he could have noted, nonnaturalized Irish), Stephens declared that the simple act of muster entitled one to all the pay and bounties awarded to any other soldier, and that military service trumped race. Another soldier in the same regiment, James Henry Gooding, believed that "too many of our comrades' bones lie bleaching near the walls of Fort Wagner to subtract even one *cent* from our hard earned pay." Gooding vowed that, if the nation could not afford to pay them, the men of the Fifty-fourth Massachusetts would do their duty "without murmur," but they would not "sell our manhood for ten dollars per month." Meanwhile, officers of the Fifty-fifth Massachusetts felt stunned at this "breach of faith," and many of them declined to accept pay for themselves until late November 1863, after their men assured that they could do so.[31]

In protest, many black soldiers refused to accept unequal pay. The Fifty-fourth and Fifty-fifth Massachusetts regiments also rejected supplemental pay appropriated by their state to make up the difference between what white soldiers received, feeling that to accept a portion of their pay from the Commonwealth would be to acknowledge a right by the United States to distinguish between them and other soldiers from Massachusetts. A member of the Fifty-fifth Massachusetts explained that black soldiers enlisted out of a sense of duty and preferred to serve without pay rather than "acknowledge ourselves the inferiors of our white comrades in arms, and thus by our own actions, destroy the very fabric we originally intended to erect."[32]

While the fight over pay hurt the morale of black troops, it also energized long-term demands for recognition of black equality and manhood. Days after learning about the reduction in pay, the noncommissioned officers of the Fifty-fourth Massachusetts resolved the need for "true, manly action" so as "to secure to us a full recognition of our rights as men by the controlling masses of this nation." Joseph Walker wrote from Florida that, while the ensuing privation to families "would cause the blush of shame to mantle the cheek of a cannibal, were he our paymaster," such suffering became acceptable if it proved that "we are making men (and women) of our race."[33]

Refusing to accept unequal pay thus provided blacks with a vehicle to assert their courage of conviction, as a member of the Fifty-fifth Massachusetts responded to white critics that blacks stood on their principles. Another soldier, John H. B. Payne, critiqued the legal climate by challenging the country to live up to its betrayed ideals: "Colored men fought to establish the Declaration of Independence, and for the star-spangled banner, the emblem of the white man. After colored men had helped to establish those great blessings, General Washington was the man who presented both the stars and stripes to white men, and suffered the slave-holder to present the stripes alone to colored men." Payne insisted as a native-born American, "Give me my rights, the rights that this Government owes me, the same rights that the white man has." Edward D. Washington of the Fifty-fourth Massachusetts noted that in combat, bullets struck black and white soldiers without distinction, and he resented being put "put beneath the very lowest rioters of New York."[34]

Some black soldiers wrote directly to high-ranking officials to assert their impatient demand for change. James Henry Gooding pointedly asked Lincoln by letter, "Are we *Soldiers,* or are we *Labourers?*" Noting that his regiment shared with whites all the perils of reducing Charleston, "the first stronghold that flaunted a Traitor's Flag," Gooding challenged Lincoln through the president's own proclamation to the South that the "United States knows no distinction in her Soldiers." Invoking the memory of the "rich mould" of dead black soldiers surrounding the parapet of Fort Wagner, Gooding emphasized that he and his comrades affirmed their place as members of the nation, and their demand for equal treatment, through native birth and military service.[35]

Other black soldiers averred breach of contract to describe the decision of the government not to pay them equal to white soldiers. In seeking clemency from the War Department on his three-year sentence for desertion, seventeen-year-old Warren Hamilton of the Seventy-third USCI offered his services if the government still needed them and explained that he regretted his actions, but felt that "one breack of enlissment was quite sufficient to justify another perticulurly when it was transacted on the part of the gov." Hamilton cleverly asked, if a general's promise could be broken, what could one expect of a "poor soldier (pri.)[?]"[36]

White advocates of arming blacks also spoke out against unequal pay. Members of the Fifty-fourth Massachusetts recruitment committee wrote Governor Andrew that black recruits suffered a deception after they had received assurances that they would enjoy equal treatment and added that because blacks "cannot even be permitted to die for their country on an equality with other soldiers, they have been made to feel that they still are only *niggars* not men." Governor Andrew, for his part, wrote to Lincoln, cabinet secretaries, and other government officials to advocate a change in policy. Andrew also proclaimed in a published letter that black troops, "showed themselves to be true soldiers of Massachusetts" at Fort Wagner, and he acknowledged black activism with a sympathetic vow not to rest until "you have secured all of your rights."[37]

For some black soldiers, frustration at unequal pay generated more than rhetoric and a refusal to accept less money. As one general reported from South Carolina, "The greatest discontent prevails, and in several instances a spirit of mutiny has been developed." When a transport docked at Folly Island, South Carolina, in April 1864, some members of the Fifty-fourth Massachusetts refused to disembark, forcing Major John W. M. Appleton to reboard and physically pull one soldier off while others followed, muttering "money or blood!" and "muster us out or pay us," in the pouring rain. Trouble continued in the Fifty-fourth Massachusetts for several months. Some USCT officers responded unfavorably to the pay protest, heightening tension even more. One soldier from the Thirty-second USCI, for example, reported that "after the officers found out that the men would not take the seven dollars, they began to treat the men like dogs."[38]

Some black troops rejected the protest against unequal pay, however, and feared that it would cause a backlash from whites. Garland H. White of the Twenty-eighth USCI complained *after* resolution of the pay issue that "those few colored regiments from Massachusetts make more fuss, and complain more than all the rest of the colored troops in the nation. They are doing themselves and their race a serious injury. I sincerely hope they will stop such nonsense, and learn to take things as soldiers should."[39]

For still other blacks, hardship eclipsed their resolve to stand against inferior pay. "Letters have been constantly arriving for six months in these regiments in which the wives of the enlisted men describe their sufferings," reported one general in South Carolina. One draftee in the Sixth USCI, organized in Pennsylvania, writing under the acronym "Bought and Sold," nearly deserted on reading his wife's letters. "Our officers tell us now, that we are not soldiers," he wrote, though he had felt "very patriotic" and "proud to think that

I had a right to fight for Uncle Sam." His wife's letters, and the realization that so many men could not send their families a penny, chilled that patriotism to the "freezing point," and he poignantly added that it had little chance of thawing. One member of the First USCI grew so despondent he shot the fingers off his right hand as a way to be discharged. Other black troops angered their comrades by breaking solidarity with the rejection of unequal pay. A member of the Thirty-second USCI, organized in Pennsylvania and a regiment that suffered terrible morale after having to endure rotten rations and backbreaking labor, cast Sergeant Major George W. Clemens to the *Christian Recorder* as a traitor after he signed the payroll to accept seven dollars.[40]

In light of these tensions, "Wolverine" in the Fifty-fifth Massachusetts asked those at home to "show their love by suffering with us," but not to write "down-hearted letters to the soldiers." "Every heart-burning letter…gives us a very bad disposition," he warned, and poor behavior among black troops threatened to affirm racial stereotyping of all blacks. Another member of the Fifty-fifth Massachusetts recognized that families suffered, but insisted that black "children would blush with shame" if their fathers accepted inferior treatment. While many of them agreed that, through resistance, blacks contended "manfully for our rights," the fact that families endured tremendous hardship as a result of the protest also weighed heavily on many minds.[41]

In addition to learning of protests and tension within the black corps, Congress received petitions on the issue from whites and blacks. Some appeals came from sympathetic officers of black regiments, such as those of the Fourth, Fifth, and Sixth USCI, and from those stationed at Helena, Arkansas. Other petitions came from black troops themselves, such as one from black noncommissioned officers at the post at Benedict, Maryland. The Rhode Island, Iowa, and Vermont legislatures petitioned Congress to equalize pay, as did multiple Union League chapters, and private citizens from such states as Maine, New York, Massachusetts, Ohio, and Wisconsin. In a July 1863 speech in Philadelphia to promote black enlistments, Pennsylvania Republican congressman W. D. Kelley appealed to black manhood but also asked cheering whites to pour in "upon Congress memorials in overwhelming numbers, demanding that, as to pay and pension, they [black soldiers] shall be treated as liberally as others will."[42]

By February 1864, Congress turned to the issue of equalizing pay for the black troops. On the Senate floor, Republican Henry Wilson from Massachusetts cited letters from four colonels commanding black troops, but he focused attention on the black protest as well, describing how the Fifty-fourth Massachusetts refused to take a single dollar and declined pay appropriated by its state legislature, "because they were promised the same compensation as other troops, and they demand it as a right." Republican senators William Pitt Fessenden and John Conness agreed that no distinction based on color should be made in pay but voiced concern for the Treasury, and suggested that equalization of pay should go forward only from the date of passage of appropriate legislation. Other senators, such as Republicans Charles Sumner of Massachusetts and James H. Lane and Samuel C. Pomeroy of Kansas, countered that justice should trump concern for the national coffers.[43]

A few days later, Republican senator Henry S. Lane of Indiana generated a debate among members of his party. Lane argued his purported concern for the Treasury by identifying blacks as refugees "fighting for a higher boon than money. They are fighting for their freedom," before he contended that "no man in his sober senses will say that their services are worth as much, or that they are as good soldiers, or that they should be paid as much." While agreeing with Lane that black troops fought "for something higher and nobler than pay," Wilson countered Lane by citing Fort Wagner, and he stood firm that justice dictated a retroactive correction.[44]

The senators also debated whether distinction should be made in pay and bounties between free blacks and slaves who enlisted in the army. While blacks argued for equal standing regardless of former lives as slaves, the Senate debate highlighted continued uncertainty as to whether the simple act of serving in the Union army created for all blacks equality before the law. Minnesota Republican senator Morton Wilkinson powerfully argued on the payment of bounties, "Are not the services of a slave soldier, if he perils his life, just as good as the services of a free man? If a slave regiment or a slave army can save this Constitution and Union, do we not owe those men just as deep a debt of gratitude as we owe the white soldiers or the free black soldiers?" Realizing the wrongs endured by slaves for so long, and claiming that "the greater wonder is that after having been treated by this nation as they have been treated, one of them can be found to raise his arm for the defense of the Union," Wilkinson pushed further: "Indeed, we owe them more."[45]

On March 10, the Senate compromised to pass a bill equalizing pay retroactively to January 1, 1864, with the exception that where a person authorized by the War Department promised enlistees the same pay as whites (such as the soldiers of the Fifty-fourth and Fifty-fifth Massachusetts regiments), that unit would receive equal pay retroactive to the date of muster. Because the House of Representatives had not yet acted on the measure, Senator Wilson on April 22, 1864, moved impatiently to add its text to an army appropriations bill. Wilson's advocacy reached its crescendo in a speech before the Senate approved his amendment by a vote of 32–5. The Massachusetts senator not only described the "obedient, faithful, brave" soldiers who "proved their courage, constancy, and devotion" at Port Hudson, Milliken's Bend, and forts Wagner and Pillow, but also the "discontent bordering on insubordination and mutiny" in some regiments on account of unequal pay. "Thousands of colored men have entered the service of the country under the plighted faith of officers of the Government," Wilson thundered, and in the breach of their promises, "discontent in these regiments has become so great that a mutiny broke out in the third South Carolina volunteers, and the leader of it, who was a sergeant [Sgt. William Walker], has been shot for mutiny, and others are under arrest and they too may be tried and shot for violation of discipline, impelled by a burning sense of our injustice."[46]

In the end, the 1864 appropriations bill passed into law held that all blacks mustered into the armed forces were entitled to the same equipment and pay dating to January 1, 1864, all persons enlisted under the October 17, 1863, call for volunteers stood entitled to the same bounty without regard to color, and all blacks free as of April 19, 1861, who had enlisted in the armed services stood entitled from the time of their enlistment to the same pay, bounty, and clothing to which whites were entitled at the time of the enlistment. The following year, blacks earlier mustered into service in South Carolina under Major General David Hunter and Brigadier General Rufus Saxton under authority from the Secretary of War dated August 25, 1862, were deemed entitled to the same pay and allowances, without distinction by color, from the time of their enlistment.[47]

When officers in the Fifty-fifth Massachusetts learned that Congress equalized black pay, they judged it best, "after so many disappointments," to remain silent until official confirmation arrived. Even then, a final wrinkle caused black soldiers to balk: the law required some blacks to swear that they were free on April 19, 1861, the day the Union first called on states to provide volunteer troops, in order to receive equal pay. Colonel Edward N. Hallowell of the Fifty-fourth Massachusetts devised a so-called Quaker Oath, whereby each soldier could swear that "no man had the right to demand unrequited labor" of them, so that either slave or free could answer in the affirmative. The necessity of this Quaker Oath angered many of Hallowell's soldiers, although they understood his good intentions and consented to take it. Some blacks felt it a "step backward" to have to swear on their freedom in order to get equal pay when they had not had their free status questioned when they enlisted in the first place. Some members of the Fifty-fifth Massachusetts even feared that the oath was a trap to identify slaves for return to their owners after the war.[48]

George E. Stephens of the Fifty-fourth Massachusetts, meanwhile, continued to seethe with rage in May 1864 that, although blacks proved themselves "just like white troops" in bravery, *Dred Scott* persisted in army pay, civilian segregation in city passenger cars, and strictures against black purchase of public lands. Lamenting that real legal change continued to elude blacks, Stephens called for a new order in which blacks would be "let alone, and treated just like other men," earning their wages when they worked, receiving praise when they fought, and being punished when warranted. Stephens promised that, where foreign-born soldiers received the same pay as the native born, and blacks had taken the same pay as whites when they served in prior wars, denying blacks their due now would only energize their resolve to oppose discrimination. As late as August 1864, in light of delays in paying the men after passage of the 1864 appropriations bill, Stephens stridently asked, "Do you think that we will tamely submit like spaniels to every indignity?" In noting that "because I am black, they tamper with my rights," Stephens expressed his conviction that whites interfered with rights and privileges inalienably vested in him through a higher law.[49]

Nonetheless, victory in the quest for equal pay gave rise to celebration in the black regiments overall. Officers of the black troops felt relieved, not only because of improved morale but for justice. An officer in the Fifty-fifth Massachusetts described the "relief experienced" by the regiment's officers as "like the loosening of a cord, long drawn to extreme tension," while Lieutenant Charles M. Duren of the Fifty-fourth Massachusetts praised black resistance and predicted that now "we shall have better men—a better Army." In the ranks of the Fifty-fourth Massachusetts, a "petty carnival" prevailed on payday, as music, dancing, and feasting marked the celebration that their resistance had earned blacks a measure of equality. Sergeant John C. Brock reported that the men of the Forty-third USCI "fell in the ranks with more alacrity than they ever did" to receive their equal pay. The troops felt further joy to send money to their families—the Fifty-fourth Massachusetts sent sixty-four thousand dollars and the Fifty-fifth Massachusetts sent sixty-five thousand dollars home by one express company alone. On October 10, 1864, the men of the Fifty-fifth Massachusetts held a commemorative service in which they equated their actions to colonial American resistance against the British and resolved their determination to prove themselves worthy for "liberty and citizenship in the new order of things now arising in this our native land."[50]

The successful fight against unequal pay proved one of the first civil rights victories borne of black protest, and it powerfully indicated their refusal to abide by any notion of second-class citizenship, even where Congress still refrained from recognizing black national citizenship in the law. Through blazing letters and petitions to government officials and newspapers, refusals to accept any pay except the same as whites, and even mutinies despite the specter of facing capital punishment, black soldiers articulated their vision of a constitutional regime that respected their equality. Historian Joseph T. Glatthaar claims that this protest from the ranks against unequal pay "served no purpose" other than to alienate blacks' more effective advocates on the issue, their white officers. Glatthaar's argument erroneously discounts the importance of black action on this matter. The protest of black soldiers not only proved vital to their ultimate success as to unequal pay, it had consequences far broader than three dollars a month. In prevailing on the issue, blacks validated their new status and demands for equality. At a time when Southern slaves had no influence and were punished for protest on the plantation, and free Northern blacks enjoyed little more clout, a protest conducted by black soldiers caught the attention of white officers, politicians, and civilians, and it bore important fruits. Led by noncommissioned African American officers who organized the protest, maintained group cohesion, and prevented degeneration into open mutiny, this major victory marked the emergence of a new class of black leaders.[51]

Aspiring to Leadership

In contrast to the pay issue, wartime black protest failed to convince the War Department to promote blacks to a rank higher than sergeant. In December 1864, Colonel Charles W. Foster of the Bureau of Colored Troops argued that, even were the military inclined to commission black officers, removing the stricture against doing so would exceed the boundaries of society's acceptance. Black officers would sometimes outrank whites, and Foster questioned whether "white officers and men [are] prepared to acknowledge and obey the colored man, or officer, as a military superior?" If so, Foster contended, there would be "no harm in giving the colored man a commission," but if such action came "in advance of public opinion," it would cause "serious injury to the service." During the War Department's prosecution of a massive Civil War, victory trumped principle on this issue.[52]

Alexander T. Augusta's experience confirmed Foster's argument. Augusta accepted a surgeon's commission and assignment to Camp Stanton, Maryland. In February 1864, six white surgeons at the camp protested to President Lincoln that the black doctor outranked them by virtue of the date of his appointment. The white doctors found it degrading that a black officer commanded them, and Augusta soon found himself examining black recruits passing through Baltimore. In the Fifty-fourth Massachusetts, all but three officers supported a petition to promote a black doctor who, as a hospital steward, had ministered to a sick captain. The three holdouts admitted that the doctor had demonstrated his medical skill, but they opposed his advancement simply because they did not want a black surgeon. The regimental commander destroyed the petition. Such events offer insight into the black experience in the army: acceptance by some whites, denial by others, and often, a general ambivalence motivated by a desire to avoid confrontation generated by pushing change too far or too quickly.[53]

On the home front, blacks opposed the prohibition against their being commissioned as officers, and they used this protest as another means by which to critique the legal structure. In aspiring to hold command positions routinely, African Americans displayed their citizenship expectations as well: not content to follow whites, blacks expected equality and even leadership opportunities. Participants in a July 1864 meeting of black Philadelphians complained that white civilians received commissions but not black veterans. Octavius V. Catto declared during a February 1865 black convention in Pennsylvania that military service had entitled blacks to at least the same rights granted to white immigrants, and if the army included "Germans commanding Germans, even Irishmen commanding Irishmen," then blacks should command blacks. Frederick Douglass told blacks in Philadelphia that refusing to enlist because they would be commanded by white officers made no sense considering that "we are everywhere commanded by white men in time of peace." Nonetheless, Douglass predicted, "I have not the slightest doubt that in the progress of this war we shall see black officers, black colonels, and generals even."[54]

In early 1865, a petition signed by hundreds of blacks and whites, including senators Charles Sumner, Henry Wilson, and Edwin Morgan, New York Tribune editor Horace Greeley, generals James S. Negley and Franz Sigel, Frederick Douglass, and Charles Lenox Remond, called for any new USCT regiments to be officered by blacks. Noting that many blacks sprang to the Union's defense at the first opportunity afforded them, the petition offered that others had hesitated because the hope of promotion remained closed to them. The petition declared that removing this bar would result in a surge of enlistments, the men to be officered by the "hundreds of non-commissioned officers in colored regiments" who stood qualified by experience to serve in higher capacities.[55]

Blacks argued further that the army could discipline whites in the armed forces who refused to respect them as officers, pursuant to the Articles of War, and they also publicized military operations successfully led by African American noncommissioned officers as evidence of their ability to command. A letter published in the *Christian Recorder* announced that a successful raid into Florida's interior led by Sergeant Major Henry James of the Third USCI in the war's closing days, comprised of twenty-two black soldiers, seven black civilians, and a member of the 107th Ohio, gave "proof" that "a colored man with proper training can command among his fellows and succeed where others have failed."[56]

In the end, only about a hundred blacks (and fourteen of 133 USCT chaplains, holding a titular rank of major) held officer's commissions during the war. Three Louisiana regiments under Major General Benjamin Butler in 1862 contained about seventy-five of the commissioned blacks, though Major General Nathaniel Banks purged them when he assumed command of the department. Six sergeants in the Fifty-fourth and Fifty-fifth Massachusetts Infantry regiments received lieutenant's bars at the end of war, and three members of a light artillery battery in Kansas accepted commissions. Eight black surgeons received medical commissions as majors, and in February 1865, Martin R. Delany accepted a commission as major of the 104th USCI, though he served on detached recruiting duty. Even where black protest on this issue proved largely unsuccessful, it reveals the aspirations blacks embraced. Delaney's commission heartened one sergeant in the Fifty-fourth Massachusetts to assert, in direct reference to language in Justice Taney's opinion in *Dred Scott,* "that we have got rights that the white man is bound to respect." The soldier anticipated that, "before the suppression of this rebellion that the colored man will not only wear the plain straps, but the spread eagle."[57]

Learning in the Ranks

As another important component of the political awareness they gained in the army, black soldiers developed a deep appreciation for education as well as the economic worth of their labor. Blacks incorporated both concepts, which also fit well with the Republican Party's free labor ideology, into their definition of citizenship. Few black troops had formal schooling, and most of those who could read or write enlisted from Northern or Border states or Louisiana. Military necessity required the education of at least a portion of these soldiers so that literate noncommissioned officers could understand sign posts, command parties on missions that did not warrant an officer, or read passes while on guard duty. One officer requested a guard detail from a white regiment not because of prejudice but because the soldiers from a nearby black regiment proved insufficient due to their illiteracy: when sent to make arrests, for example, they were "just as apt to get the wrong as the right Person, if they get any at all," and in one case, showed a wanted man an arrest summons and believed his response when he told them that the warrant named a different individual. The requesting officer received his white detail.[58]

Inspectors in Maryland began educating promising prospects when they realized that barely any of the recruits enlisting there could read sufficiently to discharge the duties of a noncommissioned officer. Encouraged by the chance to become noncommissioned officers, twenty-one blacks accordingly enrolled by the end of March 1864 at a school set up in nearby Philadelphia by the Supervisory Committee for Recruiting Colored Regiments. By June 1864, meanwhile, nine military schools in New Orleans taught an average of 2,400 soldiers/students a day, and by December 1864, twenty teachers staffed thirteen schools for 1,549 black soldiers at Memphis. Similarly, civilians operated a school in a large tent at Camp William Penn outside Philadelphia, where eleven black regiments trained.[59]

Many officers in the USCT, even those not classified as abolitionists, began to promote the idea that education should be available to African Americans. Black soldiers enthusiastically seized this opportunity, asking for regimental schools, purchasing books and paying teachers with money they raised, and studying with more educated comrades when teachers were unavailable. Like many black civilians, these soldiers saw education as a means of self-improvement as well as an important way in which to prepare to enjoy the rights for which they fought. Black chaplain Henry M. Turner petitioned the army's adjutant general for five hundred spelling books, and identified education as a "means to make brave soldiers" but also "good and intelligent citizens." Turner argued that where the regiment compiled a record of bravery in nine battles, its military service earned a right to both citizenship and educational opportunity. Churches, relief associations, and other donors, but not the government, eventually provided the books Turner sought.[60]

Regimental schools proved one of the most important ways in which military service impacted blacks' quest for self-sufficiency. The Union army did not promulgate an official or universal schooling system for soldiers in the field, but schools developed in many of the USCT regiments with the support of chaplains, unit officers, and those at home. Regimental chaplains typically had charge of these schools and usually found assistance from other officers, and occasionally the wives of officers or teachers from benevolent societies. In a letter to the *Christian Recorder*, Sergeant John C. Brock implored friends at home to send newspapers to black soldiers so that they had material to read, explaining that part of the time spent in the nation's service would also be "days of instruction, to fit us for good citizens" on the return of peace. Other times, regimental commanders supported education by purchasing supplies using their unit's regimental fund.[61]

Orders to promote education of black troops sometimes issued from the department, army, or corps level. Major General Nathaniel Banks appointed members of the American Missionary Association as lieutenants in several black regiments for the purpose of helping educate the nearly nineteen thousand African American troops in the Department of the Gulf. During winter quarters 1864–65, Major General Benjamin Butler instructed that each USCT regiment in the Army of the James build a schoolhouse so that chaplains and officers who volunteered could educate these soldiers, and Twenty-fifth Corps commander Brigadier General Godfrey Weitzel taxed sutlers to fund this educational initiative.[62]

Sometimes, scarce resources meant that only a limited number of soldiers had the opportunity to attend schools. In other cases, schools served as many soldiers as possible, and sometimes included as students the wives and children of soldiers, and people without any connection with the regiment. The overall education effort had mixed results: some units achieved a high level of literacy while in others, most reached some ability to read but still could not write. The voracity with which the men sought to learn, however, was undeniable. By January 1866, the colonel of the Sixty-second USCI, from Missouri, reported that of 431 men in the regiment, 99 had learned to read, write, and cipher; 200 could read and write; and 337 could spell words of more than two syllables. Colonel James Shaw Jr. of the Seventh USCI, organized in Maryland of ex-slaves from the Chesapeake Bay area, reported about the reaction of his men to a donation by Rhode Island citizens of five hundred spelling books: "'Give me a spelling book,' says one, 'and me,' 'and me,' said others, with eager, anxious faces that showed their interest and desire to learn." Shaw reported that barely fifty men in the regiment initially knew the alphabet but three-fourths had learned it two months later. The unit's regimental historian later recalled that by the time the Seventh USCI disbanded, nearly all could read and most could write, though, "what was of even greater importance, they had learned self-reliance and self-respect, and went back to their homes with views enlarged, sympathies quickened, and their interest in the outside world thoroughly awakened."[63]

Black soldiers embraced the sentiment of one member of the Fifty-fifth Massachusetts, who reminded them, "If ever we expect to become a people we must try and educate ourselves and our children." When the trustees of Wilberforce University in Ohio, the first college run by African Americans, appealed for money, black soldiers responded swiftly. While pursuing Lee's army to Appomattox Court House, the men of the Eighth USCI, organized at Camp William Penn, Pennsylvania, collected more than $200 from among their ranks to donate to the school. To supplement $5,000 raised by the Sixty-second USCI, a fellow Missouri regiment, the Sixty-fifth USCI contributed $1,379.50 to establish in 1866 the school now known as Lincoln University in Jefferson City, Missouri. And fittingly, when soldiers of the Fifty-fourth Massachusetts, former slaves, and Northern blacks donated money for a monument to Robert Gould Shaw in the shadow of Fort Wagner's parapet, the threat of Morris

Island's unstable sand and the potential for damage to the monument by racist vandals led to the fund's use for a different, living monument: the Shaw School founded to educate black Charlestonians.[64]

Many black soldiers also began to appreciate the financial meaning of their labor for the first time, especially ex-slaves who now earned money, and those who protested unequal pay. When the Seventh USCI, organized at Baltimore, mustered out, George R. Sherman estimated that its men had saved nearly ninety thousand dollars in Baltimore and Washington banks. Banks established for use by black soldiers, such as those in Colonel Thomas W. Higginson's Thirty-third USCI or the Department of Norfolk, Virginia, also helped some of them learn about sound fiscal practices and good financial planning.[65]

The *Christian Recorder* also noted (along with swipes at Irish Americans) that at least in Philadelphia, the war improved living conditions for blacks: "Men have been drafted and others have volunteered, and thus got their bounty, and given it to their wives and children, many of whom you would hardly know if you were to meet them on the street, they are so much changed and a great deal better clad.... They seem to enjoy it to some extent, and make a better appearance than their IRISH neighbors, who are citizens and have the rights of freemen." Moreover, many of the blacks remaining in Philadelphia, "now seek for work, their minds having been stirred up by UNCLE SAM. They have come to the conclusion to be industrious instead of lounging about in IRISH and other doggeries, day and night."[66]

That black soldiers gained a new appreciation for education and greater understanding of the value of their labor helped inform their consideration of what rights they deserved as citizens. Sergeant Joseph H. Barquet of the Fifty-fourth Massachusetts Infantry argued that education would permit blacks to capitalize on opportunities opened in the war's wake. Barquet additionally called for black land ownership and for products made by blacks to bring "in market the same value as that produced by others." In the closing days of the war, Sergeant Major George S. Massey of Pittsburgh similarly argued, as any free labor Republican would, that "homes and property" would support improvements in the status of blacks, and he called on them to earnestly pursue respectable and profitable occupations. Massey did not expect all blacks to become lawyers and doctors, but he valued all profitable labor. Massey warned that political equality would "do but comparatively little towards elevating our race or condition when we are wanting in every other respect," and he understood the need for black self-help: "While we have to look to others for equality before the law, we must depend entirely on our own hands and heads for equality in financial resources."[67]

Soldiering Side By Side

The African American military experience did more than create an opportunity for thousands of blacks from across the United States to unite, it also forced interracial collaboration in a common cause. Whites and blacks shared the triumphs and privations of a soldier's life. Members of both races had to contend with the ramifications arming blacks had on African American status. Once in uniform, positive interactions with whites supported a growing sense among blacks that they had an American identity and caused at least some whites to rethink the prewar exclusion of blacks from citizenship. Both changes were prerequisites for a new legal concept of citizenship, which excluded race as a governing factor, to emerge.

Many whites who originally enlisted in the Union army fought neither for blacks nor abolition, and some openly disdained emancipation and arming African Americans. As a black war correspondent traveling with the Army of the Potomac early in the war, George E. Stephens noted varying degrees of hostility toward African Americans among the troops. Stephens recounted that some members of the Excelsior Brigade raided the house of a free black man, and that federal officers sometimes returned fugitives to slavery. Congress itself did not pass legislation prohibiting officers from aiding in the return of fugitive slaves until March 1862.[68]

Accordingly, the U.S. Sanitary Commission and the Loyal Publication Society anticipated opposition to arming black troops, and distributed pamphlets through the army to generate acceptance of this policy. One such pamphlet described African American service in 1776 and 1812, and questioned what valid reason against arming blacks could exist when "our bravest and most patriotic generals, our Washington, and our Jackson, did not hesitate to solicit, to employ, and to reward the military services of Negroes."[69]

In fairness, some Union soldiers had probably never even seen a black person before the war. For example, the 1860 census for New York's Cattaraugus and Chautauqua counties, from which the soldiers who comprised the 154th New York Infantry hailed, listed a negligible number of black residents. On first reaching the South, members of the regiment viewed blacks they encountered as a part of the landscape, though some of them also decried slavery as an institution that debilitated the land. Eventually, members of the unit developed a multitude of reactions to blacks. Some men of the 154th New York continued to feel racist disdain for blacks, while others resented them as having caused the war in the first place, along with their own loss of freedom at having to submit to a soldier's life. Others, however, felt honored to serve as an instrument of slavery's eradication. Additionally, some members of the 154th New York who originally scorned blacks gradually changed their minds in the face of positive interactions. One opponent of emancipation converted when he went to a house near Savannah, Georgia, to purchase food at the end of Sherman's March to the Sea. There, a family of ex-slaves cooked the soldier a hoe cake, told him how they had assisted escaped Union prisoners in the past, and refused his offer to pay for his meal. On returning to camp, the soldier told his tentmate, "I went away a Democrat but I have come back an abolitionist. When a party asks me to vote to enslave such a people as...I have seen today, then I cease to be one of their number any longer."[70]

Seeing the whipping posts, and hearing of cruel treatment against slaves, convinced some white soldiers not only of the military necessity but also the justice of freeing and arming blacks. After spending six months in the South, one New Yorker reflected, "I would just like to see a man whipping a negro I would try the virtue of my sword if he did not stop it." After hearing about the thrashings endured by a fifteen-year-old escaped slave, one future USCT officer from the Seventieth Indiana wrote that it "is enough to make a man feel like it would be God's service to shoot them [slave masters] down like buzzards." After he personally encountered slaves, Meschack Purington Larry from Maine wrote his sister, "Instead of thinking les of a negroe I have sadly learned to think them beter than many wight meen that hold responsible positions." A member of the Twenty-fifth Wisconsin wrote home that the slaves he met in Kentucky could not talk for two minutes before tears welled in their eyes, as they praised God for the coming of Lincoln's soldiers.[71]

On the other hand, deep-seated racism persisted in some soldiers no matter what. These attitudes reflected relentless opposition from a portion of society against the idea of recognizing blacks as equals or citizens. Such sentiments threatened the egalitarian features of black military service as well as the notion that these aspects could someday be made permanent in the law. While a board of examination reviewed the military competence of applicants for USCT commissions, it did not screen for racists who viewed the black regiments only as an avenue for promotion. A veteran of the black Twenty-ninth Connecticut Infantry recalled at least one officer who "ought to have been with the Greys instead of the Blues, he had so little use for the Colored troops," until the regiment's colonel arrested the offender. In other cases, officers who ordered excess fatigue duty exhausted black troops, increased their sickness rates, and made them feel like little more than uniformed laborers.[72]

The racism of some high ranking officers fueled white-on-black abuse. Brigadier General John P. Hatch routinely referred to his command as "Niggers," and Major General Lovell H. Rousseau prohibited black soldiers from arresting women. On September 30, 1863, Colonel James Montgomery of the Second South Carolina (African Descent) demoralized a detachment of the Fifty-fourth Massachusetts with a harangue delivered in the middle of its protest against unequal pay. Professing to be their friend, Montgomery told the soldiers that they should feel "glad to pay for the privilege to fight, instead of squabbling about money" and argued that the government had already paid them a generous bounty in setting them free. "You are a race of slaves," Montgomery told the aghast men, "A few years ago your fathers worshipped snakes and crocodiles in Africa. Your features partake of a beastly character....I am disgusted with the mean, low habits you have learned from the low whites," who supported their refusal to take this pay. Montgomery concluded by encouraging the black soldiers to pursue education, observing that "Irishmen come to this country and in a few years become the same as other white men," and he advised them to try to improve their features by having the lightest blacks marry the darkest women. Brigade commander Milton S. Littlefield followed Montgomery with a speech pledging his honor that the men would receive their full salary, though he could do little to soothe the sting of Montgomery's nearly hour long diatribe.[73]

White soldiers could viciously insult their black comrades. During an expedition in southwestern Virginia, a detachment of six hundred black cavalry from the Fifth USCC "patiently" endured jeering whites who pulled off their caps, stole their horses, and taunted their courage. Later, four hundred of the black cavalry lost a quarter of their men in a charge, making "those who had scoffed at the Colored Troops on the march out...silent." Although Confederates brutally murdered some prisoners from the regiment, the cavalrymen gave Rebel wounded water. Some USCT officers feared the possibility of more violent racial fights. Thomas W. Higginson noted in April 1863, "There has been no quarrelling or chafing as yet" between his black regiment and nearby white troops. But, Higginson continued, "At the same time it always makes me anxious, for if a quarrel should arise, even slight, the whole slumbering hostility would awaken instantly & might be the destruction of all of us."[74]

Even some praise attributed black military acumen to the prior experience most of them had as slaves, an especially ironic commentary on perceptions of the soldier's life. Adjutant General Lorenzo Thomas reported in May 1864 that Southern whites inculcated an attitude of strict deference in their slaves, and freedmen in the army carried "this habit of obedience with them"—a statement that omitted the agitation black troops mounted against unequal pay and other perceived injustices. While deeming them to be "a most important addition to our forces," and acknowledging their valor at Port Hudson, Thomas emphasized that the greatest value of black troops lay in their performing garrison duty, thus freeing white units for combat service.[75]

On the other hand, tense racial moments sometimes resolved in a way that emphasized black rights. Some USCT officers actively defended their men and earned their admiration in the process. In March 1864, an Irish American soldier called one of the Fifty-fifth Massachusetts Infantry a "nigger" before having to flee for fear of physical retaliation. Lieutenant Colonel Charles B. Fox immediately rushed to the scene, tracked down and arrested the culprit, and had him escorted to the provost guard "by at least two files of good brave colored soldiers." Colonel John H. Holman earned black correspondent Thomas M. Chester's praise for disciplining and removing a lieutenant from the division staff for "inwarrantable treatment" to a black sergeant, and George E. Stephens reported the court-martial and dishonorable discharge of a lieutenant from the Fifty-second Pennsylvania who refused to do duty with black troops.[76]

Opportunities for blacks to parade alongside whites accentuated in a happier way their sense of equality and American identity that came with the blue uniform. While briefly assigned as the only black unit in Brigadier General Thomas G. Stevenson's brigade in August 1863, the Fifty-fourth Massachusetts drew in line with colors flying to march in review alongside white troops from Massachusetts, New Hampshire, Connecticut, Pennsylvania, and New York. Thanksgiving 1863 on Morris Island, South Carolina, included all soldiers there, black and white, assembling near the ocean for a religious observance,

3. "Emancipation Day in South Carolina." The Color Sergeant of the First South Carolina (African Descent) addressing the regiment at Port Royal, South Carolina, January 1, 1863. *Frank Leslie's Illustrated Newspaper,* January 24, 1863. Courtesy Library of Congress.

before each regiment celebrated the day on its own with sports and feasting. At other times, black troops paraded by themselves but in honor of a universal American holiday, such as when the First Division of the Twenty-fifth Corps of black troops held a "grand review" on February 22, 1865, to honor George Washington's birthday.[77]

Blacks also commemorated events specific to their experience, and they expressed in these internal ceremonies pride in the changes wrought by their service. The Fifty-fourth Massachusetts observed January 1, 1864, the first anniversary of the Emancipation Proclamation, by assembling on Morris Island, South Carolina, along with large delegations from the Second South Carolina (African Descent) and the Third USCI organized in Pennsylvania. Inspirational speeches emphasized that on the very ground where slavery previously oppressed them, blacks now stood "upright as living men."[78]

Shifts in the Racial Climate

Black soldiers took notice of the possibilities of this changing racial climate, a recognition that helped animate calls for changes in the law after the war. When a drunken white soldier told one of the First USCI to "get out of the road you damned nigger," the soldier replied defiantly, "Look at what you say...[you] can't call me a nigger no more." A corporal corrected one USCT captain who threatened to shoot him as a "damned nigger," after the corporal halted the officer for trying to leave camp without a pass. The guardsman confidently identified himself not as a "nigger" but a "Federal soldier" who wore the "Federal uniform," adding, "I have taken the same oath that you have." A court-martial later dismissed the captain.[79]

Furthermore, the fact that blacks stood against inequality earned the respect of at least some whites, another circumstance that illuminated the potential of the moment for blacks in their calls for equal rights. Members of the Fifty-fifth Massachusetts found that white soldiers encamped nearby called their unit the "Independent Colored Regiment" and encouraged them to maintain their protest against unequal pay.[80]

Combat performance also helped earn black soldiers the respect of some white troops. After their baptism of fire, the men of the Fifty-fourth Massachusetts marched past the camps of several white regiments to hear those soldiers shout, "Well done! We heard your guns!" and, "Hurrah, boys! You saved the Tenth Connecticut!" Daniel W. Sawtelle of the Eighth Maine wrote in spring 1863, "I have thought that the negroes would not make good soldiers and so did most of the men in this regt, but in the several skirmishes they have had with the rebels they have won the prasses of all and the rebels are as afraid of them as they would be of so many tigers." Sawtelle continued, "If I disliked [slavery] before I utterly detest it now and I am not alone. Men that called themselves negro haterers a while ago are compelled to say they are better than they thought they were." Following the Fourteenth USCI's performance in battle at Dalton, Georgia, on August 15, 1864, the Fifty-first Indiana reportedly honored their comrades by replying, when asked what regiment they were, "Fifty-first Colored." For the home front, a woodcut published in *Harper's Weekly* on November 11, 1865, depicted dead black and white soldiers lying together on the same battlefield.[81]

Black soldier Thomas B. Wester of the Forty-third USCI, fighting in Virginia, thus recognized war as an exercise uniting both races together in a common cause. According to Wester, blacks fought "side-by-side with the white men," the "bones of the black man...whitening the battle-fields, while their blood simultaneously with the white man's oozes into the soil" that former slaves earlier cultivated. During a march from Barrancas, Florida, to Blakely, Alabama, in the closing days of the war, Chaplain C. W. Buckley "never witnessed such a friendly feeling between white and colored troops....I have seen the two divisions exchange gifts, and talk with each other with apparent equality. All seemed to realize that they were marching from victory to victory beneath the same flag;—that their arms were alike raised in defence of our endangered liberties." When the Fifty-fifth Massachusetts broke camp to return to the Bay State, a white regiment in its brigade, the Fifty-fourth New York, drew up to bid it farewell, and each regiment gave the other "loud and hearty" cheers.

And perhaps most poignantly, in walking over the battlefield after a charge on September 29, 1864, at New Market Heights (Chaffin's Farm), Virginia, John McMurray, an officer in the Sixth USCI, "couldn't help shedding a few tears" on finding one of his men, "Big Sam" Johnson, dead. McMurray had developed a friendship with Big Sam, often listening to his stories while on the march. Decades later, McMurray recollected sadly that "even now when I think of him I feel a pang of sorrow that his cheerful light of life was extinguished so early. . . . I looked at him a few moments, said 'good bye, Sam,' and was compelled to go on without seeing that he was decently buried."[82]

Compliments from superior officers also fueled black soldiers' burgeoning sense of self-confidence and American identity, both necessary if African Americans were to continue making more defined calls for change in the law after the war. Colonel Thomas J. Morgan of the Fourteenth USCI praised his soldiers after they defended Decatur, Alabama, in October 1864 with words that highlighted changing attitudes among some whites in the army. Morgan declared to his men, the "blood of those who fell has hushed the mouths of our Enemies while the conduct of those who live Elicited praises and cheers from *all* who witnessed it—It is no small event for a black regiment to receive three hearty cheers from a regiment of white men." Morgan reminded his command that "one year ago . . . it was considered by most of the army and a large number of the people of the United States very doubtful whether Negroes would make good soldiers and it was esteemed no honor to be an Officer in a black regiment—Today the regiment is known throughout the army and the North and is honored—The Col commanding is proud of the regiment and would not [exchange] its command for that of the best white regiment in the U.S. service."[83]

Blacks accordingly linked battlefield performance with demands for equality. In the *Christian Recorder,* Chaplain William H. Hunter of the Fourth USCI identified June 15, 1864, when black troops breached the Southern works in front of Petersburg before having to fall back due to lack of reinforcements, as "the day when prejudice died in the entire Army of the U.S. of America. It is the day when it was admitted that colored men were equal to the severest ordeal. It is the day in which was secured to us rights of equality in the Army and service of the Government of the United States."[84]

Complimentary accounts of black troops in action printed in white newspapers helped emphasize this point to a broader audience. While covering combat on the Richmond/Petersburg front, African American correspondent Thomas M. Chester's articles in the *Philadelphia Press* publicized black prowess in combat and promoted the idea of racial union through shared military experience. A Democratic newspaper founded in 1857, the *Press* traditionally showed little attention to promoting the interests of blacks, and it is unknown why its editor hired a black correspondent. In mid-August 1864, Chester noted that, through joint service, both whites and blacks earned fame and glory. Chester related details of black valor for a twofold purpose: while continued displays of loyal bravery would "soon eradicate the last vestige of prejudice and oppression from the grand Army of the Potomac," it also reinforced black resolve and pride.[85]

Chester provided casualty lists not only for informational purposes but to publish tangible proof of black men shedding their blood for the Union and their own rights. For Chester, assignment of black troops to hazardous duty showed that they had established a reputation for both discipline and valor, and he found it a compliment that even after the fall of Richmond, the government intended to keep black troops in the service until their terms of enlistment expired. Chester proudly reported the details of blacks engaged in combat, describing "no flinching" as African Americans "manfully received and returned fire" at the Battle of New Market Heights, where a black division endured Confederate artillery fire, charged the Rebel earthworks, and earned fourteen Medals of Honor. Chester concluded that such gallantry "wiped out effectually the imputation against the fighting qualities of the colored troops."[86]

Conclusion

In the end, black soldiers met mixed reactions and treatment. Some encounters confirmed deep-seated racism within American society that could not be easily expunged and stood in contrast to the more welcoming reception Irish American soldiers enjoyed. Other experiences, however, affirmed a promising sense of the equality of blacks. As a member of the Fifty-fourth Massachusetts recalled, on first landing on Folly Island, South Carolina, his comrades "were liable to be insulted by any of the white soldiers," but eventually "they have come to see that they are bound to treat us as men and soldiers, fighting for the same common cause." While instances where black soldiers earned the respect of white troops or civilians did not lead to a radical and immediate shift in racial relations, they did sow seeds of acceptance that gradually germinated and merged with other impulses within at least a portion of American society. Moreover, black soldiers mobilized as active opponents to anyone or any rule that distinguished them from white soldiers, and they increasingly asserted their role as leaders of the black community. Whether helping inspire civilian freedpeople or successfully rejecting second-class citizenship by opposing unequal pay, these black soldiers also became civil rights leaders, and their influence had a profound impact both on personal attitudes (both white and black) as well as official policies.[87]

The African American military experience afforded free Northern blacks and less-educated Southern slaves an opportunity to interact with one another, as well as whites, in a shared experience and common cause. Wartime moments symbolizing the admittedly incomplete integration of blacks into the fabric of Union society—from exchanging slave garb for the soldier's uniform to helping strike slavery's death blow—generated a confidence and sense of American identity among them that began to manifest in political ways. These experiences heightened black appreciation for an American allegiance denied them by slavery in the South and persistent racism in the North, and familiarized them with the possibilities of equal treatment.

This new appreciation of their self-elevation and awareness of their American allegiance led blacks increasingly to assert their demands for a new legal order that included them as part of "the people." Black troops impatiently engaged with political issues beyond emancipation, and they challenged racist treatment that sought to distinguish them from whites. The presence of black troops in uniform, their performance in combat, and their developing American identity, political awareness, and organization, shifted the dynamic of black-white interactions. Blacks began to modify the paradigm of race relations during the Civil War era not only by enlisting, but by asserting demands for inclusion and equality as well. Experiences in the army also informed developing black definitions of citizenship.

Additionally, Confederate policy that captured black soldiers did not qualify as prisoners of war led to articulation by the federal government that any man wearing Union blue stood entitled to the same treatment regardless of race. Major General David Hunter wrote directly to Jefferson Davis and, after equating the South's fight to maintain slavery as "the liberty to do wrong—which Satan, Chief of the fallen Angels, was contending for when he was cast into Hell," informed the Confederate president that the "United States flag must protect all its defenders, white, black or yellow," and every black soldier "cruelly murdered" would result in the execution of the highest-ranking Confederate in Hunter's possession. President Lincoln adopted this policy as well, and the *New York Times* declared to readers that "a black-skinned loyalist is of more account than a black-hearted traitor anyday," when it suggested executing Confederate prisoners for every black prisoner murdered. On the other hand, such threats (no retaliatory executions ever took place) did not stop atrocities such as the Confederate massacre of black prisoners taken at Fort Pillow, Tennessee, and other instances where Confederate soldiers executed captured or wounded black federal soldiers.[88]

During the war, African American civilians used black military service to emphasize their call for equal rights. On June 5, 1864, more than a thousand black men from New Orleans, including twenty-seven veterans of the 1815 battle there, petitioned President Lincoln and Congress. Claiming to be "loyal citizens" who owned property, engaged in commerce, paid taxes, and had fathers who served in the War of 1812, the petitioners added that blacks "have spilled their blood, and are still pouring it out for the maintenance of the Constitution of the United States; in a word, they are soldiers of the union." Lincoln accordingly wrote to Governor Michael Hahn, an opponent of black suffrage, to ask "whether some of the colored people may not be let in [to vote]—as, for instance, the very intelligent, and especially those who have fought gallantly in our ranks." When the new Louisiana constitution failed to grant suffrage to African Americans, the black newspaper *L'Union* nonetheless argued that "from the day that bayonets were placed in the hands of the blacks...the Negro became a citizen of the United States," and it prophesied that, as the "war has broken the chains of the slave," it was also "written in the heavens that from this war shall grow the seeds of the political enfranchisement of the oppressed race."[89]

The Reverend Henry Highland Garnet similarly linked the service of black soldiers to political rights when he delivered on February 12, 1865, at Lincoln's invitation, the first sermon by a black in the House of Representatives. After scorning slavery from the perspective of one whose "first sight...was a Christian mother enslaved by professed Christians," Garnet declared that God "stamped on [the] forehead" of all men, regardless of race, "title to his inalienable rights." Moreover, Garnet argued, the military service of blacks to the Union sanctified equality, men who "for a season were scorned and rejected, but who came quickly and cheerfully when they were at last invited, bearing a heavy burden of proscriptions upon their shoulders, and having faith in God, and in their generous fellow-countrymen, they went forth to fight a double battle. The foes of their country were before them, while the enemies of freedom and of their race surrounded them." Garnet demanded more than emancipation in name only, looking forward to a time in the near future

> when emancipation shall be followed by enfranchisement, and all men holding allegiance to the government shall enjoy every right of American citizenship.... When the men who endure the sufferings and perils of the battle-field in the defence of their county, and in order to keep our rulers in their places, shall enjoy the well-earned privilege of voting for them. When in the army and navy, and in every legitimate and honorable occupation, promotion shall smile upon merit without the slightest regard to the complexion of a man's face.

Speaking for his racial community, Garnet demanded that blacks be held "in every respect...equal before the law, and...left to make [their]...own way in the social walks of life," with the "right to live, and labor, and to enjoy the fruits of our toil."[90]

Yet, despite recognizing themselves as citizens, and acting accordingly, blacks remained excluded throughout the duration of the Civil War from national citizenship in the eyes of the law. Moreover, while experiences in the military altered black soldiers' sense of identity, blacks also had a legacy of participating in past American wars only to experience continued racism and exclusion once the crisis passed. What remained to be seen was whether blacks could translate their wartime experiences into permanent changes in the legal concept of citizenship.

CHAPTER 4

Equal Rights and the Experience of Military Justice for African American Soldiers

While at camp on Folly Island, South Carolina, on May 1, 1864, Wallace Baker of the Fifty-fifth Massachusetts Volunteer Infantry mutinied against Lieutenant Thomas F. Ellsworth, a twenty-three-year-old from Ipswich, Massachusetts, who earned a corporal's stripe for bravery at Gettysburg before he joined the Fifty-fifth Massachusetts as an officer. Slightly younger and hailing from Kentucky, Baker lost his temper when Ellsworth sent him to his quarters for arriving at an inspection unprepared. Baker returned before Ellsworth dismissed the company and, exasperated at his command's laughter, the lieutenant repeatedly ordered Baker to his tent. In response, Baker muttered that he would "be damned" before doing so, and he then exclaimed, "I won't stand to attention for you or any other damned white officer." At that, Ellsworth angrily seized Baker by the collar and the incident turned into a full-out brawl. Baker repeatedly struck Ellsworth and tried to take the lieutenant's sword, exclaiming, "You damned white officer, do you think that you can strike me, and I not strike you back again? I will do it. I'm damned if I don't." Two nearby black sergeants ignored Ellsworth's call for assistance but the lieutenant eventually gained the advantage, seized Baker by the neck, and escorted him to the guardhouse.[1]

Baker's commanders knew why trouble simmered within the unit. The men had refused to accept unequal pay and now, letters from family members at home begged them to send any money they could. "Patience has an end," one member of the Fifty-fifth vowed, as the "picture of our desolate house-holds" haunted and hung between them and "our starry flag upon the battle-field." In the same letter, however, the author vowed that black soldiers could not accept anything except equal pay if they were to stand as citizens. For him, "We have been tried in the fire both of affliction and of the rebels, and nothing remains but pure metal. We took our first lessons at Forts Wagner and Gregg, and our last we are now taking in the field of want, and under the guns of prejudice and hate." Alternating between impatience, anger, defiance, and pride, this soldier ran the gamut of emotions connected with his unit's resistance.[2]

The pay disparity energized the demands of black soldiers for equal treatment but it also undermined discipline. In February 1864, Colonel Alfred Hartwell received an anonymous letter declaring that the Fifty-fifth Massachusetts would stack arms if it had not received pay by the first of March. On April 19, 1864, less than two weeks before Baker's incident, a mutiny erupted aboard a steamer transporting the regiment between Hilton Head and Folly Island, South Carolina, as Sampson Goliah freed himself from being tied to the ship's rigging while other soldiers revolted. A week after Baker's mutiny, Hartwell and another officer testified at Goliah's court-martial and cited the pay issue as the salient cause of tension within the unit. In a successful plea to spare the defendant from execution, the prosecutor did the same. As other white officers came to realize, most black soldiers mutinied not out of nervous energy generated by camp malaise, or the privations of combat service, but as political action.[3]

A court-martial comprised mostly of the same officers who tried Goliah convened to try Baker on mutiny charges on May 17, 1864. Members from the Fifty-fifth's brother regiment, the Fifty-fourth Massachusetts Volunteer Infantry, served as president and judge advocate, with a twenty-five-year-old Philadelphia lawyer, Captain James M. Walton—the same man who prosecuted Goliah and successfully argued against punishing him with death—filling the latter position.[4]

Baker received due process, an opportunity for defense counsel, and questioned both a white office and fellow blacks—a level of procedural fairness surprisingly typical of general courts-martial of black soldiers. Ellsworth testified first and, having declined counsel, Baker directly questioned him with Judge Advocate Walton's assistance. Although ineffective as a defense, the moment proved significant in that a black soldier cross-examined his white lieutenant. Similarly dramatic was Henry Way's testimony, not so much for his corroboration of Ellsworth's testimony but because he, as a black witness for the prosecution, played an integral role in the judicial proceedings. Baker then questioned several black defense witnesses, who admitted that they considered him "awkward" and "foolish," with a "strange" way of addressing people, and that when his comrades "wanted to play he would misunderstand them and want to fight."[5]

Baker offered no final statement and was found guilty. Influenced by its perception of increasing rebelliousness in the regiment, the court went beyond the imprisonment it ordered for Goliah and condemned Baker to death, a sentence well within its purview regardless of any mitigating factors about Baker's mental sophistication. On the other hand, George Stephens, a black soldier in the Fifty-fourth Massachusetts Infantry, squarely blamed Baker's insubordination on the "unjust treatment" endured by black soldiers. Lieutenant Colonel Charles Fox of the Fifty-fifth Massachusetts agreed, later offering that the "sad but necessary execution no doubt saved the lives of others by showing the inevitable result of such a course; but, had justice been done the enlisted men in regard to their position as soldiers, no such example would have been needed."[6]

Meanwhile, Baker's execution in June did little to quell dissidence within the regiment. Seventy-four members of the Fifty-fifth Massachusetts directly petitioned Lincoln in July 1864, explaining, "to us money is no object we came to fight for Liberty justice & Equality," but also demanding full pay from the date of their enlistment and "immediate Discharge Having Been enlisted under False Prentence." Despite Baker's recent execution, the petitioners ominously warned Lincoln that if their grievances went unresolved, they planned to "resort to more stringent measures."[7]

The record of Baker's court-martial reveals a striking juncture between black demands for equal rights and their encounter with the concept of due process through military justice. Baker mutinied out of his expectation for equal treatment and frustration at racism in the army. On the other hand, Baker received the same procedural safeguards afforded to white soldiers, and he stood as equal to whites before military law. As did many other courts-martial that tried black mutineers, the panel attempted to balance between the legitimacy of the defendant's frustration and the need to maintain military discipline. Black troops encountered in general courts-martial the ideas that they could be treated as equals before the law and that the same law could apply to whites and blacks regardless of race, even where this led to severe punishment in certain cases.

The African American experience with military justice greatly differed from that of Irish Americans. No question ever arose as to whether a different code would govern discipline or trial procedure for Irish Americans in the army. For most Irish American defendants, courts-martial were simply a way of adjudicating typical charges such as desertion, absence without leave, drunkenness while on duty, and conduct unbecoming. As Colonel Patrick Guiney of the Irish American Ninth Massachusetts noted, "Irish soldiers cannot be governed by a military dove with the rank of colonel. They need to be handled as severely as justice will permit, when they do wrong," so as to improve military effectiveness and discipline. In other instances, courts-martial in Irish American regiments arose out of political conflict between unit officers, but usually not related to nativism or inequality.[8]

For black troops, the War Department's decision to apply the same code as for whites comprised a huge step toward equal standing. Moreover, courts-martial of black soldiers served as a crossroads between equal rights and military justice, as they more frequently involved offenses with broad political implications.

The records reveal that courts-martial became an important forum for debate at a moment when blacks and whites struggled with the fluid contours of blacks' changing status. Thus James S. Brisbin, a Pennsylvania abolitionist, newspaper editor, and attorney who obtained a commission in the regular army early in the war, argued during his representation of a black soldier accused of murder that the country's collective treatment of blacks transferred blame for African American crimes to whites. Brisbin conceded that the judge advocate proved the crime but argued that the country had responsibility for the incident, "because we have permitted this man to be made a beast of burden and an ignorant savage hesitating between right and wrong, vacilating between bad and good." The court should not sentence the defendant to death, Brisbin asserted, because its members had been party to the "barbarism of the age" which led to his degraded status. "We made him what he is," Brisbin continued, "We blinded him and that made him the ignorant wretch he is and he did not know the amount of danger there was to himself in taking the life of Thomas McGrath." The judge advocate, a self-described "*radical* abolitionist," replied strongly by offering that freeing and arming the slaves gave them individual responsibility and placed them on the path from subjugation to equality. "*I* am not responsible when a negro commits murder. *You* are not responsible," Lieutenant Colonel William H. Coyl of the Ninth Iowa Volunteer Infantry contended, and he claimed it as an error to think that "our object has been to free the slaves...simply to allow them to run wild and kill people and then say, that they have been slaves and are irresponsible." As Coyl explained to the court, "Our object has been to raise up the negro" and to "put a gun in his hand, and make him useful to free him; to make him a *man*, as responsible as we are, for every act." Coyl found Brisbin's plea misplaced because they now stood "on the broad platform of 'rights to all,' and say that the negro is able to take care of himself." These words clinched the defendant's death sentence and on June 13, 1865, a black Union soldier was hanged at Louisville, Kentucky, alongside a separately convicted white civilian guerilla. The closing statements also underscored a broader debate: whether blacks could, and should, stand as equal citizens, or if a special category should be carved out that recognized their American citizenship but also a doctrine of their distinction or racial inferiority.[9]

The courts-martial records also uncover a previously unexplored avenue through which to examine how black soldiers vigorously refuted past lives as slaves now to claim rights as freedmen, soldiers, and citizens. Black mutineers embraced an alternative legal order, seeking to change laws which distinguished between whites and blacks and to bring official legal practices into conformity with their vision. Blacks turned the court-martial into an important way station on the road to freedom and citizenship, even where it punished those who violated military law. Besides revealing a surprising level of due process, general courts-martial records show the extent to which blacks situated themselves as American citizens by opposing discrimination, defying legal precedents that failed to acknowledge their equality, and advancing their interpretation of legal meanings and practices. The cases reflect black anger at white discrimination but also demonstrate how the empowerment some African Americans felt on donning Union blue led them to protest further inequity. These black soldiers *demanded* equal treatment and rights, sometimes at the cost of their lives.

Moreover, the experiences black troops, including many former slaves, had in courts-martial proceedings helped to shape their postwar agenda of legal change. Once in the courtroom, blacks encountered, sometimes for the first time, the concepts of the rule of law, equality before the law, and due process protection. While not the sole source of these concepts, courts-martial in the armed forces nonetheless provided blacks with an unexpected, and neglected, encounter with these core ideas, which they incorporated into their developing definition of citizenship.

The Procedure of Military Justice

Military justice in the U.S. Army dates to June 30, 1775, when the Continental Congress enacted the first Articles of War. Based on the British model in effect at the time, this code prescribed basic procedure for both general and regimental courts-martial. In September 1789, Congress affirmed that the Articles of War governed the army, thus continuing the existence of the courts-martial system as established before the Constitution. A revision in 1806 drew the Articles of War into the form that remained in force until 1874. In addition to the Articles of War, soldiers had to obey regulations issued by the War Department as well as department, corps, brigade, post, regiment, and company rules.[10]

Along with congressional legislation, the Articles of War defined the means by which the army administered justice during the Civil War. A regiment's or garrison's commander could appoint courts-martial consisting of three commissioned officers to try soldiers charged with noncapital crimes. Regimental or garrison courts-martial could order corporal punishment but could neither try a commissioned officer, nor inflict a fine exceeding one month's pay, nor sentence a soldier to imprisonment or hard labor for a term longer than a month. A single officer in a regiment could be detailed to form a field officer court, created by Congress during the Civil War to replace regimental and garrison courts-martial. The field officer court allowed for summary disposition of minor cases while a unit was on active field service. With identical jurisdiction as a regimental court-martial, the field officer court was to forward more serious cases to a general court-martial. General courts-martial also had jurisdiction over capital-level cases and those involving commissioned officers, and could be appointed only by the commander of an army, military division, or department, or the president. A general court-martial was to have thirteen members, though where thirteen could not be assembled due to illness, manifest injury to the service, or other good cause, a lesser number could serve so long as the panel did not drop below at least five sitting members. No death sentence could be imposed unless two-thirds of the panel concurred, though other available punishments included confinement (including solitary or while on a bread and water diet), hard labor, the wearing of a ball and chain, pay forfeiture, discharge, reprimands, and reduction to the ranks for noncommissioned officers. An August 1861 statute abolished flogging in the army. Finally, military commissions could be convened with a minimum of three officers on the panel. These smaller bodies could impose capital punishment and usually dealt with civilians in places where civil courts had ceased to function, but had jurisdiction over soldiers during time of war or rebellion in cases of spying, murder, manslaughter, mayhem, robbery, arson, burglary, rape, and other serious crimes not of a purely military nature as defined in the Articles of War.[11]

Most general courts-martial transcripts are marked by the businesslike conduct of officers determined to do their duty as members of the court. Based on his service on one, Colonel Thomas W. Higginson deemed general courts-martial "an accurate & admirable, though most tedious, method of sifting the truth," though he acknowledged that these military courts tried capital cases and considered issues so grave that only the highest courts addressed them in civil life. Nonetheless, Higginson found the "rules of Court Martial…so much more formal & careful than those of civil courts that one may venture among them with less risk of error."[12]

On the other hand, regardless of a defendant's race, court-martial panels could impose justice harshly. Captain John McMurray recalled his service on a panel at Yorktown, Virginia, that considered cases involving about thirty soldiers, primarily deserters from the white Second New Hampshire. After it sentenced two defendants to execution prior to McMurray's joining the proceedings, the court felt that it had provided sufficient deterrence, found only one more individual guilty, and sentenced him to several months of hard labor. Two officers on the panel, however, both from the Second New Hampshire, voted guilty nearly every time, and wished to inflict death at every opportunity. McMurray remembered decades later, "I shudder when I recall their votes in case after case tried before us." Fortunately for the defendants in these cases, the overzealous officers represented a minority of the court."[13]

While the regulations did not provide for them, drumhead courts-martial dispensing summary justice were occasionally held in the field on order of higher authorities, despite the mandate in the Articles of War that no soldier should suffer death except by concurrence of two-thirds of the members of a *general* court-martial. Though the availability of records and extent to which executions were reported makes certainty difficult, it seems that, contrary to conventional wisdom, few of the proceedings involving execution of black soldiers were drumhead in nature.[14]

More common, if just as severe, were instances in which officers lawfully shot men without trial. For example, Lieutenant Colonel Harai Robinson of the First Louisiana Cavalry believed "decisive action" necessary when the Second Rhode Island Cavalry mutinied in late August 1863 to protest orders to consolidate with the Louisianan unit (both were white regiments). Robinson surrounded the camp with his troops, selected two ringleaders, and wrote the order for their execution from his saddle. Both an investigating military commission and the department commander regretted the loss of life but found

Robinson's action justifiable, and by August 1864 he found himself serving as provost-marshal of the Department of the Gulf.[15]

While general courts-martial gained greater publicity, the discipline administered by single officers or regimental and field officer courts-martial had greater impact on the everyday lives of soldiers. Individual officers usually ordered an offender to serve extra duty, though other possible punishments included standing at attention on a barrel head, riding a wooden horse (a rail set several feet above ground), being struck with the flat side of a sword, flogging (despite regulations prohibiting it), tying up by the thumbs so that the soldier's toes barely touched the ground, or bucking and gagging, where the offender sat with arms around his knees and tied at the wrists with a piece of wood in his mouth. Abuse or arbitrariness most frequently occurred on this level in the administration of army discipline, and most commonly generated tension between white officers and black subordinates.[16]

Soldiers in all regiments, black or white, commonly experienced firsthand encounters with official military discipline. While punishment pursuant to an individual officer's orders was by far the most common disciplinary method, some form of court-martial tried 137 of 1,707 enlisted men who served in the Sixty-fifth USCI for more serious infractions. Seven men were two-time offenders while two faced a court-martial three times. The most common offenses included assault, conduct prejudicial to good order and military discipline, neglect of duty, sleeping on post, disobedience, and absence without leave. Notably, seventeen men who faced courts-martial stayed in the regular army after the expiration of their terms of service and volunteered for the Ninth U.S. Cavalry in 1866. The regimental history of the Ninth USCI, meanwhile, shows that, at least in that regiment, noncommissioned officers were frequently reduced to the ranks. At least eighty men who served as corporal or sergeant were reduced and one was also placed in confinement. Though nine received later promotion, one was reduced a second time. One can assume that day-to-day discipline of individual soldiers was vigorous in both units as well.[17]

The Black Experience with Military Justice

Traditional generalizations assume that racism and unfairness pervaded the treatment of black Civil War soldiers even by the official military justice system. Historians examining this particular issue, however, have differed on whether general courts-martial provided black defendants with procedural fairness and treatment equal to that afforded white soldiers. Ira Berlin noted that army regulations applied safeguards both to whites and blacks, and that general courts-martial accordingly afforded blacks substantially more rights than slaves had ever hoped to claim. Joseph T. Glatthaar maintained that race represented a critical factor in executions, but he also admitted that a review of capital-level courts-martial proceedings reveals a "surprising degree of fairness." On the other hand, Steven J. Ramold more critically appraised the army's administration of justice, and he contrasted "intense racism and stereotyping that black soldiers overcame to serve in the Union army," with the navy's "highly credible record of race relations during the Civil War" based on integrated crews, equal pay, benefits, and health care.[18]

Racism in the Union army tainted the disciplinary process on other levels, but the records reveal that officers on general court-martial panels wrestled with providing fair judicial process to black defendants while maintaining necessary discipline. Black soldiers often received equal treatment and justice in cases involving capital-level crimes. While most mutineers' protests were well grounded in legitimate grievances, and for that reason some may argue with merit that they were unfairly punished by definition, that did not change the gravity of their crime in the eyes of military law. Nonetheless, in many cases, authorities tried to avoid imposition of the death penalty even where the Articles of War called for it.

For blacks, military discipline proved especially critical in transforming former slaves into soldiers and, all excesses aside, it served as a force for unit cohesiveness. Military regulations also provided blacks with a paradoxical relationship between freedom and equality. Most black soldiers learned the difference between the army's rule of law and the capricious wielding of individual authority under slavery, though a few soldiers nonetheless resisted white officers as the replacement of one master by another. Meanwhile, USCT officers faced a difficult position. Their perceptions of black troops reinforced the need to maintain strict discipline at the same time many black troops explored their uncharted experience with liberty. Black soldiers gave up some liberties they would have enjoyed as civilians on emancipation, yet they also earned a greater level of equality pursuant to their service. In this tension, blacks probed the boundaries of acceptable behavior, while many white officers attempted to maintain strict discipline with legal and extralegal punishments, which they had learned during their service in white regiments. Some of these admittedly cruel punishments proved inappropriate for black troops, especially ex-slaves. Complicating matters, not only did unequal pay undermine discipline in its own right, it generated skepticism among black soldiers that they would receive justice on other issues. The ensuing level of distrust this situation caused between black soldiers and white officers continued even after resolution of the pay issue.[19]

Colonel Thomas W. Higginson, an abolitionist Unitarian clergyman turned commander of the First South Carolina (African Descent) (later designated the Thirty-third USCI), perceived that close supervision tempered with consideration of his men's past experiences resonated best with black troops. Higginson sought to use military discipline and regulations as a way to "develop self respect" in his men and help their transition from slavery to freedom. Higginson sought to impress on his men "that they do not obey officers because they are white, but because they are officers." Similarly, Lieutenant Colonel Henry Stone reminded the officers of the One Hundredth USCI that "men must be made to feel that it is law and orders that have been violated when an offense is brought to punishment, not merely the directions of the individual officer." Lieutenant Colonel David Branson prohibited officers in his Sixty-second USCI from ordering corporal punishment, warning that "men will not obey; as promptly, an officer who adopts the customs of the slave driver to maintain authority, as they will him who punishes by a system consistent with the character and enormity of offences and the spirit of the age." Some court-martial panels even considered the defendant's familiarity with military regulations, in keeping with initiatives to ensure that black troops understood that military discipline was not based on the rule of individuals but a codified structure of law. Other officers, however, showed little sensitivity to black experiences and prescribed punishments such as gagging or tying for even petty offenses in an effort to inculcate discipline in men they saw as degraded by slavery. While many black soldiers respected officers who were firm but just, they resented those who used punishments that recalled those administered on the plantation. Understanding that their status had changed, and that free people experienced procedural rights in lieu of arbitrary punishment, black soldiers balked at penalties that echoed slavery. Black soldiers also refused to revert to old practices of discipline after their early encounters with the concepts of due process and a standardized rule of law that could apply regardless of race.[20]

Black noncommissioned officers played integral roles in mediating discipline. Their place in the chain of command put them in the occasionally uncomfortable position of carrying out officers' orders, but many of them understood the need for discipline to ensure military effectiveness as well as to lay the foundation for more general black improvement. Sergeant Samuel Green told potential mutineers about to protest the tying up of comrades

> that all armies had to have regulations and all men were sworn in to obey orders. it was no use for them to cut up about the boys for if they cut the boys loose they would want to fight them[.] I told them that just such men as they were cutting up about started the rebellion in the commencement and I didn[']t see the use of 10 men rebelling against a regiment or a regiment against the United States Army. I told them that it had not been but a few weeks since the Colonel had talked to us about such things and now it was awful to think about let alone to do it. Then some wild fellow said that some men who upheld the officers were no better than they were and that they could destroy them as well as the officers. I replied that I didn[']t tie the man and didn[']t have it done and that I wasn[']t going to have anything to do with them[.]

The mediation of noncommissioned officers did not always succeed, and black soldiers sometimes resented their enforcement of orders issued by whites. Noncommissioned officers also faced additional charges, as a result of their rank, when they participated in a mutiny or failed to try to stop one.[21]

Some commanders of black troops overstepped their authority and, in situations in which soldiers resisted orders or acted violently, shot soldiers where a lesser punishment, or at least a general court-martial, was appropriate.

Troubling for its callousness was Colonel James Montgomery's enforcement in the early summer of 1863 of an order he issued in trying to stop his men from leaving camp to visit their nearby families. Montgomery directed the execution of those who did not return voluntarily. After the capture of one such soldier, the colonel asked him if there were any good reason why he should not be shot. When the prisoner replied in the negative, Montgomery simply answered, "Very well; you die at half past nine o'clock this morning." According to Colonel Thomas W. Higginson, who deemed Montgomery a "sore disappointment," Montgomery intended to shoot two more soldiers before a surgeon convinced him not to do so. In other cases, even officers generally complimentary of black troops sometimes felt driven to such drastic means, especially in the context of a violent threat.[22]

Procedurally, regardless of race or former slave status, a defendant facing a general court-martial during the Civil War had the right to challenge members of the panel to recuse themselves and was informed of his right to retain counsel, with whom he could meet to prepare his defense. If a defendant declined counsel, a court-martial panel could not interfere with his conducting his own defense, no matter how "unskilful or troublesome," except "to enforce... decorum and respect for the law." While the judge advocate prosecuted on behalf of the United States, in the absence of defense counsel, the judge advocate also had the duty to act as counsel for the prisoner after the accused made his plea. This safeguard did not afford a full defense, but the judge advocate had a duty to object to any leading question to any witness, or any question to the accused in which he might incriminate himself. Furthermore, the judge advocate was supposed to take care that a defendant without counsel did not suffer from ignorance of his legal rights and had a full opportunity to bring out any extenuating circumstances of his case.[23]

In order to increase the participation of officers thought likely to be less biased against blacks, some courts were composed entirely, or at least in part, by officers assigned to the USCT. Black or white, no prisoner could be sentenced to death by court-martial except by concurrence of two-thirds of its members. While procedural irregularities existed in some cases, these deviations likely reflected the fact that soldiers, not attorneys, conducted these trials. Across the board in the extant files, black defendants had the opportunity to object to members of the court and whether they took advantage of it or not, were advised that they had the right to representation. Black defendants who declined counsel still had the right to question white witnesses, while black testimony, even that offered by slaves, frequently played a prominent role in their trials. While judge advocates and defense counsels sometimes placed race in issue, or witnesses used it as an identifying factor, the records do not indicate altered procedure or standards because of a defendant's race. When crimes occurred at night, panels sought to establish if sufficient light had existed for witnesses to accurately establish identification. Moreover, in June 1864, before Lincoln, on July 4, 1864, signed legislation opening federal courts to black witnesses, the judge advocate's office affirmed that blacks could testify before military courts regardless of any disqualifying laws in the state in which the court sat. Black soldiers enjoyed rights and opportunities previously denied them in ci-vilian life, because as soldiers they were entitled to uniform application of the Articles of War and other regulations concerning military discipline and trial. Rather than devise a separate scheme to address discipline within the USCT, the federal government treated blacks on par with white soldiers in this regard from the beginning of their army service during the Civil War.[24]

Some proceedings relied exclusively on African American testimony, affirming blacks' right to testify and familiarizing these soldier-witnesses with the legal process. At times, the court-martial process also validated the idea that black civilians, and not just black soldiers, had the right to testify. For example, no distinction was made concerning slave Sophia Cummins's testimony in a murder trial at Lexington, Kentucky, in July 1865. Astonishingly, both free blacks and emancipated slaves experienced something formerly unavailable to almost all of them: the privilege of testifying against white defendants. Black soldiers and civilians offered testimony against white officers and enlisted men who engaged in improper recruitment practices or committed financial crimes against soldiers.[25]

In some cases, counsel for African American defendants questioned notions of racial equality by casting aspersion on black testimony. The testimony of two black civilian witnesses was integral to the prosecution of William Henderson, charged with murdering two white women in Arkansas in November 1864. Bolstering the eyewitness testimony the civilians provided, a black corporal recalled Henderson talking about the murders, and a lieutenant colonel testified about finding the deceased's property under Henderson's bunk the night after the shootings.[26]

Represented by a lieutenant from his regiment, Henderson's defense went poorly. One defense witness responded to a question about Henderson's character that he was a "first rate soldier but a wicked man." Wisely, the defense ended its questioning and instead submitted a written statement that mirrored the Brisbin-Coyl debate discussed earlier. The statement urged the panel to discount the testimony of all the black witnesses on the theory such witnesses often swore falsely because they had been held in bondage, frequently had to steal their food and lie about it, and "having thus been raised in slavery and in ignorance, they do not value their oath as sacred, as white men do." In an attempt to cast doubt on the identification of Henderson by two black civilians, the defense argued that whites had a hard time differentiating between blacks and observed that the vision of a white man and a black man was the same. The statement concluded by tugging at any racial bias of the panel: "Is there a person who would not shudder at the thought of having his life placed in the hands of [the two black civilian witnesses]?" The panel rejected these arguments, and Henderson was executed.[27]

Frequently, black defendants were found guilty because of solid evidence or testimony. In many instances, a feeble defense, or none at all, contributed to conviction; in others, a confession doomed the accused from the start. In some trials, however, valid defenses or mitigating factors proved decisive. In light of his verifiable alibi that he was already under arrest at the time, Private Street Humphrey of the Forty-ninth USCI found himself deemed innocent of mutiny charges against him. While the court sentenced two ringleaders of this mutiny to be shot and seventeen others to hard labor for life, the court also sentenced the last defendant, Robert Randall, to hard labor for the remainder of his service. No apparent reason justified this lighter sentence other than one witness's testimony that Randall did not go with the others to stack arms because they had left without him while he was looking for his bayonet. Although not reflected in the record, perhaps the panel wondered if he had deliberately stalled and gave him the benefit of that doubt.[28]

Similarly, Henry Cox, who participated in a fifteen-person conspiracy that ransacked a house near Vicksburg and murdered a white civilian, had his death sentence remitted and was returned to duty based on testimony that he had tried to prevent the death. In another case, William Jackson shot at and intended to kill a slave who had destroyed letters to his wife, told her that Jackson had died, and impregnated her. Yet, the court exonerated Jackson with the finding that "a man that wantonly violates the domestic relations of a soldier, by seducing his wife, while he is absent in the service of his country deserves the heaviest punishment known to the law; and the aggravation arising from such a damning wrong inflicted on the Accused, in the opinion of the Commission justified the shooting of the perpetrator of the wrong."[29]

Due process afforded Sergeant Samuel Green, who defended himself without counsel, acquittal based on his cross-examination of a white officer and testimony he elicited by questioning two black defense witnesses. Green allegedly mutinied aboard a transport steamer with his 109th USCI. When some men in the regiment grew agitated after several of their comrades were tied up on deck for neglect of duty, Green went to an officer in his unit, Captain Aaron H. Keene, to ask for the prisoners' release. Keene interpreted Green's warning that if they were not freed, "it will raise the devil," as a threat. A black witness for the prosecution, however, stated that Green had expressly advised the men *not* to create a disturbance. Two defense witnesses offered that the sergeant exerted himself to calm the men and went to the captain to *prevent* a possible mutiny in the first place while a group of soldiers gathered nearby—an example of a noncommissioned officer mediating between military discipline, white officers, and black troops. After hearing that Green told his comrades that armies had regulations that had to be followed, the court found him not guilty and restored him to duty.[30]

Because court-martial panels could impose justice harshly, regulations required army or department commanders to review proceedings involving capital sentences and these officers sometimes commuted the sentence. George Douglas placed the point of his bayonet near the chests of two officers aboard a transport steamer near New Orleans on June 19, 1865, and told them that "no white son of a bitch can tie a man up here" while other soldiers released a man tied up as punishment. Douglas mounted no defense and received a death sentence which his department commander, Major General Horatio G. Wright, mitigated to ten years hard labor without further explanation for his leniency.[31]

Capital sentences involving spying, desertion, mutiny, or murder did not require examination by the War Department or the president during time of war or rebellion, though regulations required army or department commanders to forward proceedings that involved a questionable issue, possible defect, or mitigating factor to Washington for review. This action suspended the sentence until the president's "pleasure be made known." Moreover, procedurally defective proceedings could result in the defendant's release from sentence despite clear evidence of guilt. On May 7, 1865, privates Lewis Dickinson and John Shaw of the Fifty-fifth Massachusetts argued while cleaning their guns. Shaw threatened to kill Dickinson but no one took his threat seriously. After roll call that day, however, Shaw approached Dickinson and struck him on the head with a large branch, fracturing his skull and killing him. A court-martial convicted the teenaged Shaw for murder, but a defect in the proceedings regarding the calling of the court negated his punishment and he returned to duty. Shaw subsequently faced at least two more courts-martial, one for threatening to kill two members of his company and another for deserting from the guard house in Orangeburg, South Carolina, on July 2, 1865.[32]

The War Department also showed occasional leniency when it felt racist officers had provoked mutineers, even when a mutiny had been violent. Such favorable conduct toward blacks persisted after the war. In July 1867, for instance, Judge Advocate General Holt recommended commutation of several death sentences in the mutiny of a black regular army cavalry regiment—one in which a white lieutenant died at the hands of African American subordinates (a black soldier also died). After contending that he had never considered a "more shocking illustration of the brutal tyranny which an officer has it in his power to exercise," Holt condemned the "savage treatment" exhibited by Lieutenant Edward M. Heyl toward his command. Heyl, the court discovered, had tied three subordinates to a tree by the wrists so that their feet were off the ground, struck them several times with the flat of his sword and stabbed at least one of them three times. While finding it indisputable that the defendants had mutinied, Holt considered their actions the result of "great provocation" and "terror," and declared that Heyl's conduct was "the immediate, indeed the only, cause" of their outburst. Holt recommended leniency toward the defendants, who returned to duty, and expressed more concern that the "malignant cruelty with which the men were treated" would destroy military discipline and the esteem in which people held the service. Holt recommended that the troubled lieutenant, who survived the mutiny, be tried by general court-martial.[33]

General courts-martial had significant impact. They involved not only defendants, witnesses, and the court panels but also the members of the units of these individuals who likely learned about both case and proceeding. Orders promulgating death sentences often required that these executions take place in front of the condemned man's brigade or division, and large numbers of soldiers likely inquired about the background of the executions they witnessed. Dissemination of knowledge about court-martial procedure, whether or not involving capital charges, prepared black soldiers to face the rule of law in civilian life. Former soldiers applied their knowledge of the military judicial system to file complaints, pursue opportunities to testify, and appeal judicial holdings when they thought such actions appropriate. Moreover, firsthand experiences with general courts-martial helped instill in blacks awareness of the concepts of due process and equal application of the law, regardless of race or slave status, and the idea that courts could protect black rights written into the law. These doctrines became core components of the vision of American citizenship that blacks asserted after the Civil War.[34]

Mutinies, Courts-Martial, and the Black Civil War Soldier

Mutiny cases often revealed a sense among blacks that their status had changed, as they made demands for equal treatment. Additionally, mutiny cases earned the attention of antislavery leaders and politicians who, like the mutineers, advocated a new legal order. While mutineers suffered punishment for their breaches of military discipline, their resistance against inequity in support of a vision of black equality did not pass unnoticed by members of either race. Mutiny proceedings became a crossroads between military justice and equal rights because the heat of the courtroom, and trials in which life literally hung in the balance, uncovered the character of race relations in both the Union army and broader society.[35]

Writing during the Civil War, military law commentator Stephen V. Benet defined mutiny as "resistance to lawful military authority," whether "active or passive," encompassing "not only extreme insubordination, as individually resisting by force, or collectively rising against or opposing military authority, but a murmuring or muttering against the exercise of authority, tending to create disquiet and dissatisfaction in the army." The Articles of War did not precisely define mutiny, but provided that any officer or soldier could be executed who began, caused, or joined one, did not do his utmost to suppress such an uprising that took place in his presence, or knew about an impending mutiny and failed to tell his commanding officer. The Articles of War further emphasized that anyone who so much as lifted a weapon, or offered violence, against an officer while in the execution of his duty could be sentenced to death.[36]

Black soldiers frequently faced mutiny charges because they lashed out against racially based injustices they suffered in the armed services. The most obvious example remains resistance to unequal pay, though other grievances early on earned black protest as well. Despite the strictures of military discipline, many of these men asserted their rights and demanded redress when they felt their terms of enlistment had been violated, or they had otherwise suffered unacceptable treatment. While historian Joseph T. Glatthaar accurately observed that many of the mutinies involved "non-violent protests for legitimate reasons," even more aggressive demonstrations generally had their roots in complaint about valid grievances. Examining both types of demonstrations illuminates the extent of the racism that black soldiers had to face, whether in official policies or inexcusable actions by some of their officers but also emphasizes their immediate demands for equality and unwillingness to suffer continued prejudice.[37]

Unfortunately for black mutineers, their protests occurred well into the war, after the initial impulse for lenience toward violators of military law and tolerance for dissent had disintegrated. Although flawed as a comprehensive record, the *List of U.S. Soldiers Executed by United States Military Authorities during the Late War* suggests that disciplinary leniency diminished as the war progressed. According to the *List,* only 7 and 14 federal soldiers were executed in 1861 and 1862, respectively. These numbers rose dramatically, though this also likely encompasses the greater numbers of men under arms as the war progressed: 67 in 1863, 95 in 1864, and 79 in 1865. Only 5 executions took place in 1866, for a total of 267 named on the admittedly incomplete list. Almost all of the 56 black soldiers listed on the *List* were executed in either 1864 or 1865. Fifteen of approximately 253 blacks charged with mutiny were executed by the sentence of a general court-martial, as were 4 white mutineers. Despite the gravity of the crimes committed by black mutineers, court-martial panels tried to confine capital punishment to either ringleaders or situations where a mutineer threatened the life of a white officer, and seem to have been generally cognizant that these mutineers' protests were political and not simply a release of frustration at a soldier's life. In some cases, defendants faced lesser charges even where their conduct constituted mutiny, or authorities asserted grounds for ameliorating death sentences. David Washington, a bugler in the Third USCC, faced a charge of insubordination, not mutiny, for striking a captain and refusing to be tied up as ordered for absence without leave. Even after defense witnesses made damaging statements at trial, and where Washington faced other serious charges, the court-martial panel sentenced him to only a year's hard labor without pay. Furthermore, officers permitted soldiers to refuse pay even though this technically constituted mutiny.[38]

Sampson Goliah's case sheds light on black resistance to inequality and hatred of punishments reminiscent of those inflicted on the plantation, as well as the court's location as a meeting point in balancing the rule of law with sympathy for legitimate grievances. In the course of the Fifty-fifth Massachusetts's transfer from Hilton Head to Folly Island, South Carolina, aboard a steamer on April 19, 1864, the officer of the guard, Lieutenant Jacob A. Bean, heard talking below deck after taps and repeatedly ordered the men to be quiet. Bean ordered Goliah up on deck after he continued to talk loudly and use profanity. Goliah angrily refused to go "for any damned white officer," and threatened to "smash" Bean if he laid hands on him. Another officer, Captain William Nutt, overheard the conversation as well as Goliah's declaration that "you Massachusetts men have bene humbugging us long enough" and "we are going to do as we please after this." Nutt came to Bean's assistance and handcuffed Goliah when they got the soldier on deck. Regimental commander Colonel Alfred S. Hartwell ordered the boat's captain to rope Goliah to the rigging for two hours unless Goliah ended his resistance (neither Hartwell nor Bean knew how to tie a man to ship's rigging).[39]

Ninety minutes later, more than a dozen men gathered on deck and announced that they intended to free Goliah because he "had been tied there long enough," and by a civilian no less. Bean ordered the single available guardsman to fix his bayonet and commanded the men to leave, but they taunted Bean, asking what one man could do when "there are five Companies of us and they will all be on deck in a few moments." Goliah freed himself by untying the rope with his teeth, and when Bean drew a pistol, Goliah grabbed it with both hands and cocked it. In the dark of night, a terrified Bean tussled with Goliah and the others until Goliah escaped below deck. Meanwhile, another soldier later found guilty of mutiny, Nelson Browning, told Hartwell that "other ways [existed] of punishing a man without having him tied up." When a company commander, Captain William Crane, tried to convince Browning that it served no purpose to participate in the uprising, the aggrieved soldier replied, "I know that Capt. Crane, but we have had enough of our men killed already"—a reference to Benjamin Hayes, shot at Readville, Massachusetts, for resisting an officer's authority during training, and several others hanged at Jacksonville, Florida, for rape pursuant to the sentence of a military commission. Hartwell ordered three sergeants to retrieve Goliah and he was again handcuffed.[40]

On May 7, 1864, nearly a week after Wallace Baker's mutiny in the Fifty-fifth Massachusetts, Goliah pled not guilty to seven specifications of mutiny. The judge advocate solicited Nutt's testimony that discontent existed in the regiment "because they...had not been paid according to the *terms* of their Enlistment." Colonel Hartwell reiterated that tension developed "because the Regiment had not been paid at all—nor offered pay according to terms of enlistment." Hartwell then described Goliah's outburst as "the first violent or mutinous expression of their feelings," and he expressed that he had "reason to think that very few men sympathize with these proceedings." Within days of testifying, a frustrated Hartwell wrote Massachusetts governor Andrew, "For God's sake, how long is the injustice of the government to be continued toward these men?" asking if the government meant to "goad them into mutiny" only to "quench the mutiny with blood." The next month, Hartwell wrote the secretary of war to ask for the muster out of his Fifty-fifth Massachusetts, while at the same time he and his officers struggled to prevent further disciplinary outbreaks among the men. Despite the inequities suffered by their troops, the regimental officers determined to enforce military regulations as the only method for handling the situation.[41]

Goliah questioned his commanding officer, Hartwell, and several witnesses corroborated that Goliah verbally resisted Bean. In keeping with his duty to bring out any exculpatory evidence, Judge Advocate Walton asked one witness if Goliah seemed willing to go up on deck if unmolested, to which the witness replied that he did. Goliah rested his defense on this point, stating in his final argument that he intended to go and told Bean as much, but that he would not suffer the indignity of being dragged. Goliah potentially faced a death sentence for his actions but Walton made a powerful plea for his life. "Your oath to 'well and truly try and determine the matter now before you' calls upon you to declare whether the acts of the prisoner are of that aggravated nature called mutiny," Walton pointed out. Arguing that "a grave offense has unquestionably been committed, and one to which heavy penalties should be affixed," Walton simultaneously questioned if it constituted "mutiny in the highest degree" such that "the extreme rigor of the law" need apply. Citing his duty as judge advocate to call the court's attention to mitigating circumstances, Walton highlighted Hartwell's testimony about discontent in the regiment due to the pay issue and concluded, "It is for the Court to see that the dignity of the law is maintained as well as the rights of the prisoner secured." Fifteen minutes later, the court sentenced Goliah to hard labor for the remainder of his term of enlistment, forfeiture of all pay, and dishonorable discharge, but not death.[42]

A protest in Battery F, Second USCA (Light) reveals the resentment black noncommissioned officers sometimes faced in trying to maintain military discipline, as well as the expectation of those noncommissioned officers that they would be treated the same as their white counterparts. Sergeant Horatio Price, a white sergeant detailed from the Seventh Wisconsin Artillery to act as the battery's lieutenant, ordered Corporal John Heskins tied spread eagle across the spare wheel of a caisson after Heskins drunkenly broke into a sutler's establishment. Sergeant Anderson Tolliver and others in the battery went to Price to discuss the punishment and things grew heated despite Captain Francis Marion's efforts to resolve the situation peacefully. Tolliver turned to the men and told them they should fight it out, and either Tolliver or Sergeant John Hall defiantly told Marion that they would not allow "any damned white man from another company to punish them." Armed soldiers gathered and defied Marion's order for everyone to return to quarters, vowing that "he is but one white man anyhow."[43]

Some black soldiers resisted the mutineers, however. Tolliver struck Sergeant John W. Chandler on learning that Chandler had carried out Price's orders, telling him that he "had tied up that man for them damned white sons of Bitches." In reply, Chandler declared that he acted pursuant to orders and announced that, while restraining himself for the moment, he would shoot the next person to lay hands on him. Corporal of the guard James Paydon threatened to shoot the first man who tried to untie Heskins and ordered another member of his guard to "let no one touch that rope." Nonetheless, someone did untie Heskins in the pandemonium and it seemed that the party intended to overpower the provost guard sent to quell the rebellion. Once reinforcements arrived, however, Marion arrested Tolliver and others from the crowd.[44]

Eight soldiers faced trial together for mutiny in Memphis, Tennessee, on March 30, 1864. Most of the defendants offered statements after a vigorous defense conducted by counsel formerly assigned to the court-martial detail. Tolliver and Hall averred that it was customary in the battery that noncommissioned officers would not be tied up. Hall did not justify his actions, and even confessed that he did not expect acquittal, but observed that the fact that a fellow noncommissioned officer from outside the unit meted out the punishment exacerbated the situation. Hall argued that all noncommissioned officers stood as equals, with certain privileges regardless of race, and claimed that "it is not surprising that it should have caused a general excitement among the men, and that expressions should have been used and threats made, which under ordinary circumstances would deserve severe punishment." Four of the defendants received sentences of three years imprisonment, while Tolliver received four years. Meanwhile, the court exonerated two defendants based on their statement that no evidence existed against them other than their presence in a crowd watching the disturbance. The court also returned to duty bugler Isaac Reeves, even though he loudly proclaimed during the mutiny, "fall in boys and let us clean them fellows out." An officer testified that Reeves did this for braggadocio's sake, and Reeves asserted in his defense that he used "indiscreet expressions" in jest after the mutiny ended.[45]

Asserting their role as protectors of other blacks, soldiers of the Ninth Louisiana Infantry of African Descent came close to execution after they protested the beating of a black civilian in camp near Memphis, Tennessee, and orders that their families were going to be relocated out of easy reach. On January 28, 1864, Lieutenant William Striblen and another officer physically subdued the civilian, who had resisted arrest, leaving him bloodied from several bayonet wounds. Seven or eight armed soldiers left a fatigue detail without orders to confront what they perceived as two unacceptable violations. Striblen later testified that the men "looked very defiant and scowled as I came to them." As Striblen disarmed one of the men, they demanded to see their families and expressed anger at the relocation policy. Charles Davis then noticed that Striblen had a partially concealed pistol and called out that Striblen intended to shoot. One of Davis's comrades, Sterling Bradley, stabbed Striblen and penetrated his right lung, before another soldier knocked the officer to the ground. Becoming weak from the loss of blood, Striblen staggered to his tent, turning and indiscriminately firing his pistol on the way. Striblen denied that he had ever told the mutinous troops that he had nearly killed one black that day and intended to kill another before nightfall, though a black witness confirmed that Striblen often treated the men poorly and corroborated that he passed the comment.[46]

Captain J. A. Staley represented both Davis and Bradley in their individual proceedings and argued that the excited men armed themselves "to prevent some person, or persons from removing their families beyond their reach," which they saw as violating their original agreement to enlist. Furthermore, Staley argued, the men showed understandable anger after "one of their own blood is brought before them bleeding, and suffering from wounds unnecessarily severe, (if indeed necessary at all) inflicted by two Officers, one of whom is their own commander." Both issues caused the outburst, Staley asserted, and he scorned Striblen's clumsy handling of the day's events (and the behavior of other USCT officers who acted similarly) in that "like many others he was in

attempting to do by force, what could be better accomplished by kindness."
Yet, while arguing that blacks acted just as whites would have done because
"nothing so quickly and certainly arouses the belligerent feelings of men, who
have a proper regard and affection for their wives and children, as indignity,
insult, or injustice offered to them," defense counsel also argued differentiation
between the races for which whites were responsible. Staley blamed society
for creating an "unfortunate, enslaved race, shut out from the enlightening
influence of refining associations, the means of education, and the benign and
elevating tendency of true religion," and found it "unreasonable to expect" a
black "could bring his passions in as complete control of his judgment as the
man who has enjoyed a part or all of those blessings, nor can it be expected
of him to have as correct an appreciation of his duties and responsibilities as a
soldier, as others who have been more favorably situated."[47]

The courts-martial sentenced both Bradley and Davis to death. On review, Judge Advocate General Holt found no extenuating circumstances and
added that

> it is vitally important to the success of the great and promising experiment of
> employing negroes as soldiers that—while no unjust distinctions should be made
> between them and other troops—neither benevolence nor sympathy should deter
> us from the enforcement of a rigorous discipline, alike adapted to their training
> and to the necessities of the service. It is indispensable that such grave offences,
> as those committed by the prisoners, should be so dealt with as to prevent their
> repetition. The good of the whole sometimes requires the infliction of severe pun-
> ishments in individual instances, where were the offenders the only ones to be
> affected, milder penalties might be mercifully awarded.

Defense counsel, the court-martial panel, and Judge Advocate General Holt
sought to balance consideration of the conditions in which many blacks lived
prior to joining the army versus the concept of blacks standing as equal before
the law, even where this placed demands on blacks to act in the same way the
military (and later, society) expected of whites. At the nexus of this debate lay
a broader question still unresolved: could blacks take a place as citizens equal
to whites, or did their prior lives as slaves render them unsuited for such equality? Luckily for the condemned men, Lincoln disagreed with Holt's report and
commuted both of their sentences to six months confinement at hard labor.[48]

Other mutiny cases resulted in actual execution, however. These sentences
frequently involved situations where authorities felt they needed to enforce
stricter discipline as a deterrent to further unrest. Shortly after not imposing
a death sentence in the Goliah and Browning court-martials, substantially the
same panel sentenced Wallace Baker to death, perhaps troubled by what they
perceived to be growing dissidence in the Fifty-fifth Massachusetts. In some
ways, the trial of the first black Union soldier executed for mutiny provides one
of the most effective examples to illuminate how blacks and whites wrestled
with military discipline, the meaning of arming African Americans, and black

calls for equality within the context of a changing social landscape. A history of disciplinary trouble marked the military record of Sergeant William Walker, a twenty-three-year-old in the Third South Carolina (African Descent) (Twenty-first USCI). A court-martial convened at Hilton Head, South Carolina, not far from the Port Royal area where Walker formerly labored as a slave, on January 11, 1864, to arraign Walker on multiple charges stemming from various instances in which he resisted authority of all sorts: threatening to shoot a lieutenant, refusing a captain's order to go into his tent under arrest, defying a black sergeant's order to fall in, preventing a black drum major from making an arrest, helping release a prisoner being punished for absence, and leaving his tent while under arrest.[49]

A charge of mutiny based on the events of November 19, 1863, however, reveals the motivation behind Walker's resistance. Walker marched his company, along with other men from the regiment, to commanding officer Lieutenant Colonel Augustus G. Bennett's tent. There, Walker ordered the men to stack arms in protest of the black soldiers' unequal pay and explained that they "would not do duty any longer for seven dollars per month." The men's willingness to mutiny had been exacerbated by their resentment over the high proportion of inexperienced officers who led them, some of whom openly displayed racially based disdain, as well as the excess fatigue duty they had endured. Bennett explained that the mutineers would be shot if they did not return to duty, but Walker moved among the men, telling them to leave their guns and go to their company street. The soldiers obeyed Walker's command.[50]

Despite the fact that Walker later faced a court-martial, the protest gained the attention of the regiment's officers and had some larger effect. Within days, Bennett and twelve of his officers signed a petition protesting that unequal pay "plighted" the "honor" of the country and breached the government's promise of equal treatment. On November 25, department commander Major General Quincy Gillmore ordered that black troops were not to be a labor force for white use but instead, should receive the same treatment and opportunity for drill. By the end of the month, Bennett requested that rations be furnished to his troops' families until the equalization of their pay. Although department headquarters denied the request, Bennett's act indicates his consciousness of the men's situation as well as the dilemma he faced in maintaining discipline. Several months later, Governor Andrew of Massachusetts called attention to Walker's execution in a scathing letter to Lincoln. Demanding equal pay for black soldiers, Andrew denounced "the Government which found no law *to pay him except as a nondescript or a contraband,* nevertheless found law enough *to shoot him as a soldier.*" While punishment had to be meted out to the vocal leader of the serious act of mutiny, at least some white officers and officials took heed of the rationale behind the protest and argued that upholding the law in this case violated other principles of justice.[51]

Furthermore, no one else received serious punishment for participating in the mutiny. A report in June 1864 noted that the regiment had endured inferior equipment, officers, treatment, and pay, and that the men protested without realizing that they could not simply lay down their arms. The report continued that once "good officers" explained that fact, "*all at once entered willingly to their duties,*" and that the regiment had become "one of the best" under Bennett's direction. In successfully urging the return to duty of nine mutineers without stoppage of pay, the report also noted that the men had faced partiality in their trials, with "irregularities of the records" that "rendered it impossible for these men to have Justice." Acknowledging that the discipline of black troops could sometimes be carried out in an arbitrary manner, this statement serves as an example of white officers seeking uniform administration of justice.[52]

Nonetheless, the tempestuous sergeant who led the mutiny had to face trial. After introducing a lieutenant from the Forty-seventh New York Infantry as defense counsel, Walker pleaded not guilty to all charges. Bennett testified as to the events of November 19, and two lieutenants corroborated his narrative and offered testimony about other charges. A black acting drum major testified that he declined to discipline a subordinate because Walker "eyed me sharply," and made him "afraid." Sergeant Sussex Brown also offered that he once found Walker playing cards instead of falling in for inspection. Walker wanted to "play on" and when the other card players left, let forth a stream of curses and threatened to shoot Brown.[53]

Walker tried to mitigate these damaging statements with testimony from three sergeants and three privates of his regiment. Walker then articulated a criticism of treatment in the army and his expectations for equality. Conceding in a written statement that there existed "many points" for which he was "justly blamable, and for which he cannot hope to escape without punishment," Walker also hoped that "an enlightened understanding" would make the court panel realize that his action was more an error of judgment than a desire to violate the law. Walker asserted his military service and the unequal treatment his unit and race had endured as defenses. He explained that he served as a pilot of the USS *Wissahickon* when he received a pass to visit his family ashore. Although exempt from conscription, Walker enlisted in reliance on the "promise solemnly made by some who are now officers in my regiment, that I should receive the same pay and allowances as were given to all soldiers in the U.S. Army." Claiming that nine-tenths of the men in his regiment would agree that their officers had been "tyrannical in the extreme" and "beneath the standard of gentlemanly conduct...pertaining to officers wearing the uniform of a government that had declared 'freedom to all,'"—despite the petition supporting equalization of pay signed by those same officers within hours of the mutiny—Walker stated that racist treatment and unequal pay precipitated the incident. Walker further suggested that the officers had overblown the situation, informing the court panel that the assemblage "only contemplated a peaceful demand for the rights and benefits that had been guaranteed them."[54]

Walker concluded by asserting that a "spirit of persecution" toward him existed, that "every part of my military history has been ransacked to procure a conviction" and added that he did not act alone on November 19, 1863. Claiming his ignorance of military law, Walker argued that he and his comrades had "been allowed to stumble along" and gain "knowledge of the services required of us as best we might." Walker vowed that "many things have occurred that might have been made entirely different had we known the responsibility of our position." With his mark, Walker concluded with a request that the court give as favorable a consideration as the rules of the service would permit.[55]

The court sentenced Walker to death. When only one of eleven shots of the firing squad hit Walker, a reserve squad completed the execution. George E. Stephens criticized the "strange means" by which black soldiers were shot under military law and felt that as to Walker's execution, the government "required a victim to show the colored soldiers…what they must expect if they don't take the money [the] government offers them, however paltry." Colonel Thomas W. Higginson condemned the practice of forcing officers to be "executioners for those soldiers who, like Sergeant Walker, refuse to fulfill their share of a contract where the Government has openly repudiated the other share." Massachusetts senator Henry Wilson potently cited Walker's case when he called on his fellow lawmakers to place black soldiers on equal footing with white troops in all respects, explaining that Walker had rebelled out of "a burning sense of our injustice." Over four decades later, former colonel of the Fifty-fifth Massachusetts Norwood Hallowell deemed Walker's position that black soldiers had been released from duty because the government failed to fulfill its contract as "logical," but explained that because it was time of war, Walker had to be tried and punished.[56]

Walker's case stands at the intersection of conflicting impulses generated by the army service of blacks during the Civil War. An ex-slave turned U.S. Army sergeant, Walker repeatedly bucked military authority but then relied on the rule of law for his defense. A vocal opponent of the inequality he suffered in the army, Walker experienced due process at trial and was executed pursuant to the same law and procedure mandated for white defendants. Walker's hope on donning the blue uniform melted into disenchantment because of unequal pay, and his protest against it led directly to his lawful execution, but in launching that protest Walker became symbolic of black demands for a new legal order embracing and enforcing equality.

Some cases that resulted in execution concerned the threat of violence against a superior officer. Henry Hamilton of the Second USCI was the only person to suffer death for a mutiny that involved several hundred soldiers. When an officer ordered Hamilton to return to quarters, he fixed his bayonet and declared that he would run through the first person who touched him. In other cases, noncommissioned officers occasionally received a death penalty even where they led a nonviolent mutiny. Sergeants William Kease and Doctor Moore of the 116th USCI were sentenced to death for leading more than forty armed men of their company to the quarters of Captain Sumner H. Warren on May 11, 1865, to demand the release of a private under arrest. Both sergeants faced further charges because they failed to use their authority as noncommissioned officers to prevent the mutiny, and neither of them offered any defense.[57]

Arguably the most violent mutiny of black soldiers erupted in the Third USCI while stationed in Jacksonville, Florida, on October 29, 1865. Ordered to perform tedious occupation duty amid a hostile population, many of the soldiers resorted to alcohol and resented strict maintenance of discipline in the unit after the war had ended. White officers' treatment of black female camp followers generated further complaints, as one soldier deemed the officers "loathsome" because they "apparently think that their commissions are licenses to debauch and mingle with deluded freewomen under cover of darkness." Young lieutenant colonel John L. Brower, assuming command of the unit a few weeks earlier, earned a reputation for strict discipline as he tried to combat the growing disobedience and drunkenness in his command.[58]

A harsh punishment administered to a pilferer two days before the regiment's scheduled muster out sparked the tinder. A lieutenant ordered the soldier, who had tried to steal some molasses, stripped to the waist and tied by the thumbs with his toes barely touching the ground. A crowd of soldiers, possibly unarmed, vowed to release the man, especially after others in the regiment goaded them by asking, "What kind of a company is yours, that let your men be tied up[?]" When Brower fired into the crowd with his revolver, wounding Private Joseph Green, the situation exploded. Some soldiers got their muskets and engaged in a firefight with Brower, while others attacked or shot at officers. One soldier convinced a captain to take off his sword lest an enlisted soldier injure him and then tied up the disarmed captain. In contrast, some noncommissioned officers sought to restore order, and after Brower's finger was shot off, one of the original instigators, Richard Lee, rushed to his aid and took him to safety in the cookhouse. Only the arrival of the unit's former commander, Colonel Bardwell, on the scene restored order.[59]

By October 31, 1865, court-martial proceedings began with six officers of the Third USCI and two from the Thirty-fourth USCI comprising the panel (panels could include officers from the same unit as the defendant). Fourteen soldiers stood trial for mutiny while one who did not participate in it, Archibald Roberts, faced lesser charges for saying, "Lt. Colonel Brower, the God-Damned Son of a Bitch, he shot my cousin. Where is he, let me see him." The proceedings moved swiftly, with only a few witnesses on each side answering but one or two questions each. Nonetheless, while the judge advocate seemed to ignore his mandate to assist defendants not represented by counsel, the panel's president worked to ensure substantially full and fair trials.[60]

By November 13, the court convicted thirteen soldiers of mutiny, and Roberts of conduct prejudicial to good order. Six received death sentences and of those, at least four shot or tried to shoot at officers, while one had been among the most active instigators of the incident. Yet, the court acquitted one, Theodore Waters, of mutiny despite testimony from the regimental surgeon that Waters drew nearer to the tied up man than anyone else. One defense witness countered that Waters only went with the crowd to try to get permission to free the punished soldier and another offered that Waters was in his tent when the mutiny ended. Furthermore, some instigators—privates Richard Lee, who aided Brower after helping start the riot, and John Miller, who shouted, "Let's take him down, we are not going to have any more of tying men up by the thumbs" and swore "like a mad man" during the disturbance—received only two years at hard labor. One soldier who struck a lieutenant received fifteen years at hard labor, two others received ten, and two more, including one who tried to cut down the punished man, received two years. In late 1866, the Bureau of Military Justice commuted the sentences of the surviving mutineers (the six executions had been carried out and one more died from typhoid fever) and by January 1867 had released them.[61]

Although not technically mutiny, some black soldiers who were executed lashed out against prejudice they experienced from other sources. A court-martial which met in Natchez, Mississippi, in June 1864 sentenced Roger Johnson to death for shooting a white private serving as a cook in the hospital in which Johnson convalesced (the private lingered for about a month before he died). The cook had refused to serve Johnson until a white man present had finished eating, and then threw plates at Johnson.[62]

Racial tensions between black soldiers and Southern white civilians also sometimes resulted in violence. One court-martial illuminates the seething rage some black soldiers felt against former slaveholders. On May 2, 1865, a court-martial convened in the Vicksburg courthouse to try twelve soldiers of the Fifty-second USCI, and one from the Fifth USCHA. The thirteen men were charged with entering Jared R. Cook's nearby house in conspiracy on the evening of April 3, 1865, taking money and goods, and then shooting both Cook and his wife, Minerva (he survived while she later died). Each of the accused refused representation by counsel and each pled not guilty.[63]

Thomas Richardson of the Fifty-second USCI, an accomplice turned prosecutor's witness, testified that the defendants premeditatedly went "out after rebels." Claiming that all except him were armed, Richardson explained how they had conducted the maneuver with military precision, dividing into two squads as they approached Cook's house, with one squad entering while the other stood guard outside. Some of the men ransacked the house, while Thomas Four and Ephraim McDowell shot the Cooks. Henry Cox told them not to shoot and, in Richardson's words, "they cussed him" and threatened to shoot him as well. Fifteen-year-old Alexander Cook corroborated that "some nigger soldiers" had ransacked the house, though he slipped out and hid in a woods two hundred yards away before any shots were fired. On his return the next day, Alexander found many things missing and two black women tending his wounded mother, shot in the stomach, her face showing the bruises of having been beaten and her blood all over the floor. Thirteen-year-old William Cook also corroborated that "nigger soldiers" had ransacked the house. William described watching his parents get shot. Because Cook still recuperated, the court-martial heard his testimony at his plantation. Cook recounted that his dogs woke him as the black soldiers approached, and that he saw them "rushing in in a very demon-like manner seeming to be very much infuriated from some cause," before describing the defendants' threats and demands, his ineffective protest that he had protection papers, and how the black soldiers ransacked his house and shot him and his wife. Cook added that he heard no one attempt to prevent the violence and also that after he and his wife had been shot, he heard his thirteen-year-old son tussle with one, crying "don['[t kill me, oh! Lord don['[t kill me."[64]

The accused declined to call a single witness in their defense, but all except one made an oral statement. Each defendant individually pled his defense to the court while his codefendants stood outside. All those who made a statement admitted their presence and claimed simply to have wanted to catch Rebels or to go along with the crowd. As Bannestor Washington stated, "I always like to be in that kind of a crowd that goes after rebels," while Henry Johnson reminded the court that as "colored soldiers used to be treated badly by the rebels...that makes them hate the rebels more than the white soldiers do. It[']s natural that they should feel so." Johnson admitted that he left the Cooks two and a half years earlier, and while claiming that he "had nothing personal against Mr. Cook or his family," and that he told his comrades, "I wouldn't have you do any harm here for the world," he also does not seem to have exerted himself for the protection of his former owner or his family. Morrison admitted to striking Minerva Cook. The court-martial panel found all of the defendants guilty of all charges and sentenced them to hang.[65]

Yet, the very day they sentenced the thirteen men to death, five members of the nine-man panel petitioned for clemency for Cox, despite Cook's testimony that he heard no one try to prevent the shootings. Two more panel members recommended that "in consequence of the mitigating circumstances connected in this case we would most respectfully and cheerfully recommend clemency to all of the accused with the exception of the following: James Morrison, Ephraim McDowell and Thomas Four." Major General Napoleon J. T. Dana released Cox from confinement and returned him to duty and the War Department remitted the sentences of three other defendants, though the other nine—including Johnson—suffered execution.[66]

Conclusion

Examining the courts-martial records of black soldiers illuminates the tensions military authorities experienced in trying to maintain military discipline while administering justice to African American troops. Despite the gravity of mutineers' crimes, many officers seem to have realized that they grounded their protests in legitimate grievances. Thus usually only ringleaders or those who threatened violence to an officer received capital punishment. In many instances, authorities searched for mitigating factors and defendants frequently received lighter sentences than those sanctioned by the Articles of War. Moreover black soldiers enjoyed high standards of due process when facing general courts-martial. Generally, a confession, strong evidence of culpability, and/or the complete lack of a plausible defense resulted in conviction. In other cases, such as Samuel Green's vigorous self-defense resulting in his exoneration of a mutiny charge, a black soldier's questioning of African American witnesses trumped the testimony of a white officer. Such moments emphasized to blacks and whites the possibilities of African Americans standing equal to whites before the law, and underscored for blacks the concept that they could use the rule of law and procedural due process to defend their rights.

Rather than sanction a different disciplinary scheme for black troops, the federal government considered them as entitled from the beginning to the same application of military justice and court-martial procedures that whites enjoyed. The army's embrace of procedural due process regardless of color, a doctrine mandated by the War Department and affirmed in general courts-martial proceedings, stood as one paradigm for the nation to consider as it reconstituted itself. Even though not accomplished on a wider scale within either the army or civilian society during the Civil War, the experience of general courts-martial emphasized the possibility that a pattern of fair and equal treatment of blacks could be more broadly applied.

Courts-martial proceedings demonstrated to blacks that there need not be two sets of laws, or two forms of citizenship status, but that the same legal rights, expectations, and concept of citizenship could apply to all individuals regardless of race. These wartime experiences helped inform black demands during Reconstruction for color-blind justice as a component of American citizenship and their sense that the law could serve as a bulwark to protect their newfound freedom and changed status, and showed that a new overall legal regime—one more protective of blacks' rights—could emerge from the fluidity of war.

Moreover, the proceedings of courts-martial of mutineers reveal the impatient claims for equality black soldiers made, whether protesting unequal pay or inequitable treatment. Black soldiers began to ascertain how to operate within a rule of law previously denied to nearly all of them, but they also demanded its equal enforcement and recognition of their changed status. Black soldiers loudly voiced their call, using extralegal means, for this revised constitutional and societal norm based on presumptions of their equality. That this path proved more elusive than many of these soldiers, who comprised a new corps of leadership within the black community, had hoped does not diminish the importance of the fact that it lay open at all in the federal army, or that blacks demanded it not just with words but also with action that sometimes earned them imprisonment or death.

CHAPTER 5

Irish Americans in Arms

In March 1863, an Irish-born sergeant in the Ninth Massachusetts presented his young lieutenant, an Irish American born in Boston, with a sword on behalf of their company. Sergeant Frank Lawler anticipated that the recipient would "tarnish its bright hue in the crimson tide of those recreants who would rend to pieces our beloved adopted country." A notion of agency pervaded that phrase commonly used by Irish American leaders, "adopted country," in contrast to the harsh realities of the Famine which forced most of the Irish to migrate in the first place. Irish Americans and the native-born embraced each other in the 1860s in bonds strengthened by the shared experience of war. Participation in the Civil War intensified the demands of Irish Americans for inclusion and equal treatment but also their sense of American allegiance, even as they maintained facets of their ethnic culture and an enduring concern for Ireland's liberation. Many Irish Americans increasingly came to recognize during the Civil War an American identity in addition to an Irish one.[1]

Most Irish American volunteers enlisted for a mixture of reasons, which combined in different proportions, including, prominently, money. On the other hand, Civil War soldiers, including Irish Americans, were highly ideological. Even where influenced by money, Irish American soldiers understood that their service had importance other than bounties and salaries. Moreover, while keeping in mind the individual backgrounds and motivations of Irish American soldiers, it is important to consider the communal meanings of their service. Individuals did not explicitly declare that their enlistment made them a true American at the moment they signed the muster roll. Nonetheless, aggregate wartime experiences, and the public pronouncements of Irish American leaders and newspapers, reveal intensification in the ethnic community's under-standing that its choice of allegiance to the Union consummated membership in the nation.[2]

Soldiers in the field most immediately experienced this wartime develop-ment, and they transmitted their perspective to a wider audience by writing to families and for newspaper publication. Other individuals, unable to serve in the armed forces, participated in it by contributing time, offering money, or enduring the absence of loved ones engaged in the war effort. Irish Ameri-can leaders made public pronouncements to interethnic audiences on behalf of their community, while government officials articulated in speeches and poli-cies a new understanding of Irish America's place in the United States.

On one hand, examining the Irish American military experience highlights the distinctiveness of the African American experience in the Union's armed forces. Major differences in status and treatment are easily apparent, and at first glance, the two groups shared little in common during their service. On the other hand, the shifts in Irish American identity that took place during the Civil War bear striking resemblance to those of African Americans in terms of how they developed. These changes also served as a catalyst for the expecta-tions both groups expressed about change in the legal concept of citizenship during the later 1860s.

Pageantry and Calls for Legal Change

Flag presentations to Irish American regiments early on emphasized recogni-tion by the native-born and members of the ethnic community that Irish Ameri-cans could have an American identity along with their Irish one. Both commu-nities reciprocally used wartime pageantry to solidify Irish America's position within the American people. Symbols and ceremonies assist the formation of nationalist ideas by transmitting certain messages to an intended audience and bringing people together in expressions of public unity. Most Union regiments went through "standard rites of passage" shortly after organization. The pre-sentation of silk regimental banners and American flags, held as sacred symbols of unit identity and coveted by opponents as battle trophies, capped off these rites by linking communities, the soldiers they sent to war, and the national cause for which they fought. Similar to what occurred for some African Ameri-can regiments, flags and flag presentations joined in a visible public way Irish American service, identity, and wartime claims to inclusion.[3]

The regimental banners presented to the Irish American Ninth Connecticut and Sixty-ninth Pennsylvania in 1861 displayed the respective state seal on one side and Irish symbols on the other. Both states had a potent Know Nothing presence in the 1850s, and Connecticut had even disbanded militia companies comprised of the foreign-born. In December 1862, native-born New Yorkers donated a new set of flags to the Sixty-third, Sixty-ninth, and Eighty-eighth

New York regiments of the Irish Brigade. One presenter proclaimed, "Here are your green flags and the Stars and Stripes. Allow us, American-born citizens, to present them in grateful commemoration of the gallant deeds of your Brigade," before he announced his hope that soon would "old Erin's harp be tuned afresh to the proud song of 'The Land of the Free and the Home of the Brave.' Then shall we represent 'one country, one constitution, one destiny.'"[4]

The regimental colors and sendoff of the Ninth Massachusetts, comprised of Irish American volunteers recruited from around Boston, illuminates the public culture of wartime Irish American patriotism. In late June 1861, the Ninth Massachusetts received an American flag and an emerald silk regimental banner bearing the inscription, "THY SONS BY ADOPTION, THY FIRM SUPPORTERS AND DEFENDERS, FROM DUTY, AFFECTION AND CHOICE" above the American coat of arms. On the reverse, thirty-four stars and a shamrock wreath surrounded an Irish harp with red, white, and blue strings. Along with two wolf dogs emblematic of Ireland read the mottos, "Gentle when stroked, but fierce when provoked," and "As aliens and strangers thou didst us befriend, As sons and true patriots, we do thee defend." The Ninth Massachusetts's banner thus publicly acknowledged Irish and American identities under the rubric of the United States.[5]

The day before the Ninth Massachusetts departed for the seat of war, Bostonians greeted the men as they arrived at Long Wharf via steamer from their training camp located on a Boston Harbor island. Similar to a later sendoff for the black Fifty-fourth Massachusetts, Gilmore's band and an escort seven hundred strong preceded the regiment as it marched through the heart of Boston to the approbation of throngs of onlookers who crowded the streets. At the State House, Governor John Andrew presented the Irish American regiment with another flag, this one bearing the seal of the Commonwealth of Massachusetts. A color sergeant, flanked by two others holding aloft the Stars and Stripes and rich green banner, received this flag after Andrew assured all present that "the United States of America knows no distinction between its native born citizens and those born in other countries," and requested the men to always "remember that you are American citizens." Andrew's words emphasized the inclusion symbolically consummated by the flags and probably made the meal provided for the men by the city of Boston taste even more savory.[6]

It was not entirely a day of solidarity between native and immigrant, and one person in the crowd exclaimed on the Ninth Massachusetts's departure, "There goes a load of Irish rubbish out of the city." Nonetheless, the *Courier* noted that the cheering onlookers included both Catholics and "Old native Americans," and the *Atlas and Bee* offered that whatever "complaint may be made of the clannishness" of Irish, German, and French immigrants, "they are clannish only as Americans in London, Paris and Florence are clannish; they love their native country. But when foreign war or domestic rebellion lifts its head against our government and threatens our national life, they are equally ready, with native-born citizens, to rally to the public defense." For itself, the *Pilot* noted that the impressive appearance of the Ninth Massachusetts caused the "narrow and dark spirit of Know-nothingism," to shrink "back abashed in the presence of the splendid civil and military Celtic procession." Moreover, according to the newspaper, a fusion of nationalities took place in the United States to create a new one: all those who "waved their flags" along the route, declared the *Pilot*, were "unconscious of any distinction between the loyalty of the Anglo Saxon and Celtic races, which make up the American people."[7]

A few weeks later, the *Pilot* recalled the disbandment in 1855 of the Irish American Columbian Artillery militia company that now formed the core of the Ninth Massachusetts. Just as later articles contrasted the Twentieth USCI's march through New York City with the Draft Riots there, the *Pilot* proclaimed, "Boston forgot her ancient prejudices as she gazed upon the noble column presented by the 'Irish regiment,'" while Know Nothing ex-Governor Gardner, who disbanded the Irish American militia companies, "hid his diminished head." For soldiers such as Colonel Thomas Cass, who had commanded the Columbian Artillery when it was disbanded, the flag presentation held particularly potent meaning.[8]

To the men of the Ninth Massachusetts in the field, the emerald banner served as a dual symbol of remembrance of Ireland and service to their new country. According to one officer, "We always carry our 'Green Flag.' We shall never abandon it, even though it should go to atoms. It is the emblem of all our hopes and the source of all our pride. Whilst we behold it before us, exhibiting to our gaze the Harp and the Shamrock of Ireland, we cannot forget the glorious memories associated with these emblems of our nationality." The green flag illuminated the Irish American identity of the men during reviews and in battle, while simultaneously showing that they served alongside native-born troops with equal station and bearing. In his report of the regiment's first action, Colonel Cass described how the "starry banner of the Union, side by side with our green flag throughout the fight, came out of it unscathed, while the latter was pierced by eight buck-and-ball shots."[9]

A new spirit regarding Irish American inclusion pervaded the Bay State in the weeks following the departure of the Ninth Massachusetts. The city of Boston honored the Irish flag for the first time by having it raised, along with the flags of other nations, during July Fourth celebrations. Harvard in July 1861 honored a Catholic prelate for the first time by bestowing on Bishop Fitzpatrick an honorary doctorate in divinity. The state legislature compromised on the issue of requiring Catholic children in the public schools to read from the Protestant Bible. New legislation required daily reading of the Bible but without written or oral discussion. Furthermore, students would not be compelled to read from a version of the Bible that contravened the religious faith of their parents.[10]

The Irish American press, as well as soldiers in the field, vigorously called for additional changes in the law. Perceiving shifts as early as October 1861, the *Pilot* proclaimed the triumph of "the sons of St. Patrick," who "trampled" over the "worst insult ever offered to human freedom": the principle "that political liberty should be confined entirely to those born" in the United States. While the *Pilot* here conveniently forgot about slavery, it cast Irish Americans as the dedicated defenders of *true* American ideals, in contrast to the exclusion and false patriotism preached by Know Nothings. The *Pilot* identified "the squelching out of '*nativism*'" as an Irish American triumph that "removed from republican freedom its most scandalous foe," and redeemed America amongst other nations. "The very citizens," the *Pilot* announced, "those same liars reviled the most, and charged in every possible way with treachery to the Union" now filled army regiments, demonstrating "the devotion of our people to their oaths of citizenship."[11]

Noting that many Irish Americans served in the Bay State's regiments, the *Pilot* viewed Massachusetts's November 1861 election as an opportunity "when the repeal of the 'two years' amendment' may justly be urged.... The adopted citizens have shown their devotion to the stars and stripes, and now is the time to demand all the rights and privileges to be enjoyed under them." By mid-December 1861, the newspaper reiterated how Irish Americans had become "wedded" to the "glorious Stars and Stripes," and starting in September 1862, called attention to the point by beginning to publish a column entitled "Records of Irish-American Patriotism."[12]

Meanwhile, soldiers' letters published in the *Pilot* underscored the demand for an end to nativist exclusion. In October 1861, Michael Finnerty of the Ninth Massachusetts rhetorically asked, "What would the government do in this crisis without her naturalized citizens, or who will ever again dare to point the finger of scorn against the humblest of them?" Demanding the promotion of Irish American officers that winter, Captain John W. Mahan of the same regiment claimed that casualties formed a "record proof that everywhere, fighting side by side with their brethren, 'to the manor born,' Irishmen have shown themselves not only worthy to have confided to them the honor of the American flag, but also, forgetting the 'two years' amendment, forgetting the past prejudices and errors of Massachusetts, have in the heat of battle proudly borne aloft the banner of the old Bay State, and shed their blood in its defence."[13]

Members of the Ninth Massachusetts also used the green banner to make their point. Although some members of the regiment wanted to keep the old colors on receiving a new green flag in October 1862, its colonel sent the tattered banner to Governor Andrew for display in the State House, where "it can be pointed to with pride, and must forever stifle the voice of bigotry and Know-nothingism" in the legislature's halls. Colonel Guiney used his tender of "these shreds" to emphasize the change in Irish American status that came as a result of their service, and he thanked Andrew for his "efforts to expunge from the Constitution of Massachusetts that provision [the two-years amendment] which would make political distinction between us and our brothers in hope, conviction, disaster, and victory." Andrew responded to Guiney's gesture by complimenting the bravery of the Ninth Massachusetts, and placing Irish Americans within the fold of all of Massachusetts's soldiers. More concretely, by 1862, popular sentiment had shifted and the successive 1862 and 1863 state legislatures made the legal point by passing an act of repeal of Massachusetts's two-year amendment. A slim majority of voters approved the measure in a spring 1863 referendum.[14]

Wartime Experiences

Outside of legal change, such as the "fast-track" to naturalization offered by the Act of July 17, 1862, and repeal of nativist state-level legislation, other experiences during the war nurtured a sense of American identity among Irish Americans. Military journeys afforded Irish American soldiers in blue access to important American landmarks and inspired in some of them a nationalizing sense of communion with the heritage of the United States. Just as it does for tourists today, Mount Vernon left an indelible impression on Irish Americans who passed by it. Traveling with his Ninth Massachusetts aboard a steamer, Irish-born Michael Finnerty felt "awe and reverence" when gazing, "on the spot where repose the ashes of the great and illustrious George Washington." Finnerty believed that Washington's spirit "smiled benignantly" on the Irish American regiment, and his comrades uncovered their heads as the ship's bell tolled to honor Washington's memory. Irish-born shoemaker Daniel Crotty of the Third Michigan felt that he and Washington were of the same country while he walked on the land where the "great man" lived and paid his respects at the First Couple's tombs.[15]

Defending the federal capital early in the war similarly afforded Irish Americans an opportunity to feel that they comprised part of the country. Five of the Ninth Massachusetts's officers visited the White House and cheered from the congressional gallery, with "all the fashionable of Washington and elsewhere," on announcement of Lincoln's call for men to crush the Confederate rebellion. One of the party afterward described the Capitol as "the most magnificent building I have ever seen," reminiscent of "ancient Rome or Greece in the days of their greatest splendor." Daniel Crotty watched Congress open in special session on July 4, 1861, and slowly walked around the Capitol to savor its beauty. A singer who spontaneously broke out into the "Star Spangled Banner," and seeing Lincoln and his cabinet outside the White House, capped off the patriotic day and steeled Crotty to fight for the United States.[16]

Sharing in the tribulations and triumphs of supporting the Union cause also nourished such nationalizing sentiments. Despite a torrential February 1862 rainstorm, the Ninth Massachusetts drew up in a hollow square so that its adjutant could announce the victories at Forts Henry and Donelson and on Roanoke Island. Cheers rent the air while a band played patriotic music, and one man stepped forward to sing the "Star Spangled Banner." Irish Americans played a prominent role at several critical sectors of the Union line at Gettysburg: the Irish Brigade charged the Wheatfield, Irish-born colonel Patrick O'Rorke died while leading the ethnically mixed 140th New York in helping secure Little Round Top, and the Sixty-ninth Pennsylvania helped blunt Pickett's charge by holding the Angle. The role played by these loyal Irish

American warriors remained well-known in future years, especially as Gettysburg's prominence in America's memory increased.[17]

As it did for African Americans, the Irish American experience of gathering to support a common American cause, even if temporarily defined by sectional realities, helped melt parochialism. Geographical proximity enabled frequent visits between men of the Irish American units and allowed them easier communications within their own community. The war's first winter quarters also afforded an excellent opportunity for men of the Irish American regiments to spend time together.[18]

Serving in the army also fostered contact between immigrants and the native-born, and energized a sense of Irish American unity with the larger national community. Shared allegiance to the Union, and experiencing privations in its service, served as a unifying force between the groups. Near Washington, D.C., in the early days of the war, members of the Fifth Massachusetts went to the Sixty-ninth NYSM's camp on the grounds on Georgetown College and saluted the Irish Americans, before both regiments drew up in line and cheered each other. One correspondent recalled the "exciting scene...[of] Puritan New Englanders and Catholic Irishmen thus fraternizing." Praising the military courtesies shown toward the Sixty-ninth NYSM by Colonel Abram Vosburgh of the Seventy-first NYSM, a regiment of native-born Americans, Brigadier General Theodore Runyon noted that "common danger appears to have made native and foreigners common friends."[19]

In some instances, which show marked contrast with the experience of black solders, native-born soldiers even identified themselves as Irish Americans and sought inclusion in a group identified with martial prowess. During the war's first Christmas, members of the Ninth Massachusetts decorated their camp with evergreen and adorned tents with crosses and green wreaths. That evening, the unit's officers hosted a Christmas banquet furnished by a Washington caterer, and officers from the entire division joined in the food, dancing, and speeches that lasted long into the night. Afterward, Patrick R. Guiney of the Ninth recorded that the others "all confessed that they were Irish," though he believed it "Blarney" of some of them. Such statements reveal that shared service slowly began to erode the liability associated with being identified as an Irish American, even before major combat operations, and the bonds that it generated, began in earnest.[20]

The army high command's participation in Irish American or Catholic festivities, including Christmas and Saint Patrick's Day celebrations, helped reinforce and sanction interethnic camaraderie. In September 1864, generals Hancock, Miles, Birney, Gibbon, Mott, and DeTrobriand joined the Irish Brigade first in the celebration of Mass and then a special luncheon to commemorate the anniversary of the brigade's formation. The biggest laughs of the day went to DeTrobriand's statement that the Irishmen in his command claimed him as one of their own by stating that his name was but a Frenchification of O'Brien.[21]

The realities of service made it inevitable that interethnic contact went beyond the officer corps. Likely almost all federal regiments included at least some members of Irish descent, and even ethnically identified federal regiments were amalgams of men with different backgrounds. Although mostly comprised of men of Irish Catholic heritage, the Sixty-ninth Pennsylvania included men of native-birth and other nationalities in its ranks, as well as representatives of various religions including several Quakers and Jews. Native-born Americans and Germans helped fill the ranks of Connecticut's Irish American Ninth regiment. Nearly half of the volunteers who in July 1861 formed the Twentieth Massachusetts, the "Harvard Regiment," hailed from abroad (though less than one quarter of the officers did), with the Irish, at 23 percent, comprising the largest group of the unit's foreign-born. Rochester's 140th New York went off to war with Irish-born Colonel Patrick O'Rorke, German-born Lieutenant Colonel Louis Ernst, and native-born Major Isaiah Force at its head, a reflection of that unit's interethnic composition.[22]

Good interethnic relations did not always develop easily. Reports of vandalism by federal troops against Catholic churches in the South made clear that nativism survived among some native-born soldiers. Officers of the Eighth Maine reportedly stole sacramental vessels from a church in Fernandina, Florida, and during the firing of Jacksonville, Florida, in spring 1863, soldiers from the regiment ransacked a church and wore vestments in a mocking fashion before the entire building burned to the ground. An Irish American from the Fourth New Hampshire angrily wrote in April 1863 about the "petty insults" he witnessed by "New England bigots" against members of his ethnic community. The member of the Fourth asked, "Are we at war with traitors or with Catholicity?" and he declared that, while "Catholics are ever ready to offer our lives on our country's altar…we did not enlist to see our Churches burned and robbed by a horde of miserable scoundrels," adding simply, "We saw plenty of that at home."[23]

For their part, Irish Americans could show insularism. One non-Irish officer of the Twenty-eighth Massachusetts complained that "an American is entirely out of place in an *Irish* Regiment, and they make this hard as possible for me." Irish Americans also sometimes displayed rivalry not only with African Americans but other European immigrants as well. Colonel Guiney of the Ninth Massachusetts ascribed the defeat at Chancellorsville to the "cowardice of the 11th Corps." Despite his own background as an immigrant, Guiney showed no sympathy for the heavily German corps and instead condemned it for leaving the Army of the Potomac beaten by "*want of numbers, and the disgraceful flight of the flying Dutchmen.*"[24]

Generally, however, close proximity and shared experiences helped dissolve interethnic tensions. A particular friendship developed between the Ninth Massachusetts and the Sixty-second Pennsylvania, comprised of industrial workers, miners, and farmers from around Pittsburgh, during their service in the same brigade. At Hanover Court House, Virginia, early in the 1862 Peninsula campaign, one Pennsylvanian called out, "How will we take Richmond[?]," and another replied, "Why, the Sixty-second will fire, and the Ninth will charge," before both units swept the field. The Ninth's regimental historian recalled, "They joined in our little festivities and we engaged in theirs." A Boston recruit who described celebration of St. Patrick's Day in the Irish Brigade in 1863 as outlandish participated in the merriment the following year. Meagher in June 1863 complimented New York's German American soldiers, in contrast to his friend Guiney's criticism. Even Irish Americans and African Americans sometimes found camaraderie on the battlefield: on June 16, 1864, the 116th Pennsylvania passed by a black division whose men "liberally shared" their hardtack and pork with the exhausted Pennsylvanians.[25]

On the home front, supporting the Union included an economic component beneficial to Irish Americans. Army service offered a relatively profitable option for struggling laborers, something that provided one of the most compelling reasons many Irish Americans enlisted. In addition to drawing rations for themselves, army salaries, enlistment bounties, and local assistance programs for soldiers' families provided much needed support. After one pay day, the men of the Irish Brigade sent more than thirty-five thousand dollars to their families. Investing in the war cut across national and class lines and also helped link economics with nationalism. Moreover, as the army drew more men into it, and the industrial stimulation provided by the massive Union war effort increased the demand for laborers, conditions improved in slim but meaningful ways for even some of those on the bottom rungs of the Irish American community. For example, predominantly Irish Catholic South Boston hummed with vibrant wartime manufacturing producing guns, cannon, ammunition, and helping construct warships.[26]

The Civil War failed to deter immigration from Ireland, particularly as its blighted land continued to generate poor crop outputs. Lincoln's administration, meanwhile, encouraged immigration as a potential source of soldiers and labor. In July 1862, Consul Henry W. Lord wrote Seward that many British subjects sought to serve in the federal army and suggested that "these would become perhaps all the better citizens of our country for having exposed their lives to sustain its integrity." That August, Seward asked consular officers abroad to publicize the demand for labor in America caused by so many men serving in the armed forces. Although Seward avoided any mention of military service, and qualified that the government could not offer "any pecuniary inducements" to attract "industrious foreigners," for fear of angering foreign governments, recipients of it understood the military implication of his dispatch, especially after he sent a copy of his statement to Secretary of War Stanton. The number of Irish coming to the United States increased in 1863 to fifty-six thousand and the following year to sixty-four thousand, the highest total for any year after 1854 and higher than in any year before 1847. Some of these immigrants blended into civilian society and sought jobs in industry or agriculture, while others enlisted in the army.[27]

Articulating and Appreciating an American Identity

Similar to the way African Americans interpreted and made use of the meaning of their service, Irish Americans took the lead in affirming during the war that the glory earned, and sacrifices endured, by Irish American soldiers power-fully reinforced the ties of American identity and inclusion as citizens. Irish Americans continued to maintain their ethnic culture but, under the leadership of Thomas F. Meagher and others, placed this culture within an American context and emphasized an American allegiance alongside support for Irish nationalism. Public arguments articulated by Meagher, Charles G. Halpine, and Michael Corcoran helped to define the meaning of Irish American service to the ethnic community, as well as assert it to a more-accepting native-born population. Yet personal changes also took place during this time. Some Irish Americans gained a greater appreciation for their American identity, as re-vealed in personal letters written by Peter Welsh to his family, and Irish-born Colonel Patrick Guiney to his wife.

Through newspaper columns and two popular book compilations of his work, Charles G. Halpine publicized the communal meanings of Irish Ameri-can service. An Irish-born Episcopal educated at Trinity College in Dublin, Halpine broke from his father's views to sympathize with Irish revolutionar-ies and respect Catholicism. Halpine became involved in the Young Ireland movement in the late 1840s and immigrated to the United States in 1851, where he became a newspaper correspondent and an ardent Democrat. Hal-pine's early derision of Lincoln vanished once the Confederates fired on Fort Sumter. Although he remained a partisan Democrat, Halpine enlisted in the army and wrote regular columns for the *New York Herald* urging vigorous prosecution of the war and professing to care more about the American flag than whether blacks were slave or free. *New York Tribune* editor Horace Gree-ley later identified Halpine as having "done more than any other man to popu-larize and strengthen the War with the Irish Democracy" in New York City.[28]

Halpine employed the fictional character of army private Miles O'Reilly as his vehicle to weigh in on political issues and pronounce the meaning of Irish American support for the Union, as well as to provide an appealing Irish Ameri-can figure to the larger public. With his simple but good-natured personality, O'Reilly grew popular among both Irish Americans and the country at large, and the first book collection of Halpine's writings sold three thousand copies on the first day of its release in early 1864.[29]

Echoing black correspondent Thomas M. Chester, Halpine focused on the Americanizing, communal experience of military service as one of his primary themes:

> Camps, in their own queer way, are places of very thorough national instruction. Regiments of men from all quarters of the loyal states are aggregated and mixed together in the larger organizations of our armies. They march, fight, and sleep under the same banner. No matter what their former habits or stations in life, the same food is served out to all. Equal promotion awaits their merit; and if struck down by weapons or disease, they lie side by side in one general hospital, their attendance the same, and their nursing as affectionate. Falling on the battle-field they have common graves, and living they will have a common destiny.[30]

In "Song of the Soldiers," Halpine recounted that marches, danger, wounds, and illnesses "bound" those who served together, and his final stanza, frequently recited at Grand Army of the Republic gatherings into the 1880s, resoundingly concluded,

> By communion of the banner,
> Battle-scarred but victor banner,
> By the baptism of the banner,
>> Brothers of one church are we;
> Creed nor faction can divide us;
> Race nor language can divide us;
> Still, whatever fate betide us,
>> Brothers of the heart are we!

Using the metaphor of having "drunk from the same canteen," Halpine in another poem argued that soldiers did so in the communion of military service—the sharing of hard marches and empty stomachs, the excitement of battle and the doldrums of camp life, and most sublime of all, crawling to a wounded comrade on the battlefield to give him a drink.[31]

In late November 1863, Halpine had O'Reilly pay a fictional visit to the White House. As with other O'Reilly columns, the *Herald* published the story as if it had actually happened, and some historians have believed erroneously that the column recounted a visit of Halpine to the White House. Halpine had Thomas F. Meagher present O'Reilly to Lincoln and argue a claim to equality of citizenship in the process: one of the most powerful motivations for the "Irish soldier" in the field, Meagher told the president, "was the thought that he was thus earning a title...to the full equality and fraternity of an American citizen." While Lincoln concurred, Meagher continued that "ugly and venomous as was the toad of civil strife, it yet carried in its head for the Irish race in America this precious, this inestimable jewel. By adoption of the banner, and by the communion of bloody grave trenches on every field...the race that were heretofore only exiles...are now proud peers of the proudest and brave brothers of the best."[32]

Michael Corcoran's capture at First Bull Run afforded the Irish American community a hero early in the war as well as another prominent vehicle through which to publicize the meaning of their service and assert an American identity. Like Meagher, Irish-born Michael Corcoran enjoyed excellent credentials as an Irish nationalist. After emigrating to the United States in 1849, Corcoran joined the Sixty-ninth NYSM as a private and became its colonel by 1860. Corcoran faced a quandary, however, when the Civil War erupted: as one of Fenianism's founders, he recognized that too many Irish American recruits for the Union might jeopardize manpower for Ireland's own liberation movement. Before he went off to war at the head of an Irish American regiment, Corcoran told fellow members of the Brotherhood in New York City to stay out of the army unless already in it.[33]

After his capture at First Bull Run, it seemed Corcoran would never have the opportunity to fight for Ireland. Shortly after the Confederates took him prisoner, the federal government sentenced to execution the crew of a Confederate privateer. The Confederates retaliated by selecting Corcoran to likewise face execution. Instead, on exchange after thirteen months of captivity, Corcoran found himself the Union's newest brigadier general. Corcoran dined with Lincoln in Washington, D.C., before addressing a massive gathering outside of the Willard Hotel on August 18, 1862. Gaslights arranged to spell the word "Union" backlit the speaker's stand, and the uniformed men of the Sixty-ninth NYSM proudly displayed their green regimental flag. Republican congressman Alfred Ely, himself taken captive during the rout of First Bull Run and imprisoned with Corcoran, introduced the hero to the crowd, honoring Irish Americans for their zeal for the Union before he welcomed the "chieftain of our adopted citizens from the Emerald Isle" to "the capital of your country."[34]

Mirroring statements by Thomas Meagher, Corcoran pled with Irish Americans to fight for the United States until it defeated the Confederacy. While he looked forward to fighting for Ireland in the future, Corcoran urged that the "work…here" needed successful resolution first. Rejoicing at the sight of the Sixty-ninth's green flag next to the Stars and Stripes, Corcoran wished to take the field again "with more of my countrymen, to endeavor to preserve this country for our people." Corcoran concluded his speech with the touch of a Fenian, deeming the Union army "a splendid school for military training," and alluding to Irish Americans fighting abroad after the Republic's victory.[35]

Corcoran attended similar receptions and delivered comparable orations as he traveled northward to New York. In Philadelphia, crowds wearing badges bearing Corcoran's likeness thronged through flag-festooned streets to cheer the new general and watch a parade, which included Hibernian and Fenian chapters. After lunch, Corcoran marched to Independence Hall, where he embraced the symbolism of his stage, "where our patriotic fathers met and deliberated." Although he vowed to fight for the restoration of the Constitution and Union "just as it was"—an obvious swipe at abolitionism and the Republican agenda—Corcoran in another speech that day declared himself a Democrat who supported Lincoln no matter what the president needed to do to quash the rebellion, even to the extent that Lincoln infringed on the Constitution, so long as the effect could be repaired after the war. Corcoran vowed that he would even shake the hand of any nativist or abolitionist who stood with him in the fight for the Union.[36]

From Philadelphia, Corcoran traveled through cities in New Jersey, which all honored him with ceremonies, before he reached New York City and the throngs that packed Broadway waiting to see him. The day after the festivities, the *New York Times* hailed Corcoran as a patriot hero, but it also placed the event in the context of the city's ethnic politics. The day proved "peculiarly one of exultation to the Irish," wrote the *Times,* because "never were nationalities more entirely forgotten," and the "spontaneous enthusiasm of the masses fused all hearts and united them in one glowing expression of honor to him who had proved worthy of the cause of Freedom." Moreover, argued the editorial, the native-born realized an even greater appreciation of the event because it illuminated the devotion Irish Americans had shown the American government and its republican principles. The *Times* declared Corcoran a paradigm of American civic virtue, standing as both a "hero" and a "*General of the Republic.*"[37]

Abandoning his early advice for Fenians to avoid the war, Corcoran now raised four New York regiments to form the Corcoran Legion. The Irishman also wrote a memoir of his imprisonment, a carefully crafted public pronouncement of Irish American loyalty that offered as one of its primary themes the "gratification" Corcoran felt in leading "his men into battle bearing side by side the Star Spangled Banner of his American home, and the Emerald Standard of his Native isle." Corcoran recognized both sides of the phrase Irish American, declaring that "one half of my heart is Erin's, and the other half is America's." Corcoran recalled leaving his "native isle in sorrow" and experiencing "a stranger's anxiety" on arriving in the United States, but he also appreciated that America "gave me all the opportunities I longed so for." Moreover, Corcoran proclaimed, in the United States he had the freedom to embrace his ethnicity. "I am happy because I have achieved the honor of being counted a representative of Irish nationality," he declared, and "it now increases my pleasure tenfold when I hear loyal Americans, in refering to me, say, 'Michael Corcoran is an Irishman.'"[38]

While he embraced his Irish heritage, Corcoran also easily referred to "our Republic" with a sense of belonging and membership. In global terms, Corcoran "prayed that, like that distant dome above, the azure field of our own Starry Standard would in the future be studded as thickly with stars, each representing some nation or people of the earth." For Corcoran, loyalty recognized but trumped ethnic background, and while he remained fiercely devoted to Ireland, he just as powerfully argued that nationalities could come under the rubric of the United States and the ideals of "the best and mightiest Republic that earth has ever seen." Corcoran proclaimed to all Americans that suffering for the United States, whether by wounds, time spent languishing in captivity, or other service, linked that individual to the country's heritage and generated a living connection to its ideals. Corcoran emphasized that allegiance, not ethnicity, defined one's identity and standing during the war.[39]

Corcoran ended his account by vowing never to sheathe his sword "until victory perches upon the National banner of America, or Michael Corcoran is numbered among those who return not from the battle-field." Sadly, Corcoran did not return. Not fated to fall while leading a desperate charge on the field of battle, Corcoran tumbled from his horse on December 22, 1863, lost consciousness, and died. Much as Meagher had, Corcoran revised his views through the experience of Civil War, and it would have been fascinating to watch the direction of these transformations in the postwar period had he lived. Corcoran did not undergo the political conversion Meagher did, and he stands as an exemplar of the conservative nature of Irish American loyalty, but that adds a further cast to Corcoran. Corcoran's words and actions illuminate how a diehard Irish nationalist transformed his focus to argue that serving and suffering in the Civil War linked Irish immigrants to America's Founding Fathers and earned them a place as American citizens, but also supported Ireland at the same time by bolstering the great international hope of republicanism and providing an asylum for future Irish immigrants.[40]

Patrick R. Guiney's letters home reveal an embrace of Corcoran's public message on a personal level, and they show a private individual's evolution to have a greater appreciation for his American identity alongside his Irish one. Born in County Tipperary in January 1835, Guiney emigrated to Maine at age seven. After working in factories and machine shops in boyhood, Guiney attended the College of the Holy Cross for a year before studying law. In 1858, Guiney relocated to Boston where he practiced law and wrote for the *Boston Times*. Guiney married in January 1859, moved to Roxbury, Massachusetts, and won a seat on its town council (a striking deviation from Massachusetts nativism at the time), and soon had his only child, the future poet Louise Imogen Guiney. Guiney parted from his young family to enlist in the Ninth Massachusetts when the Civil War erupted, rising to lieutenant colonel in the coming months. During the June 27, 1862, battle of Gaines' Mill, the Ninth's Colonel Cass fell ill and relinquished command to Guiney. The "Fighting Ninth" formed the retreating federal column's rearguard, and Guiney led multiple charges to stall the pressing Confederates. When Cass fell mortally wounded a few days later, Guiney received promotion to colonel, and he commanded the regiment until he suffered a bullet in the eye leading a charge at the Wilderness.[41]

Guiney remembered his Irish heritage, even though there is no evidence that he participated in the Fenian circle that existed in the Ninth Massachusetts. In accepting a sword from one of his companies in the summer of 1862, Guiney vowed to make his regiment "a testimony of Irish devotion to the vindication and establishment of human liberty." In sending the regiment's green banner, shredded in combat during the Peninsula campaign, to Governor John Andrew that fall, the young colonel informed him, "Sometimes when all else looked vague and battle-fortune seemed to be against us, there was a certain magic in the light of this old symbol of our enslaved but hopeful Ireland, that made the Ninth fight superhumanly hard."[42]

Yet Guiney's letters display how his devotion to the Republic, and recognition of his American identity, deepened with time. Almost immediately, Guiney feared for the welfare of his family and wrote his wife that he regretted the "possible rashness" of his enlisting. Nevertheless, he explained, honor and loyalty to the Union precluded his resignation. After reaching Washington in early July 1861, Guiney described both the beauty of the location of the Ninth's camp and the glory of the cause for which its men volunteered. In another letter, Guiney acknowledged that his commission might result in his death, but explained that friendships within the regiment, the fact that military service would benefit his future ambitions, and his allegiance to a cause "that will entitle those who labor in the achievement of its success to the gratitude and

4. Irish Americans of the Ninth Massachusetts Infantry before celebrating
Mass at Camp Cass, Virginia, near Washington, D.C., in 1861. Patrick R. Guiney is
seated third from the left in the first row on the right-hand side. Thomas Cass is the
first man standing nearest the cross on the right-hand side. Courtesy Library of Congress.

remembrance of the present, as well as of unborn generations—one that of itself compensates by its sublimity and goodness for all which may be sacrificed
in its defense," foreclosed him from leaving the service.[43]

By August 1861, Guiney replied to his wife that he could not oblige her
pleas to return home because resignation would blight his honor, and he stood
in defense of a "cause bright and grand as the Sun." While Democrats criticized the war, Guiney observed, "The cause is to me the same as it was when
I left Boston. Not a hue of it is changed. I care not who becomes corrupt, the
cause is pure." A sense of honor, personal opportunity, and friendships within
his regiment reinforced Guiney's underlying loyalty to a Republic which he
recognized as worthy of preservation, even at the cost of his blood.[44]

During a low ebb in the Army of the Potomac's morale in the winter of
1862–63, Guiney revealed the intensity of his deepened devotion to the Union
cause. "If we could only be successful how proudly I could live afterwards in
the knowledge of my humble participation. If we fail I never can be half the
man," Guiney confessed to his wife, "The charm of life will be gone." Within
weeks, the Irish-born colonel declared that "if the country is to be broken—
then we will have no country to love or serve." After his near mortal wound
at the Wilderness in spring 1864, Guiney proudly wrote, "God gave me an
opportunity and of which I availed myself, to shed my blood for our beloved
Republic. This is a source of great pleasure to me and one in which the pain
and consequences of my wound are entirely lost."[45]

In contrast to many Irish Americans, Guiney even grew during the war to openly support abolitionism and its more expansive idea of universal human rights, if not the nativist streak that ran through the movement. Similar to Meagher, Guiney, who started the war as a Democrat, staunchly supported the Lincoln administration and its Republican agenda, although this generated strong opposition to him from some of the Ninth's officers and several Irish American civilians back in Boston. While campaigning for Lincoln during the 1864 election, Guiney maintained that he "was the only member of that regiment [the Ninth Massachusetts] who called himself a Republican," likely an exaggeration but a revealing statement nonetheless.[46]

Maintaining Religious and Ethnic Identity in the Army

Experiences in the Union army strengthened in many Irish Americans a greater recognition of their American identity but at the same time permitted them to practice their Catholic religion and ethnic identity without apology. Some historians view this persistent ethnic culture as evidence of continued alienation from the rest of society and resistance to Americanization. More accurately, Irish Americans' firmer placement as part of the people, cemented by their military service, allowed them to practice their religious and ethnic traditions more securely within an American context. In the aftermath of the war, the *Pilot* argued that "true strength, and our highest worldly interests as Catholics, rests in our becoming Americans." Many Irish Americans embraced this idea while serving in the army, and transmitted it to families at home, but coupled it with more open celebration of ethnic practices.[47]

Spiritual devotion increased for many Irish American soldiers, as the consoling aspects of religion had a powerful allure to men enduring loneliness, privation, and possible death. Religious activities provided some soldiers with a sense of community and helped assuage their feeling of isolation from friends and family. Believing that God's will prevailed helped soothe for soldiers the psychological trauma they suffered while facing the random nature of death in battle, as well as feelings of personal guilt for participating in combat.[48]

George Tipping, an Irish immigrant born in 1842, reported to his wife in October 1862 that about a thousand men received confirmation when New York's archbishop Hughes visited the camp of his 155th New York on Staten Island. When the regiment relocated to Newport News, Virginia, the following month, Tipping wrote his wife that Mass was celebrated every morning and confessions heard every afternoon—something that no doubt comforted the devout soldier who wore an Agnus Dei and crucifix around his neck. The regimental priest gave his blessing to the kneeling men of the 155th New York before their first engagement, though Tipping honestly told his wife that despite the benediction, "there was terror in every heart." By early 1863, the 155th New York's priest baptized some men, and Tipping believed that combat had put "the fear of God" into a previously "wicked set of fellows."[49]

As chaplain of the Thirty-fifth Indiana, Irish-born Father Peter Paul Cooney, C.S.C., heard confessions straight through one night, as he helped the men prepare for anticipated battle during the Perryville campaign. Every morning for five days during the Murfreesboro campaign, Cooney gave absolution to the regiment as it knelt in line of battle. Similarly, when battle loomed on November 30, 1863, the chaplain of the Ninth Massachusetts asked Colonel Guiney to form the regiment into a square. Catholics from other units broke from the ranks to participate as the priest led the kneeling men in making an Act of Contrition, and then roused them with his reminder that they fought for liberty, justice, and global human rights. The most famous absolution involved Father William Corby, an Irish Brigade chaplain and president of the University of Notre Dame after the war, at Gettysburg, and expressive statutes on both the battlefield and the Notre Dame campus commemorate the event. As Union soldiers prepared to charge into the maelstrom of the Wheatfield on July 2, 1863, everyone knelt to receive an absolution Corby intended for those of all faiths. Nearby, Major General Winfield S. Hancock bowed his uncovered head as well. A week later, a non-Catholic captain who observed the moment asked Corby to teach him about Catholicism.[50]

In the West, Cooney also noted the effect of this interreligious mixing while serving as brigade chaplain. A Protestant soldier spoke to Cooney about converting after one Mass and celebrated his baptism a few days later. Major General William Rosecrans, commander of the Army of the Cumberland and a prewar convert to Catholicism whose brother became a Catholic bishop, attended Cooney's Mass every Sunday in the summer of 1863. Rosecrans's staff attended as well, even though none of them were Catholic. Cooney believed that "by the power of his noble example he [Rosecrans] has been the principal cause, under God, of almost entirely dissipating the unreasonable prejudice against our holy religion which the men of his army brought from home with them." Cooney also felt that the example of Catholic soldiers, the work of Catholic chaplains, and the open practice of that faith in the Army of the Cumberland led to a lessening of prejudice. By April 1864, Cooney reported to his brother that Protestants attended Catholic sermons "by thousands," that he baptized many of them, including division commander Major General David S. Stanley, and that "prejudice to the Church is gone almost entirely."[51]

St. Patrick's Day also afforded Irish Americans an opportunity to celebrate an ethnic holiday in the company of Protestant and native-born comrades, and openly embrace their Catholic culture in an American context. The Irish Brigade celebrated on a clear blue March 17, 1863, morning with a Mass followed by races and games topped off by a grand steeplechase horse race on a course that included hurdles, ditch fences, and two artificial rivers fifteen feet wide and six deep. Thousands of soldiers, including army commander Major General Joseph Hooker, observed the race, which had a five hundred dollar purse at stake. Afterward, an elaborate banquet featured thirty-five hams, pigs stuffed with chickens or turkeys, chicken, game birds, champagne, rum, and whiskey. Thousands of men gathered in the camp of the Irish Brigade from among the different corps of the Army of the Potomac, including generals Hancock, Slocum, Griffin, Sedgwick, and Franklin.[52]

Fenianism

Even Irish nationalism in America evolved during the Civil War into a context of loyalty to the United States. Some diehard Irish nationalists in the United States grew irritated at this development, but for the most part, the Fenian movement reveals a surprising level of Americanization within Irish America, even where dualism and great interest in Irish liberation persisted. Striking similarities existed between Irish nationalism and black nationalism in America at this time: members of both groups used the language of separate nationality as a means to gain inclusion and earn respect within the United States as a whole. Moreover, both groups espoused the expansion of republicanism, even where blacks focused on America while Irish nationalists included exportation of American values abroad as part of their mission.[53]

The impact of Fenianism was not confined to attendees to Fenian conventions. Whether explicitly or implicitly, many common Irish American soldiers, such as Peter Welsh, embraced Fenian ideals such as liberation for Ireland, and hostility toward England, and they placed their Civil War service in an American context as well as one of transnational republicanism. Moreover, rather than acting to hinder other Americanizing impulses, the Fenian movement helped reinforce and support loyalty to the United States even in the face of duality. That many native-born Americans went so far as to tolerate, even embrace Fenianism, during the 1860s shows that they accepted the new position that Irish Americans asserted.

Examining the Fenian movement reveals paradoxical impulses within it, considering the Brotherhood's professed devotion to Ireland. Historian Thomas N. Brown found the overall Irish nationalist movement to be "riddled with ambiguities," and he cites Fenianism as an example. While operating as an autonomous Irish government from a capital in New York City shortly after the war, the Brotherhood focused much of its energy on Irish American issues and served as a political "pressure group" within this country, even where many American Fenians did want to return to Ireland, liberate it, and reverse the consequences of the famine.[54]

Founded in New York as the Emmet Monument Association in the mid-1850s, the organization changed its name to the Fenian Brotherhood in 1858, after mythological warrior defenders of Ireland called Fianna, and sought the overthrow of British rule in Ireland. Ultimately, the Fenians achieved neither the numbers nor the goals to which they aspired. While the movement thrived within Irish American units, the Brotherhood never fielded the forces its commanders hoped would mobilize to liberate Ireland after the war. Even at its peak after the Civil War, the Brotherhood never numbered more than forty-five thousand members, and it probably numbered less. Of those members, only a fraction participated in any actual maneuver against British interests.[55]

It comes as little surprise that Americanism so thoroughly affected Fenianism: it developed as an American movement and flourished in the Union ranks. Large portions of some circles enlisted to defend the Union when the war erupted. The Milford, Massachusetts, chapter sent 80 out of 115 members into the Ninth Massachusetts. By November 1863, the Irish-born head of the Rappahannock Circle in that regiment believed that three hundred soldiers from the Ninth alone would subsequently fight in the Fenian ranks, though only "in accordance with our duties and obligations to the U.S. Government." As of January 1865, Fenian circles met within several regiments and on certain naval vessels, as well as larger units such as the Corcoran Legion and federal forces on Morris Island, South Carolina. In addition to activity generated by Fenians already in the ranks, the Brotherhood dispatched delegates, sometimes bearing passes from the army, to address Union troops.[56]

Moreover, many prominent Fenian leaders served in the Union army. At an 1863 Fenian convention, Brigadier General Michael Corcoran and Colonel Matthew Murphy of the Sixty-ninth New York won election to a five-man central council, and several federal soldiers and veterans signed the convention's resolutions in person or by proxy. At a January 1865 convention in Cincinnati, Irish Brigade commander Brigadier General Thomas A. Smyth—already Centre of the Fenians in the Army of the Potomac after Corcoran's death—won election to the central council. The convention also appointed thirteen federal army officers to a committee for military affairs, which it formed in its self-proclaimed capacity as a national assembly for Ireland.[57]

When the first Fenian convention met in Chicago on November 3–5, 1863, 82 delegates attended from twelve states, the District of Columbia, and the federal Armies of the Cumberland, Tennessee, and Potomac. Under Head Centre John O'Mahoney's leadership, the delegates drafted a constitution mandating annual conventions and an elected leadership. These Fenians consciously tracked tenets of American republicanism to render themselves "in better accord with the democratic institutions of America, and thus secure for [the organization] a greater popularity...among our fellow citizens born in this country," but also because most of the organization's members expected the Brotherhood to have a democratic "system of government and direction in accordance with the institutions and customs of America."[58]

Closely reading the proceedings of this first convention reveals the dual pull felt by some in attendance, a striking phenomenon in that the delegates comprised the most vocal members of the Irish American community in professing devotion to Ireland and its liberation. In welcoming the delegates, O'Mahoney set the convention's agenda: to organize for the time "when we will have to strike a blow for the Independence of Ireland." In another speech, O'Mahoney identified the Civil War as an impediment to Fenianism because so many Irish Americans enlisted in the Union army, though he simultaneously declared that the cause would benefit from their battle training. As expected, Fenian del-egates at the convention gushed with "love of Ireland," expressed their "long-ing for her liberation," and declared the island's people a distinct nationality entitled to all rights of self-government. While one participant proudly noted that so many Irish fought for their adopted country, he also assured that many in the Union ranks would fight and die for the "dear *old* land."[59]

Yet, many of the convention's resolutions focused on themes of loyalty to the United States, defining what wartime sacrifice earned them, and linking America and Fenianism in a global struggle for republicanism. The delegates explained that, while mostly composed of American citizens of Irish birth or descent, the Brotherhood remained open to all who sympathized with Ireland's liberation by any "honorable means," though disclaiming, "except such means as may be in violation of the constitution and laws under which we live and to which all of us, who are citizens of the United States, owe our allegiance." Furthermore, the delegates argued, their overarching devotion to the Republic earned them every right to act under its laws: "We further boldly and firmly assert our unquestionable right under the said constitution and laws to associ-ate together for the above named object, or for any similar one; and to assist with our money, our moral and political influence, or, if it so pleases ourselves, with our persons and our lives in liberating any enslaved land under the sun." The delegates stated that they did not contemplate breaking any American law but argued that if they failed to exercise fully their "civic and social privilege as Freemen under the American constitution," they rendered themselves "unwor-thy of participating in the great political privileges wherewith the naturalized citizens of America are invested."[60]

Noting that "exiles of every country," but particularly the Irish, "found a home, personal freedom, and equal political rights, in this American Repub-lic," the Fenians declared their unwavering allegiance to the United States. Placing their loyalty to America in a global context, members of the conven-tion emphasized the "supreme importance" of the "preservation and success" of the Constitution not only for Ireland's future but the "well being and social elevation of the whole human race." The Fenians further argued that their ob-jectives benefited not only the Irish but "all sincere lovers of human freedom," and that Americans especially gained because Irish sons kept "watch and ward for the United States at the thresholds of the despots of Europe." Believing that English sympathy for the Confederacy had caused an irreparable rift with the United States, the convention urged young Fenians to study military tactics and stand ready to offer their services to the U.S. government. As did other Irish Americans, the Fenians thus styled themselves as defenders of American interests through loyalty to the Constitution, antipathy to the English, and a desire to propagate the American mission of spreading liberty. The Fenians cast themselves as an elite guard crusading for American principles worldwide.[61]

The Fenian movement grew in popularity so that when its second conven-tion opened in Cincinnati on January 17, 1865, 273 circles sent delegates, a substantial increase from the 63 circles represented at Chicago. This assembly again wrestled with the dualities of striving for Ireland's liberation within the context of allegiance and service to the U.S. flag. Despite paradoxically deeming this Fenian convocation a national congress in exile for an Irish Republic, O'Mahoney inextricably linked its cause with that of the Union. Although he grieved at the losses Fenians suffered during the Civil War, O'Mahoney proclaimed that these "brothers have died for the Republic." Noting that "thousands" of the "most ardent and best working" Fenians "rushed to the defense of the Union," O'Mahoney now exaggeratedly described the Brotherhood as the bulwark that prevented Britain's entry into the Civil War. Lamenting that the Union did not help the Fenians to the extent Britain assisted the Confederacy, O'Mahoney nonetheless declared that the Brotherhood served "the best interests of America" at the same time it worked for the liberation of Ireland. Moreover, in calling for Fenians to stand prepared to sail for Europe or attack Canada "at once," he also cautioned that such movement should occur only "at the command of the United States authorities."[62]

At the same time, the Fenian delegates realized the implications of straying too far from the Brotherhood's Irish focus, and some of them sought to counter this trend by drafting an address to their "fellow-exiles in America" which highlighted devotion to the cause of Ireland. "Though forced by oppression and dire necessity into foreign countries, Ireland is still your faithful heritage," the convention reminded its audience. "You are strangers wherever else you go, and no matter how fortune may favor you, if your hearts are true, upon your lips the bread of exile will prove bitter. You owe to that dear land your first and warmest love."[63]

Furthermore, the convention criticized America in its address to the Irish people as part of its effort to stifle Ireland's depopulation. In 1845–55, Ireland's population plummeted from 8.5 million to 6 million. Irish nationalists feared that, in light of famine deaths and continued emigration, the Irish nationality would soon cease to exist, and the scattering of Ireland's people would render it unable to take its rightful place as a nation. Calling for the Irish to remain "at your posts" and not "to forsake your country," the Brotherhood portrayed a bleak life in America. "The fate of the emigrant is seldom an enviable one," the convention proclaimed. "We who address you know by bitter experience that the instances are few in which men and women of Irish birth ever find themselves at home or happy in a foreign land. It is unnecessary to do more than remind you of the poverty, the misery, and too frequently the crime with which very many of the Irish people sink after their arrival in America." The convention presented to the people of Ireland a far different picture than the honored and glorious republic it otherwise celebrated, and for which Irish American soldiers fell during the war.[64]

Diverging views, as well as the Brotherhood's continued growth, led to dissension within the organization's ranks. As chapters proliferated (67 new circles formed by mid-April 1865, followed by 67 more the following month), members called for greater democratization. More than six hundred delegates gathered in another convention held in Philadelphia on October 16, 1865, and they revised the Fenian charter so as to even more closely duplicate the American governmental structure. This new constitution mandated governance by a Senate, a House of Delegates with representatives chosen in proportion to the number and size of constituent circles, and a president advised by cabinet members he appointed with the advice of the senate. By the end of the year, O'Mahoney rejected this constitution, which increased the senate's power at his expense, and a schism opened up between two wings of the Brotherhood. Another divergence motivated the split: while O'Mahoney's faction emphasized sending arms and troops to Ireland, the Senate wing, under future American congressman William R. Roberts, supported capturing Canada and using it as leverage in order to obtain Ireland's freedom.[65]

Meanwhile, helping to establish Fenianism as an American political group, Charles Halpine published a lengthy article about the organization in the May 5, 1865, edition of the *New York Herald*. Halpine's two themes were justifying Fenian actions based on Britain's dual hostility to Ireland and the United States, and the overarching loyalty Fenians felt for the United States. Halpine not only continued themes that pervaded his Miles O'Reilly columns, he emphasized the American loyalty and identity of all Irish Americans, including supporters of the Fenian Brotherhood. Halpine disclaimed descriptions of the Fenians as a secret society disloyal to the United States. Instead, Halpine used Irish American wartime service to gain acceptance for the organization, and he assured his readers that the "Fenian Brotherhood is loyal to the land of its adoption in every fibre; and none the less so because refusing to forget the land to which its members are bound by ties either of blood or birth." Halpine asked Americans to consider whether "an organization which...has sent over twenty-eight thousand of its active members into the armies of the Union, [should] be condemned as unfaithful to the American cause, for no other reason than that it hopes yet to grapple with the tyrant of its native land, and to place 'the Irish Green above the English Red,' while at the same time aiding to avenge America's quarrel with the government which permitted a swarm of pirates to be sent forth from its harbors to prey upon American commerce in the hour of our sorest need?" Halpine emphasized that Fenians "have been zealously and actively loyal to the cause of the Union," and he cast as martyrs for the Republic such members as Brigadier General Thomas A. Smyth and Colonel Matthew Murphy, who both died in the closing days of the war.[66]

Halpine further declared that Fenians did not sanction violation of American law in wanting to liberate Ireland. While they would "most gladly take advantage of any conflict between the Red Flag and Banner of Stars, at once to prove their fidelity and devotion both to the land of their adoption and that of their birth," Halpine promised that Fenians would not cause the war or act outside of American authority. Instead, Halpine claimed, the Fenians intended to furnish arms, supplies, and officers, "matters perfectly open to legal private enterprise under the precedents established by the British government in favor of the Southern rebellion." Halpine assured his readers that individuals in Ireland would do the rest, though, "let there be a war between the United

States and England, and not a dollar in bounty would be required to enlist from seventy-five to one hundred thousand able-bodied and pugnacious Irishmen throughout the States in that holy strife." Accordingly, in contrast to the revolutionaries in Ireland, Fenians in American were not required to be able-bodied, learn military drill, or swear to perform any military service.[67]

Halpine's lyrics for a "Fenian Rallying Song" included two stanzas that identified Fenian readiness for war as a component of their loyalty to the United States. After asking God to smile on America, Halpine noted that Irish Americans did not "forget the isle" from where they came, and he looked forward to a day "When Yankee guns shall thunder / On Britain's coast, on Britain's coast / And land, our green flag under / The Fenian host, the Fenian host!" Moreover, in keeping with men such as Peter Welsh, Thomas F. Meagher, and Michael Corcoran, Halpine located his anti-English sentiments within a larger global context. Halpine argued that the reunited United States had every right to assert its defense of republicanism in the world, whether against French designs in Mexico under the Monroe Doctrine, or by allowing the Fenians to send arms and trained Irish American veterans to Irish soil. Above all, Halpine equated being a good Fenian with good American citizenship.[68]

Other Fenian lyrics often emphasized this American link as well. Some Fenian songs waxed eloquent about Ireland and lamented its condition as well as the Irish exodus, but others focused on the Irish American experience and emphasized dual loyalty to the United States. "The Irish American Army" linked Fenianism and Unionism, and celebrated soldiers from the ethnic community who helped quash the Confederacy, while another song, "To the Fenians," proclaimed that "the Stars and Stripes, with your own flag, are with you to the death." Some songs referenced American constitutional debate, such as the "Fenian Song," with the lyrics, "Let 'equal rights' your motto be / Keep Liberty in sight," or the "Fenian Battle Song," sung to the tune of "Battle Cry of Freedom," which called for Irish Americans to "assert your rights as freemen" and refrained that they were "fighting for liberty in Erin." More explicit in terms of American loyalty, the "Fenian's Hope of Independence" announced, "We'll lower the pride of England, her yoke we'll overthrow / Long she has persecuted, and kept the Irish low / But soon with her it shall be night—with us the coming day—/ In her place we'll plant the Stars and Stripes of Sweet America!"[69]

Wartime Opposition and the Irish American Identity

Static political views among most Irish Americans complicated their relations with both the Union and some of the native born. These views greatly differed from those of blacks, who not only supported the Republican agenda but wanted it to move even faster and further. As the conflict dragged on, emancipation, conscription, and mounting casualties led to some opposition, and even violence steeped with racism, within the Irish American community at home, even while some Irish Americans began to recognize a deeper sense of their

American identity. Cynicism about the Republican Party persisted in many Irish Americans: as Irish-born Jesuit, Bernard O'Reilly, observed in 1864, the "very same puritanical race" that caused the centuries of "oppression + prostration" in Ireland formed the "most energetic, + living, + controlling element" of the Republican Party. O'Reilly found "the spirit which blazed forth in the destruction of the Ursuline Convent" in 1834 difficult to forget.[70]

Historian Susannah Ural Bruce argues that, despite early rapprochement, native-born Americans grew frustrated at Irish American political positions during the war, exacerbating nativism and contributing to a stereotype of Irish Americans as "disloyal, violent, and threatening to all that was good in America." Such resistance certainly comprises a major part of the legacy of Irish Americans during the Civil War, made more prominent because it sometimes erupted into high-profile violence such as the New York City Draft Riots.[71]

Yet the other side of that complicated legacy includes Irish Americans who pronounced support for the war effort, casualty reports from Irish American regiments, and funerals honoring fallen Irish American soldiers. As casualties mounted within Irish America's ranks, the ethnic community honored such sacrifice but also used it to strengthen the American identity of its still living members, and show evidence of Irish American devotion to the Constitution in support of claims for all the rights and privileges granted to the native-born. Local governments and individual citizens joined to pay tribute to universal sacrifice in the name of the United States, further cementing in the process Irish Americans as part of the American people. For example, the American flag hung conspicuously in St. Bridget's church in Rochester, New York, for the funeral of Irish-born Colonel Patrick O'Rorke of the 140th New York, killed at Little Round Top on July 2, 1863. Protestants, Jews, and Catholics alike attended the ceremony, and according to Rochester's historian, much of any interethnic tension that existed between Irish Americans, German Americans, and the native-born diminished shortly afterward. On July 4, 1865, O'Rorke's name hung from one of the banners that adorned a memorial arch Rochester erected, and a delegation placed a white lily atop O'Rorke's grave as part of the city's 1868 Memorial Day ceremony. Such moments visibly reaffirmed acceptance by the native-born ethnic community of Irish American pronouncements of covenanted patriotism.[72]

Moreover, while many Irish Americans resisted the Republican agenda and some of its wartime measures, many native-born Americans did as well. Many native-born Americans expressed horror at the motives behind, and racism displayed, during such outbreaks as the New York City Draft Riots, but so did many Irish Americans. Irish Americans serving in the field felt especially betrayed that members of their ethnic community participated in such atrocities. Enlisted laborer Peter Welsh equated the rioters with Confederate agents and lamented that "the Irish men of New York took so large a part in them disgracefull riots," while attorney turned colonel Patrick Guiney more succinctly hoped that, regardless of ethnicity, "the artillery *will exempt them from the Draft forever!*"[73]

Wartime privations and mounting carnage dampened initial enthusiasm for military service across all strata of the community. The devastating losses of the Seven Days, Antietam, and Fredericksburg, all engagements in which prominent Irish American units suffered grievously, and an ensuing drop in enlistments necessitated a draft that applied to both the ethnic and native-born communities alike. In Massachusetts, between January 1 and October 17, 1863, only 6,353 volunteers enlisted and mustered, white and black. The increase in financial incentives offered as the war went on, as well as the need for conscription, indicates general diminution in enthusiasm for military service (a circumstance which made the late-war influx of black troops all the more critical to the Union victory).[74]

While hardcore nativists undeniably seized on reports of Irish American draft dodgers to bolster their arguments, native-born draft dodgers faced similar societal censure. Furthermore, many Irish Americans scorned draft dodging as well. Prominent Irish American businessmen in Toledo, Ohio, denounced "cowardly and treacherous" draft dodgers. The *Pilot*, in August 1863, urged that even *non-citizen* males, if healthy, without a family to support, and of military age, had a "moral obligation" to enlist or provide a substitute in support of the Union, although the newspaper rejected *requiring* an alien to enlist.[75]

Not surprisingly, discussions regarding emancipation led to some of the most paradoxical arguments within Irish America and helped define relations with African Americans. In June 1861, the *Pilot* declared its "abhorrence" for the "curse of America": slavery. By late summer 1862, the newspaper identified abolitionists as having provoked the conflict, but argued that the North rightly wished to curtail slavery's growth. Yet, a week after arguing that Northern opposition to slavery's expansion hewed to the "fundamental law of the land," the *Pilot* glumly contemplated the ramifications of "mad philanthropy for the African." "The North is becoming black with refugee negroes from the South," wrote the Irish American organ. "These wretches crowd our cities, and by overstocking the market of labor do incalculable injury to white hands." Urging Northern states to forbid black entry across their borders, the paper admitted that the "negro...creature has the common rights of humanity living in his breast," but justified exclusion by asking, "In the country of the whites where the labor of the whites has done everything, but his, nothing, and where the whites find it difficult to earn a subsistence, what right has the negro either to preference or to equality, or to admission?" The *Pilot* queried, "What has the African done for America?" and questioned, "What great or even decent work has his head conceived, or his hands executed?" before declaring, "To white toil this nation owes every thing; but to black, nothing." Fears of competition sometimes erupted into racist violence, such as the New York City Draft Riots, or when Irish American stevedores in Toledo, Ohio, rioted along wharves on Lake Erie on July 8, 1862, to protest the use of African American strikebreakers against them. Longshoremen armed with rocks and clubs clashed with blacks brandishing knives and pistols, and the violence turned against homes and businesses in Toledo's black district after one of the white men died.[76]

The same day the Irish Brigade made its forlorn charge at Fredericksburg, the *Pilot* declared to its readers that, because millions of blacks could not live peacefully side by side with whites, bondage of one race remained the "only cure" for the "common good of both." The following month, the *Pilot* criticized emancipation as pushing the Confederacy further into "a new, direct, sweeping provocation of Southern treason" that, along with the "incompetent, fanatic, radical administration of Abraham Lincoln," threatened to permanently rend the Union.[77]

Many Irish Americans opposed the radical changes that would be wrought by freeing the slaves because of racism, the links among nativism and abolitionism, concern regarding the economic impact emancipation might have on their already tenuous socioeconomic position, and a fear that the radical Republican agenda would irreparably damage the nation's constitutionalism. In August 1862, before the Emancipation Proclamation, the *Pilot* articulated an ambivalent view toward Lincoln: while portraying Republicans as nativists and "unconstitutional enemies of the South," the *Pilot* described Lincoln as no "irrepressible Abolitionist." After declaring, "We want no better President than Abraham Lincoln," the editorial simultaneously feared the abolitionist element of the Republican Party and called for a Democratic return to power for the "safety of the nation." After the Emancipation Proclamation took effect, the *Pilot* proclaimed about Lincoln in January 1863, "He has changed and so have we. It is now every man's duty to disagree with him." At a low point in Irish American (and national) morale on the heels of successive defeats at Fredericksburg and Chancellorsville, the *Pilot* grumbled in May 1863 that Irish Americans now found themselves "engaged in an abolition war," and went so far as to declare that "the Irish spirit for the war is dead!...Our fighters are dead."[78]

In 1864, Father Bernard O'Reilly in a private letter blamed both the "fanatics of the North as well as the Conspirators of the South," for the war, and he could not decide "which my soul hates with a more thorough hatred." While O'Reilly identified slavery as a "social evil" bequeathed to the South by "other generations & other Governments than our own," he thought that abolitionists fomented a crisis when waiting for slavery to wither gradually would have been less cataclysmic. O'Reilly ascribed Irish America's waning enthusiasm for the war by early 1864 on the restructuring of society proposed by Republicans: "Oh! to save the Union, we were willing, as willing as any to make any sacrifice...we loved the Union most dearly," O'Reilly penned, but when the "radical clique of Puritans" put "the iron yoke of their own wills on that poor President who never knew his own," and used Lincoln "as a tool for their own wild theories, + ferocious emancipation schemes," O'Reilly argued, "surely the Irish Catholics throughout the Union might well pause before this Puritanical Juggernaut beneath whose wheels they were exhorted + commanded to cast themselves, their families, their fortunes, + their conscience to boot." Coupled with the remnants of nativism, emancipation and the arming of blacks represented the final straw for Irish American morale. When the "puritanical detractors" of the "ancient + chivalric" Irish went so far as to "place the negro on a level with themselves," O'Reilly explained, "no wonder the enthusiasm for the war cooled down," and he added that "nor was it among the Irish alone [that] its abatement was sensible."[79]

The Democratic Party, meanwhile, took practical steps to maintain the wartime loyalty of its Irish American base. After the New York City Draft Riots, for example, the Democratic majority in that city's Common Council appropriated money to pay bounties for any men drafted. Republican mayor George Opdyke vetoed the measure (and lost in the next election), and in response, New York's Board of Supervisors funded an Exemption Committee to purchase substitutes, especially for poor men supporting families and city workers.[80]

Complicating what Irish American wartime political affiliation meant, deep fissures marked the Democratic Party during the Civil War. Some Democrats became full-out Republicans, or joined the War Democrat/Republican coalition Union Party. Other Democrats, including Irish Americans, opposed the war as part of the Copperhead movement and urged initiatives to conclude, but not necessarily win, the war. Most Democrats embraced an intermediate position, supporting the war and restoration of the Union on antebellum terms but disapproving the Republican agenda. On the other hand, especially after resistance to the draft, many Republicans proclaimed that allegiance to their party simultaneously translated into allegiance to the United States. As Republicans energetically cast Democrats as traitors who shared party with those who governed the Confederacy, Democrats had a difficult time constructing their identity as a loyal opposition party. Ex-congressman Gerrit Smith thus wrote in 1864, "The Democratic Party is, in short, neither more nor less than the Northern wing of the Rebellion."[81]

Republicans applied this argument to native-born and foreign-born Democrats alike. Even Irish-born Patrick Guiney exclaimed, during an 1868 speech supporting Ulysses S. Grant for president, "The great bulk of the democratic party therein went into rebellion against the country that received my father and his children." Guiney declared, "The republican party have got all that was good for anything, all that was truly democratic, in the old democratic party." In another postwar speech, Guiney argued that the chiefs of the rebellion still led the Democratic Party. While admitting that well-meaning men existed in both parties, Guiney criticized the Democrats for aiding the rebellion by rioting against the draft, and he intertwined the Republican Party and the federal army by claiming that there existed a "union of hearts between the two." Guiney in this way scorned, regardless of ethnicity, anyone who failed to support the Republic(ans).[82]

Many Democrats countered such attacks by arguing that opposition to the Republican agenda did not automatically translate into support for the Confederacy. Boston's and New York's Irish American newspapers endorsed George B. McClellan's 1864 presidential candidacy but justified doing so by arguing that only the election of a Democrat could restore the nation, on the conservative terms they desired. The *Irish-American* called on readers "to save their country" from lurching toward "despotism," while the *Pilot* argued that Irish American opposition to Lincoln stemmed from their "desire to see the Union re-established, peace and prosperity return to bless the land once more, and the Constitution to be restored over all." Democratic victory in 1864 likely would have proved disastrous for the objective of preserving the Union, but many Democrats, including Irish Americans, did not necessarily view their acts as ones of sympathy with Copperhead Peace Democrats. Lincoln received 2,213,665 votes to McClellan's 1,802,237 during the 1864 presidential election. Northern civilians in general hotly debated the issues of civil liberties, the transformation of federalism, emancipation and what to do with blacks afterward, and changes to traditionally racially exclusionary policies. Irish Americans participated in this societywide debate by asserting largely conservative views.[83]

Moreover, for many Irish Americans, overall loyalty to the Union, even if it was conservative in nature, prevailed over fears regarding parts of the Republican agenda they opposed. Irish Americans mirrored the beliefs of many Northerners in the beginning of the war: they wanted to preserve the Constitution and Union as they were before the firing on Fort Sumter, although Irish Americans as a whole generally remained more resistant to legal evolution than did other groups as the war progressed. Few Irish Americans enthusiastically supported the full Republican agenda, but many of them did want the United States restored, and they did not necessarily see their opposition to the Republican Party as contradictory to having an American identity. In describing a fictional banquet given in honor of his literary creation, Miles O'Reilly, Charles Halpine urged that the issues of emancipation, conscription, and the suspension of the writ of habeas corpus stood subsidiary to overall loyalty to the country. Halpine declared that

> To the flag we are pledged, all its foes we abhor,
> And we ain't for the nigger, but are for the war.

At a packed March 1863 Union rally at Cooper Institute in New York City, James T. Brady comparably assured the audience of the loyalty of Irish American Democrats: "I differ with many of you in regard to the causes, the conduct, the prosecution, and the probable results of the war in which we are engaged. But...I would be false to the Irish race...if I did not use my last breath, and employ the last quiver of my lips, in the utterance of a prayer to Heaven against all assailants, internal and external, for the preservation of the American Government." Within days of Lincoln's reelection, the *Pilot* called on its readers to support the administration, for "the integrity of the constitution, the preservation of the Union, and the restoration of peace."[84]

Intense opposition by some Irish Americans to the Republican agenda, and hostility to African American aspirations for equality and citizenship, did not mean rejection of an increasing sense of American identity. The politicizing experience of military service caused some Irish American soldiers in the field to reconsider their former positions. Many Irish American soldiers held on to racist hostility against blacks, to be sure. Irish-born William Jones scorned the Emancipation Proclamation, vowing that he "did not enlist to fight for those black devils" and grumbling that a soldier's salary was low enough without the injustice of now "fighting for blacks." A soldier in the Irish American 155th New York likewise noted the dissatisfaction "one and all" of his comrades "because of the Nigger proclamation."[85]

Yet other Irish American soldiers criticized slavery on encountering it. Michael Finnerty of the Ninth Massachusetts identified slavery's "blighting influences" as the reason that the nation's capital lacked the "bustle" of New York and Boston. While on picket duty near Big Bethel, Virginia, in March 1862, Patrick Guiney received five black females into his lines and proclaimed "In the name of old Ireland and Massachusetts, I set you free." A few weeks later, Guiney sent his wife some "fragrant Virginia leaves" given to him "by the only Virginia lady I met on the march—*she was black.*"[86]

Writing shortly after the war, Michael Macnamara of the Ninth Massachusetts stereotyped African Americans, occasionally calling a black woman "wench" and referring to a black boy as having the "agility of a monkey." On the other hand, Macnamara described an encounter with an eighty-year-old man who had worked his entire life as a slave, his strength sapped from a now withered body, and recounted, "We felt, more than ever, in heart and principle, an uncompromising enmity to human slavery."[87]

Not all Irish Americans objected to arming blacks, moreover, although egalitarianism did not always motivate their position. In October 1863, Charles G. Halpine reminded his audience that "every black regiment in garrison would relieve a white regiment for service in the field," and "every ball stopped by a black man would save the life of a white soldier." In a poem, "Sambo's Right to Be Kilt," Halpine argued that whites could arm blacks for these reasons while disclaiming any admission of social or political equality. The poem included lines such as, "In battles wild commotion / I shouldn't at all object / If Sambo's body should stop a ball / That was comin' for me direct," and ended, "The right to be kilt we'll divide wid him, / And give him the largest half!" Halpine argued elsewhere that military discipline would provide the "best school" in which the "elevation" of freedmen "to the plane of freedom can be conducted."[88]

Moreover, a few Irish Americans even became Republicans. By October 1863, former Irish Brigade commander Thomas Meagher wrote another Irish American who faced opposition for his new Republican allegiance, Patrick Guiney, to condemn Irish Americans who blindly followed the Democratic Party. Meagher expressed his intense frustration that "to their own discredit and degradation, they [Irish Americans] have suffered themselves to be bamboozled into being obstinate herds in the political field," and that "Democrats they profess themselves to be from the start—the instant the baggage-smashers and cut-throat lodging-house-keepers lay hands on them—and Democrats they remain until the day of their deaths, miserably and repulsively regardless of the conflicting meanings that name acquires through the progressive workings of the great world about them." Meagher further asserted that "under the captivating pretexts of the States-Rights, Habeas Corpus, and the popular claims and rights of the kind," the Democratic Party "would cripple the national power." Meagher's statements, and outspoken Republican support at the time, crippled his position within the Irish American community, and he sought a fresh start as acting governor of the Montana Territory after the war, a position he held until his death on July 1, 1867.[89]

Thus, while Irish American civilians and soldiers engaged in the same debates as native-born Northerners about the prosecution of the war, as well as freedom for the slaves, some adhered to racism while others embraced egalitarianism, or at least accepted a pragmatic approach so as to win the war. Many Irish Americans maintained devotion to the Democratic Party even where it became associated with slavery and secession. On the other hand, at this moment of intense debate and party fluidity, some former Irish American Democrats altered their views, and a few even went so far as to join the Republicans.

Conclusion

Nativism undoubtedly survived the war. Intractable nativists cited Irish American participation in the Draft Riots and their hostility to emancipation, and it seems certain that dissent from Irish Americans was more frequently linked to assertions of disloyalty than was the case with other groups. In March 1863, the Ladies Aid Society in Dubuque, Iowa, refused to help the wives of Irish Catholic soldiers, advising them to "look to Catholics" for assistance. In February 1864, a Protestant mob attacked a Catholic parish fair in Mount Pleasant, Iowa, damaging property before cursing the Irish Americans there and calling them traitors, while the mob's leader, former probate judge and army chaplain Thomas W. Newman, cautioned "that every Catholic priest and Bishop in America prepare very soon to lose their heads."[90]

Lingering criticism and isolated instances of anti-Irish action, however, do not amount to a widespread resurgence of nativism. The interaction of different groups united in support of the Union, as well as other changes wrought by the Civil War, crippled the nativist impulse of the 1850s. The largest nonpolitical nativist association at the time, the Order of United Americans, preached disdain of immigrants and Catholics across sixteen states in the early 1850s, but could not even maintain a quorum at its last recorded meeting in 1862. The Sons of America, which wielded great influence in Pennsylvania, crumbled with the outbreak of the Civil War, as did the Order of United American Mechanics.[91]

The decay of nativist organizations during the Civil War did not mean that nativism vanished, never to reappear in the United States. Nonetheless, the service of Irish Americans allowed for them to assert that they deserved greater inclusion in American society and equality of citizenship based on the proof of loyalty offered by their military service. The diminution of nativism eliminated the main challenge to Irish American inclusion and equal citizenship, in contrast to the challenges African Americans would face after the war, and allowed Irish Americans to assert claims for further legal change during Reconstruction.

More broadly, Irish American soldiers experienced acceptance, not hostility, in the ranks, as they more openly practiced their religion, celebrated their ethnic culture, and even continued to proclaim their support for Irish nationalism. Celebrating Irish American culture, practicing Catholicism during the Civil War, and remembering one's native land or heritage did not indicate an unwillingness to Americanize, any more than Irish American celebrations of St. Patrick's Day, Italian American feasts in Boston's North End, or continued Catholicism does today. Instead, the openness with which Irish Americans held their ethnic identity and religion in the 1860s accompanied the corresponding shifts generated by the meaning of Irish American service and support for the Union. Irish Americans felt it increasingly possible to celebrate their ethnic identity within an American context, and they incorporated an American identity alongside their Irish one. These changes reveal that Irish Americans increasingly felt they could be considered Americans even where they did not completely abandon their ethnicity, or eschew Catholicism to embrace the Protestant majority, as some argue they would have had to do to assimilate. Instead, Irish Americans even placed Fenianism within the context of good American citizenship, identity, and allegiance.

Moreover, some Irish Americans reconsidered their political views based on their military experiences, and even Irish nationalists adjusted their focus. While many Irish Americans at home remained resistant to the Republican agenda, the Civil War nonetheless helped awaken for Irish America as a whole a new appreciation for the United States as a beacon of republicanism and a belief that its perpetuation would help Ireland and the entire world. In this climate, Irish Americans increasingly recognized the American component of their identity and allegiance, and these changes generated the potential to lead to growing calls, after the war, for a more nationalized and broadened understanding of what American citizenship meant.

CHAPTER 6

African Americans and the Call for Rights

In 1868, Kentucky's superintendent of freedmen's affairs, Benjamin P. Runkle, announced in a speech to blacks in Louisville, "At last when the government, casting aside the last lingering remnants of prejudice, determined to use all the power it could command to crush the rebellion it offered the musket to the Black man—the musket without the promise of bounty and without the sword—How they responded let the names of 125,000 black men on the rolls of the National Army answer! How they used their arms, let Fort Wagner and Port Hudson respond!" Runkle inspired his audience by reminding them that, "amid the ringing of steel, the roar of cannon, and the crash of musketry, was a people born, from darkness to light, from bondage to freedom; and stood, their shackles broken, forever free, waiting in the dim uncertain morning of this new day," beginning "to become fitted for citizens of a free nation."[1]

Runkle distinguished between social equality, and averred that blacks did "not want, ask for, or expect it," and equality before the law sought by blacks and ordained by the Declaration of Independence: the right to live, possess property, pursue happiness, receive a fair wage, support families, have educational opportunities for children, worship as they chose, testify in courts, sit on juries, vote, and enjoy personal security. For Runkle, "every man who is liable to be called upon to bear arms in defence of his country, should have a voice in the government of that country," and he further pronounced to his audience, "when we saw 'Old Glory' surrounded by the glittering bayonets coming to the rescue, did it matter to us whether the faces in that column were white or black?...Why should we who stood side by side in the same armies...object to vote with them side by side at the same ballot box to support the same eternal principles? I do not believe we would be called upon to answer whether we fought in a white or black regiment; but on *what side we fought,* on the side of *God, liberty and humanity,* or on the side of *darkness, the Devil and Slavery.*" After recognizing the allegiance blacks showed to the United States, Runkle urged them to embrace the Republican free labor ethos by pursuing education and property, cultivating moral character, and avoiding alcohol.[2]

Little over a decade before Runkle's speech, the Supreme Court excluded blacks from American citizenship pursuant to its holding in *Dred Scott.* In March 1861, Congress sent to the states a thirteenth amendment, never ratified, to protect slavery from federal interference in the states where it existed. In the mid-to-late 1860s, however, discussion focused on the ramifications of emancipation and the place of blacks in American society, and opinions formerly viewed as belonging only to extreme abolitionists became increasingly conventional.

Black soldiers understood while in the armed forces that their status had changed as a result of their service, even if the extent and permanence of these changes remained in a state of flux. As a black newspaper pronounced in the war's waning months, "Within two years the standard of 'Justice' has been raised in our favor; an admission of our valor, our manhood, our courage, has been made by our former oppressors; *partial* equality has been extended to us, and our rights as citizens have been recognized, in a great measure." Yet, as the war wound down, whether blacks would be able to move the country to enshrine permanently in the law these wartime ways of thinking remained uncertain. Blacks had served in past American wars with no lasting change to their status, and they now faced two questions with much at stake: Would all blacks finally become part of "the people" and be considered as national citizens by the law? And what would any such citizenship status actually mean?[3]

The War's Closing Days

One of the most compelling moments experienced by many black soldiers in the war's closing days was the reception they received by freedpeople as the Union army advanced toward ultimate victory. A sergeant of the Fifty-fourth Massachusetts reported that, when his regiment entered Charleston, South Carolina, in 1865, the streets "thronged with women and children of all sizes, colors and grades." One elderly black woman threw down her crutch and "shouted that the year of jubilee had come." Another soldier rejoiced as freedom came in late February 1865 to Wilmington, North Carolina, where a major slave market had existed before the war: "Where once the slave was forbid being out after nine P.M., or to puff a 'regalia,' or to walk with a cane, or to ride in a carriage," black soldiers now marched in front of cheering black civilians, "with banners floating" and "splendid brass bands and drum corps" playing patriotic music. Some of the newly liberated distributed tobacco, bread, meat, or water to the soldiers, while one nonagenarian stood with "long white locks and his wrinkled cheeks, saying 'Welcome, welcome!'" Another touching scene came when a woman ran to embrace her son with pride as one who left as a slave but "returned in the garb of a Union soldier, free, a man."[4]

As blacks joined the festivity of triumphant unionists both in the North and South, they did so with the satisfaction of knowing that their community played a critical role in achieving the success they celebrated. Black nationalist Major Martin Delaney addressed jubilant freedmen on St. Helena Island, South Carolina, in July 1865: "Do you know that if it was not for the black man this war never would have been brought to a close with success to the Union," nor "the liberty of your race if it had not been for the negro?" Delaney thundered to his audience, "I want you to understand that—Do you know it, do you know it, do you know it[?]"[5]

Yet, these celebrations went beyond the exhilaration blacks felt at participating in the Union's triumph. Blacks realized that their military service helped create the necessary context for the ratification of the Thirteenth Amendment, which eliminated slavery. Participation in the Union victory now invigorated blacks to assert stronger calls for defined citizenship rights based on equality. A member of the 119th USCI wrote of several regiments and thousands of black civilians from a local refugee camp who partook in a "grand spectacle" at Camp Nelson, Kentucky, on July 4, 1865, congregating "in the heart of a slave State" and celebrating "the day sacred to the cause of freedom" as "an assemblage of colored people...never before beheld" in Kentucky. Together, the black troops and freedpeople enjoyed singing, speeches, a review of black regiments, and a good dinner. "By laboring for our own cause," the black veteran argued, "we show, in the first place, that we understand and appreciate what our rights are; in the second place, that we have the courage and manhood to ask for them; in the third place, that we are determined, sooner or later, to have them."[6]

On the other hand, interracial tension increased in some areas once combat ceased. "During the actual existence of the Rebellion," related a member of the Third USCI days before a mutiny in that regiment, "we have been told by our commanding officers on the eve of battle to forget old grudges and prejudices, and fight like men for a common cause." Where officers "have nothing now to fear from stray bullets," however, they tormented their black subordinates with hated punishments reminiscent of the plantation, such as tying up by the thumbs. The soldier reported that the word of the "smooth oily tongue of the white planter" often proved enough to "condemn" black soldiers and civilians, "the only true and avowed friends" of the United States in the South.[7]

The words of George M. Turner, a Third Rhode Island Artillery sergeant who served in South Carolina and Florida, reveal the struggle of a white soldier who attempted to reconcile reluctant respect for black bravery with deep-seated racism. In December 1861, Turner recounted to his cousin laughing "until our sides are nearly bursting" at the singing and dancing of contrabands, and in June 1862, he wrote his father that he "despised [blacks] more than dirt." By late July 1863, Turner showed a marked change of heart: "When you hear any one remark that nigger soldiers will not fight, please request them to come down here and judge for themselves," and he deemed the Fifty-fourth Massachusetts "as good a fighting regiment as there is in the 10th Army Corps." Yet, by the following May, Turner reverted to racism, expressing anger at the idea of black equality, resenting blacks for being "the 'bone' over which the Northern and Southern dogs are quarreling," and declaring that he was "not willing to fight shoulder to shoulder with a black dirty nigger." When Captain Charles B. Brockway addressed an August 1865 Democratic rally in Columbia County, Pennsylvania, he condemned emancipation as a divisive measure that had destroyed morale in the North and stiffened Confederate resolve in the South. Brockway called black troops "cowardly," identified them as "government pets" kept away from real danger, and he demanded an end to organizations created "especially for the care of negroes."[8]

Black soldiers witnessed grave atrocities committed by fellow whites in the blue uniform while serving on garrison duty near Charleston, South Carolina. Soldiers of the 127th New York hurled epithets and rocks at the new freedpeople, while the Twenty-first USCI (executed mutineer William Walker's regiment) attempted to shield black civilians and help them transition from slavery to freedom. Racial tensions boiled as conditions deteriorated in Charleston, a city stripped of supplies, barren of food, and facing a smallpox epidemic. Some of the New Yorkers destroyed booths in the blacks' marketplace, assaulted and reportedly raped former slaves, sacked black homes, and demanded that blacks move aside when whites wanted to pass on the sidewalks. Orders prohibiting such behavior had little effect, while blacks retaliated by hurling bottles, and brandished knives for protection.[9]

On June 18, 1865, members of the New York unit fought with those of the Thirty-fifth USCI who defended two black women from insult. Little changed after the 165th New York replaced the 127th. By July 8, skirmishing between that regiment and the Fifty-fourth Massachusetts exploded into a full-out melee that lasted until another white unit deployed on July 10 to restore order. Major General Quincy Gillmore moved the New York regiment to Morris Island, forbade its members to enter Charleston, and dispatched an officer from the Twenty-first USCI to confiscate its regimental banner, a humiliating act of punishment. Gillmore also transferred the Twenty-first USCI to Hilton Head and tried to minimize contact between white and black troops. Other attacks persisted by members of other white federal regiments, however, leading to the recall of both the Fifty-fourth and Fifty-fifth Massachusetts by the fall of 1865.[10]

Black garrisons in the South also generated tensions with the local white population. On one hand, the presence of black troops often dissuaded whites from retaliating against freedpeople—an empowering position. H. M. Turner reported that whites within reach of black troops felt "afraid to kick colored women, and abuse colored people on the Streets." According to one officer, black soldiers cheerfully rendered service because they felt they did so to advance the interests of fellow African Americans. Yet, for white Southerners who already viewed African Americans with disgust, the presence of black soldiers serving in their midst underscored the mortification of Confederate defeat and represented the societal changes associated with the end of slavery. The notion of armed black soldiers proved a terrifying social and physical threat for Southerners who before the war feared the potential for slave revolt. Rumors swirled in some areas that black soldiers would lead a widespread Christmas 1865 slaughter of white planters in the South, highlighting, in the words of one historian, the "symbolic power of African American troops and their role in fueling the fear of white southerners during the closing months of the year."[11]

Fear and resentment against black soldiers, especially as they served as a protective force for freedpeople, eventually led to brutality against African Americans in blue. In Columbus, Georgia, a black soldier overheard a drunken white man call him a "God damn black son of a bitch" before shots rang out, wounding him in the hand and each arm. Officers had to restrain the black soldier's 103rd USCI from retaliating, and the town nearly exploded in violence after a federal detachment arrested the perpetrator: hundreds of white Southern civilians, some of whom brandished pistols, turned out to demand his release. Columbus's white civilians also petitioned Georgia's governor to try to get the black garrison removed, claiming that the black soldiers had shown "a disregard of moral and legal restraints" by "robbing and insulting our citizens both male & female," and that after one of the soldiers was shot, black troops "fired indiscriminately into the street wounding one of our peaceable & orderly citizens necessitating the amputation of his leg."[12]

Yet African American soldiers also felt emboldened to take tangible action against white southerners who insulted them or black civilians. The garrisoning of Kinston, North Carolina, with "*smoked Yankees*" in 1865 exasperated local residents, but they soon saw "the *smoked Yankees* marching some of their fellow citizens to jail at the point of a bayonet." At Olustee Station, Florida, one white man found twenty guns pointed at him after he declared that "all the niggers should be in [hell]." One soldier actually fired, grazing the offender's head, but when Brigadier General Benjamin Tilghman arrived on the scene, he ignored the breach of discipline and merely led "the wounded man aside...and bid him depart in peace, lest a worse evil come upon him." Sergeant E. S. Robison wrote directly to Major General Quincy Gillmore to report that whites had ransacked the home of a black man outside Columbia, South Carolina, and that the local federal commander ignored the aggrieved man's complaint. "I am only a sergeant and of Course Should be as silent as possible," wrote Robison, "But in this I Could not hold my temper After fighting to get wrights that White men might Respect By Virtue of the Law."[13]

Such incidents reveal the strong reactionary forces that marshaled to oppose integration of blacks into society, as well as the uncertain position blacks held. At the same time, these episodes show how some blacks felt empowered to stand up against mistreatment and reject prior expectations of submission. Moreover, in the context of persistent inequality and prejudice, blacks understood that the Thirteenth Amendment would ring hollow if emancipation meant freedom in name only, especially should the states remain arbiters of what rights citizens enjoyed. Blacks especially realized, in the closing days of the war, that they needed federal protection to exercise defined rights of citizenship uniformly enforced across the country, and that the Union's victory afforded them the opportune moment to seek it.

Mustering Out from One Fight, Mobilizing for Another

As the war wound down, muster-out ceremonies helped many black soldiers transition into a civilian life formerly unknown to most of them, that of freedmen. By autumn of 1866, only thirteen thousand blacks remained in the Union army, in contrast with eighty-three thousand a year earlier. The last Civil War USCT regiment, the 117th USCI, disbanded in August 1867, though blacks would continue to serve in the regular army in the Ninth and Tenth cavalry and Twenty-fourth and Twenty-fifth infantry regiments. In most regiments, the men gathered on their last day of service to receive their discharge papers and any pay owed them, turn in equipment they did not wish to purchase, and listen to a final address from their colonel. Such moments revealed an opportunity for the redefinition of racial relations in the aftermath of the Civil War. As the Sixth USCI mustered out, its officers adopted a resolution illustrating the impact that black service made on at least some white comrades: after noting that blacks "have shown themselves to be brave, reliable, and efficient as soldiers," the resolution stated that, "being satisfied with their conduct in the high position of soldiers of the United States, we see no reason why they should not be fully recognized as equals, honorable and responsible citizens of the same."[14]

Colonel Theodore H. Barrett declared to the troops of his Sixty-second USCI, out of Missouri, "It is you yourselves, that have made yourselves soldiers and men," and that through their actions, the men and their families transformed from slaves living in "negro quarters" to freedpeople living in homes, with children who would experience not the auction block but the schoolhouse, and wives under the protection of a husband instead of the dominion of a master. Barrett reminded his men that these changes created new responsibilities and opportunities, and he counseled them to save their money, remain sober, find good wives, put a premium on education, and buy land and cultivate their own living, if possible, rather than working as wage laborers. Most importantly, Barrett told the men, "It is not the color which is hereafter to make the difference between men. You are to have an equal chance with the white man. You wish to be citizens? Show to the country then that you are capable of citizenship." Acknowledging that the law did not yet recognize blacks as American citizens (the Fourteenth Amendment had not yet overturned *Dred Scott*), Barrett declared, "If you shall deserve citizenship, you will in the end receive it, with every right and every privilege enjoyed by those who now deny these rights to you." Nonetheless, Barrett announced the inevitability of equal rights as a result of military service, and that even former slaveholders would soon have to acknowledge, "to have been a colored soldier, is to be a citizen." Identifying his veterans as leaders within the black population, with a duty to instruct the new freedpeople, Barrett closed his valediction by recalling a time when the regiment crossed the Mississippi River, so that its right rested on the Illinois side and its left remained in Missouri, "thus, uniting slave soil with free, you marched out of bondage, with muskets on your shoulders." As Barrett had, other commanders noted to blacks the opportunity for legal change as a result of African American military service, and urged them to pursue self-reliance and embrace the Republican Party's free labor ideology as well.[15]

For the Fifth USCI, recruited out of Ohio, the disbanding of the regiment juxtaposed the sadness of parting with a new confidence for future political action. As one black correspondent wrote,

> When discharged, see them turn away with a sad, lingering gaze upon that old flag which they have borne so proudly upon the many battlefields....Then, as the order is given to break ranks, see how eagerly they grasp the hand of their comrades in earnest friendship for the last time. A tear courses down their bronzed cheeks, as they hastily say the parting word in final adieu to that comrade who has with them passed through all dangers.

In discussing persistent prejudice and opposition to giving blacks the vote, the author identified in a very explicit way the expectation that these veterans would take the lead in vindicating black demands: "We will not revert to these acts of oppression again....We, who have, for the last three years, been so closely connected as to have formed a seeming brotherhood, now, when these ties are about to be dissolved, are we not willing to continue this connection in some form, which may bring us together in something like the former organization?" In proposing annual reunions of Ohio's black veterans, the author nominated thirteen sergeants from the Fifth and Twenty-seventh USCI regiments to establish "an organization which will...be a guiding star to our future advancement in the cause of liberty and justice."[16]

Black soldiers elsewhere made similar calls. From the ranks of the Twenty-second USCI, W. A. Freeman argued after Appomattox that "the blood of our comrades who have fallen upon the fields of battle, while assisting to plant the tree of liberty," and the "tears of our widows and mothers, which have watered" that tree, meant that "liberty and equality have been purchased at too great a sacrifice" to be forfeited. In August 1865, Sergeant Norman B. Sterrett recognized the inextricably linked battles black soldiers fought, one on the battlefield and the other against racism. Exasperated at the tension that existed between emancipation and prejudice, a "new idea struck" Sterrett, that "when three or four thousand brave colored soldiers, who have endured privation and suffering to crush the wicked rebellion, return to their homes in Maryland," the result would be that "respectable colored people will be able to walk the streets without being insulted." Seven hundred black Iowans of the

Sixtieth USCI convened at Davenport on October 31, 1865, to petition their state legislature for the right of suffrage on coming home from the field. The veterans resolved that Iowa had a "duty" to allow blacks to vote, reminding legislators that "he who is worthy to be trusted with the musket can and ought to be trusted with the ballot."[17]

While Americans wrestled with the ill-defined contours of the postbellum racial and political landscape, ceremonies similar to those given Irish American and native-born regiments welcomed the return of at least some black regiments recruited from the North. A week before the African American Twenty-ninth Connecticut Volunteer Infantry returned to Hartford, the state rejected a law that would have extended suffrage to blacks. In counterpoint, the Twenty-ninth Connecticut's homecoming celebration matched that given to white regiments and afforded blacks access to public space in the state's capital city. Hartford's mayor greeted the men on November 24, 1865, and the veterans followed a brass band to City Hall, where they ate a meal prepared by the city's white and black citizens. Afterward, local militia escorted the Thirty-first USCI, half recruited in Connecticut, to City Hall, where both regiments received the mayor's official salutation. Governor William Buckingham and the Twenty-ninth Connecticut's former commander praised the men's service before they marched through Hartford's flag-adorned main streets, observed by handkerchief-waving crowds.[18]

Welcome-home celebrations also provided blacks a forum with which to articulate publicly their vision of a new postwar legal scheme. On November 14, 1865, a crowd of whites and blacks thronged Harrisburg's flag-adorned streets in a ceremony hosted by the city's chapter of the Pennsylvania State Equal Rights League. Members of the 3rd, 6th, 8th, 22nd, 24th, 32nd, 41st, 43rd, 45th and 127th USCI, 11th USCHA, and the 54th and 55th Massachusetts regiments marched (and disabled soldiers rode in carriages) in a parade marshaled by black correspondent Thomas M. Chester. Wreathed banners bearing slogans such as "HE WHO DEFENDS FREEDOM IS WORTHY OF ALL ITS FRANCHISES" decorated the streets of Harrisburg's black district. When the procession reached the state Capitol, a prayer and the singing of "My Country, 'Tis of Thee" opened the program.[19]

The Harrisburg ceremony went beyond welcoming the return of thousands of black veterans in blue; it allowed African Americans to announce their constitutional views in front of a multiracial audience on the grounds of the most important governmental space in Pennsylvania. A black speaker condemned to the audience "the shame of the Keystone State...that she remands back those dark hued warriors, who risked life in her defence, to a degrading tutelage, and that she grudgingly accords to them the inalienable rights of men, while she withholds from them those governmental instrumentalities whereby alone these rights can be perfectly secured." Resolutions read aloud honored the service of thousands of black soldiers, both living and dead, and linked black claims of manhood and citizenship with the proof of loyalty validated by their sacrifice. Other resolutions held that federal power trumped that of the

5. National Convention of Colored Citizens, meeting in the House of Representatives at New Orleans, Louisiana, April 1872. *Frank Leslie's Illustrated Newspaper,* May 4, 1872. Courtesy Library of Congress.

states and declared that race-based distinctions violated both the Declaration of Independence and the Constitution's Article 4 Section 4 "guarantee to every State in this Union a republican form of government." Perceiving that states would be uncertain defenders of their rights, blacks increasingly called for a federal definition of citizenship, along with a pledge that the national government would protect the rights associated with it.[20]

Meanwhile, some blacks continued to seek advancement through military service after the war. An encouraging symbol of postwar respect came with the July 28, 1866, army reorganization act, which provided for four black infantry and two black cavalry regiments within a sixty-regiment regular army. In contrast to prewar exclusion from the army, black regiments now were to receive the same uniforms, weapons, and pay as white soldiers, and they did not serve in a separate corps. The act also provided for schools at all permanent posts. About half the blacks who joined the regular army in the late 1860s served during the Civil War. At least 533 men transferred directly from mustering out USCT regiments and about 2,500 other USCT veterans joined shortly after their discharge, many of them listing their occupation as "soldier" when enrolling.[21]

On a public level, William Wells Brown, in *The Negro in the American Rebellion: His Heroism and His Fidelity* (1867), took up William C. Nell's mantle to detail black valor at battles such as Fort Wagner and atrocities suffered at such places as Fort Pillow. Other blacks used the lessons that they learned in the army to serve as leaders in civilian life, standing within their community as individuals especially qualified to assert demands for equality. On an personal level, "If we hadn't become sojers, all might have gone back as it was before," freedman and veteran Thomas Long wrote after the war, "But now tings can neber go back, because we have showed our energy and our courage and our naturally manhood." When a white man insulted a black soldier in South Carolina by asking, "What are you, anyhow," the African American retorted, "When God made me I wasn't much but I's a man now." Black veterans assisted other freedpeople, inspired in them long-lasting pride, and helped build institutions such as churches and schools for their community. The existence of thousands of black veterans across the United States generated self-respect and energized the African American community to demand equal rights.[22]

Conventions and Equal Rights Leagues

During military service, blacks witnessed firsthand the power of large-scale organization at the same time that many, especially ex-slaves, became politically aware for the first time. While black veterans demanded that whites remove impediments against them, they also expected fellow African Americans to work actively for self-improvement. Both themes intensified as black veterans took lessons learned in the army into an energized black convention movement. The shared experiences of military service strengthened unity and American identity within the black community. Military service also helped inform black expectations of what citizenship entailed and afforded African Americans a powerful argument that those who defended the Union deserved full membership in its society. During the Civil War, blacks began to meet once again to assert their demands through national and state conventions that directly addressed governmental officials and spoke to white and black Americans. The convention movement not only showed that blacks could rationally engage with questions of constitutional importance, it allowed blacks to highlight inequality against them across the country. Through conventions, blacks further asserted their American allegiance, called on the federal government for recognition and protection as citizens, and articulated their expectations as to the contours of that citizenship.

The heritage of blacks gathering in national conventions dated to 1830, with the establishment of the National Negro Convention. Meeting eleven more times, with the final convocation in 1855, dissension prevented most of the plans discussed from ever coming to fruition. Black leaders also organized numerous state-level conventions before the Civil War. All but one of these prewar state conventions occurred in the North (the lone one on Southern soil occurred in Maryland in 1852), and they generally reflected the different priorities of Northern and Southern blacks. While Southern slaves likely would have placed full emphasis on the abolition of slavery had they been allowed to convene, Northern black antebellum conventions frequently debated voting rights and other strictures against them.[23]

This does not mean that Northern conventions ignored slavery, but many Northern blacks viewed political equality as a weapon with which to kill it and argued that improving rights for themselves would hasten emancipation in the South. Additionally, the Northern antebellum convention movement spent much of its energy debating the issues of colonization and emigration, as some blacks urged a return to Africa. These debates divided the Northern black leadership and dissipated attention from other issues facing the black community.[24]

The Emancipation Proclamation, Attorney General Bates's 1862 opinion that included blacks as American citizens, and the arming of thousands of black soldiers galvanized a new convention movement during the 1860s. Blacks seized the opportunity provided by their wartime participation to engage, with greater clarity, issues regarding their place in the polity. This reinvigorated convention movement promoted the notion that loyalty to the Union trumped race in determining citizenship status. While continuity existed from before the war in some areas, such as calls for the franchise and invocations of the Declaration of Independence as a guiding document, blacks now entered constitutional discourse with increasingly focused arguments. African Americans presented a more united front, generally eschewed emigration and colonization, and offered an expansive definition of the bundle of rights that comprised citizenship. Efforts to deny blacks their equal rights perverted the natural law, delegates declared, much as antebellum laws supporting slavery deviated from the spirit of the Declaration of Independence. Black conventioneers cast themselves as the keepers of the "true" American Founding and challenged whites to live up to its ideals.

The convention movement reflected and fed off of black military service in several ways. Experiences in the army helped inform black expectations of what citizenship meant. Moreover, the valor of black troops in uniform, both on the battlefield as well as in demanding equal pay, inspired delegates with a sense of pride in African American manhood and confidence in black leadership ability. Time and again, references to black service, whether in speeches or by the hanging of American flags sometimes literally stained with the blood of black troops, marked the proceedings. Delegates repeatedly asserted that in addition to birthright, service during the Union's crisis automatically conferred citizenship and rights on blacks.

Additionally, conventions adopted a martial spirit, rousing the black community as a whole with references to duty, sacrifice, and continued struggle. That nearly all black soldiers served in federal, not state, regiments helped bolster African American identification of the national jurisdiction as superior to that of the states. Combining entertainment and political propaganda, conventions popularized among blacks songs that linked the service of African Americans in uniform with the fight to redefine citizenship. In addition to songs like the "Battle Cry of Freedom," "Are You a Member of the League," challenged black men and women to participate in the struggle for equal rights. Equating membership in the Equal Rights League to the role black soldiers played in saving "this glorious land," the song incorporated the chorus, "They look like men of war."[25]

Black conventioneers now deployed on a different type of battlefield, one where Americans wrestled with how they would interpret the Constitution after the Civil War, and where blacks insisted that their birth within the United States and military service gave them every right to participate. Convention delegates used military service to quash any remaining impulse in support of colonization or race-based exclusion. Blacks now centered their discussions on whether a simple test of loyalty could determine whether one was a citizen, and they articulated their expectations of real freedom, not just in name only, complete with equality and better-defined and guaranteed citizenship rights.

The 1860s convention movement also stimulated greater communication within the black leadership, reflecting the breaking down of sectional boundaries begun by participation in the Union military. As African American soldiers from across the country found themselves in closer contact with one another, so also did national conventions allow for local delegates to bring their perspectives to the collective center of black debate. State Equal Rights League chapters remained subordinate to the National Equal Rights League. Moreover, because black activists realized that the goals of the black movement transcended state boundaries, greater solidarity of purpose connected local conventions. Accordingly, when black conventions met in New York and Illinois on the same day in 1866, they greeted each other by telegram.[26]

Reflecting their American identity, delegates to the black conventions believed that they acted in a spirit of representative democracy that comported with republican political practices. Conventions also distributed their proceedings in pamphlets, called for more black newspapers, and encouraged publication of appeals that disseminated their message to the black and white communities. Furthermore, whites frequently observed these conventions and, in some instances, found themselves elected as honorary members or asked to address the assembly.[27]

Conventions, and the equal rights organizations they created, flaunted white prejudice by publicly demonstrating a high level of competent black self-governance. Many conventions kept precise minutes that reveal meticulous devotion to the rules of parliamentary procedure, as delegates formed committees, debated motions, and drafted reports. The Equal Rights League set out constitutions for national and local governance, which included provisions allowing for trial and censure, suspension, or banishment of members who violated bylaws or committed offences contrary to the league's interests. In so doing, the league sought to position itself and its members within the broader rule of law and carry forth the lessons learned from black encounters with general courts-martial during the Civil War.[28]

Comparable to Irish nationalism within Irish America, an undercurrent of black nationalism ran through African America during the 1860s. Postwar black conventions rejected Martin Delaney's emigrationism but carried forth his mission to contrast racist degradation by restoring to blacks a sense of pride in their ancient heritage. Black delegates also extolled African America's accomplishments and encouraged a communal sense of responsibility to those of African lineage, calling for self-regeneration to prove, among other reasons, that blacks were as capable as whites. Talk of black pride and identity, as well as a black nation within the United States, pervaded African American conventions and organizations, and sometimes created tension between the principles of color-blindness they espoused at the same time. In 1866, the Pennsylvania Equal Rights League petitioned Congress as "true children of the Republic," but distinct, with a "color which mantles our cheeks and of which we may justly feel proud." Addressing a proposal to eliminate use of the word *African* in connection with the African Methodist Episcopal Church, George A. Rue asked, "What is there so detestable in that word?" Rue urged his readers to embrace the word *African,* reminding them, "no crime is attached" to it. Some of the paradoxes and dualities of black nationalism during the 1860s anticipate the "double consciousness" identified by W.E.B. DuBois, even where DuBois espoused a nationalism different from that of earlier black leaders such as Delaney.[29]

The first black national convention since 1855 shows how deeply the experiences of the Civil War unified and nationalized blacks, and energized their more coherent call for far-reaching rights. Its delegates gathered in 1864, before constitutional emancipation and at a time when not all Northerners accepted the idea of permanent emancipation as a prerequisite to peace. Moreover, the Republican Party seemed to blacks unsettlingly noncommittal about the matter in the face of hotly contested upcoming elections. On the evening of October 4, 1864, approximately 150 delegates from seventeen states and the District of Columbia convened in Syracuse, New York, and elected Frederick Douglass the convention's president. Although dominated by delegates from New England and the Mid-Atlantic states, attendees included representatives from Virginia, North Carolina, Florida, Louisiana, Mississippi, Tennessee, and Missouri. These delegates declared their vision of freedom both to the nation but also to equivocal Republicans, and they served as that party's broadly egalitarian conscience in calling for the irrevocable abolition of slavery, full inclusion of blacks into the American people, and a fulfillment of the nation's founding principles.[30]

On October 5, after creating several committees and determining the convention's rules of order, the delegates cheered while the battle flag of the black First Louisiana Native Guards was suspended across the main platform. Captain James H. Ingraham, present with the regiment during its attack at Port Hudson, described the assault and his fellow delegates applauded, with their multiracial audience, the black heroes and "the battle-flag which they bore." The night's session ended with the singing of "Battle Cry of Freedom," evoking in the delegates a sense that they now rallied "round the flag" in calling for equal rights for all.[31]

On October 6, the convention founded the National Equal Rights League and, despite an East-West rivalry, established its headquarters in Philadelphia, Pennsylvania. While not seeking to interfere with other organizations, the delegates called for increased unity through the league in order "to obtain by appeals to the minds and conscience of the American people, or by legal process when possible, a recognition of the rights of the colored people of the nation as American citizens." In keeping with their call for equality among all people, the delegates mandated that membership in the league should remain open regardless of color or sex.[32]

Speakers then ascended the rostrum. Dr. P. B. Randolph declared to the world, "WE ARE COMING UP!...and going up to *stay*," and honored dead black soldiers as "the seeds" of a "mighty harvest." Reminiscent of William C. Nell's prewar arguments, black Boston attorney John S. Rock vowed that the experience of their grandfathers, who fought in the Revolution only to be cheated of their rightful due, could not repeat itself. Rock further assessed that black soldiers on and off the battlefield "have done wonders for the race."[33]

The delegates identified themselves as offering the true interpretation of the Declaration of Independence and Constitution. In a powerful Declaration of Wrongs and Rights, the convention reminded all Americans that whites had "by brute force" caused blacks to suffer "every cruelty and indignity possible," divested them of ownership of their bodies and the fruits of their labor, equal pay while in the army, and the rights of trial by jury, representation in the government, and education. Accordingly, the delegates reasserted the "fundamental principle" that "all men are born free and equal," and they rejected tortured antebellum readings of the same principal that permitted racism and slavery (e.g., Chief Justice Taney's logic in his *Dred Scott* ruling that blacks were never intended to be included in the words of the Declaration of Independence). Blacks urged a racially inclusive rule of law as well as official affirmation of their citizenship, but they also proffered definitions of what rights they expected that citizenship to include by listing what had been denied them up until that point. Blacks realized that their status as citizens would remain meaningless and rhetorical unless citizenship had concrete definition in the law.[34]

In an address to their "FELLOW-CITIZENS," the delegates argued that forces conspired to reverse the progress of equality, exclude black men from the ballot box, deny the black soldier "his claims to the gratitude of his country," and "scout his pretensions to American citizenship." Concerned that the Republican Party remained equivocal, and fearing that a single military defeat could destroy the potential presented by the North's slow but ongoing march toward victory, the delegates called for a permanent abolition of slavery and granting black men the vote. Without the franchise, they argued, property ownership, and freedom and its associated rights, became mere privileges held at the sufferance of others.[35]

Tens of thousands of black soldiers grasped these rights for all African Americans, declared the convention, holding "the American people bound in honor thus to reward them." The delegates interrogated the nation,

> Are we good enough to use bullets, and not good enough to use ballots? May we defend rights in time of war, and yet be denied the exercise of those rights in

time of peace? Are we citizens when the nation is in peril, and aliens when the nation is in safety? May we shed our blood under the star-spangled banner on the battle-field, and yet be debarred from marching under it to the ballot-box? Will the brave white soldiers, bronzed by the hardships and exposures of repeated campaigns, men who have fought by the side of black men, be ashamed to cast their ballots by the side of their companions-in-arms?

In answer, these black leaders reminded all Americans, including hesitant Republicans, that where the Union "required, demanded, and in some instances compelled, us to serve with our time, our property, and our lives...we claim to have fully earned the elective franchise; and that you, the American people, have virtually contracted an obligation to grant it." Having earlier affirmed the notion that birthright and mutual service to the Republic united black and white Americans in citizenship, the address scorned conservatives who would continue to deny blacks natural rights they had additionally purchased with their blood. Having declared that the African American's right to citizenship superseded that of naturalized immigrants, these representatives also asserted that black loyalty trumped Southern treason and reminded whites that the votes of Southern ex-slaves would further safeguard the "ark of Federal Liberty" for all Americans at the ballot box. Allegiance, not race, defined the idea of citizenship espoused at the convention. Moreover, the concept of citizenship offered by the 1864 National Convention included political and civil rights linked to a national status.[36]

Following the 1864 National Convention, the first meeting of the National Equal Rights League convened in Cleveland on October 19, 1865. In good Republican terms, the national league sought "to encourage sound morality, education, temperance, frugality, industry, and promote every thing that pertains to a well-ordered and dignified life" In addition to moral suasion, the league sought to use the "legal process" to gain recognition of black citizenship in theory and practice.[37]

An oration by Philadelphia delegate William D. Forten on the last day of the meeting placed the significance of black military service in even blunter terms than did the 1864 convention. Forten recounted that the Republican Party "sprang from the sympathy...[for the] agonizing sufferings" of American-born slaves. Seeing "the rapid approach of national death," Republicans "invited us, as citizens and sons, to its bosom," Forten continued, binding themselves "before God and the world, to emancipate, enfranchise, and crown us with all the rights of citizenship, and bid us welcome within the magic circle of common brotherhood." Forten reminded his audience, and the nation, that black men "cast up their sinewy bodies as a living rampart" against Confederate forces.[38]

Forten's speech rose in tone as he reached his point: the betrayal of promises to blacks, and the response by blacks that their needs be placed at the center of postwar debate. White Republicans "begged" blacks with false promises, Forten argued, and "like the supple and fierce tiger," blacks "rushed to the battle-field." Yet, Forten fumed, these soldiers had been "wooed...to [a] deadly embrace with the soft cadence of a lover's note," and subsequently "deserted by those whom we faithfully supported, and *insolently informed that this is a white man's country, though it required the strong arms of over 200,000 black men to save it,* and that the elective franchise is not now a practical question, and we must find homes in some Territory separate to ourselves, as white and black men cannot live together upon terms of equality." Forten sought defeat of the view that blacks can *"moisten the cold ground with their warm blood, in defence of the spangled banner, but there can be no abiding place for them here, as freemen and citizens."*[39]

Forten called for the league to fill the nation with "trumpet-toned, shrill, and loud, and stern" appeals, demanding justice for the "sacrifice" of the nation's "sable *defenders."* Forten's clarion call sounded radical but he assured his audience that blacks "ask nothing new," because "every right enjoyed by the pale-skinned and highly-favored class, is ours" through "birth, by taxation, and loyalty, and sealed…with our hearts' blood." Forten demanded that the martial sense of duty displayed by black soldiers on the battlefield manifest in this constitutional fight as well, and that blacks refuse to yield until final victory, with the "same unyielding pertinacity which led us to face the iron hail of death on a hundred battle-fields."[40]

State Conventions North and South

Forten did not need to remind his fellow blacks of the opportune moment for action, however, in light of the striking proliferation of statewide or regional conventions as early as 1865: blacks convened in Louisiana in January and May, in Pennsylvania in February and August, in Virginia in June and August, in Connecticut in June, in New Jersey in July, in Tennessee in August, in Indiana in September and October, in North Carolina and Michigan in September, in California and Missouri in October, in South Carolina in November, and in Arkansas and a regional New England conference in December. In Alabama, blacks assembled to call for federal protection in the face of church burnings and other racially motivated attacks, though Mississippi blacks could not do so because their fear of violence against them was so strong. Blacks in Louisiana, Massachusetts, Missouri, New Jersey, New York, North Carolina, Ohio, Pennsylvania, Tennessee, and probably other states as well founded state Equal Rights Leagues by July 1865.[41]

Statewide meetings and organizations allowed even more black spokesmen to participate in the energetic discourse regarding Reconstruction and their own citizenship status, and to address local concerns. Statewide conventions did not occur in a vacuum, but had a broad significance for the national civil rights movement. The records show that resolutions, debates, and speeches in state conventions percolated through their national counterparts. Moreover, these local conventions asserted persuasive arguments that helped secure ratification of the Civil War amendments and passage of statewide legislation.

Many of these local conventions petitioned state legislatures and engaged the white populations of their respective states during discussions about the Civil War amendments. Southern conventions especially highlighted conditions and inequality in the former slave states, helping give rise to congressional response pursuant to the Civil Rights Act of 1866, the Fourteenth and Fifteenth amendments, and the Enforcement acts of 1870–72.

Pennsylvania's convocations serve as a microcosm of the statewide convention movement in the North during the era of the Civil War and Reconstruction. On February 8–10, 1865, ninety-six black representatives gathered in Harrisburg to assert their expectations and found a state chapter of the Equal Rights League. By the afternoon of the first day, the Pennsylvanians secured a national flag for the proceedings and praised advances such as Bates's opinion on black citizenship, the enlistment of black troops, the ratification of the Thirteenth Amendment by several states, recognition by the United States of the countries of Haiti and Liberia, and the admission of black attorney John S. Rock to the Supreme Court's bar. Nonetheless, the delegates demanded the franchise, identifying it as a right they held as a result of birthright citizenship, and they called for "every native born colored citizen over the age of twenty-one" to have the same right to vote as "their white fellow citizens." Echoing the 1864 National Convention, blacks began defining their expectations of citizenship through what had been denied them thus far: access to educational institutions, the jury, and ballot boxes, and public places such as churches, theaters, and streetcars.[42]

The Pennsylvania convention, like other national and statewide conventions, served as an opportunity for blacks to gather and consider intraracial issues as well. For example, the Pennsylvania delegates resolved that black teachers should receive preference to teach black pupils, "not by reason of their complexion, but because they are better qualified by conventional circumstances outside of the school-house." Though hedging on the idea of racial preference, the resolution demonstrates a movement on the part of most delegates that blacks should educate themselves. On the other hand, after much debate, the representatives resolved that black proprietors should serve all customers, black and white, and not prefer whites for the purpose of trying to gain their business patronage. The delegates also called for members of the black community to embrace the Republican Party's free labor ideology and focus on self-improvement by obtaining real estate, pursuing education, and becoming involved in mercantile or mechanical pursuits. All of these goals linked with the definition of citizenship that blacks sought to make permanent in the law. Within months, thirty-five delegates of the state Equal Rights League again convened at Harrisburg on August 9–10, 1865, and by 1866, the state league had chartered chapters in fifty counties across the Keystone state.[43]

The state league energized blacks to promote their citizenship rights and elevate their condition by their own local efforts. The state league organized public rallies, circulated petitions, and sent letters to newspapers. By funding court cases and lobbying politicians, the state league also brought the issue of streetcar segregation to the foreground, until state legislators enacted a bill in 1867 prohibiting segregation or exclusion of blacks by railways. The state league encouraged local chapters to conduct "literary exercises, lectures, essays" to attract attendees, raise funds, and educate the black community, as well as to combat "rowdyism, intemperance, gambling, profanity and Sabbath breaking." Local chapters proved active: the 220 members of Philadelphia's Garnet League, for example, established schools, sponsored essay contests, and hired lawyers for wronged black soldiers.[44]

Even more dramatic, the aftermath of war generated a round of statewide conventions across the South, where blacks had formerly been unable to gather, much less weigh in on constitutional issues. Though mirroring many of the same themes as the conventions held in Northern states, the Southern state conventions more directly dealt with the impact of slavery, emancipation, and the more virulent white racism their delegates experienced. These conventions even more vividly contrasted black loyalty against the treason of white Confederates, even more stridently argued that choice of allegiance trumped race, and they articulated consistent definitions as to what they thought citizenship meant.

Unsatisfied with a legal freedom that rang hollow, Southern blacks particularly highlighted the inequalities of Black Codes passed across the South in the immediate aftermath of the Civil War. Black Codes gave African Americans some rights, but heavily restricted them at the same time, including labor provisions that governed contracts and wages, licensing at exorbitant fees for certain crafts or occupations, and the arrest of blacks who without "good cause" quit their employment. In many former slave states, legislation applicable to loosely defined vagrants (for instance, Alabama included in its definition of vagrant a "stubborn or refractory servant," or a "laborer or servant who loiters away his time") subjected unemployed blacks to heavy fines, and sometimes authorized their being hired out or forced to labor as part of a chain gang. Some states, such as Alabama, instituted apprenticeships, whereby a white "master or mistress" assumed responsibility for children whose parents were judged unable to support them. Preference was to be given to the "former owner of said minor," who had a duty to provide medical care, food, clothing, and education to his or her ward, but also the authority to inflict "moderate corporal chastisement." Florida authorized thirty-nine lashes to any black who possessed a bowie-knife, sword, or gun without a license obtained from the probate court on recommendation of two "respectable citizens of the county," or entered into any "religious or other public assembly of white persons," or any railroad car set aside for whites. South Carolina obliged blacks who migrated into that state to pay a bond or face expulsion, and required black shopkeepers to pay an annual license fee of a hundred dollars, and mechanics, artisans, and tradesmen to pay an annual license fee of ten dollars, all subject to satisfying a judge of their sufficient skill and moral character. The concepts embodied in the Black Codes diametrically opposed the idea of citizenship proffered by blacks and Republicans. Black Codes perpetuated the continuing economic dependence of blacks and made it excruciatingly difficult for them to pursue self-sufficiency and land ownership on a meaningful scale. Along with continued racist treatment by many white Southerners, the Black Codes demonstrated for blacks and Republicans what would occur in the absence of a federal arbiter of citizenship rights.[45]

Within two months of Appomattox, blacks in Norfolk, Virginia, occupied by the Union army in May 1862, acknowledged the Thirteenth Amendment under consideration by the states, but demanded more than just abolition in the name of the law. Instead, the delegates sought to define what freedom and citizenship entailed by calling for an end to race-based legislation and for blacks to be granted the right to education, legal recognition for their marriages, the ability to hold real estate, the freedom to move about on public ways, make and enforce contracts, testify in court, and have political representation.[46]

In another powerful display soon after Appomattox, sixty black Virginians gathered in Alexandria for a statewide convention in early August 1865. One speaker rejected white contentions about black laziness by noting that blacks had supported both themselves and their former owners with their labor. The delegates diplomatically (and likely, grudgingly) assured the American people that they felt "no ill-will or prejudice toward our former oppressors," but they also took note of the "chaos and disorganization" of the moment and called for equal protection by the law and the right to vote. The delegates rejoiced at the death of slavery and expressed a willingness to "forgive all those who have treated us as the beasts of the field" but also reminded whites, "while we forget all the innumerable wrongs which our people have endured for hundreds of years past, let our opposers remember that we are now free." One speaker noted that former slaveholders had tried to prevent some delegates from attending, while another "contended that there was no real prejudice between the white and black race of this State. We had slept together in childhood—we had toiled together in manhood, until our interests had become common."[47]

Another address, however, proved more vocal about the realities of blacks in Virginia. Declaring that they had been "denied the ownership of our bodies, or a right to our *wives,* our *children,* and the *products* of our *labor,*" and "compelled, under pain of death, to submit to injuries deeper and darker than the earth ever witnessed in the case of any other people," these black delegates rejected slavery and prejudice with a boiling hatred. "We have been forced to silence and inaction; to look on the infernal spectacle of our sons groaning under the lash; our daughters ravished, our wives *violated,* and our firesides desolated," the authors raged; even when "the nation in her hour of trial called her sable sons to arms, we gladly went and fought her battles, but were denied the pay accorded to others until public opinion demanded it." The Virginians demanded their equal rights as native-born American citizens, and in a subsequent resolution, explicitly rejected *Dred Scott* exclusion:

> We claim to be a part of the United States, as represented in the preamble to
> the Constitution of the United States. Also as a part of the people which the

Declaration of Independence declares to be free and equal, and we believe that the framers of the Constitution and originator and signers of the Declaration of Independence never contemplated otherwise than a perfect equality before the law to all the inhabitants of the Government.

Contrasting the loyalty shown by blacks, from hiding escaped Union prisoners to fighting as soldiers, with Confederate betrayal of the country, these blacks demanded more than the closing of the "auction block." Instead, these Virginians claimed the ballot as the only way to defend themselves, and they located their expectations at the heart of national debate.[48]

Blacks in other slave states followed the Virginians' lead. A convention in Nashville, Tennessee, in August 1865 emphasized the role of black veterans and included as delegates and honorary delegates veterans of the Second Light Artillery USCT and the Thirteenth, Fourteenth, Fifteenth, and Seventeenth USCI regiments. Openly recognizing their former life of "chains, lashes, bloodhounds and slave marts," black Missourians in October 1865 met to "demand" (a word used repeatedly in their address) suffrage based on the principles of the Founders as well as their nativity, labor, good character, and in contrast to Confederate treason, the nine thousand loyal black troops "enlisted under the banner of Missouri."[49]

The following month, black delegates gathered for six days in the bastion of secessionism and slave power: Charleston, South Carolina. Forty-five delegates urged the establishment of schools and declared that "we cherish on our hearts no hatred or malice toward those who have held our brethren as slaves, but we extend the right hand of fellowship to *all,* and make it our special aim to establish unity, peace and love amongst all men." The attendees proclaimed to the people of South Carolina that they "resolved to come forward, and, like MEN, speak and *act* for ourselves." Reminding all South Carolinians that blacks embraced the Declaration of Independence and the Constitution with the same pride felt by native-born white Americans, the delegates contrasted black loyalty to the United States with the treasonous sectionalism of Southern whites, and assured whites that they addressed them, "not as enemies, but as friends and fellow-countrymen, who desire to dwell among you in peace, and whose destinies are interwoven, and linked with those of the American people." Calling for "*even-handed Justice,*" the convention rebuffed Black Codes and the lack of suffrage that kept them from equality. Instead, the South Carolinian blacks announced a different vision that also served as a coherent theory of what citizenship meant: "We simply desire that we shall be recognized as men; that we have no obstructions placed in our way; that the same laws which govern white men shall direct colored men; that we have the right of trial by a jury of our peers, that schools be opened or established for our children; that we be permitted to acquire homesteads for ourselves and children; that we be dealt with as others, in equity and justice."[50]

In Little Rock, Arkansas, William H. Grey, who became the first black to address a national nominating convention when he seconded President Grant's renomination by the Republican Party in 1872, placed black calls for equal rights squarely within traditional American legal values. Grey claimed that "we are not asking that the people should try any new experiment in this matter; we do not ask them to go outside the great charter of American liberty—the Constitution and the Declaration of Independence—but rather that they should strictly conform to the letter and spirit of those time-honored documents."[51]

In Augusta, Georgia, black conventioneers wrote the state legislature in poignant terms. After recounting that they passed on the opportunity to arise in a slave insurrection during the Civil War and endured the "degradation of two hundred and forty-six years' enslavement," the delegates also pronounced their willingness "to bury the past, and forget the ills of slavery, and assume the attitude of a free people." At the same time, the black Georgians warned, "We shall expect your encouragement by the creation of such laws as are equitable and progressive." Gratified by a recent law permitting black testimony in court, the Georgian delegates reminded whites that "we trust you will not stop there." In exchange for their promise to loyally defend the United States against any foe, and to "maintain the honor of our State," Georgian blacks asked for schools and colleges for their children who aspired now to become "doctors, lawyers, ministers, army officers," and for suffrage, jury rights, self-control of labor through reasonable wages, equal treatment on railroads and public conveyances, and the end of antiblack prejudice and white vows of reprisal once the Union army and Freedmen's Bureau withdrew.[52]

The thread of military service connected all of these black conventions, whether national or local, Northern or Southern, and delegates pressed for some of the lessons learned in the armed forces, such as encounters with due process in general courts-martial, to be recognized by civil law. The new freedpeople demanded concrete rights that gave a broader definition to their freedom beyond emancipation in name only. Ex-slaves in the South particularly delighted in their opportunity to convene in gatherings after the war where formerly they could not, a powerful extension of their newfound freedom to move about, vote, speak, and do other things formerly prohibited to them when in bondage (including, for black maids in Mississippi, wearing buttons into the homes of their employers that portrayed General Ulysses Grant during the 1868 presidential campaign). Moreover, blacks used the convention movement, and organizations such as the Equal Rights League, to keep their claims and definition of citizenship at the forefront of complex Reconstruction era discussions.[53]

Blacks, Global Republicanism, and Human Rights

Strikingly, just as Irish Americans did, Reconstruction-era African Americans located their movement within a global context, breaking national boundaries to embrace the idea of a broader international drive for human rights and liberal democracy. Blacks from Illinois argued in 1866 that America could not cede the first place on the cutting edge of the tide of liberalism, while they identified all over the world the rights of sovereign citizen advancing toward triumph. When Californian blacks gathered in a convention in late October 1865, they not only addressed local concerns but also debated the Fenian movement. Subscribing to universal liberty, equating Ireland's oppression with that of American slaves, and resentful at Britain's actions during the Civil War, W. H. Yates went so far as to offer that "we should be willing to assist our Irish brethren in their struggle for National Independence; and 40,000 colored troops could be raised to butt the horns off the hypocritical English bull." The Reverend J. H. Hubbard countered Yates, scorning Ireland as "the most deceitful of all nations" and controlled by the Roman Catholic Church, but another delegate responded that it was Democratic politicians who had prejudiced Irish Americans against blacks. Robert H. Small declared that "one of the proudest things a black man could do would be to assist with forty thousand men, or more, in writing Emmett's epitaph." Another delegate suggested a more broadly worded resolution, noting that "the Chinese and Indians in our very midst stand in need of our sympathy and encouragement." The black Californians eventually adopted a resolution stating that they "sympathized with the oppressed of all nations," lamented the failures of the Polish and Hungarian revolts, and declared that "notwithstanding the opposition we receive from Irish immigrants in America, whose prejudices are excited against us by the misnamed Democratic Party, every effort to rid Ireland of English bondage, and establish Irish independence meets our cordial approbation."[54]

This confrontation of African American idealism with the realities of Irish American racism created a complicated and unexpected intersection in the 1860s. African American calls for integration into political life at times echoed nativist sentiments, just as Irish Americans sometimes employed racist rhetoric in advancing their own points. Entering the juncture of birthright and naturalized citizenship, "You allow the foreigner to come here and enjoy the privileges of a free citizen after the short residence of five years," complained the *Christian Recorder* in mid-1865,

> without even inquiring into his previous character. He may be a banished convict from the country which gave him birth, it matters not; the magnanimity of our republican institutions gives him free access to the best society, which he not infrequently poisons with his monarchical heresies, while the respectable colored man, born and reared under the influence of freedom, and instilled with the principles of civil and religious liberty from the cradle up, is cut off from the rights he was born to inherit, by the same magnanimous laws which cry "welcome" to every illustrious foreigner who may set foot on our shores.[55]

On the other hand, black leaders found the ideal of Irish liberation appealing, even where they honored British abolitionism which helped energize that movement in this country. In 1866, John Mercer Langston linked "that tendency towards an enlarged freedom which distinguishes our age; which in England bears the name of Reform; in Ireland the title of Fenianism; in Europe the name of Progress; and in our Government the name of Radicalism; impresses us with the firm conviction that our claims to universal suffrage will, with no long delay, be...decided by the rule of pure and speedy justice." Moreover, blacks recalled abolitionism in Ireland as embodied by Irish nationalist Daniel O'Connell, who attacked slavery and organized a petition signed by thousands of Irish asking their brethren in America to support the abolitionist cause. Strikingly, J. F. Quarles, speaking in 1871 to a convention of Southern blacks, equated the cause of Irish liberation with that of the Union:

> On the one hand were arrayed the friends of human liberty and human progress; on the other were marshaled all the hosts of despotism and caste. The principles involved were the same as those which produced the English revolution of 1688; the same for which the patriots of '76 so earnestly contended, in the struggle between the colonies and the mother country; the same for which Ireland, that deeply wronged, but unconquerable people, struggles to-day.[56]

The *Christian Recorder* proved more equivocal toward Fenianism. In mid-1866, the black newspaper printed an article that jokingly began: a man asked "if we had done any thing for the Fenians" and learned "that we had bought a *half peck* of Irish potatoes the day before." Yet the newspaper at the same time reported (with surprise) that a deputation of black Philadelphians offered to the Fenians a hundred veteran troops to march immediately to the Canadian border. While vowing that "colored Fenianism will be as scarce as apple trees in the desert of Sahara," and scorning the invasion of Canada as "wicked and absurd," the article also stated, "We had no justification to offer for the tyranny of the English Government in Ireland, and can fully appreciate their desire for riddance of its merciless exactions." In another editorial, the newspaper even foreshadowed efforts of the Irish National Land League by calling generally for "more equal distribution of property" and asking "if Irish character seems more brittle and less dignified, more open to temptation and less elevated in moral tone, than that of England, are we not in justice compelled to trace back the cause...to the crime of England in wresting from the people their legitimate right to the Irish soil?"[57]

By early 1868, the *Christian Recorder* printed one article which used Fenian statements that the Civil War served as training for future fighters of Irish liberation to question the meaning of Irish American service for the Union. The paper argued that Irish Americans acted only out of self-interest and relied on traditionally nativist language to lament that the "unquestioning submission to the command of the Priest," and the "violence of Irish Catholic bigotry" seen in the United States would occur in Ireland should the Fenians triumph. Yet the same paper within two months reprinted an article announcing, "Hope for Ireland, it seems, is dawning at last," after passage of legislation disestablishing the Anglican Church of Ireland, which all Irish, regardless of their faith, had to support with their taxes. "With all our heart," the article offered, "we extend to the Irish people—in whom beats as noble a spirit as in any other people under the sun—the hand of warm congratulation in view of this beginning of still better and grander things to come."[58]

For Frederick Douglass, the tension between English and Irish mirrored the racial conflict in the United States. Douglass could, in 1861, announce his hope that the United States would soon take its place "side by side with noble old England" in terms of emancipation, but in 1871, also describe English governance of Ireland as "tyrannical and oppressive." In 1872, Douglass went so far as to declare himself, "something of an Irishman as well as a Negro," linking radical thought in both populations. Yet Douglass also resented Irish American racism, describing members of that community as "warm-hearted, generous, and sympathizing with the oppressed everywhere when they stand on their own green island" but taught to "hate and despise" blacks on arriving in America. Douglass sometimes characterized Irish Americans in nativist terms, protesting the treatment of "native born colored Americans" compared to Irish "foreigners swarming in your midst, those who *fill* your jails, and almhouses *as well as build them.*"[59]

In January 1865, Douglass juxtaposed his equation of Irish and black degradation with scorn for Irish American behavior. Douglass declared that "wherever men oppress their fellows...they will endeavor to find the needed apology for such enslavement and oppression in the character of the people oppressed and enslaved," so that "when England wants to set the heel of her power more firmly in the quivering heart of old Ireland, the Celts are 'an inferior race.' So, too, the negro, when he is to be robbed of any right which is justly his, is 'an inferior man.'" Yet lines later, Douglass noted that if the black man could fight in the army and pay taxes, "he knows enough to vote. If he knows as much when he is sober as an Irishman knows when drunk, he knows enough to vote, on good American principles."[60]

In late 1869, speaking about America's "composite nationality," Douglass scorned anti-Chinese violence in California, as did the *Christian Recorder* earlier that year. Douglass lamented that "already have our Celtic brothers, never slow to execute the behests of popular prejudice against the weak and defenceless, recognized in the heads of these people, fit targets for their shil[l]alahs." Douglass instead dreamed of an egalitarian America open to all, just as Wendell Phillips proclaimed to his audience of Bostonians in April 1861, and Michael Corcoran wrote about in *The Captivity of General Corcoran,* published in 1865. "We should welcome to our ample continent all nations," Douglass pronounced, "kindreds, tongues and peoples, and as fast as they learn our language and comprehend the duties of citizenship, we should incorporate them into the American body politic. The outspread wings of the American eagle are broad enough to shelter all who are likely to come." Douglass credited "the arm of the negro and the muscle of the Irishman" as generating and spreading "much of the wealth, leisure, culture, refinement and civilization of the country" across the land, and asserted that without them, "English civilization" would have "still lingered this side of the Alleghenies, and the wolf still be howling on their summits." Declaring that "man is man the world over," Douglass professed his wish that "we shall spread the network of our science and our civilization over all who seek their shelter, whether from Asia, Africa, or the Isles of the Sea. We shall mould them all, each after his kind, into Americans; Indian and Celt, negro and Saxon, Latin and Teuton, Mongolian and Caucasian, Jew and gentile, all shall here bow to the same law, speak the same language, support the same government, enjoy the same liberty, vibrate with the same national enthusiasm, and seek the same national ends."[61]

Douglass thus linked Ireland to oppressed nations such as Poland and Hungary, and noted how "Ireland keeps us in chronic tears by her wail from across the sea." Douglass embodied the duality of black thought about Irish Americans during the postwar era: hostility toward them based on their behavior and prejudice, resentment at avenues open to them that remained closed to blacks, but also empathy for Ireland and genuine hope for its liberation as part of a global dawn of freedom that both Irish Americans and African Americans welcomed.[62]

Such moments of fraternity show that not all African Americans and Irish Americans expressed insurmountable hostility between them, and even pointed to a brief hope that racial tensions between the two groups would dissipate in the changed climate after the war. On the afternoon of April 4, 1865, for example, a public meeting convened in Boston's Faneuil Hall to celebrate the fall of Richmond included blacks and Irish-born alongside white native-born Bostonians. Two black men sang a spiritual, followed by speeches from Irish-born Colonel Patrick R. Guiney, Frederick Douglass, and Massachusetts's senator Henry Wilson and ex-senator Robert C. Winthrop. In 1875, a joint ceremony by Irish Americans and blacks in St. Paul, Minnesota, commemorated the birth of Daniel O'Connell, and blacks in Baltimore planned to participate in that city's St. Patrick's Day celebration. Even Boston's Irish American newspaper, the *Pilot,* showed a little more sympathy for blacks in the aftermath of the Civil War. Editor John Boyle O'Reilly, fervently interested in the cause of Irish nationalism and Catholicism but also in all the downtrodden, helped fuel this brief but hopeful shift.[63]

Citizenship Defined

Congress took note of the arguments that came out of black conventions, and Massachusetts senator Charles Sumner and others routinely presented their petitions for consideration. On December 21, 1865, Sumner presented a memorial from the August 1865 Tennessee convention, before Republican senator Jacob Howard presented a petition of South Carolina's blacks calling for protection of their civil rights in light of "their unquestioned loyalty, exhibited by them alike as bond or free, as soldier or laborer, in the Union lines under the protection of the Government, or within the rebel lines under the domination of the rebellion." Similarly, on January 5, 1866, Sumner presented a petition from a convention of Alabaman blacks who assembled in Mobile, "represent-ing four hundred and thirty-six thousand nine hundred and thirty citizens of the United States," and called for federal protection in the face of church burn-ings and violence against them, along with a petition from Mississippi blacks who could not meet in convention due to the fear of violence against them. At the same time he highlighted the explosive situation in the Deep South, Sumner submitted petitions from the citizens of Philadelphia and half a dozen other Pennsylvania towns calling for implementation of the Constitution's guarantee to every state of a republican form of government.[64]

Reports issued by black conventions about the racial inequities of state legislation and conditions in the South, as well as their demand for definition of what rights they enjoyed as citizens, helped bring about passage of the Civil Rights Act of 1866. Republicans in Congress recognized that deferring to the states to define the rights and privileges of citizenship, as was done before the war, would render that title hollow for millions of blacks. The act mandated, in harmony with the Republican Party's free labor ideology, that "all persons born in the United States and not subject to any foreign power, excluding Indi-ans not taxed, are…citizens of the United States," and that

> citizens, of every race and color…shall have the same right, in every State and Territory in the United States, to make and enforce contracts, to sue, be parties, and give evidence, to inherit, purchase, lease, sell, hold, and convey real and per-sonal property, and to full and equal benefit of all laws and proceedings for the security of person and property, as is enjoyed by white citizens, and shall be sub-ject to like punishment, pains, and penalties, and to none other, any law, statute, ordinance, regulation, or custom, to the contrary notwithstanding.[65]

Congress went beyond simply prohibiting a reconstitution of slavery under a different name. The act provided a definition of national citizenship rights in the law for the first time, including economic rights of contract and property, as well as access to court enforcement so as to ensure practical enjoyment of these rights. Alongside the activities of the Freedmen's Bureau, created in March 1865, and with agents who, among other things, worked to ensure fair and consensual contracts between black laborers and white landowners in the South, the Civil Rights Act of 1866 sought to provide blacks, and all Americans, with access to the growing capitalist economy and the means for self-sufficiency as a right of citizenship. Moreover the Civil Rights Act of 1866 altered the practice of fed-eralism by recognizing the federal government's responsibility to protect these rights. Federal, not state, courts had jurisdiction over offences under the bill.[66]

On January 5, 1866, Senator Lyman Trumbull of Illinois, chair of the Sen-ate Judiciary Committee, introduced what would become the Civil Rights Act of 1866. During debate, Trumbull noted that the act meant "to give effect to [the Thirteenth Amendment] and secure to all persons within the United States practical freedom." Referencing Black Codes that discriminated against Af-rican Americans, "deny them certain rights, subject them to severe penalties, and still impose upon them the very restrictions which were imposed upon them in consequence of the existence of slavery," Trumbull emphasized that "there is very little importance in the general declaration of abstract truths and principles"—the freedom of the slaves and the principles of the Declaration of Independence—"unless they can be carried into effect." Revealing how citizenship expanded gradually to incorporate both civil and political rights during the 1860s, Trumbull assured his fellow senators that this act concerned itself only with civil rights, and not political ones.[67]

Some opponents challenged the act on the grounds that it subverted federalism: it applied nationwide, went beyond protection for freedpeople alone, and truncated the traditional view that state law created citizenship rights. "Can any man believe that the founders of this Republic...would have ever entered into the Union," asked Democrat senator Eli Saulsbury of Delaware, "if they had supposed that in the short term of eighty years their children would be subjected to the absolute control and the omnipotent will of the Federal Congress?" Saulsbury further queried, "What becomes of the powers of the States? What becomes of the rights of the States? Sir, they have not even the privilege of administering their criminal laws; they have not the privilege of saying who shall give evidence and who shall not in their own courts; they have not the privilege of saying who shall hold property and who shall not." Kentucky Senator Garrett Davis bluntly summed up a racial objection to the act: "This is a white man's Government," and "the negro is not a citizen here" unless made so by force.[68]

On the other hand, Republican senator Jacob Howard of Michigan asserted that the act did not invade the "legitimate rights of the States," but "simply gives to persons who are of different races or colors the same civil rights." Moreover, Howard trusted that, having employed "nearly two hundred thousand" blacks "in the prosecution of our just and righteous war," the nation could not "now be found so recreant to duty, so wanting in simple justice, as to turn our backs upon the race and say to them, 'We set you free, but beyond this we give you no protection; we allow you again to be reduced to slavery by your old masters, because it is the right of the State which has enslaved you for two hundred years thus to do.'" In response to Senator Davis's admonition that "the power to change the Constitution is a power simply to amend; it is not a power to revolutionize...it is not a power to change our form of Government," Republican senator Lot Morrill of Maine asked, "Are we not in the midst of a civil and political revolution which has changed the fundamental principles of our Government in some respects? Sir, is it no revolution that you have changed the entire system of servitude in this country?" According to Morrill, the changes comprised a "revolution grander and sublimer in its consequences than the world has witnessed hitherto." Trumbull reminded the Senate that the act applied to whites as well as blacks, and asked what could be so repugnant about legislation providing that all people shall have equal rights.[69]

Toward the end of the debates in the Senate, Massachusetts Republican Henry Wilson provided an eloquent summation on February 2, 1866, reminding his colleagues that at least six of the former Confederate states "passed laws wholly incompatible with the freedom of these freedmen," laws "as iniquitous as the old slave codes." Wilson proclaimed to the Senate that, by the Thirteenth Amendment, and

> by the will of the nation freedom and free institutions for all, chains and fetters for none, are forever incorporated in the fundamental law of regenerated and united America. Slave codes and auction blocks, chains and fetters and bloodhounds are things of the past, and the chattel stands forth a man with the rights and the powers of the freemen. For the better security of these new-born civil rights we are now about to pass the greatest and the grandest act in this series of acts that have emancipated a race and disenthralled a nation.

Later that day, the Senate approved the act by a vote of 33 to 12, with 5 not voting; the House followed suit by a vote of 111 to 38, with 34 not voting, on March 13, 1866.[70]

President Johnson vetoed the act on March 27, 1866, because, in his opinion, the freedpeople were not fit for citizenship, and the legislation inappropriately revised the relationship between the federal and state governments by now allowing the federal government to interfere with a state's ability to discriminate between the races as its government saw fit. On April 9, 1866, exactly a year after Lee's surrender at Appomattox, the House of Representatives joined the Senate's vote a few days earlier to overturn Johnson's veto. The first national civil rights legislation in American history became law, and at long last, national citizenship began to have practical meaning.[71]

In the context of legislative uncertainty—a future Congress could repeal the act, for example, especially where Democrats had mounted a vigorous challenge against it—Republicans sought a further, more permanent safeguard for the new, national definition of citizenship. On June 13, 1866, Congress passed and sent to the states for ratification the Fourteenth Amendment. The amendment, declared ratified by the nation on July 28, 1868, defined in the law that "all persons born or naturalized in the United States...are citizens of the United States and of the State wherein they reside," without distinction as to color or race. The Fourteenth Amendment further mandated that "no State shall make or enforce any law which shall abridge the privileges or immunities of citizens of the United States; nor shall any State deprive any person of life, liberty, or property, without due process of law; nor deny to any person within its jurisdiction the equal protection of the laws."

Calling for Political Rights

Although welcoming the passage of the Civil Rights Act of 1866 and the proposed Fourteenth Amendment sent to the states, blacks continued to exert pressure for their political rights. This objective became especially urgent in light of the race-based opposition articulated by leaders such as Senator Davis and President Johnson, and the specter of increasing violence against freed-people by white supremacists.

African Americans asserted both idealistic and pragmatic arguments to support this call, and their contentions gradually helped persuade Republicans to support the idea of giving black men the vote. Frederick Douglass forcefully argued as early as December 1863 that "when this rebellion shall have been put down, when the arms shall have fallen from the guilty hands of traitors, you will need the friendship of the slaves of the South." Douglass foresaw that enfranchised blacks would be "your best protector against the traitors and the descendants of those traitors, who will inherit the hate, the bitter revenge which will crystallize all over the South, and seek to circumvent the Government that they could not throw off." As Douglass, and subsequent black conventions, argued, "You will need the black man there, as a watchman and patrol; and you may need him as a soldier. You may need him to uphold in peace, as he is now upholding in war, the star-spangled banner."[72]

In autumn 1866, four black men thus wrote "to the People of the United States" that the black vote would not only "lift us from the lap of hate and scorn" and "place us on the footing of full citizenship, where we ought to be, and where God intended men should be," but also safeguard the Union victory. "We will act as we did when we became Soldiers in the Army of the Republic," the four men assured the country in a letter published in the *Christian Recorder*. "Give us the ballot and the country is safe." The authors identified depriving blacks of equal political rights as not only an immoral breach of their natural rights and manhood but also a betrayal of the Constitution, which jeopardized the safety of the Union at a time when it was reintegrating millions of ex-Confederates. Instead, they argued, blacks had proved their allegiance and thus had a higher claim to the franchise than former Rebels who tried to destroy the Union. The letter stemmed from a resolution, passed at a convention of the Colored Soldiers and Sailors League in October 1866, to convene another national meeting of black veterans in Philadelphia on January 8, 1867, to demand the vote. The day chosen for the meeting held great symbolism: the anniversary of the Battle of New Orleans during the War of 1812, in which blacks played a prominent part, highlighted the length of African American loyalty and contribution to the United States. Through such meetings and activities, black veterans stood as the vanguard of the effort to gain equal political rights as part of the definition of American citizenship.[73]

Black citations of their loyalty, in counterpoint to Southern white treason, gradually resonated with white Republicans, especially after Lincoln's assassination. By the fall of 1865, Ohio Republican (and formerly, unofficial advisor to Lincoln) William M. Dickson identified black loyalty to the Union as *the* decisive factor for the federal victory. "While I am not one of those who place the bravery of the negro soldiers above that of the white," Dickson assured, "it is a fact which will hardly be denied, that but for the opposition of the entire negro population to the rebel cause, we could scarcely have succeeded."

Dickson wished to see blacks "continue this good work" because "if [the president] may confide reconstruction to the loyal whites, he may also to the loyal blacks." Dickson echoed African American conventions in his support of granting blacks the ballot:

> The protection of the black man himself requires it; gratitude for his devoted loyalty requires it; the protection of our civilization from the influence of a degraded and barbarous element requires it; the protection of ourselves from the insidious rebel ballot requires it; the speedy restoration of the rebel states to their proper relation to the General Government requires it; the fundamental principles of our Government require it; the Golden Rule of our most holy religion commanding us to do unto others as we would that they should do unto us, requires it.

Massachusetts Republican George B. Loring similarly claimed that "the government which can make soldiers of its people, should also make citizens, and of citizens, voters." For Loring, "whatever means are required to secure to the American citizen everywhere, the privileges of the church, the school house, the ballot box and jury box, should become a part of the machinery of reconstruction," and he vowed to reopen the Civil War if need be to accomplish these goals.[74]

Blacks thus shrewdly connected their loyalty to ongoing debates about suffrage and the success of the Republican agenda at a time when determinations on these issues had not yet been made. Immediately after the war, Massachusetts Republican congressman George S. Boutwell took up the point articulated by African Americans, recognizing that "the black man, despised, down-trodden, with no reason to cheer or bless the flag of the Republic...has proved true to the country." Boutwell asked, *Can it be* in the heart of any man of the twenty million inhabitants in the North, with an ingratitude unexampled save in the instance of Judas Iscariot, now to consign these people, their race, and their posterity to the tender mercies of the men who instituted Libby Prison and Andersonville...and finally closed their career of systematic and organized crime by the assassination of the President of the Republic?" Boutwell could think of "no excuse that we can offer to mankind in the coming ages, if, after having accepted the services and the blood of these men in defence of the flag, of liberty and of the Union, we turn and conspire with these their ancient oppressors and trample our faithful allies in the dust." Yet, at the same time, Boutwell asked for suffrage for blacks not "because they are competent to judge of questions of public policy, but...because they are in favor of this government, and the white people of the South are against it." Blending idealism and pragmatism, Boutwell argued, "I am in favor of allowing him to vote, without going into any inquiry whether he can read and write, because his power at the ballot-box is now essential to us, just exactly as his power in the field with the bayonet was essential to us during the war."[75]

Republican Pennsylvania congressman William D. Kelley echoed a black argument that failing to reorder society so as to reflect racial equality comprised a continuation of treason and jeopardized the rights of all. Kelley urged inclusion for blacks not only out of self-interest for white northerners ("Make him secure, and your own rights can never be infringed") but because of the contrast between Confederate treason and black loyalty. As many Republicans of both races sought a genuine definition to freedom, Kelley warned that "you may change the name without changing the thing," and he argued that leaving millions of blacks without rights to testify, make contracts, or pursue education permitted the anti-republican and treasonous machinations of the slave power to survive. Only in eliminating race prejudice, Kelley further argued, could America "harmonize the practical workings of our institutions and the sublime truths that underlie them." Yet Kelley also cast the choice as one between "the poor, ignorant masses who, during the war, have been your friends" or taking the "brothers and friends and associates of John C. Breckinridge and Jefferson Davis as your rulers."[76]

The impact of black arguments about obtaining the vote shows how idealism and pragmatism converged to effect legal change during the 1860s. Blacks used their military service as the cornerstone of their demands for political and civil rights, and to thrust these claims into the center of Reconstruction debate, but they also shrewdly connected their loyalty to deliberations over suffrage, the fate of the Union, and the success of the Republican agenda at a time when even most Republicans remained unenthusiastic at best about giving the vote to the black man nationwide. African Americans persuaded Republicans that blacks could help support their agenda for reconstituting the country, just as blacks aided the Union's military victory. This point became especially important after emancipation nullified a clause in the Constitution under which slaves counted as three-fifths of a person for the purpose of apportioning congressional representation and would permit the South to send even more representatives to Congress than before the war.[77]

Pursuant to three Reconstruction acts passed by Congress in 1867, blacks not only gained the vote in the former Confederate states but, in a stunning moment, began to attend state constitutional conventions as delegates and hold important elected federal, state, and local offices in those states as well. Of the slightly more than a thousand delegates who attended state constitutional conventions held in the South between 1867 and 1869, 268 were black. During Reconstruction, in addition to local offices, 682 black men served as representatives and 112 as senators in their state legislatures, six served as lieutenant governor, and one, P. B. S. Pinchback, briefly served in December 1872 and January 1873 as Louisiana's acting governor. Attorney Jonathan J. Wright served as a justice on South Carolina's Supreme Court until he resigned his seat in 1877, facing a threat of impeachment by the Democratic state legislature on unsubstantiated corruption charges. Fourteen blacks served as U.S. congressman and two, Blanche K. Bruce and Hiram Revels, represented Mississippi in the Senate. Blacks represented the United States abroad for the first time in history, with Don Carlos Bassett as ambassador to Haiti (1869–77) and James M. Turner as ambassador to Liberia (1871–78).[78]

Military service launched some blacks into politics. For example, Josiah T. Walls had been a Virginia slave before his capture by Union forces. After receiving some education and enlisting in the Third USCI, Walls mustered out in Florida with the rank of sergeant, and he represented that state in Congress from 1871 to 1873. On the whole, black veterans were underrepresented as Reconstruction officeholders: they comprised 16 percent of America's adult black male population at the war's conclusion but made up less than a tenth of 1,510 documented black officeholders between 1867 and 1877. Historian Donald Shaffer found that nearly 80 percent of veteran officeholders (and 60 percent of black lawmakers overall) served in Louisiana, Mississippi, and both Carolinas. Shaffer further noted that relatively few black veterans hailed from Florida, Georgia, Virginia, and Alabama, and that many black veterans came from Border or Northern states where the opportunity for postwar office remained largely unavailable.[79]

Many Northerners, however, including Republicans, initially showed apathy or opposition to allowing blacks to vote in their own states. Accordingly, African American conventions and organizations maintained the black call, petitioning and agitating for the vote nationwide. Conditions for success became more favorable when, in 1868, a resurgent Democratic Party jolted Republicans to the realities earlier raised by Frederick Douglass when it took both houses of the New York, New Jersey, and Ohio legislatures, and the governorships of Connecticut, Maine, and California. In that year's presidential election, Republican candidate Ulysses S. Grant won against Democrat Horatio Seymour by only slightly more than 300,000 votes out of a total of 5.7 million votes cast, with an electoral vote of 214 to 80 (of the former Confederate states, Texas, Mississippi, and Virginia cast no electoral votes, Louisiana and Georgia went to Seymour, and Grant carried Arkansas, Alabama, Florida, Tennessee, North Carolina, and South Carolina). Half a million black Republican votes in the South, cast pursuant to the Reconstruction acts of 1867, proved decisive to Grant's winning the popular vote.[80]

Persistent black pressure, coupled with political realities, thus helped set the climate for ratification of the Fifteenth Amendment. Blacks continued to demand suffrage and other measures so as to make reality comport with the Thirteenth and Fourteenth Amendment rights their actions had also helped to secure. Another National Convention of Colored Men met in Washington, D.C., on January 13, 1869, in the context of the recently adopted Fourteenth Amendment. Delegates from twenty-one states, North and South, as well as the District of Columbia, focused on divergences between the ideals of the Fourteenth Amendment and its practical application. A letter read from Bishop D. A. Payne of Ohio emphasized an urgent need for blacks to address federal and state legislatures about increasing violence against them in the South. In all but five eastern states and two western states, Payne cautioned, "the heel of the oppressor is still upon the neck of the colored American."[81]

From this convention, nine black delegates met with the House of Representatives Judiciary Committee on February 16, 1869. After some flattery of the committee members, Pennsylvanian Isaiah C. Weir lectured the committee on constitutional doctrine in a lengthy speech (it seems he enjoyed his chance to address the committee) that argued the superiority of the Constitution over state law and urged the necessity of granting suffrage to blacks. Weir pointed to the naturalization debate discussed in the next chapter and asked, "Is it not folly to talk about protecting our naturalized citizens in their rights abroad, by war, if needs be, with one of the greatest powers of the earth, while the smallest State at home can strip them of all their rights?" After attacking the power of the states to impact suffrage and other citizenship rights, Weir argued that regulating who could vote by color jeopardized property rights, the right to personal liberty, and the right to life itself.[82]

Weir then adopted a more radical tone, shaking the argument that uneducated blacks were not fit for the franchise by observing that whites "used it so stupidly" that they brought about a massive Civil War. The "fidelity and splendid soldiership" of "black heroes," Weir claimed, "entitled themselves not only to liberty, but to citizenship," and he identified as "unworthy to participate" in national affairs those Democrats or conservative Republicans who would deny blacks their rights. Suffrage was no more a bestowal, according to Weir, than allowing blacks to "eat our own victuals, wear our own clothes, go to market with our own money, pay our own debts," and he declared that the "community that releases to us our rights…long withheld from us…has no right to demand our gratitude." The right to vote, Weir instructed the committee, "is ours because it is yours, and for the same reason that it is yours."[83]

In the end, several factors, many of them underpinned by black military service and illuminated by black conventions, converged to establish the conditions for the Fifteenth Amendment. Just as African American military service helped fuel the push for the Thirteenth and Fourteenth amendments, continued black pressure helped bring about the Fifteenth Amendment as well. Many Republicans came to embrace a genuine moral commitment to blacks, desired to formalize black status (at the urging of African Americans), and wished to resolve the paradox whereby the black suffrage imposed in the South by the Reconstruction acts of 1867 remained optional in the North (by 1868, blacks could not vote in eleven of twenty-one Northern states and five Border states). As their concern mounted over the Democratic Party's postwar resurgence, Republicans coupled these ideological impulses with the need to consolidate their agenda after the Union victory won, in part, by black participation. Black agitation, Republican moral commitment to civil rights enforcement, and the idea that citizens stood entitled to protection in exchange for their service, themes all buttressed by the black military experience, converged with Republican pragmatism at a moment when idealism and expediency overcame racism.[84]

Many Americans hailed the Fifteenth Amendment's ratification in the spring of 1870 as the end of the "black question." Blacks celebrated across the land, from a gathering of three thousand in Boston that included veterans of the Fifty-fourth and Fifty-fifth Massachusetts regiments to one in Detroit where blacks carried likenesses of Lincoln, Grant, and John Brown and sang about voting. Wendell Phillips's American Anti-Slavery Society disbanded ten days after ratification of the Fifteenth Amendment, and Frederick Douglass jubilantly announced, "Never was revolution more complete," creating "a new world" where "the black man is free, the black man is a citizen, the black man is enfranchised...no more a despised and hated creature, but a man, and, what is more a man among men." According to Douglass, blacks now stood "upon an equal footing with all other men, and that the glory or shame of our future is to be wholly our own," with access to the means of self-sufficiency in a new country where "character, not color, is to be the criterion," and blacks had the opportunity to rise or fall, succeed or fail, as their own actions and choices dictated.[85]

Counterrevolution in the South

On the other hand, states remained free to define voting qualifications so long as they avoided exclusion based on race, color, or previous condition of slavery, leaving open their use of poll taxes and literacy tests. Such provisions seemed race-neutral on their face but had a disparate impact in excluding blacks. Even more troubling was the rise of a vicious racist counterrevolution, organized and implemented from the highest to the local levels across the South, with apologists in the North, which sought to tamp out blacks' new enjoyment of citizenship rights and intimidate white Republican governments. In opposition to legislation and constitutional amendments enshrining the Union victory and blacks' rights in law, the Ku Klux Klan operated across the South by 1868 to preserve white dominance and the political and economic subordination of blacks. Through the murder and beatings of black students and those involved in politics, attacks on whites seeking to assist the freedpeople, and the burning of black churches, schools, and homes, Southern white racists spread a wave of intimidation and terror through the South by the time black troops had demobilized. A night attack on the family of Jackson and Jane Surratt in South Carolina involved Klansmen thugs ordering everyone out of their house, snatching an infant from his mother's arms, and having everyone lie down, nearly naked. Jackson escaped but his wife and children suffered a lashing; Jane staggered away in such bad shape she could not hold her son to suckle him, and a daughter whipped in the assault exhibited signs of post-traumatic stress. On July 30, 1868, three days after the Tennessee state legislature convened an emergency session to deal with the Klan, the Klan attacked ex-slave and army veteran Richard Moore by administering 175 lashes with a buckled whip. Highlighting the tension that existed between Moore's roles as Union veteran and citizen versus conceptions that he was a disrespectful black man, a Republican paper in Cincinnati reported that Moore's offense was his Union military service, vocal opposition to white racism, and supposed defamation of a white woman, while a local paper announced that Moore was a bad slave. Ten percent of black delegates to state constitutional conventions in the

South in 1867–68 became victims of racist violence, and seven of them were murdered.[86]

In contrast to focus on political rights, an early 1871 state convention of black Tennesseans petitioned Congress about Klan violence and asked assistance to gain property, access to education, fair treatment of laborers, and an end to de facto slavery and poll taxes. An October 1871 Southern States Convention of Colored Men met in the House chamber in Columbia, South Carolina, to contend literally with matters of life and death. Delegates from Alabama, Arkansas, Florida, Georgia, Louisiana, Maryland, Mississippi, North Carolina, South Carolina, Tennessee, Texas, and the District of Columbia demanded an end to the persistent injustice of state legislation against them, and Southern white attempts to circumvent the Union's military victory and the Civil War amendments through the use of vicious extralegal secret organizations such as the Klan. J. H. Burch of Baton Rouge called for legal doctrine and real life practice to converge: "If we look all over the Southern States, we will find the highways and the byways marked by the bleaching bones of white and colored men, who have fought, bled and died that colored men might assume, even in South Carolina, the rights and privileges of manhood. We stand here in the hall of the House of Representatives of South Carolina, a body of colored men discussing American politics, civil rights, education and labor. Let me ask those gentlemen who now look me in the face, how long is it since they dared walk the streets without a pass after the clock struck nine at night?" J. F. Quarles of Georgia similarly called for strict, swift enforcement of laws to quash extralegal violence, ensure just remuneration to laborers, allow exercise of a truly free ballot, secure a commitment to educational advancement, provide equality of rights to all citizens without any distinction, and reject not only state discrimination but, anticipating the Civil Rights Act of 1875, also prejudice by private individuals on street cars, hotels, and theaters.[87]

Congress responded to this resurgence of open warfare in parts of the South with five Enforcement acts passed between 1870 and 1872, which recognized that without security of person, other citizenship rights became meaningless because they could not be enjoyed in practice. The first Enforcement Act of May 31, 1870, reiterated that American citizens could vote without regard to race, color, or previous slavery, provided enforcement provisions to secure this Fifteenth Amendment right, and mandated that the civil rights secured by prior legislation such as the Civil Rights Act of 1866 applied to everyone, including aliens. Subsequent Enforcement acts emphasized the link between civil and political rights, and mandated an increasingly nationalized system of elections, complete with federal supervision. The Enforcement acts highlight a debate within the Republican Party on the need to protect black rights versus conservative constitutional tenets; the expansion of the federal government to secure enforcement of federal laws versus the danger of centralization and damage to federalism; and protection of black rights versus the possibility that doing so would injure the rights of whites. The Enforcement acts imposed criminal penalties against those who tried to interfere with black voting rights and sought to suppress organizations such as the Ku Klux Klan, including by presidential suspension of the writ of habeas corpus and use of federal troops.[88]

The Department of Justice, established in 1870, punished civil rights violations in the South in the early part of that decade. Pursuant to the Enforcement acts and other civil rights legislation, hundreds of members of white supremacist groups faced prosecution, conviction, and imprisonment. While this again vindicated black rights and equal enjoyment of equal citizenship rights before the law, it also illuminated in no uncertain terms that powerful forces of resistance would challenge the developments of the Civil War era, and that these changes would not go untested. If contingency and choice of action led to the advancement of rights in the Civil War era, they also allowed for their erosion for African Americans.[89]

Moreover, Congress passed in early 1875 an act signed by President Grant that desegregated public accommodations and outlawed racial discrimination in inns, public conveyances, and theaters, though not schools. First proposed years earlier by Charles Sumner, the Civil Rights Act of 1875 recognized that permitting the humiliating exclusion of blacks from public accommodations destroyed equal citizenship by allowing whites to impose on blacks a race-based caste system. Blacks serving in Congress reminded their white colleagues how segregation contradicted civil and political equality, and threatened to truncate black access to the market economy as well. According to free-born black Alabama congressman James T. Rapier, "Just think that the law recognizes my right upon this floor as a law-maker, but that there is no law to secure to me any accommodations whatever while traveling here to discharge my duties as Representative of a large and wealthy constituency. Here I am the peer of the proudest, but on a steamboat or car I am not equal to the most degraded. Is not this most anomalous and ridiculous?" Despite its potential, however, the Civil Rights Act of 1875 went poorly enforced until the Supreme Court declared it unconstitutional in 1883.[90]

Conclusion

As Frederick Douglass pointed out at a recruiting rally in Philadelphia within days after the battle of Gettysburg, accepting the blue uniform and federal musket turned the lowliest ex-slave into a man and citizen. Regardless of prejudice in the armed forces and society at large, blacks used their participation in the Civil War to place their expectations squarely at the center of Reconstruction debate and make sure that Douglass's 1863 declaration of citizenship became enshrined in the law and meant something concrete. Many black soldiers equated their military service and bravery as validating their worthiness for equal citizenship, even while the broadness of that concept remained vague. As James H. Hall of the Fifty-fourth Massachusetts declared in the summer of 1864, "If we fight to maintain a Republican Government, we want Republican privileges." After assuring whites that blacks did "not covet your wives nor your daughters," Hall informed them, "All we ask is the proper enjoyment of the rights of citizenship, and a free title and acknowledged share in our own noble birthplace."[91]

Black soldiers drew on their experience in the army when contemplating what rights they expected as a result of this citizenship status. Moreover, the political awareness black soldiers gained during their service percolated throughout the entire African American community and resulted in a more powerful and unified movement demanding equal rights. In the 1860s, African American leaders and tens of thousands of black soldiers in blue built on William C. Nell's important theme that their service to the Republic affirmed and guaranteed their citizenship. After the war, through participation in conventions, service as local leaders within the black community, and appeals such as one listing the names of the officers and men of Company C of the Tenth USCHA under the words "We fight for our Rights, Liberty, Justice and Union," black soldiers kept prominent the meaning of their service and what they expected to result from it.[92]

Moreover, blacks acted with unprecedented vigor and success; they had participated in past American wars but never on the scale made possible by the Civil War. Changes wrought by the war allowed conventions patterned after antebellum meetings to have stronger focus and a greater impact. Personal, geographical, and philosophical differences persisted, but the elimination of slavery and the new history of blacks in the Union's armed services allowed for a greater sense of unity, and a more national emphasis, to pervade these meetings.

In the end, blacks identified two inextricably interrelated battles, one waged on the battlefield and the other to make permanent their interpretations of what their loyalty to the Union meant in terms of citizenship. Rejecting second-class citizenship or caste, African Americans energetically called for tangible definitions of inclusion, striving for a freedom that went beyond the death of slavery in name only. Blacks engaged in constitutional debate and addressed the multiracial nation on an unparalleled scale and with great impact. Delegates used the conventions to commemorate black veterans and their sacrifices, but they also capitalized on this military service as the cornerstone to buttress their new vision of citizenship, demand equal rights and the vote, and speak out against antiblack violence. Mobilizing in local, state, and national organizations and leagues, black leaders not only discussed the contours of citizenship amongst themselves but directed their views—and their expectations—to governmental leaders and the general polity. Casting their position as one of orthodoxy maintaining the true spirit and meaning of the Revolutionary generation, these blacks embraced the ideas of participating in republican democracy and society as a whole.

While the nation as a whole considered how to reconstitute the nation after the Civil War, blacks asserted their American identity, moral calls based on their military service, and the pragmatic argument that their votes could help safeguard the Union victory and consolidate Republican power at the polls. At the same time, the loyalty African Americans showed to the Republic, as well as continued Democratic power at the polls and persistent tension in the South, led at least some whites to change formerly exclusionary opinions and accept the idea of black citizenship and voting rights for men.

Action and argument from African Americans thus helped bring about measures which expanded and more fully defined both their rights and ideas of American citizenship as a whole. Black pressure helped secure national ratification of the Thirteenth, Fourteenth, and Fifteenth amendments (in 1865, 1868, and 1870, respectively), as well as the Civil Rights acts of 1866 and 1875, the Reconstruction acts of 1867, and the Enforcement acts of 1870–72. In addition to helping save the Union, promoting a broadened definition of freedom and citizenship became another great legacy of African American Civil War soldiers. Now, the concept of citizenship became primarily national, and a formerly hollow vessel began to be filled with certain civil, economic, and political rights. Even where rights victories eroded in the 1870s, and confronted the dark and violent opposition of white racist groups, future generations brought to fruition the hard-won ideals of black citizenship championed during the Civil War era.

CHAPTER 7

The Affirmation of Naturalized
Citizenship in America

On June 15, 1864, the men of the Ninth Massachusetts gathered at Faneuil Hall in Boston to celebrate their homecoming after the expiration of their three-year term of enlistment. The city's mayor thanked the veterans for doing as much as any citizens had to sustain the Union, and Massachusetts adjutant general William Schouler declared that their service helped to undermine prewar nativism. Afterward, the regiment marched to Boston's Irish American district in the North End for a grand reception. Before spread tables in a decorated hall, a band played "St. Patrick's Day in the Morning" and an officer of the Columbian Association welcomed the men and noted how they had proved that Irish Americans upheld the government of their adopted country. Meanwhile, a militia company and band escorted Colonel Patrick Guiney, still recuperating from a severe head wound suffered just weeks earlier at the Wilderness, from a reception at the Parker House downtown to his home in Roxbury.[1]

As the war wound down, ceremonies honoring Irish American service to the Republic underscored the inclusion such loyalty earned them within the American people. On April 19, 1865, sergeants from the Sixty-third, Sixty-ninth, and Eighty-eighth New York Infantry regiments carried the Irish Brigade's banners in Lincoln's funeral procession from the White House to the Capitol. Elderly General Winfield Scott wistfully raised his hat to the green flags, carried besides the Stars and Stripes, as they passed by him on the somber day. The Irish American Sixty-ninth Pennsylvania, 116th Pennsylvania, and the regiments of the Irish Brigade (which later marched in a triumphant July 4, 1865, parade in New York City), participated on May 23, 1865, in a more festive pageant: the Grand Review. Two hundred thousand people lined Pennsylvania Avenue to watch 150,000 troops from the Army of the Potomac and Sherman's army parade over two days from the Capitol to the White House and then to Georgetown. The Grand Review celebrated the Union victory and linked regiments from across the country, including Irish American ones but excluding African American ones, in a triumphant and nationalizing spectacle through the reunited nation's capital.[2]

Through the war, a sense of American identity strengthened within many Irish Americans over time. Irish Americans did not abandon the ethnic component of their identity, yet, just as it did for African Americans, the Civil War era marked a moment when many Irish Americans became an integral part of U.S. society. During the war, Irish Americans advanced an interpretation of American nationalism that incorporated immigrants, and they argued that their defense of republicanism in the United States benefited Ireland and the entire world. Irish Americans openly practiced their culture and Catholic religion in the army, something which the nativists of the 1850s would have vigorously opposed. Now, as they did for many African Americans, mustering-out and homecoming ceremonies in the war's closing days publicly cemented Irish Americans into the broader community. In some ways, the typicality of such ceremonies emphasized society's acceptance of the new Irish American position: most regiments, whether ethnically identified or not, experienced similar events.

In assessing the impact of Irish American service, the *Boston Pilot* in July 1865 accordingly declared, "When the next generation records with flushed cheeks...this heroic age, they can say with proud consciousness 'we too, are Americans, and our fathers bled and died to establish this beloved country.'" The following year, the *Pilot* reported that "there is a large, an honorable, and influential, a liberal and an increasing number of Americans who welcome Irish American citizens to an equal share in the prizes of business and political life, and who are proud to associate with them upon the same social plane. There is neither patronage nor condescension in this but simply a full and cordial recognition of political and social equality." More dramatically, Irish-born Colonel Guiney seized on the ripe moment to juxtapose military service with a new order that more generally accepted Irish Americans as members of "the people." In a pro-Grant speech before the 1868 presidential election, Guiney declared to his audience, "Go up to the State House and you will find the torn and faded banners of the Ninth Regiment, and so long as they remain there no man will ever be heard to say that the Irish people living in Massachusetts are enemies of the republic."[3]

One tangible display of this shift came as Irish American veterans and civilians attained political positions with increasing frequency soon after the war. Irish-born officer Charles G. Halpine won election as register of New York City in 1866 with the endorsement of Union Democrats and Republicans, while Irish-born St. Clair A. Mulholland, commander of the 116th Pennsylvania, served as Philadelphia's police chief from 1869 until early 1871. By 1870, the voters of Albany, New York, elected a number of Irish-born representatives to the State Assembly, and in 1878 elected an Irish-born Democrat as mayor. Irish-born Patrick Guiney, who started a political career before the war by serving on the Roxbury Common Council, won appointment in 1865 as an assistant district attorney for Suffolk County, Massachusetts, and won election as register of Probate and Insolvency for that county in late 1871. In 1868, Irish-born Democrat Patrick A. Collins served in the Massachusetts House of Representatives, and by 1870 he took a seat in the state Senate; he later represented the Bay State in Congress from 1883 to 1889. Moreover, the need for additional labor generated by economic expansion and industrialization helped foster increased tolerance of immigrants. Capitalist development and slow but sustained financial improvement for some Irish Americans increasingly trumped nativism.[4]

Ethnic celebrations, such as the Saint Patrick's Day celebrations in the Army of the Potomac, continued in civilian life after the war and emphasized an Irish American identity. In 1871, as many as sixty thousand people marched through New York City's muddy streets on a two-hour-long St. Patrick's Day parade. Mayor A. Oakey Hall, a Tweed Ring henchman, observed the parade wearing a suit of green and black striped cashmere, and common council members wore green kid gloves and a sprig of shamrock in their buttonholes. The Sixty-ninth New York participated in the parade, along with five hundred members of the Legion of St. Patrick, two Fenian companies, divisions of the Ancient Order of Hibernians, sections of the Quarrymen's United Protective Society and Longshoremen's Union Benevolent Society, eighteen temperance groups, and fifty bands. After the parade, working-class Irish Americans celebrated in various bars, the noncommissioned officers of the Sixty-Ninth New York enjoyed a ball in Irving Hall, and members of the Knights of St. Patrick and the Friendly Sons of St. Patrick attended banquets. The Irish American upper-class packed Steinway Hall for a concert to benefit a church in Ireland.[5]

The *Pilot* accordingly declared, in April 1865, that Irish Americans could "be proud" of their "race and religion." At a meeting of the Irish Republican Campaign Club held in New York on September 30, 1868, Irish-born Democrat turned Republican senator from California John Conness similarly announced, "It should be our boast particularly that we are Americans...not forgetting our origins, not forgetting the trials of the land that we came from, and the race from which we spring, for that but sharpens the mental appetite for liberty as we find it here; but as American citizens simply, owning a part in the great cause of the Republic established by the fathers, maintained by their sons, to go down, I trust, forever to posterity."[6]

The Uncertain Meaning of Naturalized Citizenship

In this context, Irish Americans sought a more defined meaning of naturalized citizenship in the law in America, as well as when naturalized Americans traveled abroad. Understandably, blacks had little interest in this issue, being preoccupied with their own agenda for obtaining recognition of their American citizenship in the first place, as well as defining the rights this citizenship encompassed. When blacks did address the naturalization debate, they generally did so to highlight reasons why they, too, should be included as citizens.

By 1865, most of Europe still adhered to the principle of perpetual (or indefeasible) allegiance, that a subject could not disclaim birth allegiance even by swearing an oath of loyalty to another country. For centuries, for example, British legal doctrine held that subjects born within the realm owed inalienable allegiance to their sovereign from birth, and that the sovereign protected these subjects as a natural and reciprocal obligation. Under this bright-line rule, no act by that subject, not even naturalization in a foreign land, could remove this allegiance (although certain acts could forfeit the sovereign's protection). Britain accordingly considered naturalized American citizens born in the United Kingdom, including Irish Americans, to be subjects. This status exposed them to treason and other charges. British law also attached subjectship to the children of subjects even if those children were born abroad and, in 1731, to the second generation born abroad.[7]

Strict legal doctrine wavered in the New World regarding the nature of allegiance. In the 1700s, Parliament promoted naturalization of foreigners within the North American colonies, in contrast to its position on the naturalization of British subjects. Meanwhile, colonists sometimes naturalized newcomers out of military and economic necessity, and some colonial assemblies claimed their own right to admit the foreign-born to the ranks of British subjects, until Britain disallowed such local admissions in 1773. The realities of a diverse colonial society, which included settlers from the United Kingdom but also French Huguenots and large numbers of German immigrants, among others, further blurred the applicability of the doctrine of perpetual allegiance. Colonists increasingly viewed citizenship as based on a consensual, contractual relationship, in which a foreigner could naturalize and claim citizenship by committing allegiance, and much-welcomed labor, to the commonwealth.[8]

As Britain's North American empire fell apart, so also did the United States' adherence to the doctrine of perpetual allegiance. Both the disruption and the ideals fostered by the War of Independence motivated many states to embrace the idea that citizenship, in contrast to subjectship, originated through an individual's right to choose allegiance. Although not adopted uniformly or in unison, for the most part states during the Revolution gave residents a period of time to elect whether to remain within the state, acknowledge its independence and the legitimacy of its laws, and accept the protection it gave in return for allegiance. In the alternative, individuals could leave. More broadly, while the revolutionaries recognized the need for regulation to govern how one went about changing one's allegiance in the future, they held the individual's right to do so as inalienable and undeniable.[9]

The United States thus embraced expatriation rights, the notion that one could relinquish one's birthright citizenship, without permission from one's native government, and choose allegiance to a different country. Yet, at the same time, the United States failed to articulate a coherent policy regarding the practical mechanics and boundaries involved in the exercise of expatriation rights. In the decades before the Civil War, various authorities stood in conflict regarding the limits of an individual's right to expatriate, and what role both native and naturalizing country played in its exercise.[10]

For starters, the meaning of naturalization remained nebulous. Congress did not address the nature of citizenship even when obvious opportunities to do so arose: early naturalization regulations, passed in 1790, 1795, 1798, and 1802, instead focused on procedural issues and the length of time one should acclimate to the United States. This idea that one should serve as an "apprentice" in the Republic before becoming a citizen implicitly affirmed the idea that individuals created citizenship by embracing the ideals of the Constitution, in exchange for protection granted by the state. While national security threats occasionally produced severe reactions, as historian James Kettner noted, the overarching theme marking federal policy was that "citizenship should ultimately depend not on some magical result of birth alone, but on belief, will, consent, and choice." Yet early legislation failed to define what rights, privileges, protections, and duties attached to naturalized citizens, or address their relation to their native country.[11]

Thomas Jefferson identified expatriation as a natural right, while Hamiltonian Federalists maintained that one could not renounce allegiance without the sovereign's consent (even though at first glance, this position conflicted with the Revolution). The federal and state judiciaries failed to clarify the matter. Some judges continued to look to British law for guidance, and they upheld perpetual allegiance. Other jurists recognized a qualified right of expatriation, if not always the absolute right identified by Jefferson, and held that one could change allegiance but not by unilateral action. In the absence of explicit federal legislation, the judiciary failed to agree that expatriation existed as an unqualified right, much less create a consensus of case law defining its boundaries.[12]

Britain, on the other hand, relied on the doctrine of perpetual allegiance to justify the impressment of British-born sailors on American vessels. In the wake of a June 1807 incident, during which sailors of the HMS *Leopard* boarded the USS *Chesapeake* to search for deserters after firing three broadsides into the ship, killing or wounding twenty-one of its sailors, a royal proclamation on October 16, 1807, restated the doctrine that foreign naturalization did not absolve the relationship of British-born sailors to their crown. After war with Britain erupted in 1812, the United States offered as part of a peace proposal that it would prohibit further use of British subjects on public or private American ships except those who had already naturalized. Britain responded by asking the United States to deliver up these naturalized sailors. The Treaty of Ghent, which ended the war, failed to settle the issue of British impressment.[13]

Meanwhile, the State Department vacillated on the rights of naturalized citizens when they returned to their native country. In 1840, ambassador to

Prussia Henry Wheaton wrote an influential opinion on the issue, which adhered to a modified policy of perpetual allegiance. Wheaton held that the United States could not shield a Prussian-born naturalized American from compulsory military service while in his native country. "Had you remained in the United States, or visited any other foreign country, (except Prussia,) on your lawful business," Wheaton informed the naturalized American, "you would have been protected by the American authorities, at home and abroad, in the enjoyment of all your rights and privileges as a naturalized citizen of the United States. But, having returned to the country of your birth, *your native domicile and natural character* revert, (so long as you remain in the Prussian dominions,) and you are bound in all respects to obey the laws exactly as if you had never emigrated."[14]

Permutations of Wheaton's doctrine dominated American foreign policy on this issue through the Civil War. As Democrat James K. Polk's secretary of state, James Buchanan vigorously called for equal protection of naturalized American citizens, but he also recognized that the United States would have a difficult time enforcing the principle. Buchanan accordingly advised naturalized Americans to remain in the United States if possible. Buchanan's successors in Whig Millard Fillmore's administration, Daniel Webster and Edward Everett, supported the right of expatriation but they affirmed Wheaton's doctrine and held a naturalized citizen's status unconditional and unqualified anywhere *except* in the naturalized citizen's homeland.[15]

Franklin Pierce's Democratic administration weakened the Wheaton doctrine. Austria in 1853 seized Hungarian Martin Koszta while he was in Turkey. Koszta, a refugee of the 1848 revolution, had declared his intent to become an American citizen while previously in the United States. Captain Duncan Ingraham of the USS *Saint Louis* secured Koszta's release under the threat of force, and Secretary of State William L. Marcy refused Austria's demand for reparation. Marcy joined the right to pursue happiness elsewhere with the doctrine that allowed people to resist oppressive government, and he extended American protection even to those aliens merely domiciled in the United States. Marcy backtracked two years later when he gave the minister to Sardinia instructions consistent with Wheaton's doctrine. In October 1856, Pierce's attorney general Caleb Cushing affirmed that the American Revolution promoted granting individuals as much personal freedom as possible within regulation for the general welfare, and bitingly noted that British law affirmed perpetual allegiance but simultaneously permitted aliens to naturalize in Britain, leading him to condemn "jurisprudence of England [which] asserts an assumed rule of public law, or denies it, according to the caprices of apparent local interest."[16]

Buchanan's Democratic administration continued the Pierce administration's break with the Wheaton doctrine, though slow steps and vacillation marked official policy changes. Secretary of State Lewis Cass mildly limited Wheaton's doctrine in April 1859 by applying it to naturalized citizens who were in their native country's army, or actually called into it, at the time they left. Edward Bates, Lincoln's future attorney general, scorned Cass's cautious approach: "The right of expatriation is denied by many of the Governments of Europe," Bates confided to his diary, "but our Government has always affirmed it." According to Bates, once naturalized, a person "*is a citizen,* as perfectly and absolutely as any native born," and he questioned why such an individual should be "less entitled to the protection of this country than a native born American citizen." Years later, Bates affirmed his belief that taking the oath of naturalization transformed foreign-born individuals into Americans, after they spent the "few years of probation, required for the very purpose of changing them into *Americans,*" and he added that this also made them "the political equals of natural-born citizens."[17]

Under presidential and public pressure, Cass subsequently criticized perpetual allegiance in a letter to one of his ambassadors abroad as "a relic of barbarism." Despite more tentative language elsewhere in the letter, Cass held, "The moment a foreigner becomes naturalized, his allegiance to his native country is severed forever. He experiences a new political birth.... Should he return to his native country he returns as an American citizen, and in no other character. In order to entitle his original government to punish him for an offense, this must have been committed while he was a subject and owed allegiance to that government."[18]

By the eve of the Civil War, at least the executive branch had developed a general rule extending diplomatic protection to naturalized citizens except where native governments, within their own jurisdiction, sought enforcement of obligations owed by the expatriate prior to departure. Buchanan as president declared in his fourth annual message to Congress, "Our Government is bound to protect the rights of our naturalized citizens everywhere to the same extent as though they had drawn their first breath in this country. We can recognize no distinction between our native and naturalized citizens." The legislature did not codify Buchanan's policy, however, and it remained open to rejection by subsequent administrations, as well as a judiciary that had never resolved the issue. At roughly the same time, Prime Minister Lord Palmerston affirmed Britain's adherence to the doctrine of perpetual allegiance, though he noted that one could, by misconduct, lose British protection. In short, decades after the Revolution, America remained diametrically opposed to Britain's doctrine of perpetual allegiance in theory, but the practical meaning of naturalization and the boundaries of expatriation rights remained unsettled.[19]

During the Civil War, maintaining the delicate balance of European nonintervention precluded any strong American stance on expatriation rights. Furthermore, Secretary of State Seward complained of instances where naturalized American citizens returned to their homeland to avoid serving their new country in the federal army but then invoked the protection of the United States to screen them from military duty there. Not intending to expend diplomatic capital on naturalized citizens who fled the Union in its time of need, and then sought its protection after shirking service to it, Seward ordered his minister in Prussia, "You will make no further applications in these military cases without specific instructions." Meanwhile, the issue received little mention in either the letters of Irish American soldiers or ethnic newspapers.[20]

Immediately after the war, the debate over expatriation rights and perpetual allegiance resurfaced. The United States emerged from the war conscious of its increased power and ability to exert influence on the international stage. Moreover, the participation of tens of thousands of immigrants in direct military service, as well as Irish American calls for the equalization of citizenship status and growing political clout, renewed the federal government's commitment to enforce expatriation. In the end, the actions of the Fenian Brotherhood unexpectedly brought the issue of expatriation to the forefront at a time when the United States was in the process of defining for itself what national citizenship meant in America. While Fenianism did not succeed in liberating Ireland, Britain reacted to its potential. The ensuing diplomatic crisis, and Irish America's coalescence as a political bloc, directly generated changes both in American and British citizenship doctrine and practice.

Britain's Reaction to Fenianism

Across the Atlantic, the growth of the Fenian movement, and the fact that many of its members wore Union blue, generated Britain's protest against the openness with which the Brotherhood operated in the United States. By 1865, Britain acknowledged that American law made it more difficult for authorities in this country to interfere with Fenian meetings but complained that the participation of military and civil officials implied federal sanction. How could the United States protest British actions during the Civil War, the United Kingdom further questioned, in light of Fenian activity in America? The War Department's grant of a fortnight's leave of absence to Colonel John H. Gleason so that he could attend a Fenian convention particularly earned Britain's protest. In response, Secretary of State Seward assured the British of the sufficiency of existing neutrality laws and that the American government foresaw no imminent crimes, "unless renewed and systematic aggressions from the British ports and provinces should defeat all the efforts of this government to maintain and preserve peace with Great Britain." British protests against Thomas W. Sweeny proved more effective. An Irish-born division commander in the Army of the Tennessee who lost his right arm in the Mexican War, Sweeny accepted an appointment as Secretary of War in the Senate wing of the Fenian Brotherhood in late 1865. After reports arose that Sweeny conferred with U.S. Secretary of War Stanton about the possibility of transferring surplus military supplies to the Fenians, the British minister to the United States, Sir Frederick Bruce, contacted Seward. "It seems to me that he ought to be called to choose between the North American and the Irish Republic," Bruce urged Seward, and he added, "The effect of his acting as Secretary of War is to confirm the Fenian dupes in the belief that the Government of the United States favours the movement." Within two weeks, the army cited absence without leave to dismiss Sweeny from the service.[21]

British authorities arrested about a hundred suspected Fenians in Ireland between mid-September and mid-October 1865 and began searching the baggage of visiting Union veterans. The acting consul in Dublin, William B. West, wrote to Seward with concern that some of those confined claimed American citizenship and that this would cause a problem when they stood trial for treason as British subjects under the doctrine of perpetual allegiance. To complicate already tangled matters, the British arrested several Union veterans, among them Captain James Murphy of the Twentieth Massachusetts, and Lieutenant Colonel John W. Byron of the Eighty-eighth New York, who West described as "the hero of 32 fights in the service of his adopted country," and who Britain released relatively quickly. Captain Michael O'Boyle of the Sixty-Ninth New York claimed naturalized status but was committed for trial, while another naturalized American who served four years in the Ninth Connecticut, Lieutenant Joseph H. Lawlor, fumed at his imprisonment for a week in solitary confinement before his release. The secretary to the American legation in London, Benjamin Moran, dreaded the "trouble" he anticipated the "insane Fenians are about to give us." In Dublin, West scorned "Fenian mania," which "induced a great many of our adopted Irish citizens to visit this country . . . and many of them are now suffering most severely, and, I might add, justly punished for their folly, in abandoning the comforts and happiness of their American homes for the insane project of aiding revolution here."[22]

Limited arrests failed to allay British fears, as increasing numbers of Irish Americans, many of them Civil War veterans, continued arriving in Ireland. At the urging of the Lord Lieutenant of Ireland, Parliament suspended the writ of habeas corpus in Ireland on February 17, 1866, out of fear of an impending Fenian attack. Prime Minister Lord John Russell justified to Parliament that, after the Civil War, Irish Americans—many of whom had participated in the war and became American citizens—conspired to assist an Irish insurrection. The suspension bill met with little opposition, and by the end of the day, a hundred fifty suspected Fenians found themselves under arrest in Dublin alone, about a third of them claiming naturalized or native-born American status. Though he disapproved of Fenianism, William West criticized the arbitrary measures implemented as the British imprisoned Americans regardless of whether probable cause for suspicion existed, and simply because they came from the United States or served in its army. On the other hand, West wrote one prisoner, "It is to be regretted that so many of our Irish-born citizens should leave their adopted country, when they have all they can reasonably desire, and if sober and industrious, could never experience the want and misery which you now complain of." West also recognized that some Fenians who urged the United States to take "decisive measures" sought to "bring about a collision that will redound to their benefit."[23]

Within a week of the suspension of the writ of habeas corpus in Ireland, American ambassador Charles Francis Adams complained of the difficulties presented by the conflicting views America and Britain held regarding expatriation and allegiance. Adams realized that the arrests reopened the issue of expatriation rights during a time when the American public, at least the Unionist portion, felt aggrieved at British pro-Confederate actions during the Civil War. This state of affairs, Adams also knew, afforded Fenians an opportunity to promote their own interests. Adams had always cast a wary eye on Irish America. Though not a full nativist, Adams worried that large-scale Irish immigration would affect detrimentally American institutions. Over a decade earlier, Adams admitted that he understood why so many people worked for the "exclusion of foreign-born persons and Roman Catholics from all share of power over public affairs": because "neither of these classes has yet shown any thing else than a great repugnance to embrace the doctrines which we uphold," a notion which Irish Americans later claimed their support for the Union discredited. Yet, at the same time, Adams had scorned the nativist movement as detracting focus from the more important issue of abolition and rejected the philosophical paradox of antislavery Know Nothings who declared "that the slaveholder is a tyrant, who puts his heel on the neck of his slave, only because God made him of a different color from his own, and set him in Africa instead of in Europe," but would "to-morrow build a wall between themselves and others of their fellow-men, because God placed them, at the time of their birth, somewhere else than in the United States."[24]

Now, issues generated by and about Irish Americans overshadowed another matter Adams identified as more important: obtaining reparations for British violations of strict neutrality during the Civil War. The United States, Adams believed, would cede the moral high ground in negotiations if it protected or even ignored the activities of American Fenians. Furthermore, Adams noted the recent inclusion of Irish Americans into the broader society of the United States, and he questioned the duality of the Fenian movement when he wrote William West that "it behooves...all such as desire to enjoy the benefit of their incorporation into the people of the United States to take particular care not to forfeit their rights by taking part in political struggles of what to them should be nothing but a foreign country." By the end of 1865, Adams enforced a policy less vigorous than Seward would have liked and sought to protect innocent Irish Americans but not those who "justly subjected themselves to suspicion of complicity with treasonable projects."[25]

British authorities had temporarily averted a full-blown Anglo-American controversy by quickly releasing most of the men arrested in 1865 on the condition that they return to America, but arrests after the suspension of habeas corpus in February 1866 reheated the issue. On February 28, the under secretary for Ireland told West that he could see any native-born American prisoner but refused to allow the Dublin consul to interview three men bearing certificates of American naturalization, claiming them "as ordinary subjects of her Majesty," who "must be dealt with accordingly." As arrests proliferated, Adams called on the British foreign secretary, Earl Clarendon, on March 5, 1866, to release the naturalized Americans, or at least for the British to articulate some rationale for their imprisonment, before they became objects of American sympathy. Clarendon relied on perpetual allegiance to respond that Britain recognized no interference from any foreign country on behalf of any subject naturalized abroad. The Lord Lieutenant of Ireland similarly refused to communicate with American diplomats about the prisoners, and the British law officers on March 9, 1866, held it "impossible that Her Majesty's Government should recognize any title in a Foreign Power to interfere on behalf of natural born subjects of Her Majesty...on ground that such natural born subjects have become naturalized...in a Foreign Country."[26]

In America, Seward reminded Bruce that American politicians could not ignore the rights of naturalized citizens, especially in light of Irish American service during the Civil War and American resentment at British actions during the conflict. Bruce further assessed for his superiors that the Johnson administration would not actively combat Fenianism due to the power of Irish American votes. Seward proposed a resolution in which Britain did not concede the doctrine of perpetual allegiance, but allowed American consuls to intercede for all Americans nevertheless. Seward's plan would thereby eliminate distinction between native and naturalized Americans as a practical matter.[27]

Around the same time, Seward urged Adams to bring separate pressure to bear on the British government and reminded him that, under American policy, naturalization "completely absolves the person complying with it, from foreign allegiance" and invests him with protection from the U.S. government equal to that of native-born citizens. Seward's statement echoed sentiments by some of his Democratic predecessors at the State Department, particularly Buchanan, but circumstances in 1866 greatly differed from the ones existing before the Civil War. The United States now had the military and industrial strength to assert itself and, as Seward recognized, could not as a matter of principle allow Britain to imprison Union veterans. Additionally, Seward pointed out something Adams already knew: if unresolved, the controversy would energize anti-English hostility in the United States. Seward also recognized the growing political influence held by the Irish American community, and the power their votes potentially held in upcoming elections, a circumstance that stood in marked contrast to the almost wholly disfranchised African American community at that time.[28]

After Adams showed Seward's missive to Clarendon, the British gradually released both naturalized and native-born American citizens so long as they agreed to return to the United States. Clemency did not solve the disagreement between Britain and America regarding the meaning of naturalization, however, and Clarendon refused to concede the doctrine of perpetual allegiance after another conference with Adams at the end of May. Seward remained unsatisfied at this response, as did the Fenians and the Irish American community at large, and none of them intended to rest on this issue until America both codified and enforced the idea that naturalized citizens enjoyed the same protections as the native-born. Continuing Fenian activities, and the Habeas Corpus Suspension Act Continuance Bill passed in August 1866, guaranteed that the questions surrounding expatriation rights would persist until resolved once and for all.[29]

Irish American Mobilization

Britain's actions in arresting Irish Americans, coupled with already tense Anglo-American relations, made it the perfect time for the Fenians to take their cause to the American public. Britain's recognition of the Confederacy as a belligerent power, and its failure to prevent the outfitting in British ports of Confederate privateers such as the *Alabama,* generated immense American hostility. By early 1865, both British prime minister Lord Palmerston and Queen Victoria feared the strong possibility that the United States would attack Britain or Canada after the Civil War concluded. Rallies in America now raised funds for the Brotherhood and afforded opportunities for Irish Americans to further explore the paradox of concern for Ireland and loyalty to the United States. Moreover, while Irish American votes comprised important blocs in local elections in the past, this moment allowed for the construction of a broader constituency worthy of greater attention from American political leaders. Public meetings focused increasing attention on the status and protections afforded to naturalized citizens and gave birth to Fenianism's unintended but lasting legacy in the United States: the opportunity for Irish Americans to resolve successfully their demands for equality of citizenship before the law. Charles Francis Adams already recognized that Irish Americans gained recent "incorporation into the people of the United States"; they now acted accordingly by asserting their desires within the context of the American legal and political traditions, and further linking Irish and American nationalism through shared antipathy toward Britain.[30]

George Archdeacon, a naturalized American imprisoned by the British during the arrests of autumn 1865, summarized to President Johnson the urgency with which Irish Americans now held the issue of expatriation rights. Archdeacon informed Johnson that he felt "a deep interest, in common with hundreds of thousands of true Irish American citizens, in the question of our rights as openly sworn citizens of the United States," and he asked the federal government to "set this matter at rest, so that adopted citizens generally may know their real standing in foreign countries, and the value from home of that citizenship of which they are so proud here."[31]

Meanwhile, Fenian rallies pressured politicians and inspired an American public already livid at Britain. Rallies in New York City on Sunday, March 4, 1866, and similar meetings held the same day at Troy, New York, and Rivington, Vermont, indicate the level to which this sympathy spread. Although New York archbishop John McCloskey condemned the meeting as a profanation of the Lord's day (especially as the Catholic Church opposed Fenianism), and the portent of a winter storm hung in the air (it did snow toward the end of the meeting), an estimated hundred thousand attendees poured in from Brooklyn,

Westchester, and New Jersey to gather at Jones's Wood. Music played and booths provided billiards, bowling, and liquor. Fenian bonds on sale depicted Erin pointing to a sword lying on the ground, while a kneeling Union soldier readied to take the sword and leave for Ireland. Speeches delivered that afternoon from stands decorated with American and Irish flags proved the main attraction. After several orators exhorted the audience to donate money to the cause, Fenian Stephen J. Meaney rose to condemn Adams and other American diplomats as "English hirelings" for not acting more vigorously to free imprisoned Americans.[32]

A few days later, people paid a fifty-cent admission fee and packed into a meeting at Cooper Institute on March 9. While speakers addressed the cause in Ireland, two American flags adorned the stage alongside a banner displaying the Fenian sunburst and harp. Just as African Americans used USCT banners at their conventions, the regimental colors presented to the Ninety-ninth New York State Militia for its brief Civil War service evoked Irish American support for the Union. In contrast to African American efforts, however, George Francis Train criticized nationwide concern about the "oppressed and degraded black" instead of the "holy cause" of Irish liberation before he linked Fenianism to Irish Americanism. Train recalled speaking near Independence Hall in Philadelphia the week before, and reminded his audience that several Irish had signed the Declaration of Independence and thus helped establish "our magnificent Republic." Invoking these Founders, and the tens of thousands of Irish Americans who fought in the Civil War, Train "demanded" congressional assistance for the Irish cause. Train further reminded Irish Americans that they could use their position in this country to influence its policy. Identifying President Johnson as an ally of the Fenian movement, and predicting that a "neutral" Secretary of State Seward would do little to halt their activities, Train summoned his audience to boycott British goods, pressure the government to discourage British trade, and donate money to the cause.[33]

Another event drew further attention to the Brotherhood, though it did little for the liberation of Ireland: from May 31 to June 5, 1866, the Fenians invaded Canada. As concern for Canada's safety mounted in the months leading up to this operation, Seward sought to balance Irish American interests and British calls for preventative action with a policy of conscious inactivity, hoping that Fenian enthusiasm for invasion would chill with time. President Johnson, wrestling with the Republican Congress over Reconstruction, and wary of alienating traditionally Democratic Irish American voters, similarly vowed to respond only to an overt act of Fenian aggression. The Fenians, meanwhile, interpreted the U.S. government's position as one of approval for their plans or, in the least, neutrality. Once the attack began, however, the United States prevented thousands of reinforcements from joining the Fenian invasion's advance force under Colonel John O'Neill, dooming the assault to failure. At Britain's urging, as the invasion entered its death throes, Johnson ordered the arrest of "all prominent, leading or conspicuous persons" acting in violation of American neutrality laws. In the end, the invasion left several thousand members of the Brotherhood stranded and feeling betrayed. The government and New York Democratic leaders like William M. "Boss" Tweed and Mayor John T. Hoffman paid their return fares home. The invasion had turned into a debacle but it kept the issues surrounding Irish Americans and the meaning of naturalization in the public eye.[34]

Irish Americans, Politics, and Equal Rights in the mid-1860s

In the fluid context of Reconstruction, politicians from both parties used the Fenian/expatriation issue to connect with traditionally Democratic Irish American constituents. Both Democrats and Republicans linked support for Ireland's liberation with a more global struggle for republicanism under the leadership of the United States. During the invasion of Canada, Republican Reader W. Clarke from Ohio asked the House to grant the Fenians belligerent's rights on June 4, 1866. On June 11, Pennsylvanian Democrat Sydenham E. Ancona urged a bill repealing the Neutrality Law of 1818, which punished persons who, within the United States, began or aided any military expedition against any foreign state with which the United States was at peace. Ancona condemned British actions during the Civil War, and further noted that "the active sympathies of the people of the United States are naturally with all men who struggle to achieve" Ireland's independence, "especially when those engaged therein are the acknowledged friends of our government, as are the Irish race, they having shed their blood in defence of our flag in every battle of every war in which the republic has been engaged." In response, Republican Robert C. Schenck of Ohio (later minister to England from 1870 to 1876) called for strict neutrality, recognizing both parties as belligerents but, as Schenck explained, "'Hands off,' is the motto I would prefer." Republican Abner Harding of Illinois immediately offered a substitute to Ancona's resolution that would recognize the Irish nation as a belligerent power, express further sympathy with "all true Irishmen in their holy struggles for freedom," and "remember with gratitude that many brave Irishmen periled their lives and mingled their blood with the patriots of the Union Army on many hard-fought fields against rebels...aided by England with ships and money and materials of war." Both Ancona's and Harding's proposals were referred to the Committee on Foreign Affairs for its consideration. Adding to the moment, the House of Representatives on June 21 welcomed into its chamber future congressman William Roberts, then president of the Brotherhood's Senate wing, arrested on the Canadian border and nearly prosecuted by the American government. Roberts spent the next night meeting with congressmen and senators.[35]

More important, and with indelible constitutional implications, something quietly occurred in the drafting of the Fourteenth Amendment. Where the original version proposed by the House of Representatives remained silent, on June 8, 1866, as the Senate considered amendments to the House version, moderate Republican senator William Pitt Fessenden from Maine inserted without objection the phrase "or naturalized" into the amendment's first section so that it read, "All persons born or naturalized in the United States, and subject to the jurisdiction thereof, are citizens of the United States and of the State wherein they reside." Without debate or fanfare, the Senate adopted the revision and on June 13, the House assented to the Senate version and adopted the amendment for ratification by the states.[36]

In this moment lost on scholars of the Fourteenth Amendment or the Reconstruction-era Congress, naturalized citizens were constitutionally affirmed as part of "the people." Nativist measures targeting naturalized citizens became unconstitutional pursuant to the remainder of Section 1, that "no State...shall abridge the privileges or immunities of citizens of the United States," "deprive any person of life, liberty, or property, without due process or law," or "deny to any person within its jurisdiction the equal protection of the laws." Inclusion recently confirmed by the military service of Irish American and German American soldiers, as well as the understanding that if ex-slaves could comprise citizens so also must naturalized Americans, perhaps rendered the moment uncontroversial and thus unnoticed. Nonetheless, Fessenden's addition to the Fourteenth Amendment, made within days of the Fenian invasion of Canada, represented a profound constitutional sanction, prior naturalization laws notwithstanding. Where the Civil Rights Act passed on April 9, 1866, remained silent about naturalized citizens, and dealt only with birthright citizens, the Fourteenth Amendment constitutionally expanded the concept of citizenship to mandate equality for people in either category, at the same time the rights associated with national citizenship began to be defined in the law for the first time.

Some Irish Americans and Republicans even began a surprising rapprochement at this time. On one level, pragmatism motivated the alliance: Fenians sought Republican support, and Republicans courted Irish American votes, especially because every one obtained increased their party's vote totals and weakened a traditionally Democratic base as well. Republican campaigners cast Johnson as a turncoat who encouraged the Fenians to invade Canada and then betrayed them once on British soil. The alliance rested on more than Machiavellianism, however, and provides another example of intertwining ideology and political pragmatism similar to the circumstances that led to suffrage rights for black men. As many Fenians defined their movement within a broader transnational one that promoted republicanism across the globe, an unexpected, albeit temporary, alliance of principle developed between some Irish Americans and Republicans who advanced universal respect for liberty and rights.[37]

During the Civil War, some Irish Americans, such as Thomas F. Meagher and Patrick R. Guiney, embraced the Republican Party and its broader view of rights. A number of prominent Fenians officered black regiments, a surprising moment of radicalism linking some Irish Americans with African Americans during the Civil War, and blurring the boundaries of antagonism between both groups. John O'Neill, for instance, served as a captain in the Seventeenth USCI before he led a Fenian detachment in the June 1866 raid on Canada. Of Belgo-Italian lineage, Octave Fariola served as lieutenant colonel of the Ninety-sixth

USCI, during which time he vigorously sought clemency for one of his soldiers convicted of murder by a general court-martial and sentenced to death, before he became adjutant general of the Fenian self-proclaimed Irish Republic. Building on these seeds, Irish Americans now held themselves out as a source of votes but some of them also argued in petitions, rallies, Fenian conventions, and private letters in favor of the egalitarianism espoused by Republicans, even where many members of this ethnic community still held deep-seated prejudice against blacks.[38]

As the Republican *New York Tribune* explained, increasing numbers of Irish Americans began to realize "that the direct and sure way to win liberty and opportunity for [their] race is to concede...that [there] are...natural, inalienable rights, not of superior races, but of every race." This growing impulse within the Irish American leadership and community converged with Radical Republicans' promotion of equal rights and rejection of distinction based on racial or ethnic differences. In articulating an inclusive vision of the United States that embraced the assimilation of different people into a unified American nationality based on loyalty to republican values, Fenians, their Irish American supporters, and Radical Republicans found themselves in ideological agreement.[39]

Thus, in Philadelphia, the local Republican Party actively recruited Irish Americans into its machine. Irish Americans shouted their support at a Republican rally in Milwaukee in 1866, infuriated by what they perceived as the Johnson administration's lack of support for the Fenian cause. Illinois Republican governor Richard J. Oglesby, Senator Lyman Trumbull (at various times affiliated with the Democrats, Republicans, Liberal Republicans, and then Democrats again), and Republican speaker of the House Schuyler Colfax joined John O'Neill at a Fenian picnic in Chicago on August 15, 1866. Among speeches criticizing Britain, praising Irish American Civil War service, and urging attendees to vote Republican, Colfax spoke of the philosophical convergence between Republicans and some Irish Americans. Colfax, an early supporter of the Fenians, described the Brotherhood as promoting "liberty to all and justice to all" and declared that this "noble and patriotic motto...thrills my heart" and inspired him to "clasp the hand of every man as a brother who proclaims that noble sentiment in our land." While taking the opportunity to attack the Democrats and impugn Andrew Johnson as "acting under the dictation of the British Minister," Colfax found a brotherhood of liberty that linked both the racial agenda of the Republicans and the global defense of republicanism Fenians espoused, and he declared to Irish Americans: "You have stood together on the battlefield. Now stand together at the ballot box. If you believe in liberty for Ireland, you must go to work and speak for liberty in America. The true way to aid your cause is to fight as the great Union Republican organization does, for human rights and impartial justice, and for the downfall of tyranny and oppression wherever it may exist." At another Fenian picnic, Massachusetts Republican senator Henry Wilson similarly quoted a definition that Fenianism supported "the cause of liberty everywhere" and declared, "If that be Fenianism, then I am a Fenian."[40]

Meanwhile, postwar Fenian meetings manifested the increasingly American focus that developed during the Civil War. Echoing arguments made by African Americans in their own call for inclusion, William Roberts invoked the history of Irish American service to the United States at a convention his wing of the Brotherhood held in Cleveland in early September 1867, declaring that "from the first shot at Lexington in 1775, to the last in 1865, the citizens of Irish birth gave the noblest proofs of their devotion to America and her institutions." Addressing the issue of dual allegiance, Roberts proclaimed that activities of Irish Americans on behalf of their natal land in no way diminished their loyalty to the United States but instead showed themselves to be the defender of its republican ideals. Roberts declared illogical the argument that, "because we love the mother that bore us, we cannot adore the bride of our choice," and he interpreted this contention as asserting that because Fenians sought to spread the freedoms enjoyed in America, they somehow rendered themselves "not in harmony with the spirit of free institutions, or conscientiously true to our oath of citizenship." Assuring his audience, and those who would read a printed version of his speech, that "the Republic has nothing to fear from her Fenian citizens, who hope to establish a similar government on Irish soil," Roberts also cast Irish Americans who supported the Brotherhood as following the noble example foreigners such as the Marquis de Lafayette, Thaddeus Kosciusko, and Friedrich Wilhelm von Steuben, who helped secure American independence.[41]

Moreover, during this September 1867 convention came a stunning moment that reveals the broader recognition, in at least some Irish Americans, of a more expansive understanding of liberty and human rights, and further blurred the lines of hostility with African Americans. The delegates learned that several thousand black men of New Orleans offered to fight for Irish freedom and, despite any antipathy between Irish Americans and African Americans, swiftly resolved to "accept the services of every man who truly loves liberty, and is willing to fight for Ireland, without distinction of race, color, or nationality." Although these blacks never did fight under the Fenian standard, the offer and its acceptance reveal the unexpected links and mutual goals affirmed by the outcome of the Civil War: multiracial and transnational promotion of liberty and republican values. In addressing the delegates, Roberts claimed that "in the ranks of the Fenian Brotherhood are men of various nationalities, many of whom, neither by the ties of blood nor education, have the slightest affinity with the Irish people. They may differ in matters of religion, politics, and even in social feelings; but there is one common bond of Union, broad, deep and strong. It is Liberty, *priceless Liberty*."[42]

By 1868, New York's *Irish People* endorsed Republican candidate Ulysses S. Grant for president, and Irish American Republican Clubs, including chapters in Chicago, Cincinnati, and Troy, New York, actively campaigned for the Republican Party. Michael Scanlon, editor of Chicago's *Irish Republic,* accused the leaders of the Democratic Party taking Irish American votes for granted and thinking "they could use them for their packing horses forever, on whose shoulders every ignorant and unprincipled ruffian could ride into office."[43]

Not all Republicans welcomed the rapprochement. In November 1868, the black newspaper the *Christian Recorder* complained of an Irish American journal that claimed that its endorsement of Grant for president converted ten thousand Irish American votes from Democratic to Republican, and then voiced its expectation that Grant would be sympathetic to the Irish. After first asking, "If loyalty to the right is to be thus liberally rewarded, what under conscience cannot the Negro demand?" the paper answered that blacks requested "*nothing.*" "The Negroes who, through fire and blood, voted for General Grant, ask no *especial* favors, they ask of him what the Negro has ever asked of the American people, *not mercy, but justice.* Let the new President treat us just as he treats the other thirty millions of the land, protect us in our rights and immunities as American citizens, and we ask no more." Earlier that year, an article in the newspaper condemned Fenians for engaging in an "illegitimate mode of warfare," which inspired "almost universal terror" in England, and questioned the dual loyalties of Irish Americans: "What is their right of citizenship, and to what government do they really belong?" Assuming that "every Fenian is a sworn subject" of the Irish government in exile, the paper observed that "perhaps hundreds of thousands of them...come up to our polls with their naturalization papers in their hands, people of another government, but allowed to use their Irish Catholic vote to press the policy of ours into the service of their own." Exposing the paradox, the article observed that "either the 'Irish Nation' is a myth, or the citizenship of these people is not American, and they have no more right to interfere in our politics than a subject of Russia."[44]

Not all Irish Americans eagerly embraced the Republican agenda either. Many Irish Americans continued to espouse a conservative viewpoint, and ethnic pro-Democratic newspapers such as the *Pilot* called on readers to ignore Republican efforts to woo them with rhetoric concerning the Fenian and expatriation issues, and to reject the purported Radical view that an African American held superiority over an Irish American. Editor John Mitchel of New York's *Irish Citizen* continued to champion the Democrats, attacked the Republican Party as threatening to bring about a race war, and accused Radical Republicans of serving British interests.[45]

The Central Executive Committee of Irish Citizens, vanishing after publishing one pamphlet in 1866, displayed concern for the shifting political allegiances of Irish Americans and argued for rejection of both the Democrat and Republican parties. Led by Irish-born Union veterans Thomas Antisell, who served as a brigade surgeon, and James R. Beirne, an officer in the Thirty-seventh New York who won a Medal of Honor for bravery at Seven Pines, the committee in some ways urged an antebellum agenda. As if the war had never happened, the committee contended that crises in Europe generally resolved by bloodshed but argued that in America, determination occurred at the ballot box. The committee then interpreted that Civil War as one initially waged by the North to preserve the Union, but which became corrupted by abolitionism, so that soldiers were "betrayed into fighting for the emancipation of the negro and the support of an intolerant and oppressive Radical majority in

Congress," which forced Confederate states to extend suffrage to blacks as a form of domination over the South. "Do you want to aid in forcing the South into rebellion again?" asked the committee, which further declared that "the Irish citizen...will not lend himself to the oppression of one-third of the country for the benefit of a small and blatant minority, who have...been ever ready to deny him that measure of political and religious liberty which is the right of every citizen of the land."[46]

Here, then, lie the committee's concern: Irish Americans had begun joining a Republican Party that "sought out the Irish patriotic societies," offering them "honeyed phrases and high-sounding promises," in order to sway the Irish American voter "from his plain duty to aid" President Johnson's efforts to restore the country "to its former political status." The committee warned that in New England, Puritan descendants maintained unabated "bigotry" through "anti-Catholic crusades," and their "hobby is now negro suffrage, and the party who persecuted the Irishman in his mode of worship, who declared him unworthy to bear arms in a New England State, or enjoy a civil office of trust in the Commonwealth, gloats with insane delight over its negro fetishism, and openly boasts that it prefers the negro to the foreign-born citizen, whether German or Irish." Joining an "unholy pact" with Republicans, the committee argued, comprised a decision to oppress the South, depress its white population by lifting up blacks, and assist despotism worldwide, including in Ireland, by aiding it in America.[47]

At its missive's end, the committee acknowledged that a new order would emerge from the cataclysm of war and urged Irish Americans to form a new, national party and elect their own officials to political office. While trying to remain loyal to a conservative agenda, the committee nonetheless supported radical doctrines by supporting a worldwide struggle for republicanism (so long as it did not include blacks) and urging the construction of a "more united and powerful" national Irish American voting bloc outside of the Republican or Democratic parties. Recognizing Reconstruction as a fluid moment, when "all old party bonds and issues are broken up, when new elements have swept into the political circle," the committee argued that "now is the time for the Irish citizens to place themselves in that position in which, instead of being at the heels of a party, they may become the arbiters of the welfare of the land." Shunning both parties as neglectful of Irish Americans once elections had been won, the committee argued that a unified Irish American vote would benefit not only the United States but Ireland as well.[48]

Thus Irish Americans of different political stripes recognized the burgeoning voting power of their community as a national voting bloc, this circumstance alone a powerful symbol of inclusion and citizenship identity that sharply contrasted with the position blacks occupied at this point in time. The day after Congress defeated, on July 2, 1866, Reader W. Clarke's proposal to grant belligerent rights to the Fenians, Fenian leader William Roberts gave a speech in Buffalo, New York, in which he warned that Fenians would vote only for candidates allied with their cause. Heeding Roberts's call, Congressman

Nathaniel P. Banks, formerly elected to Congress in 1854 as a member of the Know Nothing Party before becoming a Republican and serving as a second-rate general during the Civil War, earned Irish American praise by reporting a bill in the House to weaken U.S. neutrality laws. With Roberts prominently canvassing the congressional floor, the House passed the bill on July 26, 1866, without a negative vote and with 123 in favor (though with 63 abstentions).[49]

Within days, Banks found himself a popular figure among Fenian circles, hailed by Roberts as a "great statesman" who had secured "the love and lasting friendship of all Irishmen." A letter noted to Banks that his resolution might even help the Republicans take New York, insofar as "all the Irish ask is an expression of sympathy; that being given, their leaders, who are already right, will be ready to break openly with the Democratic Party." Banks's bill provided that expression, showing that Republicans, "sympathize with [the Irish] in their patriotic purposes and endeavors." Of course, Fenian disappointment mounted when a split between Republicans led the Senate to fail to act on the bill. Radical Republican Zacariah Chandler of Michigan tried to convince the Foreign Relations Committee to amend the nation's neutrality laws even before Banks's bill came up, but Charles Sumner of Massachusetts killed any such initiatives with inaction (though he shrewdly left Banks's bill pending through the election). The Senate's refusal to act prompted Roberts to remind Banks that if the Republicans eschewed their preelection promises of support, "our disappointment and chagrin would be intense."[50]

Whether accurate or not, many contemporaries ascribed the Republican victory in the 1866 congressional elections to fluid Irish American political allegiance. In Massachusetts, a substantial portion of Irish Americans normally very loyal to the Democrats recognized the Republican stance on Fenianism and expatriation rights, and refrained from voting in the 1866 election. While this may not indicate a pervasive or permanent defection by Irish Americans into the Republican ranks, this behavior, in a state that had a potent nativist heritage, is surprising and significant. Some Irish American voters could not bear to vote Republican, but their abstention produced the same effect nonetheless. A Democratic leader in Rochester, New York, wrote Samuel J. Tilden that "we were beaten by the Fenian vote. We had the state by 25,000 majority if we had received our accustomed Irish strength," while the defeated Democratic gubernatorial candidate, New York City mayor (and Fenian sympathizer) John T. Hoffman, declared that "it looks as if the Radicals have succeeded in capturing by their false statements a large number of Fenian votes and that accounts for our losses." Hoffman learned his lesson and became more vocal in his pro-Fenian statements.[51]

Conclusion

Fenianism brought to the forefront postwar discussions of Irish American citizenship status. The movement served as a vehicle though which many Irish

Americans, particularly those who served in the Civil War, further expressed their inclusion in the American polity and called for additional changes in American citizenship doctrine. In contrast to Know Nothingism's halcyon days, Irish Americans now addressed the ethnic community and the broader public in open rallies, forging in the process a national constituency worthy of the attention of American political leaders. Irish Americans acted as citizens not only by gathering in public spaces but by asserting their wishes within the context of American political traditions.

Although an easier political mobilization than that of blacks, this moment proved similarly critical regarding legal change. The emergence of an Irish American national political bloc helped consummate inclusion in the American people, and it allowed this ethnic community to assert coherent arguments about changes it expected to be made to the legal concept of American citizenship. The experience of African American and Irish American political mobilization at this point also reveals a major contrast between the status of both groups during this period. African Americans at this time sought to attain even the right to vote, much less the political inclusion more readily granted to Irish Americans. This circumstance helps to explain why African Americans placed emphasis during this time on defining what rights national citizenship encompassed, along with the concepts of equality before the law, while Irish Americans focused on eliminating distinction between native-born and naturalized citizens but spoke less about what that citizenship meant in practice in the United States.

Fenian activism in the 1860s would have terrified nativists a decade earlier as an example of purported Irish American disloyalty, especially after the Brotherhood declared itself the Irish government in exile, invaded Canada, and flew a harp and sunburst flag outside its "capital" at the Moffat mansion near Union Square in New York City. Instead, the Fenian movement gained popularity with both the Irish American and native-born communities after the Civil War, even as it continued to highlight the dualities present in Irish America. Fenian activities afforded Irish Americans, whether members of the Brotherhood or not, an opportunity to demand that the United States provide equal protection to its citizens regardless of their naturalized status. Moreover, Fenianism allowed Irish Americans a way to more fully explore and engage in the egalitarian impulse of the Radical Republican movement, and helped blur, at least for some Irish Americans, racism against African Americans.[52]

In courting Fenianism for political and ideological reasons, both Democrats and Republicans recognized and affirmed the new location Irish Americans claimed for themselves within the American polity. Praising Irish American service, and agreeing that it consummated American citizenship, these leaders also accepted and publicized a new identity for members of this community: that of the guard of republican principles, even where this required them to ignore continuing Irish American racism against African Americans. Instead of viewing Fenians in particular, and Irish Americans in general, as a threat to the United States, as nativists had, American political leaders now publicly embraced the idea that Irish Americans acted as global leaders furthering a transnational republican movement with the United States located at its apex. These officials also joined with the Irish American community to demand equality of citizenship between naturalized and the native-born, something enshrined in the Fourteenth Amendment.

In the end, the intense pressure applied by this ethnic community, supported by society at large, compelled the United States to more fully define what rights and protections naturalized American citizenship afforded. As another factor that fueled the increasing importance and definition of federal citizenship, the debate over expatriation rights precisely coincided with and influenced national consideration of the Fourteenth Amendment, and the movement reinforced the amendment's principles even where it did not specifically discuss its language. While antebellum nativist elements sought to limit Irish American influence in politics, an Irish American–led movement now gained in widespread popularity. Irish Americans helped successfully motivate a major reconsideration of American citizenship doctrine and established themselves as a national political bloc in the process.

Yet, at the same time Americans considered the Fourteenth Amendment, Britain stood fast in its policy of indefeasible allegiance, and the meaning of naturalized citizenship abroad remained unresolved. Continued Fenian activities, and the pressure of Irish American activism, had the potential to cause a war or, in the alternative, force Britain and the United States to resolve their differences over expatriation rights once and for all. As naturalized citizenship became equalized to birthright citizenship as a legal concept in the United States, Irish Americans and the larger American community now turned to resolving its meaning abroad.

CHAPTER 8

The Affirmation of Naturalized
Citizenship Abroad

In the spring of 1867, Fenians dispatched arms and men to Ireland aboard a ship they named *Erin's Hope*. Britain arrested twenty-eight of thirty-one men within a day of their landing on Irish soil, including native-born American William J. Nagle and naturalized American John Warren. According to Nagle, the British arrested the two former Civil War officers on June 1 and kept them in the local prison at Youghal until June 4 before marching them in handcuffs through the streets of Cork to the jail in that city—"the penalty of being an American soldier with Irish blood in my veins, so far offending the majesty of British law as to be found upon Irish soil." Secretary of State William H. Seward instructed the American minister in London, Charles Francis Adams, to intercede for the two officers, reminding Adams, "faithful service in the armies or navy of the United States during the rebellion constitutes an enhanced claim of persons so serving to the consideration of the Government which they have helped to perpetuate." Britain nonetheless recognized Warren as a British subject and charged him accordingly.[1]

Another incident later that summer exacerbated tension between Britain and America. Early on the morning of September 11, 1867, British authorities arrested Thomas J. Kelly and Timothy Deasy, two former Union officers and now, active Fenians, on a street in Manchester. On September 18, twelve unarmed police guarded the two handcuffed prisoners during their transfer to the county jail. As the police van passed under a railway arch, up to fifty armed Fenians stopped it, shot one of its horses, and called for the prisoners' freedom. When this request went unheeded, the Fenians accidentally killed a policeman inside the van as they shot a lock off its door so as to release Kelly and Deasy.

Adams accurately assessed that this bloodshed would enflame British public opinion and force the government to treat the Fenians with more severity, just at the moment he hoped for a release of confined Irish Americans. While Kelly and Deasy escaped to America, the British arrested twenty-six men for the policeman's death, and by early November 1867, convicted five on capital charges. British authorities mitigated the sentence for two of the defendants but executed the other three on November 23, 1867, including one who claimed American citizenship. The next day, Irish Americans in New York City and across the United States held funerary processions for the "Manchester Martyrs." Even the *New York Times,* generally hostile to Fenianism, condemned the executions.[2]

The *Erin's Hope* expedition and the Manchester Martyrs episode did more than create an Anglo-American diplomatic crisis. Both incidents heightened popular response in America in a way congressional resolutions could not, and they illuminated the opposing positions Britain and the United States asserted about expatriation rights. Moreover, while Americans were working toward resolving the meaning of naturalized citizenship within the United States, through the process of ratifying the Fourteenth Amendment, both incidents underscored for Americans that the question of what naturalized citizenship meant abroad still remained unsettled. In this context, Fenian John Savage challenged the American people and government to provide a strong national response when he concluded his book, *Fenian Heroes and Martyrs* (1868), "It is full time the people should know what is the meaning of the phrase *American Citizen,* or if it has any meaning at all, and having a meaning, does it embrace a distinction between and a difference of protection to, a native and an adopted 'citizen.'" According to Savage, the imbroglio between America and Britain resulted from the blurry boundaries of expatriation rights, and the vagueness about what American citizenship meant: "If the Government had its mind made up as to what constitutes a citizen and his rights, its Minister and Consuls in Great Britain would no doubt have shown some prompt dignity and decision, when the national sentiment and character were outraged by the wanton arrest and contemptuous treatment of American citizens so-called, both native and adopted." In the end, both naturalized and native-born Americans called for either war or diplomacy to vindicate naturalized citizenship abroad, and their efforts helped to change citizenship doctrine on both sides of the Atlantic.[3]

Martyrs and Trials

By the fall of 1866, some British officials held out hope for an Anglo-American truce over the expatriation issue, believing that the completion of congressional elections would lessen Irish American political influence at a time when dissension, low morale after the failed invasion of Canada, and a diminished treasury afflicted the Brotherhood. Optimistic that Fenianism had entered its death throes, the British government even intimated that it would not seek renewal of the Habeas Corpus Suspension Act when a new session of Parliament opened on February 1867. On the other hand, Adams reported ongoing uneasiness in Ireland, as defiant rhetoric continued to emanate from America. Britain's moment of hope proved short lived as Fenianism resurged within the United Kingdom, leading to continued suspension of habeas corpus and imprisonment of Irish Americans as subjects. With their Civil War veterans in the lead, Irish Americans agitated for a strong American response.[4]

In March 1867, renewed resolutions in Congress called for America to grant the Irish belligerent rights and expressed sympathy for their efforts to establish a republican government in Ireland. On a more popular level, ten thousand people attended a rally at Union Square in New York City in the pouring rain on the evening of March 13, 1867. Colored paper lanterns bearing the Stars and Stripes and the motto, "Union forever," joined Irish Americans, American nationalism, and Irish nationalism without acknowledging any contradiction. Speakers vowed twelve British dead for every executed Irishman, and a unanimous resolution linked Ireland's suffering with American resentment toward Britain for acts it committed during the Civil War: "The Crown and oligarchy of Great Britain have forfeited all claim to international courtesy from the government and citizens of the United States by the treacherous and hostile conduct pursued by them towards this republic during the recent civil war," and "we deem it our right to retaliate upon her in a war for Irish independence" because the "attempts made by them to destroy our commerce, overthrow our institutions, and perpetuate discord and bloodshed on the American continent demands swift and speedy vengeance." On March 14, 1867, hundreds of Fenians gathered at City Hall in Detroit and a large rally took place at Boston's Faneuil Hall, keeping Irish Americans in the press and national consciousness.[5]

After meeting with Seward on May 20, 1867, Britain's conciliatory minister to the United States, Sir Frederick Bruce, informed his superior that Irish Americans "so pressed" Johnson's administration that it had no choice but to promote expatriation rights. Bruce further reported that the administration sought Irish American support, particularly with upcoming elections in mind. "American orators and newspaper writers invariably talk of the Irish as an oppressed people struggling for liberty and politicians of all parties find it to their interest to adopt this view in all questions affecting Ireland," Bruce noted to Lord Stanley, the new British foreign secretary, and he saw "no remedy for this inconvenience as long as an insurrectionary spirit prevails in Ireland, unless the restoration of the Southern States to the Union and the increasing immigration from Germany diminishes the importance attached to the Irish vote."[6]

The Manchester episode on September 18 hardened the British government's position regarding Fenian prisoners, and when Adams went to the Foreign Office on September 23 to discuss a possible release of Warren and Nagle, the British responded that their trials would proceed. Further complicating matters, Bruce died suddenly on September 19. Meanwhile the London *Times* reflected British public outrage: "If the murder of a policeman is treated as a comparatively venial offence because he was assassinated in a public capacity, policemen cannot be expected to protect the public against the 'American citizens,' as they call themselves, who seem to be multiplying both in Ireland and in this country." The *Times* emphasized that "a natural-born subject cannot transfer his allegiance from one sovereign to another at pleasure" and declared to readers,

> For the restless adventurers whom the close of the American war has let loose upon the world, and who fancy they can here perpetrate with impunity deeds for which they would be hanged at home, with or without law, we can feel no compassion at all, on whichever side of the Atlantic they may have been born....They have already had fair warning, and they may be assured that if they should fall into the hands of justice no American minister will intercede for them, and no English minister will venture to reprieve them.

The Manchester incident left the British government little choice but to proceed with the trials of Nagle and Warren. By Christmas Eve of 1867, Adams informed Seward that, in London, "It may be doubted whether at any time since the discovery of the scheme of Guy Fawkes, there has been so much of panic spread among families throughout this community as at this time."[7]

Warren's and Nagle's citizenship status arose as soon as their trials commenced in Dublin in autumn 1867. The American government hired counsel to defend both men against charges of treason and, as a native-born American citizen, Nagle applied for jury *de mediatate linguae*. Literally meaning "of the half tongue," this type of jury, composed of six English subjects and six from the alien's country, determined civil and criminal cases where one party was an alien. Unable to supply such a jury, the British had to release Nagle in May 1868, and he arrived to a hero's welcome in the United States, including a reception at Cooper Institute attended by women's suffrage activists Susan B. Anthony and Elizabeth Cady Stanton.[8]

Warren's different experience galvanized Irish Americans, and the larger American public, to the cause of sanctifying expatriation rights. Born in Ireland and claiming naturalization as an American citizen, Warren squarely fit within the British definition of a subject. From Kilmainham Prison in Dublin, Warren issued a call that "it is the duty of America to immediately protect any citizen whose liberty is assailed for giving expression to opinions in American favorable to the spread of republicanism and self-government." Powerfully describing how naturalization papers and passports held no meaning in Britain, Warren called out to all Americans that "the very idea of the myrmidons of England being permitted, for one moment, to touch an American citizen and imprison him for presumed acts done in America, should rouse the indignation of every American citizen, and demand that England should be made immediately and significantly to understand that *no American citizen is amenable to her laws for acts committed within the jurisdiction of the United States.*" Warren reminded Irish Americans that "you have entered into a sacred compact with the American government. You have renounced all former allegiance and have sworn to obey and protect her laws. By your industry, by your manual labor, by your intellect, by your capital, by your devotion, by your blood on the battle field, you have, in proportion to your number, done more than any other class of citizens to raise your adopted country to the proud position which she holds to-day." In a separate letter, Warren called on President Johnson to intervene against British insult to American citizenship.[9]

Like Nagle, Warren petitioned the British for trial by jury *de mediatate linguae,* but the court denied his request by relying on Britain's long-held doctrine that "he who once is under the allegiance of the English sovereign remains so forever." The British Court cited American jurists such as Supreme Court justice Joseph Story and Chancellor Kent to support its ruling, declaring, "We in our courts have been in the habit of treating, not merely with respect, but with reverence, these two great lights of the laws of America" and ominously warned "they who in America...have ever been under the allegiance of the Crown of England" to take note "how, according to the laws of England, they may be dealt with when they are found here." With this ruling, Warren dismissed his counsel and stood trial as a British subject from October 30 to November 1, 1867.[10]

Just before the court sentenced him to fifteen years imprisonment on November 16, 1867, Warren (conveniently forgetting his Fenian activities) declared, "I am an American citizen, and as such I owe allegiance to that government and to none other. I am a soldier in the United States army...I have fought for America; I belong at present to her national militia, and in case of war to-morrow between these two countries, England and America, my position is in the army." Warren further announced, "If America does not resent England's conduct towards me; if the only allegiance I ever acknowledged is not to be vindicated, then thirteen millions of the sons of Ireland who have lived in happiness in the United States up to this will have become the slaves of England." A week later, Britain executed the three Manchester Martyrs.[11]

Adams "regretted" the "conflict between established policy of the Executive Department and the ruling of the Federal Judiciary" regarding expatriation rights, which allowed the British Court to embarrass the United States by citing American jurists in favor of a doctrine the United States opposed. President Johnson also noted the conflict in his annual message to Congress, and asked the legislature to "declare the national will unmistakably upon this important question." At Seward's request, Attorney General Henry Stanbery performed a cursory review of Warren's case and admitted that the British Court correctly denied Warren a jury *de mediate linguae* under "perfectly well established" British law. For his part, Seward protested to Britain the conviction by asserting Warren's status as a naturalized citizen and cited the agitation his imprisonment caused in the United States.[12]

Meanwhile, Warren publicly petitioned Congress in terms that would have caught the attention of any proponent of a stronger American nation-state. Warren described his situation as that of a "first-class convict in a British bastile," and he reminded the congressmen that "British law claims me to be a British subject, ignores my United States citizenship, and consequently your right to confer it." Warren challenged Congress to answer whether under the Constitution and naturalization laws, "Am I...a citizen of the United States and entitled to her full protection, or am I under the English statutes a British subject and amenable to English laws in America," and he concluded his missive with hyperbole: "In the name of our common country, in the name of freedom, in the name of God, I ask of you to take hold of this matter vigorously, and compel England to expunge from her law books every presumption bearing on the rights of the American citizen. If she does not do it, wipe her from the face of the earth, and God will bless you."[13]

The Public Response in America

Even before the Manchester executions and Warren trial, the Fenian situation energized an increasingly powerful response in America during the summer and fall of 1867. Petitions came in from more than just select Fenians acting out of self-interest, or the family members of prisoners. President Johnson received a letter from New Jersey's governor Marcus L. Ward informing that citizens of that state demanded the release of those claiming to be U.S. citizens, while another similar petition contained more than a thousand signatures, including from the mayor of Brooklyn and other governmental officials and judges. While Seward received an appeal from Detroit's Fenian circle, New York's state constitutional convention mistook Nagle and Warren as *both* native-born Americans and asked for their release in a petition signed by Irish American Union Democrat judge Charles P. Daly, Republican ex-mayor of New York City George Opdyke, Republican Horace Greeley, and fifty others. Five thousand citizens of Hamilton County, Ohio, also called on Johnson to pressure Britain to release its Irish American prisoners.[14]

Now, as the crisis intensified, William H. Grace identified the situation as "the most popular political issue of the country at present." Fenian John Savage wrote Republican congressman Banks in November that the "non action of the United States representatives in Great Britain has led to deep humiliation here and to every form of insult and outrage—including martyrdom on the scaffold—on the other side. The doctrine of once a subject always a subject is as insolent as preposterous." Savage further reminded Secretary of State Seward that "thousands of those citizens have served the republic on the field. Thousands have won these citizenships helping to save the republic. Thousands are maimed for life in the service, and bear honorable scars in testimony of their *allegiance* to the United States government." A few weeks later, after Warren's sentencing, Savage grumbled that the doctrine of perpetual allegiance violated "the compact entered into between the United States and its adopted citizens," and he vowed that the American people could not "tamely submit to such a humiliating position." Reflecting on ceremonies commemorating the

British evacuation of New York City during the Revolution, held the day before he wrote, Savage declared that if America "admitted" the British doctrine, then the Revolution meant nothing because "we are not a country, but a colony of Great Britain." This "insult to the republic" aroused a question "vital to every man," Savage pronounced, for it involved "the spirit, character, and dignity of the republic."[15]

While the country debated the Fourteenth Amendment in late 1867 and early 1868, tens of thousands of Americans, both Irish-born and native-born, attended public meetings held from Milwaukee, Wisconsin, to Bridgeport, Connecticut, from Cincinnati, Ohio, to Nashua, New Hampshire, to urge that the federal government provide equal protection to native-born and naturalized American citizens abroad. The widespread debate generated by the naturalization issue signified more than affirmation of Irish Americans in the polity in the aftermath of the Civil War, or political opportunism by those who sought their votes. Through meetings, petitions, resolutions from state legislatures, and congressional debates, Americans discussed allegiance and expatriation within the context of considering what comprised a republican government, who had rights to participate in and be protected by it, and what it meant to be an American citizen. This discussion comprises a neglected facet of the broader debates that took place in the aftermath of the Civil War. The expatriation question took prominence after Congress sent the Fourteenth Amendment to the states on June 13, 1866, but it served as a backdrop during ratification debates about a measure that affirmed U.S. citizenship for naturalized persons, prohibited states from abridging "the privileges or immunities" of such citizens, and forbade states from depriving "any person," alien or native-born, "of life, liberty, or property, without due process of law" or "equal protection of the laws."[16]

Many Republicans embraced the impulse running through the discussions about expatriation rights that recognized a stronger American nation and an expansive view of rights to be enjoyed by all persons, including the right to self-determination. Some Irish Americans, meanwhile, declared that naturalization, by comprising a choice, showed a deeper appreciation of American republicanism than felt by the native born. At the head of this debate lay the meanings and practices of Irish American citizenship status, both in the United States and abroad. Contrasting native-born Americans, "born on the soil of freedom, and inheriting, without trouble or difficulty"—and therefore, not fully appreciating—the "priceless boon" offered by America, the *Irish-American* described Irish naturalized citizens as having made a choice for freedom in relocating to the United States. Moreover, the newspaper's editors asserted, Irish Americans "honestly earned" the rights of citizenship when the "expatriated sons of Ireland" battled alongside the native-born in support of Union, "dying that the republic which gave them shelter might live." Naturalized Americans now stood with clear title, "as citizens (with a trifling limitation as to the highest executive offices) in the same sense as though we and our fathers had possessed the land for generations." Reminding readers that the United States fought Britain in 1812 over the doctrine of perpetual allegiance, the *Irish-American* declared that disrespect for American citizenship now could not go unchallenged, or the vague "definition of the rights of American citizens" remain unrevised.[17]

Irish-born Colonel Patrick Guiney wrote Massachusetts congressman Benjamin Butler an indignant summation of the Irish American position. Guiney demanded immediate resolution on behalf of "millions of American citizens" and supported the concept of a strong American nation-state capable of defining and protecting its citizens:

> I am one of those millions, and I have fought side by side with thousands of men born, as I was, in Ireland, for the flag, the integrity, and the perpetuity of this Republic. Are we British subjects or are we American citizens? We must be answered *now,* and we are ready to fight the matter out in the political field—or in any other. This country was built, has been made great and prosperous, and hopes to go on in the increase of its greatness and prosperity, upon the right of expatriation. England denies this right, and does an overt act, if not a series of them, in pursuance of that denial, and in absolute defiance of our law. Will this nation— will Congress—will you—allow us to be seized, tried, condemned, and punished *as British subjects* with only a cataplasm of cold-blooded insolence from some Charles Francis Adams, to allay our sense of outrage? I ask this question, and I want to see it answered in decisive action. Nothing else will do. Remonstrance, trifling, effete diplomacy, can never settle a matter which the War of 1812 failed to adjust. The elegant and bold words of Mr. Seward, followed as they always are with flat inaction, will not avail—are not worth a Scotch bauble to us. The first duty of a government is to protect its citizens. Mr. Seward lets the citizen take care of himself [crossed out: and goes into real estate....] the best way he can. How differently all other governments act in the interest of each of their citizens whose rights as such citizens are denied, trifled with, or trampled upon abroad! Our country must not be an exception any longer; we must assert the force of our laws, and that our Constitution is not a false light to the immigrant nor a sham to those who swear allegiance to it.
>
> I am no Fenian, properly so called; but I think well of those who are, and better of their cause. This, though, has nothing to do with the subject. American citizens and American soldiers are startled by finding themselves pronounced to be that which most they hate to be—British subjects. We want this position answered by the establishment of our *status* under the Constitution and laws of our country. Do we ask too much?[18]

Butler replied within days to blame Johnson for the lack of vigorous protection of naturalized citizens and scorn any Irish American support for the president. "I sympathize most heartily with every word you say," Butler assured Guiney, "The naturalised citizen is as much an American as is the native born. Especially is this true of those who have fought side by side with us in the country's battles. Theirs is a baptism by fire and blood in to the church of American freedom American rights and protection of American laws."[19]

Meanwhile, mass meetings protesting the expatriation issue grew in size and frequency, uniting Irish- and native-born on this topic and publicly punctuating the message that Guiney sent privately. On November 23, 1867, tens of thousands of people convened in Cincinnati to resolve that the Ohio congressional delegation should use their best efforts to urge the government to "take immediate action" regarding all American citizens, whether native-born or naturalized, imprisoned by the British. That same evening, thousands of veterans of the Irish Brigade and Corcoran Legion gathered at Cooper Institute in New York City. After appointing a committee to lobby Congress, the meeting resolved that naturalized and native-born citizens stood subject to the same rights, responsibilities, and protections, and called on the government to defend the liberties of all citizens. The veterans then reminded everyone that they and other "Irish-born citizen soldiers of this Republic" had "recently emerged from the horrors and slaughter of a great war in defense of the flag of their adopted country, which flag they did fully believe would give them its protecting shelter against the claims to their allegiance of any Power on the face of the earth." To emphasize their point that the United States owed Irish Americans protection in exchange for their allegiance, some orators wore their federal army uniforms, and they spoke under a banner that read, "The rights of the naturalized citizens must be protected. Our claim in the Republic is earned by our devotion."[20]

A few days later, on November 26, 1867, another meeting gathered at Cooper Institute, this one open to the public and chaired by Irish American judge Charles P. Daly. Echoing the words of the Irish American veterans, this meeting emphatically affirmed that, where "the Constitution and laws impose on naturalized citizens the same burdens and responsibilities as on those of native birth, they should also receive the same protection from the government to which they have sworn allegiance, and to which alone they owe obedience." Inviting war should Britain not abandon the doctrine of perpetual allegiance, the meeting called on

> our fellow-citizens throughout the Union, by the mutual interests which bind us as children, by birth or adoption, of a common country, to assemble in mass meetings in their various localities, and, in the name of the people of the United States, to demand that our representatives at Washington shall not rest until the amplest protection is insured to all our people abroad, and the name of an American citizen is respected throughout the world, as was that of the Roman of old.[21]

In Boston, six thousand people assembled at Faneuil Hall on December 7, 1867, and adopted resolutions sent to President Johnson that rejected Britain's continued application of the doctrine of perpetual allegiance and its de facto nullification of American naturalization. Resolving that "the time has come when it is no longer just, politic, wise, or expedient to suffer any foreign power to exact service or allegiance of any kind from those who have been naturalized as citizens of the United States," the Faneuil Hall assembly petitioned

Congress to declare that "the fullest legal protection while traveling in foreign countries" applied to "all citizens, native and adopted," and called for the immediate release of all American citizens presently held as British subjects. Boston's ex-mayor Joseph M. Wightman served as president of the meeting, and eleven other prominent citizens served as vice presidents, including Irish-born Union veteran Patrick R. Guiney and Irish-born editor of the *Pilot,* Patrick Donahoe, in a nativist stronghold in the 1850s.[22]

Not content to confine his thoughts to private letters, Guiney ascended the podium at the Faneuil Hall meeting, an especially moving figure in that he bore the grievous head wound received in service of the Union without an eye patch. Echoing his earlier letter to Butler, Guiney declared to this broader audience that both native and naturalized citizens stood "on precisely the same footing as to their rights and duties" pursuant to the Constitution, and he attacked Britain's imprisonment and sentencing of Irish-born American citizens without the same due process applicable to native-born American citizens in British territory. Britain alone did not earn Guiney's anger, however, as he questioned the Johnson administration's courage in protecting America's citizens and defending so fundamental a right as expatriation. Guiney cast himself as the proponent of America's strong national power by arguing that, in allowing Britain to determine the Constitution's effect according to where an American citizen was born, America ceded to Parliament the power to "alter, amend, impair or destroy" this country's fundamental charter and the rights vested in it. For Guiney, the issue could not be simpler: the naturalized citizen and his chosen government contracted for protection on one side and allegiance on the other, and on adjuring foreign allegiance and swearing loyalty to the United States, "the Constitution flings its sunshine and its promise around the new-born citizen." Guiney acknowledged that the Irish "love their native hills and valleys," and did not leave their homeland willingly but as a result of expulsion at the hands of British actions, but in referring to "our nationality," he included himself as an American.[23]

From major urban centers to rural areas, similar mass meetings swept the entire country, calling for an affirmation of expatriation rights and demanding that the nation assert its power to protect those it defined as citizens. Republican congressman George S. Boutwell forwarded to the Johnson administration the proceedings of a public meeting held in Marlborough, Massachusetts, which declared that the United States had to stop allowing "any foreign power to exact allegiance from any citizen of this republic, whether native or adopted," and called for the federal government to demand release of all those American citizens tried and convicted as British subjects. On December 22, 1867, Milwaukeeans gathered at City Hall to identify the violation of any rights of citizens abroad as a cause of war in a petition sent to Johnson, Seward, and Congress. The attendees affirmed that "expatriation is one of the inalienable rights of man," so that one naturalized in the United States "should be regarded during the continuance of such domicile as invested with our national character, and entitled to the protection of our government," and "no distinction should be tolerated between native-born and naturalized citizens of the United States in regard to immunities and privileges in foreign countries." On January 8, 1868, the Knights of St. Patrick met in New York to adopt similar resolutions, sent to Seward, and called on the United States to settle by treaty with Britain the debate over expatriation rights once and for all.[24]

On January 17, 1868, citizens of Bridgeport, Connecticut, unanimously declared, "When the government of the United States has accepted the allegiance of any person of foreign birth it is its right and its duty to give him protection as such citizen everywhere, and it is not bound to conform to the policy or traditions of any other nation." Citizens in the Adirondack Mountains of Franklin County, in northern upstate New York, convened at the courthouse in Malone to echo the resolutions passed by the Cooper Institute assembly on November 26, 1867, and the residents of Auburn, New York, a central New York town where Seward had his home since 1823 and Harriet Tubman lived after the war, likewise met in a courthouse to proclaim that through the Revolution, War of 1812, Mexican War, and Civil War "our flag has had no more faithful, tried, or noble defenders than our adopted citizens." The Auburn meeting demanded European nations to respect, and the United States to defend, the equal citizenship of naturalized Americans.[25]

A number of state legislatures also sent resolutions to Congress. On January 22, 1868, the Wisconsin state legislature rejected the doctrine of "once a subject always a subject" as "repugnant to the dictates of enlightened civilization" and identified expatriation as "one of the inalienable rights of man." Wisconsin's legislature further vowed that "no distinction should be tolerated between native-born and duly naturalized citizens of the United States in regard to their immunities and privileges in foreign countries." A month later, Wisconsin's legislature reiterated its position by announcing that "if there is a principle which is popularly precious to the heart of the country, it is that those millions of foreigners who came to our shores had the right to come, the right to stay, the right to make themselves citizens by complying with the law, and a right, as citizens, to be defended by the government." Pennsylvania's legislature instructed its senators, and requested its congressmen, to urge Seward to demand the release of all American citizens, native or naturalized, and resolve with Britain the expatriation issue. The legislatures of Minnesota, Ohio, and California passed similar resolutions.[26]

In contrast to antebellum nativism, some state legislatures explicitly affirmed equality for native and naturalized citizens in America and abroad. On January 29, 1868, Maine's governor Joshua Chamberlain (of Gettysburg fame) endorsed a resolution of his state's legislature that contrasted with antebellum nativism there. Maine's resolution declared that "the naturalized citizens of the United States are entitled to the same rights and protection, in the lawful pursuits of life, as native citizens, whether at home or abroad," and any denial of this American doctrine comprised "an offence against the United States." Maryland's legislature, where the Know Nothing party achieved success before the Civil War, similarly asked its congressional representatives to secure "to all naturalized citizens the same rights of person and property, both at home and abroad, which are now possessed by the native-born." Kansas's legislature, moreover, declared it "a cardinal doctrine of republicanism that every man has the indisputable right to transfer his allegiance from one government to another" and recognized that pursuant to the Constitution, "naturalized citizens are entitled to all the rights privileges, and immunities of the native born," save "the offices of President and Vice President."[27]

Petitions continued pouring into Congress from across the country through the summer of 1868, though with particular intensity from late 1867 through the end of March 1868. A broad and popular movement urged equal rights and protection for native and naturalized citizens, action to compel Britain to recognize expatriation rights, and affirmation of the power of the United States to define and protect its citizens. By January 1868, Seward wrote Adams that, while the American public deplored the bloodshed of the Manchester rescue, nonetheless their sympathies "are every day profoundly more moved and more general" on Ireland's behalf. British application of perpetual allegiance to naturalized American citizens, "awakened a general feeling of resentment and deeply wounded our pride of sovereignty," Seward noted, as well as that "the people are appealing to this government throughout the whole country from Portland to San Francisco and from St. Paul to Pensacola." With tensions already exacerbated by Britain's actions in the late war, Seward feared the outcome unless the expatriation issue was resolved.[28]

Expatriation Rights and the Act of July 27, 1868

Under this pressure, Seward's State Department as well as Congress took up the cause of settling the expatriation issue once and for all. The issue took on heightened prominence as pressure peaked in a presidential and congressional election year, especially in light of Republican Party's poor showing in several 1867 state elections in the North. As Seward noted in March of that year, Fenianism not only gained the sympathy of Irish America but "of the whole American people."[29]

On November 21, 1867, an Irish-born Democratic congressman from New York, William E. Robinson, moved for Charles Francis Adams's impeachment for "neglect of duty" for "failing to secure" the "rights" of American citizens in Britain. Speaking in support of this demand a few days later (which became submerged by calls for Johnson's impeachment), Robinson attacked British imprisonment of American citizens and Americans who discounted this "insult" because "the victims are Irishmen or Fenians," and felt them "unworthy of a flag for his country, or a grave beneath its soil." Assuring that he did not claim that naturalized Americans could "invade England and there commit crimes with impunity," Robinson demanded that no American traveling abroad should ever be imprisoned without proper charges and a fair, speedy trial, or be subject to distinction based on naturalized status.[30]

Robinson challenged the country, "'Are we a nation?' If so, let us show it, not by broils at home, but with backbone abroad." Robinson also conflated Irish nationalism as a natural component of Irish Americanism and announced that Britain must realize "we sympathize with Ireland, and that we have a right to do so." Robinson went so far as to proclaim, "We have just as much right to Ireland as she [Britain] has," because Britain based its claim on "fraud" and the seven-century-long attempt of an "inferior race," the English, to conquer "a superior race like the Irish." Professing that the United States itself "is Irish," reflected in a large segment of the population as well as the number of congressmen who had at least partial Irish heritage, Robinson reminded his fellow representatives of the power Irish Americans held as a voting bloc. Robinson concluded with a resolution, which the House approved, calling for the Committee on Foreign Affairs to report a bill articulating the extent to which the United States would protect the rights of her naturalized citizens, and he quoted a poem published in the *New York Herald* the day before under the name of "that gallant soldier, genuine Irishman, and true American," Charles Halpine's fictional Miles O'Reilly:

> Oh, as citizens—Americans—
>   We gloried in the name,
> And on many a field our blood we shed
>   To guard your flag of fame;
> But to-day we lie in bonds, as if
>   Mere felons we had been—
> The only charge that England brings,
>   "Those boys were for the Green!"
> We are citizens twice over,
>   By the law and by the sword,
> By adoption and by service,
>   But our claims are now ignored;
> Say, Uncle Sam, is this your wish,
>   And do you really mean,
> That you've outlawed all your faithful sons
>   Whose birth was of the Green?[31]

Within days, Robinson delivered another speech in which he exposed to his colleagues Britain's two-faced position on perpetual allegiance by quoting an 1857 letter from the British Foreign Office, in which it refused to help the mother of a dead naturalized American citizen make a claim for compensation to the United States. The Foreign Office wrote to the woman, living in Dublin, that her son's naturalization precluded its involvement because he "deliberately renounced his connection with this country, and died a citizen of the United States." Robinson also invoked Irish American participation in the Civil War, quoting the words of Patrick J. Condon, formerly an officer in the Sixty-third New York: "I believe you are aware I shared the gloom and the glory of the

Irish brigade," but now "American citizens and soldiers who had shed their blood and periled their lives in defense of the Union were marched like felons from a British dungeon escorted by constabulary." Robinson named other arrested federal veterans, such as Denis F. Burke, who "three times won the rights of citizenship, once by the regular form of naturalization, and twice afterward by honorable discharges from the American Army."[32]

Robinson concluded by naming several Irish American generals, living and dead, and he noted that the British applied the rule of perpetual allegiance even to individuals born in America of parents born in the United Kingdom. "This is a question of importance to thousands of soldiers who have risked their lives in defense of the American banner," Robinson reminded his fellow congressmen, and "they deserve the protection of the flag they fought for." While denying that anyone had a right to violate British laws while visiting its territory, Robinson upheld the right of naturalized citizens to enjoy protection while traveling abroad on business or pleasure, and he predicted, "We are going to make a change in the law of nations."[33]

Other congressmen expanded Robinson's call to include equal treatment at home. On December 20, 1867, Republican congressman Hiram Price of Iowa proposed a resolution declaring the government's "obligation...to protect and defend the subject, whether native or adopted, whether at home or abroad," and that the country would "submit to no such oppression of our citizens by any Power" and "adopt such measures as will make it safe for an American citizen, free from crime, to travel in any part of the civilized world."[34]

A few weeks later, on January 9, 1868, the House unanimously approved resolutions asking the president to intercede with Britain to secure the release of prisoners in Canada, Britain, and Ireland. On January 20, 1868, Republican congressman Robert T. Van Horn of Missouri introduced a joint resolution that demanded redress for the execution of Michael O'Brien, one of the Manchester Martyrs who claimed American citizenship, and affirmation by the United States that naturalized citizens are "entitled to all rights and protection accorded natural-born citizens" and infringement of those rights by foreign powers constituted a cause for war. The following day, California's senator John Conness, an Irish-born Democrat who switched to the Republican Party, offered a similar joint resolution authorizing the president to use armed force if necessary to obtain the immediate liberation of Americans imprisoned by Britain.[35]

Finally, on January 27, 1868, Massachusetts's Republican congressman Banks reported a bill from the foreign affairs committee that declared naturalized citizens abroad entitled to the same protection of person and property accorded to the native-born and empowered the president to use all resources at the country's disposal to enforce it. The law carved out several exceptions: where the naturalized citizen stood guilty of a crime committed within the foreign state's jurisdiction, deserted from the armed services or conscription ordered by such state, obtained naturalization through fraud, committed treason against the United States, lived abroad continually for five years, failed to make proper report of property for taxation, returned to the native country with the intent of resuming domicile there or elsewhere in a foreign state, or engaged in any foreign war as a belligerent. For the first time, Congress stood ready to put teeth behind American support for expatriation rights.[36]

Except for a provision authorizing reprisals on British subjects, many congressmen from both parties enthusiastically embraced the proposed bill. Minnesota Republican congressman Ignatius Donnelly championed the measure not only because it confirmed the legal status of millions but because he felt it furthered America's role in shining as a beacon for republicanism. Claiming that Europe's refusal to recognize American naturalization showed the "contempt" with which monarchical governments treated democracies, Donnelly offered that the Civil War decided the "destiny of all mankind" and linked "the agitation which now pervades western Europe" as "the reflex of the mighty results of our own great struggle," an "'irrepressible conflict,' not alone between slavery and liberty, but between republicanism and monarchy." After winning the "crusade against slavery in this land," the United States now embraced another mission, to "be on the side of liberty and against oppression in all the lands of this earth," even if it meant war. Democratic congressman George W. Woodward from Pennsylvania called the Declaration of Independence "the first grand naturalization act adopted by this country," affirmed by blood spilled in the War of 1812, and he proposed the bill be amended to confirm American support for expatriation rights for its own citizens.[37]

For some, Banks's bill did not provide enough protection. Iowa Republican congressman James F. Wilson feared that the bill's section authorizing the president to use all resources at his disposal to secure the principles of expatriation did not have enough specificity, and the lack of explicit enforcement provisions could render the act hollow. Wilson felt that naturalized citizens should find "the shield of this Republic as firmly held for their defense as it is for those who are born upon our soil" and declared that "it is high time that feudalism... [is] driven from our shores and eliminated from our law." Wilson demanded a clearer, more forceful bill, so that the whole world would know that "the act of naturalization is equivalent to an American birth; and that where he may thereafter go the flag of the Republic envelops him as completely as it does the person of him who first saw the light of heaven in an American home." Illinois Republican congressman Norman B. Judd objected to the list of terms by which the federal government declared it would not provide protection, claiming it inappropriate to "hunt up disabilities, imaginary or supposed difficulties" and "notify foreign Governments what points might be made against such naturalized citizens."[38]

For different reasons, Democratic congressman John Chanler, one of New York's staunchest racists and a bitter opponent of the Fourteenth Amendment, also stood as an energetic proponent of affirming expatriation rights. Chanler did so as part of his attack on efforts to uplift blacks to equality, a notion he found to be repugnant and insulting to whites. Chanler called for an international diplomatic congress to convene, and for the United States to take the lead in changing the international law of expatriation as part of its global mission. Chanler made these proposals out of gratitude to foreign-born individuals who fought for the Union, but also so as to further define American citizenship as based on whiteness. Chanler equated expatriation and emigration as principles as fundamental as the rights articulated in the Declaration of Independence, and he deemed naturalized and native citizens "identical before the law" and enjoying an "inalienable" right to protection so long as they obeyed it. Chanler opposed the use of the phrase "naturalized citizens" in Banks's bill as implying a distinction where none existed, going so far as to say that while Congress had done so much work to declare no distinction among American citizens based on color, there should be none based on birth. While calling for action, "boldly, decisively" and "at once" to vindicate the rights of American citizens abroad regardless of birth, Chanler simultaneously rejected reprisals against British subjects as a reenactment of "the brutalities of the Middle Ages."[39]

On February 20, 1868, Banks reported a new bill from the Committee on Foreign Affairs, H.R. 768, which stated that "this government has freely received emigrants from all nations and invested them with the rights of citizenship; and whereas it is claimed that all such American citizens, with the descendants, are subjects of foreign states, owing allegiance to the governments thereof...this claim of foreign allegiance should be promptly and finally disavowed." The bill mandated three points: first, that any declaration or order of a government officer that questioned or restricted the right of expatriation was null and void; second, that all naturalized citizens traveling abroad would receive from the government the same protections accorded to native-born citizens in like situation and circumstances; and third, that whenever the president learned "that any citizen of the United States has been arrested...upon the allegation that naturalization in the United States does not operate to dissolve his allegiance to his native sovereign; or if any citizen shall have been arrested and detained, whose release upon demand shall have been unreasonably delayed or refused, the President shall be, and hereby is, empowered to order the arrest and to detain in custody any subject or citizen of such foreign government who may be found within the jurisdiction of the United States."[40]

Even in Britain, the growing furor across the Atlantic caused some popular support for abandoning perpetual allegiance. On December 11, 1867, British barrister William Vernon Harcourt wrote under a pseudonym in the London *Times* to argue that perpetual allegiance made sense during the feudal period, when few people left the realm except to escape some duty or service but proved inappropriate to deal with the waves of immigrants leaving British territory in the nineteenth century. Besides, Harcourt argued, recognizing Irish Americans as U.S. citizens would place greater responsibility on the American government for their behavior abroad. Harcourt proposed the establishment of a joint American-British commission to resolve the issue that Charles Francis Adams, that same day, identified as "one of the most threatening problems to the peace of the two countries." The following month, the Law Amendment Society after debate concluded that the time had come to resolve the Anglo-American divergence on the issue. Even the London *Times,* which two months earlier upheld the doctrine of perpetual allegiance in the context of the Manchester rescue and Warren trial, in January 1868 admitted that it understood the interest shown on the issue in the United States, considering that much of its population hailed from abroad, and called for a resolution with America.[41]

As discussion and rhetoric heightened to a crescendo, the State Department urgently sought to settle the expatriation issue, hoping to preclude the passage of additional inflammatory resolutions. Seward wrote Adams that the naturalization issue generated so much controversy that it had to be resolved before any other Anglo-American difference, such as the *Alabama* claims, could even be addressed. Stanley agreed in principle but took a cautious stance, instructing Edward Thornton, Britain's new minister to the United States, to assure Seward that Britain stood ready to abandon perpetual allegiance but that a number of legal questions had to be considered first—the status of children, for example, as well as what to do if someone renounced his naturalization and wished to return to his original allegiance. Seward pressed the issue and suggested to Thornton that the two countries should at least lay down the general principles for a resolution and leave the final details for a future convention, but the British government dragged its feet.[42]

Lasting from March 5, 1868, until final acquittal on May 26, 1868, President Johnson's impeachment trial in the Senate cooled Seward's ability to press the naturalization issue. Meanwhile, the House passed a modified version of Banks's bill, including a retaliation clause, on April 20 by the vote of 104 to 4, with 81 abstentions. Additionally, Adams resigned his diplomatic post and returned to the United States. Once relieved of the threat of removal from office, Seward immediately went back to work on the expatriation issue. On May 27, Seward instructed Benjamin Moran, serving as charge d'affaires in London until a successor could be named to fill Adams's place, to continue pressing the British. On May 28, Seward replied to British minister Thornton's request for assistance in the event of another Fenian attack against Canada by using the Fenian threat to help coerce a negotiated end to perpetual allegiance: "Whatever danger there may be of a disturbance of the peace at the frontier at the present time," Seward declared, "that danger is altogether due to the omission by the British Government to reasonably remove, either by legislation or negotiation, the indefeasible features of British policy on the subject of the rights of naturalized citizens of the United States." The following month, Seward instructed Moran to remind the British of the terms of Banks's bill pending in the Senate, including its reprisal provision.[43]

Both political parties addressed the issue during what turned out to be a close 1868 presidential election, in which Republican Ulysses S. Grant won with less than 53 percent of the vote, and possibly a minority of white voters. On May 20, the Republican convention declared in its platform "sympathy with all the oppressed people which are struggling for their rights," and contrasted former nativist impulses by holding that "foreign immigration, which in the past, has added so much to the wealth, development of resources, and increase of power to this nation—the asylum of the oppressed of all nations—should be fostered and encouraged by a liberal and just policy." The convention adopted another plank:

> The doctrine of Great Britain and other European powers, that because a man is once a subject, he is always so, must be resisted, at every hazard, by the United States, as a relic of the feudal times, not authorized by the law of nations, and at war with our national honor and independence. Naturalized citizens are entitled to be protected in all their rights of citizenship, as though they were native-born; and no citizen of the United States, native or naturalized, must be liable to arrest and imprisonment by any foreign power, for acts done or words spoken in this country; and, if so arrested and imprisoned, it is the duty of the Government to interfere in his behalf.

The Democratic convention followed suit and adopted planks of "equal rights and protection for naturalized and native-born citizens at home and abroad," absolute opposition to the doctrine of perpetual allegiance, and called for "the assertion of American nationality, which shall command the respect of foreign powers, and furnish an example and encouragement to people struggling for national integrity, constitutional liberty, and individual rights."[44]

Britain remained slow to respond while the Senate debated H.R. 768. Ultimately, the powerful chair of the Senate's foreign relations committee, Charles Sumner, blocked the retaliation clause because he deemed making retaliatory arrests of British subjects a "proposal of unutterable barbarism." The Senate passed a revised version of H.R. 768 on July 25, 1868, 39 to 5 with 20 abstentions. The House quickly concurred with the revised version that same day.[45]

The act signed by President Johnson on July 27, 1868—the day before the secretary of state declared that the nation had ratified the Fourteenth Amendment—affirmed that "expatriation is a natural and inherent right of all people, indispensable to the enjoyment of the rights of life, liberty, and the pursuit of happiness." The act disavowed foreign claims of allegiance on those which America had invested with citizenship and codified the right of American citizens to expatriate and naturalize abroad as well. Declaring any order or decision of any government officer that restricted or questioned the right of expatriation to be contrary to the fundamental principles of the government, the act held that all naturalized citizens abroad "shall be entitled to, and shall receive from this government, the same protection of persons and property that is accorded to native-born citizens in like situations and circumstances." Finally, under the act, whenever the president learned that an American citizen had been "unjustly deprived of his liberty by or under the authority of any foreign government," he had a duty to "demand" of that government the reasons for such imprisonment. If the rationale given appeared "wrongful and in violation of the rights of American citizenship," the president then had a duty to "demand the release of such citizen" and "use such means, not amounting to acts of war," to effect that release.[46]

With the Fourteenth Amendment, the Constitution for the first time definitively set forth the doctrine of equality between native-born and naturalized
citizens, and with the Act of July 27, 1868, Congress declared the policy of the
United States regarding expatriation rights. The Act of July 27, 1868, still in
force today, explicitly linked expatriation rights to those listed in the Declaration of Independence, and in conjunction with the Fourteenth Amendment, it
affirmed that naturalization placed foreign-born citizens on the same footing
as those born on U.S. soil. Moreover the Act of July 27, 1868, made citizenship
consensual and voluntary, by affirming one's right to opt out of birthright citizenship and choose a new allegiance. As nation-building measures, moreover,
both the amendment and the act affirmed the power of the government of the
United States to define its citizenry as well as protect it.[47]

On the other hand, implicit in this understanding of expatriation rights and
national citizenship was the idea that the destination country had to accept
the expatriating individual for naturalization. America affirmed the right for
people to change their allegiance but expatriates had to find a nation willing
to naturalize them. American support for expatriation rights did not require or
expect that nations had to agree to naturalize every incoming foreign-born person, or any at all. Individual nations, including the United States, retained the
power to determine whether to naturalize individuals, as well as the procedure
involved to do so. Accordingly, while the United States strongly supported expatriation rights and the voluntary nature of citizenship, it could also exclude
Native Americans, who were considered to have allegiance to their tribe, from
naturalization and American citizenship without paradox. In 1882, Congress
passed an act prohibiting the naturalization of Chinese individuals as well. At
the same time that a proponent of expatriation rights could support the right of
a Chinese-born person to change allegiance and naturalize abroad, that same
proponent could also support American exclusion of the Chinese from naturalization and citizenship without perceiving any contradiction. Individuals had a
right to expatriate under the Act of July 27, 1868, but nations did not have a
duty to naturalize those who they did not wish to naturalize.

Negotiation with the British

On the diplomatic front, Seward pressed the new American minister to Britain,
former senator Reverdy Johnson, to settle the naturalization issue. Minister
Johnson reported no success after a month, but he maintained pressure on Britain, especially after passage of the Act of July 27, 1868, and Seward's reminder
that America hesitated to apply itself vigorously against any further Fenian
attacks on Canada where Britain showed insufficient interest in resolving the
perpetual allegiance issue. By September 19, 1868, Minister Johnson reminded
Stanley that the naturalization dispute precluded even discussion of the *Alabama* claims, and Stanley finally assented. Although unwilling to conclude a
formal treaty until a royal commission studying the matter issued its report,

Stanley agreed that the two countries should at least approve a protocol agreeing on certain expatriation principles.[48]

On October 9, 1868, Minister Johnson and Stanley signed a protocol establishing that Britain would now consider and treat subjects naturalized in America as "in all respects and for all purposes American citizens," and vice versa. While the protocol could not take effect until Parliament revised the law codes pursuant to the report of the royal commission, the British government officially announced that it would, at long last, abandon the doctrine of perpetual allegiance. Also by 1868, the Senate ratified or had placed before it treaties which clarified naturalization rights with the North German Union, Bavaria, Baden, Württemberg, Hesse, Belgium, and Mexico as well.[49]

On February 20, 1869, a commission appointed by the crown the previous May recommended, as expected, that Britain abandon the doctrine of perpetual allegiance. Finding perpetual allegiance "neither reasonable nor convenient," the commission declared that the doctrine conflicted with "that freedom of action which is now recognized as most conducive to the general good as well as to individual happiness and prosperity," and was inconsistent with the practices of a state that otherwise allowed its subjects freedom to emigrate. Besides, the panel urged, a change in policy would alleviate Britain of any claim for protection by people who had "severed their connection" with the empire. Around the same time, Britain announced plans to release several dozen Fenian prisoners, among them John Warren, in the near future. In exchange, and as the Brotherhood's treasury and overall potency dwindled by spring of 1869, Grant's administration (which included Fenian sympathizer Schulyer Colfax as vice president) grudgingly signaled a greater willingness to prevent any further designs on Canada.[50]

On May 12, 1870, Parliament passed an act that allowed British subjects to naturalize abroad, except if some disability to doing so existed. The next day, a treaty between Britain and the United States recognized that American citizens could naturalize as British subjects and British subjects could naturalize as American citizens and thenceforth be held "in all respects and for all purposes" as citizens or subjects of their new country. The short treaty went on to mandate that British subjects who naturalized in the United States could resume their British subjectship by publicly renouncing their naturalization by May 12, 1872. Americans could do the same, although because of the requirement of Senate approval for the treaty, the two-year period within which to renunciate began to run on exchange of the ratification of the treaty. Finally, the treaty provided that Britain or America could readmit someone to citizenship, on that person's application, who had naturalized in the other country, and allegiance based on that naturalization would fall null. The Senate consented to the treaty on July 8, the United Kingdom ratified it on July 16, and President Grant approved it on July 19. With the ratifications exchanged on August 10, 1870, an issue left unsettled since the close of the American Revolution was resolved.[51]

The debate over expatriation rights had an unintended consequence: it brought into focus corruption within naturalization procedures, helping spur on a reform movement regarding that topic. The American consul in Zurich criticized the "worthlessness" of American naturalization certificates as evidence of citizenship and urged that only federal courts issue them not just to combat election fraud at home, but also so that governments abroad would respect their meaning. Allegations of fraud, such as charges that naturalization papers could be purchased for two dollars at one New York City bar, led to a congressional committee chaired by Ohio Republican William Lawrence to investigate 1868 election fraud in New York City. Congress incorporated the Lawrence Committee's recommendations into the July 14, 1870, second Enforcement Act, which focused on naturalization reform. While this act did not tighten or restrict access to legal naturalization, it did make it a crime to commit perjury in any naturalization oath or affidavit, make or sell false naturalization certificates, knowingly use any fraudulent naturalization certificate, or falsely represent that one was an American citizen. Further reflecting greater control by the federal government over naturalization affairs, the act gave U.S. courts jurisdiction over offenses against the act. The act also authorized federal supervision of elections in cities with populations greater than twenty thousand people and appointment of federal deputy marshals to guard polling places on national election days. Accordingly, for New York's 1870 election day, the federal government appointed almost eight hundred supervisors and twelve hundred deputy marshals in a multiracial force (at least two hundred of the deputy marshals were black).[52]

Fenians in North America tried another Canadian assault around the same time resolution came on the expatriation issue. On May 25, 1870, John O'Neill led Fenians who struck at Eccles Hill on the Vermont border. A presidential proclamation published in newspapers that same day declared that anyone who attacked Canada forfeited their "right to the protection of the Government, or its interference on their behalf to rescue them from the consequences of their own acts." The Fenian attack collapsed, and the American government tried O'Neill and several of his comrades (a far cry from the Johnson administration's response of paying the return fare for many of the Fenians stranded during the 1866 raid), and sentenced them to prison terms ranging from six months to two years. President Grant pardoned them within months, just before Election Day in New York State. Britain followed suit and, on January 15, 1871, began discharging Fenian prisoners so long as they accepted return to the United States. By February 1872, all Fenian prisoners in Canada had likewise been returned across the border save one. Fenianism would no longer pose a threat to Anglo-American relations, and it gave way in coming years to other Irish nationalist organizations such as Clan na Gael.[53]

Conclusion

In the end, Fenianism failed in its objective of liberating Ireland from British rule, but its activities did accomplish a number of unanticipated goals in the

Unites States. Fenianism generated a postwar opportunity for Irish Americans to solidify their right to act as citizens and coalesce as a voting bloc recognized by local and national political leaders. Fenianism helped publicize the contribution Irish Americans made to the Union war effort, and it facilitated Irish American inclusion in the broader community on the basis of this loyalty. The Fenians and their supporters increasingly acted as an Irish American political advocacy group, lobbying both lawmakers and society at large to promote changes in American citizenship doctrine.

In stunning contrast to the nativism of the 1850s, much of American society went beyond tolerating Fenianism to embrace it in the second half of the 1860s. Now both the Fenian movement and Irish American agitation regarding expatriation rights garnered widespread approval across the land. Irish Americans successfully asserted an American identity, along with expectations for legal change, at a moment when Irish American military service, egalitarian impulses, America's emergence from the Civil War as a global power without fear of tampering from abroad, and American concern for transnational republicanism contributed to a more accepting climate. Native-born whites proved more receptive to the moral arguments Irish Americans offered based on their military service, desire to spread American-style republicanism to Ireland, and calls for the United States to act as a more vigorous nation-state in defending those it defined as citizens. Moreover, the power of Irish American votes lured politicians from both parties.[54]

Akin to black protests against caste in citizenship based on color, Irish Americans opposed distinction based on whether one held birthright or naturalized American citizenship. Popular support across America forced the clarification of citizenship doctrine pertaining to naturalized citizens at home as well as abroad. Legislation emphasized the power of the United States to define and protect its citizens, including when they traveled abroad, in the context of America's consciousness and exercise of its power as a stronger nation-state and status as the global defender of republicanism. Some Americans even expressed their willingness to go to war over the issue. At the same time, this legislation affirmed the voluntary and consensual nature of citizenship by affording expatriation rights as a way out of birthright citizenship, including for Americans. In the end, diplomatic pressure forced Britain to accept the American view on expatriation rights and abandon its adherence to the doctrine of perpetual allegiance.[55]

In 1869, a report from the House Committee on Foreign Affairs recognized the petitions "from nearly every State, and signed by representatives of all parties" on the naturalization issue. The report offered that "no subject has ever shown greater unanimity of opinion than this demand for the protection of American citizens resident or travelling in foreign states" and ascribed congressional action in passing the Act of July 27, 1868, to "obedience to the prayer of these petitions." On May 23, 1870, New York City mayor Abraham Oakey Hall and Irish-born congressman William E. Robinson used loftier words in their speeches on American citizenship delivered to a packed house at Cooper

Institute, where Irish American veterans had gathered several years earlier to discuss the issue. In introducing Robinson, Hall, an alleged henchman in the Tweed Ring, lauded American citizenship as "an insignia more honorable than those of Kings" and inclusively noted that "when the subject of American citizenship is inscribed upon any banner, I want to march under it as you do." Hall acknowledged the impact of Irish American activism in helping force the Anglo-American naturalization treaty: "Irishmen set in motion the ball which rolled in the early part of this month to the feet of England's Sovereign and compelled her to sign a bill which accords to you and to me, and to every American, the rights throughout all Great Britain of American citizenship." Irish Americans, Hall explained, raised the issue; congressmen like Robinson advocated their concerns; and, through these efforts, Britain now accepted as American citizens those they formerly considered as subjects.[56]

Robinson opened his speech by declaring it a mortification on the national character any time the government shirked its duty to guard the rights of its citizens at home or abroad. A nation was more than the power of its military and the wealth of her coffers, Robinson continued, for if it would not protect its citizens at home and abroad, its might and money were meaningless. Robinson echoed Hall's words in ascribing to Irish American agitation, and his own efforts in Congress, the fact that foreign countries now respected the United States and citizenship in it. Naming Irish American Civil War heroes such as Corcoran, Mulligan, Shields, Meagher, Logan, and Sheridan, Robinson bristled that before, Irish Americans who had sworn allegiance to the United States and fought for her preservation were held, tried, and even convicted while visiting Britain for words spoken and acts done in America. Should war have erupted between the two countries, Robinson reminded his audience, they would have been liable to suffer death as traitors to the British crown. The agitation of naturalized citizens, however, resulted in their acknowledgement as equal to the native-born before all the nations of Europe, pursuant to a bill Robinson deemed one of the most important in the history of the United States.[57]

The Legacy of National Citizenship in the Era of the Civil War and Reconstruction

Americans confronted anew during the 1860s the issues of who comprised "the people," as well as what citizenship meant, and they did so in the course of the hard-fought triumph of the Founders' ideals of liberty and freedom over the paradox of slavery. From the smoke of the Civil War battlefields, and equally hazy antebellum understandings of what national citizenship meant, Americans began to clarify citizenship doctrine and practice in ways still with us today. Citizenship as a concept became primarily national in character. It contained certain civil, political, and economic rights to be safeguarded principally by the federal government, not the states, and which applied to all citizens regardless of whether they were black or naturalized. At the same time Americans acknowledged the nation's power to define and protect its citizens at home and abroad, they affirmed the consensual nature of citizenship by defending the expatriation right individuals have to opt out of their birth citizenship without their native country's permission and choose a new allegiance.

African Americans and Irish Americans energetically helped to shape the more modern and better-defined understanding of national citizenship that Americans fashioned after the Civil War. The experience of defending the Republic strengthened for many Irish Americans and African Americans their American identity and brought greater self-recognition of their allegiance to the United States. Moreover, shouldering the federal rifle invigorated in both groups expectations of full inclusion in the American people, along with the same protection, rights, privileges, and opportunities enjoyed by native-born whites. Both groups had in the past cited their contributions to America as a response to exclusion. Now, in the wake of the Civil War, Irish Americans and

6. "Uncle Sam's Thanksgiving Dinner." A celebration by Thomas Nast of
postwar egalitarianism, in this drawing Uncle Sam carves a turkey at a table surrounded
by men, women, and children of different races and nationalities. Uncle Sam's female counterpart, Columbia, sits at the far left of the table between a black man and a Chinese family.
An Irishman sits at the far right of the illustration. A banner in the background celebrates the
Fifteenth Amendment, and the table's centerpiece is labeled "Self-Government/Universal
Suffrage." Behind Uncle Sam a painting depicts Castle Garden, a major entry point
for immigrants before Ellis Island. Thomas Nast in *Harper's Weekly*,
November 20, 1869. Courtesy Library of Congress.

African Americans reasserted that argument with greater vigor as a result of
their sharpened sense of American identity, as well as the moral foundation
provided by their military service to the Union. Both groups relied on these
military contributions to help frame and resolve the debate over the meaning
of the Union's victory and define changes made to the nation's constitutional
order. That between 188,000–196,000 African Americans, and 150,000 (if not
more) Irish Americans, fought in the Union's armed forces made some native-
born whites more receptive to the idea that members of both groups should be
included in the American people. Their military service allowed both groups to
push their expectations to the center of Civil War era debate.[1]

From this dialogue between Irish Americans, African Americans, and
native-born whites, a new understanding of national citizenship emerged in
the law: that any person born or naturalized in the United States (excluding
Native Americans) was entitled to the same rights and privileges regardless of
race or former status as a slave or alien. As Republican congressman George S.
Boutwell from Massachusetts pronounced on July 4, 1865, "The war for

freedom and the Union has been carried on by the whites and negroes born on this continent, by the Irish and the Germans, and indeed by representatives of every European race. With this fresh experience we ought to make it a part of the organic government that no State shall make any distinction in the enjoyment of the elective franchise on account of race or color." Although Boutwell spoke about the vote, his sentiments pointed to a broader understanding of citizenship rights in general.[2]

African Americans and Irish Americans significantly involved themselves, in separate but intersecting ways, in the redefinition of American citizenship that occurred during the 1860s. The uncoordinated efforts of both groups resulted in a broader concept of citizenship, the rights associated with it, and its applicability to blacks, the foreign-born, and native-born whites on an equal basis. Both groups helped eliminate the possibility of caste or second-class categorization in the law of national citizenship, consummated with the ratification of the Fourteenth Amendment, even where it existed in practice as to blacks through extralegal white discrimination and then the rise of Jim Crow. Even where tensions persisted between members of both groups, and many Irish Americans continued to define citizenship along racial lines, overall Irish American and African Americans helped to mold the more modern understanding of national citizenship that we recognize today. In the process, African Americans and Irish Americans *acted* as American citizens.

Moreover both groups successfully urged a more robust use of the national government's power, at least in terms of defining and protecting the rights associated with citizenship. In this way, African Americans and Irish Americans helped to promote the concept of a stronger American nation-state. African Americans urged the federal government to assume the authority to define citizenship rights and then enforce them, revising in the process the boundaries of federalism in the law of citizenship. Irish Americans challenged the United States to assert its power on a global stage, not only as a defender of republicanism but in terms of protecting abroad those who it identified as its citizens. Overall, the theme of a more powerful nation-state linked with Attorney General Bates's earlier recognition that national citizenship afforded to individuals rights and duties that could not be truncated by the laws of a state, and Francis Lieber's argument that the United States formed, "and ought to form, a Nation." Adding to this impulse, African Americans and Irish Americans benefited, as did the native-born, from a pension system for Civil War veterans and their families, which gradually replaced local models of assistance and strengthened the ties between the federal government and its citizens both during and after the war.[3]

Additionally, African Americans and Irish Americans experienced a kindling of American patriotism generated by their sense of inclusion during the 1860s, in contrast to cynicism and exclusion born of slavery and nativism before the war. The arguments of both groups now helped to fuel the broadening of American nationalism from a white/native form to something more willing to incorporate immigrants and blacks, even where nationalism remained hotly contested ground. Both groups thus helped to bring to gradual fruition, in practical terms, Abraham Lincoln's July 1858 declaration that something stronger than a blood nationality united Americans. Lincoln noted that "perhaps half our people...have come from Europe," without any connection to the Founding days by blood. "But when they look through that old Declaration of Independence they find that those old men say that 'We hold these truths to be self-evident, that all men are created equal' and then they feel that that moral sentiment taught in that day evidences their relation to those men," Lincoln pronounced, "that it is the father of all moral principle in them, and that they have a right to claim it as though they were blood of the blood, and flesh of the flesh of the men who wrote that Declaration...and so they are." For Lincoln, "That is the electric cord in that Declaration that links the hearts of patriotic and liberty-loving men together, that will link those patriot hearts as long as the love of freedom exists in the minds of men throughout the world."[4]

For blacks, change came in particularly profound forms during the 1860s. Ex-slaves suddenly transformed from chattel property to person and, in light of their military service, could never go back to bondage again. Both Northern and Southern blacks validated their manhood and American identity by joining the armed forces in the first place. This choice, along with other experiences in the military, helped many blacks to recognize an American allegiance from which they had been excluded by law before the war (besides the fact that consideration about their national allegiance probably never crossed the mind of most slaves).

Black soldiers bolstered their declarations of equality by successfully protesting unequal pay, opposing other inequities, and performing well in combat. Blacks seized on the ideals embodied in events such as flag presentations, the intersection of equal rights and military justice, and mustering-out ceremonies, and sought to have them permanently enshrined in citizenship doctrine. Military experiences helped blacks appreciate a greater awareness of the power of national organization, and increasingly recognize, in harmony with free labor Republican ideology, the value of education and the worth of black labor.

In this context, blacks articulated more developed and cohesive demands for rights through national and state-level conventions and organizations, including across the South within months of Appomattox. Blacks helped to shape the legal concept of citizenship that emerged during Reconstruction by calling for due process and equality before the law, civil and political rights, and economic autonomy and self-sufficiency, including intervention by the federal government to prevent de facto slavery created through disadvantageous race-based state laws and contractual interpretations. With astounding speed, blacks went from having no rights that whites were bound to respect to asserting a voice in America's governance and standing as equal citizens armed with the rifle, the vote, and other important rights, even where some whites sought to prevent them from enjoying these rights in practice. African Americans helped to motivate such changes in the law as the Civil War amendments, Civil Rights acts of 1866 and 1875, Reconstruction acts, Enforcement acts, and creation of the Department of Justice.

Additionally, more than two decades after the war, Joseph T. Wilson, who fought with the Fifty-fourth Massachusetts, lauded the effect of educational opportunities in the army: "Since the war I have known of more than one who have taken up the profession of preaching and law making, whose first letter was learned in camp; and not a few who have entered college." In the aftermath of the Civil War, the Freedmen's Bureau helped coordinate the education of ex-slaves, while various faith-based aid societies such as the American Missionary Association, American Freedmen's Union Commission, and organizations run by specific denominations, poured money, supplies, and thousands of Northern white teachers into the South during the late 1860s. Black colleges such as Fisk University in Nashville, Tennessee; Hampton University in Virginia; and Howard University in Washington, D.C., established within years of the Civil War, trained black teachers. The educational initiative comprised a long-term success of Reconstruction. By 1892, 25,000 schools existed for blacks in the South, and nearly two-thirds of the 20,000 Southern blacks who taught in them had themselves been educated in schools founded during Reconstruction. By the 1890s, more than 2 million Southern blacks had learned to read, many could write, and blacks edited more than 150 newspapers across the South.[5]

For Irish Americans, changes wrought by the Civil War were less profound, if more stable and long-lasting. Irish American military service accelerated the withering, though not the death, of nativist feelings and action against them. Irish Americans now unapologetically celebrated their ethnic character and religious identity, but felt entitled to do so as Americans. In contrast to ante-bellum nativist fears, the country embraced the Fenian movement and its self-identification as the vanguard of an American-led global impulse toward republicanism and democracy. Empowered by their military service and their votes, Irish Americans successfully demanded that the United States enforce expatriation rights and remove legal distinction between native-born and natu-ralized citizens. These changes in the law came about through the Fourteenth Amendment and the Act of July 27, 1868. In the process, Irish Americans es-tablished their power as a national voting bloc and helped to sanctify the idea that conscious embrace of Americans ideals and principles formed a basis of citizenship alongside native birth.

In the explosion of postwar industrial and geographic growth, more Ameri-cans began to view immigration not as a liability but as a boon, a way to fuel industrialization and provide the labor necessary to open still untapped resources of the American continent. According to John Higham, nativism lay substantially dormant for the two decades after Appomattox; overall, it never again came close to achieving the power it did during the zenith of Know Nothingism. This circumstance inspired Frederick Douglass, who in 1879 noted that nativist hostility against the Irish and Germans had melted, and that Boston, Baltimore, and New York were no longer scenes of violence against European newcomers. As racist forces reestablished their dominance, Douglass voiced his hope that black rights in the South would similarly "revive, survive and flourish again."[6]

Postwar changes played out for Irish Americans in different ways. The dedication in May 1879 of New York City's new St. Patrick's Cathedral, and the election in 1880 of Irish-born William R. Grace as that city's first Catholic mayor, indicated the increasing stability of Irish America and the Catholic Church in the United States. By the 1880s, accessible public transportation in many cities permitted an avenue of escape from working-class slums to places such as Brooklyn and South Boston. Irish Americans began to play increasingly critical roles in urban politics through the use of organized machines, such as New York's Tammany Hall, and by 1890 Irish American bosses led many urban Democratic machines or otherwise wielded heavy influence. The establishment of nationwide religious, political, and cultural institutions, such as the Ancient Order of Hibernians (reorganized in 1871), Philo-Celtic societies (1873), the American Irish Historical Society (1897), and the Gaelic League of America (1898), focused on creating a respectable Irish cultural identity so that members of this ethnic community could assimilate not as members of a sullen group but one noted for its culture and civilization. By 1900, two-thirds of Irish America, 5 million strong, was born in the United States, and Irish Americans had largely achieved occupational parity with native whites: 35 percent engaged in white collar work or farming, 50 percent worked as skilled laborers, and 15 percent toiled as unskilled laborers (although these proportions varied geographically).[7]

Yet, based on persistent native-born fears about Irish American political power now wielded through powerful machines noted for their corruption, political tensions continued. The New Jersey legislature in 1870 thus abolished elective government in Jersey City as a result of the election of Irish Americans there, and the 1885 Massachusetts legislature removed Boston's police force from city control when Hugh O'Brien became that city's first Irish Catholic mayor. Thomas Nast published in *Harper's Weekly* during the late 1860s and early 1870s cartoons that depicted simianlike Irish Americans. One caricature, entitled "The Day We Celebrate," represented St. Patrick's Day celebrations in 1867 by showing apelike Irish Americans wearing top hats and beating policemen. Such depictions contrasted with Nast's 1869 illustration, "Uncle Sam's Thanksgiving Dinner," which celebrated egalitarianism by depicting Uncle Sam carving a turkey at a large table surrounded by men, women, and children of different races and nationalities, including the Irish. Uncle Sam's female counterpart, Columbia, sits at the far left of the table between a black man and a Chinese family, and the table's centerpiece celebrates "Self-Government/Universal Suffrage."[8]

Citizenship status notwithstanding, uncertainty remained for increasing numbers of Irish Americans ascending into the middle class by the 1890s. Besides facing the painful separation of moving away from ethnic neighborhoods, these Irish Americans stood vulnerable to possible Yankee rejection as

7. "The Day We Celebrate." In contrast to including an Irish American
at the table in "Uncle Sam's Thanksgiving Dinner," Thomas Nast in this engraving
depicts the Irish Americans as stereotypical apelike brutes. Thomas Nast in
Harper's Weekly, April 6, 1867. Courtesy American Social History Project.

well as financial failure, which threatened to send them tumbling back to the
working-class neighborhoods they sought to escape, especially during the economic turmoil of the last quarter of the nineteenth century. The transition into
the middle class also gave rise to a vaudeville form of parody, which amused
some Irish Americans, and infuriated others, by poking fun at Irish American
aspirations, as well as class tensions within ethnic America.[9]

Moreover, the Irish American working class continued to face the realities
of industrial life. On one hand, Irish American males broke into the ranks of
the skilled and unionized trades to a surprising degree by 1900. On the other
hand, the economic turbulence that marked the period from 1873 to 1897, as
well as increasing labor tumult (from 1880 to 1905, the building trades alone
experienced ninety-five hundred strikes), created for these workers tough and
uncertain lives. Irish Americans played a prominent role in many labor actions, which led to bloody clashes between mobs and militia. Hostility among
some Americans toward organized labor blurred with attitudes toward Irish
Americans as a result of their prominence in unions. A good portion of Irish
America's unskilled laboring population, moreover, remained in squalid slums
such as Chicago's Bridgeport or Philadelphia's Skittereen.[10]

In this context, a radical form of Irish American thought emerged, creating some previously unexpected alliances and helping blur ethnic lines by

emphasizing class issues instead. According to historian Edward T. O'Donnell, one reason antebellum Irish Americans often stood on the "wrong side of all the burning social issues of mid-nineteenth-century American, be it temperance, abolition, or public education" was their pre–Civil War association of reformers with nativism. The diminution of nativism, affirmation of naturalized citizenship, and the economic situation during the 1870s and 1880s, all led to and made possible Irish American interest in causes such as antimonopolism, labor unionism, and land reform.[11]

In surprising ways, Irish American radicalism carried forward the Civil War era's discussion about human rights, and it merged with some elements of the Protestant, native-born reform tradition. These circumstances encouraged both groups to reevaluate their assessments and stereotypes of the other. Irish American organizations honored abolitionist Wendell Phillips on his death in 1884, and when a fellow crusader against bondage, James Redpath, died in 1891, Irish and American flags fluttered next to each other at his home. Both Phillips and Redpath supported the Irish National Land League, an organization that promoted Irish independence coupled with socioeconomic change, united the Irish American community across class, and introduced thousands of working-class Irish Americans to labor and reform critiques.[12]

Born in Galway in 1837, Patrick Ford became one of the most famous of the Irish American radicals. Ford's parents brought him to Boston in 1845, in flight from the Famine. At fifteen, Ford worked as a printer's apprentice for William Lloyd Garrison's *Liberator,* and in 1862, he enlisted with his brother in the Ninth Massachusetts (as a postwar letter shows, Ford had great respect for his commander, Guiney). Ford relocated to New York City in 1870 and there founded the *Irish World,* which achieved an impressive audience on both sides of the Atlantic. Ford used the *Irish World,* which he renamed the *Irish World and Industrial Liberator* in 1878, to endorse trade unions, justify labor violence, and promote issues such as women's suffrage and black inclusion in the labor movement. While calling for Irish independence, Ford also urged social reform on both sides of the Atlantic. In the mid-1880s, Ford tempered his positions in the face of intensifying labor violence and nativist condemnation of Irish American involvement in it, criticism from the Catholic Church, and denunciation by "pure" Irish nationalists who recognized the need for social and economic reform in Ireland but charged that Ford's radicalism distracted attention from the objective of Ireland's liberation.[13]

Ford also took exception to what he characterized as Anglo America's view that they "were *the* American people," along with its expectation that other groups had to reject their own identity in order to assimilate with it so as to create a nationality. Ford instead vowed that "each element has a perfect right to its own traditions, its own social usages, customs, religion, modes of living, amusements" and that "no other element has any right...to interfere or dictate in the matter." Fearing that "Anglo-Americans and Protestants" would transform America's republic into an aristocracy, Ford looked to Irish America "for the preservation of democratic principles in our government." As Frederick

Douglass tried to do for African Americans, Ford articulated an Irish American vision of the nation matching Irish American aspirations for equality.[14]

Meanwhile, even some middle-class and upper-class Irish Americans embraced the notion of labor reform. Patrick Guiney, serving as Boston's assistant district attorney after the war, did not forget his youth spent working in factories, and in 1866 he accepted the nomination of the Workingman Party to run for Congress (he came in third, behind the victorious Republican candidate and the Democratic nominee). The Workingman Party supported an improved moral, intellectual, and social culture for workers, besides practical measures such as an eight-hour work day. During the campaign, Guiney vowed to fight for laborers' rights, called for support from both Democrats and Republicans to promote the interests of common American citizens, and expressed anger that one New Hampshire company issued an 80 percent dividend to its stockholders but not so much as a cent increase in its workers' wages.[15]

On the other hand, native reformers promoting clean city governments grew angry with corrupt Irish American political machines. Eugene Lawrence's scathing articles, published between 1871 and 1876 in *Harper's Weekly*, blamed Irish Catholics for New York City's problems, and recalled their role in the wartime Draft Riots. The labor struggle forced working-class Irish Americans to confront strikebreaking and mob violence. Intensifying bloodshed associated with labor unrest helped reinvigorate nativism against Catholic and foreign-born radicals, and immigrants in general, by the later 1880s. Members of the American Protective Association, founded in 1887 and centered in the Midwest, took an oath never to vote for a Catholic, employ one if a Protestant could be found, or strike with them. While never achieving the success of antebellum nativist organizations, the group raised a cry at the flow of new immigrants.[16]

Within years of the Civil War, the Orange Riots in New York City illuminated all of these persistent tensions. On July 14, 1870 and 1871, deadly riots erupted in New York City during successive Protestant Irish parades celebrating the anniversary of William of Orange's victory over Catholic James II at the battle of the Boyne (there were eight deaths in 1870 and more than sixty deaths and one hundred injuries in 1871). The Orange Riots transcended simple, centuries-old animosity between Protestant and Catholic Irish to reveal the continuing contest in New York City between working-class Irish Catholics standing up to defend their rights against persecution versus middle- and upper-class Protestant reformers disgusted with Tammany Hall corruption and seeking the downfall of the Tweed Ring, persistent nativists who still feared the threat of Irish Catholic ascendance, and concerns overall regarding the values and increasing protest radicalism of a growing working class. Each side worried that the other threatened to subvert American republicanism, so that, as historian Michael A. Gordon wrote,

> Irish workers and many middle-class Irish allies believed that the Orangemen
> symbolized the oppression they had known in Ireland and that Orange principles

would help to subvert republicanism and 'Anglo-Saxonize' America at the same time that industrialization was causing class lines to harden. Supporters of the Orangemen, believing it was the Irish Catholics who threatened republicanism, attempted to reassert the values they believed should govern social relationships as immigrants like the Irish challenged their class authority.

Irish American veteran, author, and revolutionary D. P. Conyngham in 1871 thus distinguished between Protestantism as a "religion of toleration" but Orangeism as "the embodiment of intolerance, bigotry, and slavish degradation."[17]

Meanwhile, Irish nationalism, which figured so prominently in the redefinition of American citizenship, alienated some of its American support, as some elements of the movement shifted from romantic forms of rebellion to social revolution and terrorism by the 1880s, at the same time America faced the labor strife with which Irish Americans became increasingly associated. The stabbing murder of the new chief secretary for Ireland in Dublin in May 1882 echoed President James Garfield's September 1881 death from an assassin's bullets. Bombings by "Dynamiters" in England mirrored labor agitation in the United States such as the Haymarket episode. Increasing violence alienated Americans, and divisions appeared even within Irish America over Irish nationalism's radical tactics.[18]

Despite their uplifting transformation in the law, blacks continued to confront even greater paradox and duality, as practical realities unceasingly challenged egalitarian ideals. For example, the Union veterans' organization, the Grand Army of the Republic (GAR), officially adopted a color-blind policy for membership and permitted blacks to join it. Yet, while integrated nationally, black and white veterans often attended segregated local posts. The GAR nonetheless provided blacks with opportunities on several levels, and historian Barbara A. Gannon aptly noted that its members, "black and white, created and sustained an interracial organization in a society making giant steps backwards into an almost dark age of racial segregation. If they could not hold back the darkness, they should receive some credit for lighting a small candle against the coming of the night." By the 1880s, the GAR afforded blacks a vehicle for broadcasting their vision of the Civil War's meaning against those who sought to submerge the memory of slavery and black military service, or promote the South's Lost Cause mythology. Through GAR posts, blacks commemorated emancipation and the ratification of the Fifteenth Amendment, sponsored speeches and campfire meetings recalling their military experiences, honored local black veterans as well as white friends in naming their posts, participated alongside whites in Memorial Day observances, Fourth of July celebrations, and GAR encampments, and consistently reminded members of both races of black military service and their struggle for freedom in the process. Integrated posts existed more frequently than previously thought and allowed blacks to take part as full-fledged members, bringing together veterans regardless of race or class just as the Union army did decades earlier. Even segregated posts in the GAR represented a milestone, incorporating blacks and whites into a nationwide organization and affording black veterans a local social, charitable, and political platform. While the GAR did not vigorously challenge lynching and discrimination against blacks with action, and many GAR members held prejudiced views typical of the time, on the other hand the GAR provided an important veterans organization for blacks and kept alive memories for future generations of both blacks and whites.[19]

Some USCT officers maintained a presence in the lives of their black soldiers, while others promoted the African American cause. Internally, many black veterans maintained a close sense of comradeship with their former army friends, staying in touch whether through the GAR or private means. In some areas, USCT veterans clustered together, such as in North Carolina's northeastern central section, permitting the development of sustained security and support networks that resulted in less white-on-black violence than in other sections of the state. Moreover, an 1872 gerrymander by Democrats created the "Black Second" congressional district in that area, which elected black congressmen such as James O'Hara, Henry Plummer Cheatham, and George H. White during the last quarter of the century. Other black veterans, however, focused not on community or citizenship issues but confronted in personal ways the intensely difficult adjustment to civilian life many soldiers felt after serving in combat; others simply lost contact, especially those who moved away from the local area where their unit had been recruited. Moreover, in the South, black veterans frequently became the target of intense anger from whites who felt overlapping feelings of prejudice, betrayal by their participation in the Union victory, or simply dismissed them as willing simpletons conned by the Yankees.[20]

Not surprisingly, historian Donald R. Shaffer found that black veterans as a group lived poorer, shorter lives marked by lower status jobs, harder physical labor, and greater susceptibility to disease than did their white comrades but also achieved a level of prosperity greater than blacks who did not serve. Shaffer concluded that the Civil War "left a significant positive legacy" for black veterans, validated their manhood, created admiration for them within the black community, and permitted them to benefit from military pensions. The 1890 census also reveals a disproportionate number of black veterans in developing urban areas in both the North and South. On the other hand, Shaffer notes the partial nature of blacks' gains, the targeting of black veterans by angry white southerners, and the eventual marginalization of their contributions to the Union victory.[21]

Even the pension process provided a paradox for blacks. Shaffer found that white veterans achieved greater success in obtaining pensions than blacks did. In a sample he examined, about 92 percent of white Union veterans made at least one successful application as compared to approximately 75 percent of blacks, almost 84 percent of white widows received a pension versus 61 percent of their black counterparts, almost 70 percent of white parents succeeded in obtaining a pension in contrast to about 36 percent for blacks, and approximately half of both black and white minor children proffered successful claims.

Yet Shaffer accurately notes that bureaucratic factors, and other matters admittedly borne from overall racism against blacks, skewered these numbers, but not race-neutral pension laws. Where they did refer to blacks, these laws often sought to assist black veterans and their dependants by setting an easier standard for African American widows in terms of proving their marriage. The illiteracy of many African Americans hampered their ability to complete adequate applications, and poverty hindered their means to hire attorneys skilled in prosecuting pension claims and to pay for other related legal expenses. Racism by individual examiners at the U.S. Pension Bureau, who investigated black veterans' claims more closely than they did whites' applications, infected the process. These examiners more frequently ordered "special examinations" for black claimants, often out of racism although other times simply because defective black applications failed to offer sufficient proof of service such that the government could grant a pension.[22]

Judicially, the courts initially protected black legal rights. When defense counsel challenged a guilty jury verdict against whites who burglarized a black woman in Kentucky on a May 1866 night on the basis of a state law that a black had no right to testify against the white thieves, the circuit court of Kentucky took notice that formerly "black witnesses were excluded" so that "crimes of the deepest dye were committed by white men with impunity." "Congress met these evils," continued Supreme Court justice Noah Swayne, writing in his capacity as circuit court judge, "by giving to the colored man everywhere the same right to testify 'as is enjoyed by white citizens,' abolishing the distinction between white and colored witnesses, and by giving to the courts of the United States jurisdiction of all causes, civil and criminal, which concern him, wherever the right to testify as if he were white is denied to him or cannot be enforced in the local tribunals of the state." Swayne identified the Civil War as an "impetuous vortex" that swallowed up the "evil" of slavery, leading to a Thirteenth Amendment that "destroyed the most important relation between capital and labor in all the states where slavery existed." According to Swayne, the amendment's drafters "sought security against the recurrence of a sectional conflict" but also "felt that much was due to the African race for the part it had borne during the war," and they were "impelled by a sense of right and by a strong sense of justice to an unoffending and long-suffering people." The court upheld the constitutionality of the Civil Rights Act of 1866, relying on the Thirteenth Amendment's authorization that Congress could enforce it by appropriate legislation and prohibit a reconstitution of slavery except in name, and added that the amendment "throws its protection over every one, of every race, color, and condition within that jurisdiction, and guards them against the recurrence of the evil," slavery, so that "the constitution, thus amended, consecrates the entire territory of the republic to freedom, as well as to free institutions" for all future time.[23]

In 1873, Iowa's Supreme Court affirmed the "equality of all men before the law, which is not limited by color, nationality, religion or condition in life," and that the principle forbidding that rights could be denied "on the ground of race or color" had "become incorporated into the paramount law of the Union" by the Civil Rights Act of 1866 and the Fourteenth Amendment. In *Coger v. The North Western Union Packet Co.*, a biracial teacher of black children boarded a steamboat on the Mississippi River. When the management of the vessel, following a custom separating blacks from whites on board, sold Coger a meal ticket entitling her to eat only in a separate area of the ship, she returned the ticket and asked a man to buy for her an unrestricted ticket without informing the ticket agent that it was for a black. After seating herself at dinner, Coger was told by one of the steamboat's officers that she must leave the table and eat elsewhere, and when she refused, the captain forcibly removed her from the dining area. Coger resisted so that the table cloth was torn off and dishes broken. The court noted, "By her spirited resistance and her defiant words, as well as by her pertinacity in demanding the recognition of her rights...she has exhibited evidence of the Anglo-Saxon blood that flows in her veins. While we may consider that the evidence, as to her words and conduct, does not tend to establish that female delicacy and timidity so much praised, yet it does show an energy and firmness in defense of her rights not altogether unworthy of admiration." The court went on to affirm that all who observe reasonable rules and regulations of a common carrier had the right to receive first-class accommodations, regardless of color, that the Fourteenth Amendment and Civil Rights Act of 1866 sought to protect blacks from prejudice borne of their former condition of slavery and "protect them in person and property from its spirit," and upheld liability for damages to the plaintiff.[24]

Moreover, Cecilia Elizabeth O'Leary correctly noted that an "uneasy relationship between citizenship, racism, and nationalism would persist into the next century as a central contradiction in the construction of American identity and allegiance," something highlighted from the start by the fact that black soldiers did not march in the Grand Review of 150,000 Union soldiers in May 1865, an inspirational pageant celebrating American power and nationhood, but focused on Northern whites. Nonetheless, the process of incorporation had begun; despite setbacks and retreats, there would be no going back. As O'Leary noted just as accurately, "At no other time during the nineteenth century would blacks consider themselves so fully American as they did during Reconstruction." Thus Thomas W. Higginson, an abolitionist colonel of a black regiment, recalled a joyous service for blacks on January 1, 1863, during which he "waved the flag, which now for the first time meant anything to these poor people," and "there suddenly arose...a strong male voice (but rather cracked and elderly), into which two women's voices instantly blended," singing "My country, 'tis of thee, Sweet land of liberty, of thee I sing!" As more blacks joined in, Higginson motioned for the whites on the podium to remain silent because he "never saw anything so electric; it made all other words cheap; it seemed the choked voice of a race at last unloosed." The Civil War era proved the moment when blacks definitively asserted that the United States belonged to them as much as any other, that nothing could change the fact that this was their land too.[25]

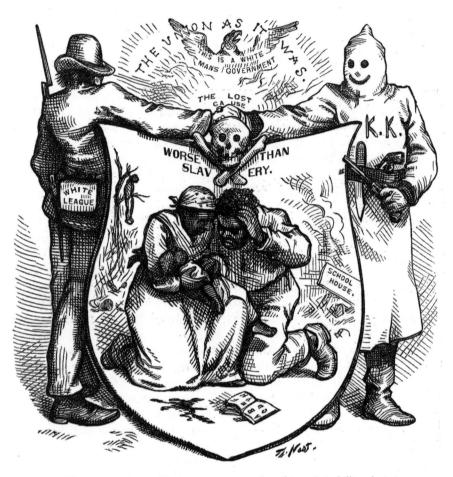

8. "The Union as it was. The lost cause, worse than slavery." A chilling depiction
of extralegal violence against blacks in the South, in contrast to their newfound rights in
the law, this engraving shows a member of the "White League" shaking hands with a member
of the Ku Klux Klan over a shield which depicts an African American couple holding a
possibly dead child, while a man hangs lynched from a tree in the background. Thomas
Nast in *Harper's Weekly*, October 24, 1874. Courtesy Library of Congress.

On the other hand, vicious racist violence across the South continued to
prevent most blacks from enjoying their rights. Such violence severely impeded
Republican voting, the efforts of the Freedman's Bureau, and the ability of
blacks to live as citizens in practical terms. In 1871–72, the Klan burned thirty
Mississippi black schools and churches, and in the period between January and
March 1871, assassinated sixty-three Mississippi blacks. In December 1874,
in Vicksburg, Mississippi, the site of one of the Union's greatest military triumphs during the Civil War, an armed White Line force ousted black veteran

Peter Crosby from his elected position as sheriff. The paramilitary force did more than that, moreover, murdering in cold blood fleeing blacks who had no intention of resisting. At least twenty-nine, if not more, blacks lay dead at the end of this violent spree, many of their bodies rotting in the open because their families feared to claim and bury them. Similar brutality erupted at Clinton, Mississippi, in early September 1875, as White Liners attended a Republican barbecue with concealed weapons. After creating a verbal confrontation, one White Liner shot into the head of a black man at point-blank range, and full-scale mayhem ensued. Some armed blacks fired back before scattering in fear for their lives, and white posses ranged through the area for days, butchering black leaders and white carpetbaggers and leaving their bodies exposed to animals and elements. Between thirty and fifty men died.[26]

By 1875, 2,141 blacks had been killed and another 2,115 wounded by white supremacists in Louisiana alone since the end of the war. Some of these deaths occurred singly, others in massacres such as one in the small hamlet of Colfax, Louisiana, where whites butchered and mutilated dozens of blacks on Easter Sunday 1873, after they sought to assert their political rights. In September 1874, a full-blown White League militia army numbering five thousand men defeated thirty-five hundred Republicans in battle on Canal Street, in the heart of New Orleans' business district, forcing the temporary flight of Governor William P. Kellogg until federal troops arrived. This was not the first time New Orleans witnessed large-scale violence aimed at curbing black and Republican power. On July 30, 1866, as Republicans sought to reconvene a state constitutional convention and enfranchise black Louisianans, a white mob stormed the convention and attacked blacks parading in support outside the Mechanics' Institute where the delegates met. Police joined whites in shooting and beating blacks, and by the end of the riot, at least thirty-four blacks (and likely more) and three white Unionists lay dead, with more than a hundred injured.[27]

After the war, the hostility Irish Americans in the South displayed against Republicans, African Americans, and Reconstruction legislation helped integrate them into regional white society. Historian Christopher Waldrep found that in Vicksburg, Mississippi, for example, whites in the 1870s unified as a racial bloc in which color trumped ethnicity or class interests. Irish Americans in the South shared in that region's particular allegiance to the United States during Reconstruction, and its unique relationship with the vision of American nationalism that ascended as a result of the Civil War.[28]

The activities of white racists contrasted with the newfound ability and courageous determination of ex-slaves in the South to hold conventions, vote, move about, and do other things formerly prohibited to them when in bondage. Poll taxes and literacy tests, coupled with extralegal intimidation and brutish violence, combined to prevent many blacks from exercising the franchise as a practical matter. For example, the Republican vote in Claiborne County, Mississippi, went from 1,844 in 1873 to 496 in 1875. In Yazoo County, in which more than twelve thousand blacks lived, only seven Republican ballots were cast in 1875, and that number dropped to two on election day in 1876.[29]

Meanwhile, the Supreme Court slowly began to whittle away the practical impact of the Civil War amendments and legislation, beginning with the *Slaughter-House Cases* (1873), which truncated an expansive interpretation of the Fourteenth Amendment. Holdings in *U.S. v. Cruikshank* (1874) and *U.S. v. Harris* (1883) undermined anti-Klan legislation. In *Cruikshank,* the Supreme Court overturned the handful of convictions the government obtained against participants in the Colfax Massacre under the Enforcement Act of 1870. After ruling that the indictments were faulty for not specifying race as the white defendants' motivation, the Supreme Court sacrificed protection for blacks on the grounds of federalism, holding that the Fourteenth Amendment permitted Congress to prohibit only state violations of black rights, while state and local governments alone had the power to punish crimes committed by individuals. Where local authorities could not or would not prosecute white racist violence, blacks now stood open to terror dispensed by the Klan. In *Harris,* a lynch mob raided a Tennessee jail and captured four white prisoners, despite the sheriff's efforts to protect them. One of the prisoners died, and the federal government prosecuted members of the mob under Section 2 of the Enforcement Act of April 1871, which made it a crime for two or more persons to conspire for the purpose of depriving anyone of the equal protection of the laws. The Supreme Court struck down the provision as unconstitutional, again ruling that the Fourteenth Amendment authorized Congress only to prohibit contravening state action, but left the acts of individuals to regulations by the states. In *U.S. v. Reese* (1875), the Supreme Court permitted the imposition of poll taxes and similar measures in a holding that the Fifteenth Amendment simply prohibited race-based exclusion in voting practices.[30]

The *Civil Rights Cases* (1883), involved defendants from New York, Missouri, Tennessee, Kansas, and California who denied blacks access to public facilities in violation of the Civil Rights Act of 1875, which desegregated public accommodations. In ruling that the Thirteenth Amendment purged badges of slavery but did not remove racial discrimination in inns, public conveyances, or theaters, and reiterating that the Fourteenth Amendment addressed state action but not private discrimination, the Supreme Court nullified much of the Civil Rights Act of 1875. By the 1880s, states across the South began enacting Jim Crow laws, formally quashing black equality in practice, disenfranchising blacks through poll taxes and literacy requirements, and mandating segregation in schools, education, and public accommodations.[31]

In the North, some Republicans recoiled at the growth of the federal government and tired of the use of federal troops in Southern states by the mid-1870s. Moreover, as the desire for sectional reconciliation flourished, Northern whites showed an increasing willingness to overlook racial injustice in the South. Overall, federal protection for black rights diminished in substantial ways and further allowed for the success of Southern white supremacists. The changing political economy that marked the last quarter of the nineteenth century also helped fuel Northern abandonment of African Americans. During and shortly after the Civil War, blacks' labor, quest for property, and thirst for education made them seem to Republicans like model free labor Americans. Thus, in 1865–67, Northern Republicans embraced the idea that blacks could be productive workers, in contrast with the view of prejudiced Southern whites who mistreated blacks through violence and swindles. Practices of racial discrimination precluded blacks from gaining meaningful prosperity, however. While this situation led to the Civil Rights Act of 1875, opponents persuasively argued that the act radically expanded governmental power for the purposes of a particular group. Even in the North, complaints arose that blacks wanted to gain social equality without working for it, as had other groups, and that they sought to rely instead on legislation that reinforced reliance on the government and undermined adherence to free labor. Republicans grew disillusioned and indifferent toward blacks they increasingly saw not as exemplars of free labor ideology but as dependents reliant on governmental assistance, and who participated in and sought to exploit class conflict and labor tension. Mounting fear among Republicans about the expanding role of government, as well as disdain for interest group politics overall, fueled skepticism about black calls for land reform and increased governmental services and protections. In this way, political mobilization by blacks actually began to work against them.[32]

The Civil War era, then, bequeathed to the nation an incomplete and divided legacy, one in which the tremendous potential of the late 1860s began eroding as early as the 1870s. The promise of the wartime years, recognized by Frederick Douglass in 1863, remained unfulfilled in significant ways. As blacks, long-standing as well as newly converted white egalitarians, and diehard racists continued to contest the new meanings of citizenship during the era of the Civil War and Reconstruction and its aftermath, the result for African Americans was not a permanent linear leap forward but one of bold steps followed by continuing contention, and of the erosion of practical enjoyment of rights even after the solidification of a legal foundation for future egalitarianism. While historian Brooks D. Simpson identifies developments of the 1860s, as revolutionary, he aptly contends that in practical terms blacks learned to live with continuity of prewar treatment by the following decade. As Donald R. Shaffer noted, glory won on the battlefield segued into a "more profound, if less dramatic" battle as blacks fought to preserve the advances made during the Civil War era and to preserve validation of African American manhood in categories such as politics, governmental relations, economic autonomy, family life, interracial and intraracial relations, and historical memory. By 1895, 1865 Medal of Honor winner Christian A. Fleetwood of the Fourth USCI noted bitterly, "After each war, of 1776, of 1812, and of 1861, history repeats itself in the absolute effacement of remembrance of the gallant deeds done for the country by its brave black defenders and their relegation to outer darkness."[33]

Notwithstanding, Americans during the 1860s laid a durable foundation for future correction. National citizenship, more important than before and now trumping that of the states, became better defined in a process that would continue to develop in the coming decades. A new paradigm ascended in which loyalty trumped race, color, and ethnicity in defining who belonged in the American people. Choice of allegiance, and the idea that one could elect to be an American and decide to embrace the ideals of the Republic regardless of race, ethnicity, or place of birth, rose to the same level as birthright as the maker of citizens. The theoretical notion that naturalized citizens should stand on equal footing as the native-born received constitutional sanction. Legislation still in force today ranked expatriation alongside the inalienable rights identified in the Declaration of Independence.

The experiences shared by native-born white, Irish American, and African American soldiers in support of the Union helped fuel this breakdown of racial and nativist distinction in the law. Even as an impulse of sectional reconciliation swept through the country and sought to submerge the race issue, blacks kept alive the memory of their service. Moreover, while some white Union veterans sought to hide from sight black participation in the war for fear of jeopardizing reconciliation, others kept alive the memory of African American loyalty by publishing papers about their service with black troops (several of which are cited in this book) or including blacks in GAR activities (whether in integrated posts or not). Even while prejudice may have persisted in many white Union veterans, so too did the mutual recognition of those who fought together to preserve the integrity of the nation.

Moreover, even as their practical enjoyment of rights eroded, the potential for blacks now existed, an indestructible template created from the storming of Fort Wagner and rejection of unequal pay, the convening of black conventions, and the ratification of the Civil War amendments and promulgation of congressional civil rights statutes. Affirmations of equality and inclusion also came in subtle yet moving ways, and not just through the law. A spirit of remembrance swept over the United States on May 29–30, 1869, with flowers placed on the graves of fallen Union veterans in 336 cities and towns across thirty-one states. As part of these commemorations, participants made a profound statement of inclusion in Wilmington, Delaware, as "native and foreign, white and black, Catholic and Protestant, orthodox and liberal, all acknowledged the binding force of patriotism and our common humanity, and joined in doing honor to the memory of those who died that the nation might live, and that 'government of the people, for the people, by the people, should not perish from the earth.'" A black band and GAR post joined city police and firefighters, a white GAR post, and "Irish Nationalists with the harp and the sunburst flag of Erin" in a procession that included more than two thousand Protestant and Catholic children from various Sunday schools. The Catholics and a detachment from the GAR turned off into the Catholic cemetery where a requiem service was celebrated, while the rest of the procession continued to the Wilmington and Brandywine Cemetery, where the principal ceremonies occurred; earlier, visits had been made to smaller cemeteries, including where the black soldiers being honored lay at rest. At West Chester, Pennsylvania, white GAR Post 31 and black Post 80 held joint ceremonies and heard an oration by the Welsh-born former commander of the Irish American Sixty-ninth

Pennsylvania Infantry, Brigadier General Joshua T. Owen, before paying tribute to veterans in Greenmount Cemetery. The entire cortege then relocated to the black cemetery, "where the same ceremonies were gone through with."[34]

Perhaps even more powerful symbolically, during a service not long after Appomattox, a well-dressed black man shocked the congregation at Richmond's St. Paul's Episcopal Church by approaching as the minister was about to administer communion. The man's action violated the tradition that blacks, confined to a special section of the church, could receive the sacrament only after all whites had. The congregation remained motionless in their seats as the black man knelt down at the rail until another distinguished, gray haired man approached and knelt down next to him: Robert E. Lee. The service then resumed.[35]

In later decades, as Jim Crow and social Darwinism ascended, and the Supreme Court affirmed the doctrine of separate but equal in *Plessy v. Ferguson* (1896), blacks held onto the memory of such uplifting moments of equality, along with others borne from their military service. For them, such moments, as well as the legal changes of the 1860s and 1870s, made up the potential for the future. Molding the legacy of the Civil War comprised a major theme of Frederick Douglass's postwar life, as he tried to maintain blacks' place as part of "the people" as well as in the national memory. Douglass declared in 1884 that the cause of blacks "may be buried under the dust and rubbish of endless discussion concerning civil service, tariff and free trade, labor and capital...but our Lazarus is not dead. He only sleeps." In 1888, Douglass noted that while "the nation may forget...the colored people of this country are bound to keep the past in lively memory till justice shall be done them." As black soldiers, leaders, ministers, and common folk debated the meaning of participation in the Civil War, and tried to maintain a voice in the American polity, they kept alive the hope of the Civil War era's achievements and potential—a memory that blacks began to define even before taking up arms in that struggle. In doing so, these individuals stoked the fire of hope and courage, and they articulated arguments that would be brought to fruition in future civil rights movements carried on by their sons and daughters, and culminating in another corrective moment a century after the Civil War.[36]

Notes

Introduction

1. 10 Op. Attorney Gen. 382, 383 (Nov. 29, 1862).

2. States chartered and incorporated towns, businesses, educational institutions, and professional and religious associations, which then self-regulated members via rules and bylaws. Novak, "Citizenship," 87–101, 105–8. Maltz, "Fourteenth Amendment," 320–21. Kaczorowski, "Revolutionary Constitutionalism," 871–72. *Barron v. Baltimore,* 32 U.S. 243, 247, 250–51 (1833) (Bill of Rights did not apply to the states; states, not the federal government, are the guarantor of individual rights); see also 10 Op. Attorney Gen. 382, 385 (Nov. 29, 1862).

3. Marshall, *Citizenship and Social Class,* 8. Foner, *Story of American Freedom,* xvi–xviii, xx. Shklar, *American Citizenship,* 1–3, 14, 26, 52, 64, 67–72, 99. Novak, "Citizenship," 84–87.

4. Citizenship links social, political, and legal history. Smith, *Civic Ideals,* 30–31. Novak, "Citizenship," 84–87.

5. Kaczorowski, "Revolutionary Constitutionalism," 873–74. Novak, "Citizenship," 105–9. Richards, *Conscience and the Constitution,* 113–14. *Cong. Globe,* 38th Cong., 1st Sess., 2615 (May 31, 1864).

6. For a synopsis of the debate about whether its drafters intended the Civil Rights Act of 1866 to reach both private and governmental discrimination, see Maltz, *Civil Rights, the Constitution, and Congress,* 70–78. See also Finkelman, "Prelude to the Fourteenth Amendment." 417 n. 12; Kaczorowski, "Revolutionary Constitutionalism," 920–21; Smith, *Civic Ideals,* 286.

7. 10 Op. Attorney Gen. 382, 389, 394–95, 401, 409 (Nov. 29, 1862). Lieber, *Amendments of the Constitution,* 15–16, 27–28, 36, 39. See also Benedict, *The Constitutional Amendment,* 2 (criticizing in 1866 that the Fourteenth Amendment "declares who *are* citizens, but does not declare, as it should do, that all citizens shall owe paramount allegiance to the United States, and to no other nation, Government or State, and shall be protected by the United States in the rights of citizenship").

8. For how emancipation led to the question of what freedom meant as a practical matter, see Michael Vorenberg, *Final Freedom.* Philadelphia *American,* quoted in Kaczorowski, "To Begin the Nation Anew," 53. Spear, *Citizen's Duty in the Present Crisis... October 7th, 1866,* 16. See also Jenkins, *Our Democratic Republic,* 26–28 (urging in 1868 uniform suffrage laws so as to form a homogenous national republic).

9. Moore, *Constitutional Rights and Powers of the People*, 3–65. Ackerman, *We the People: Transformations*.

10. Loring, *Oration...December 20, 1866*, 8. Frank, *With Ballot and Bayonet*, vii, 2, 9, 11, 23.

11. Richards, *Conscience and the Constitution*, 119, 123, 258.

12. *Addresses of the Hon. W.D. Kelley, Miss Anna E. Dickenson, and Mr. Frederick Douglass...July 6, 1863*, 7. Vorenberg, *Final Freedom*, 82–84.

13. Frederick Douglass, "Govern with Magnanimity and Courage," Philadelphia, September 6, 1866, in Blassingame and McKivigan, *Frederick Douglass Papers Series One*, vol. 4:139–46, 140 ("adopt the principles proclaimed by yourselves, by your revolutionary fathers, by the old bell in Independence Hall"). *Christian Recorder,* July 1, 1865 ("the American people" had "sadly degenerated from their first principles," and it was "time that these errors should be corrected.").

14. *Addresses by His Excellency Governor John A. Andrew...Wednesday, August 27, 1862*, 4.

15. The contrast of both groups with the experience of German-born Americans during the war is instructive by its differences. According to historian Christian Keller, language barriers and Civil War experiences, including being made scapegoats for the Union defeat at Chancellorsville, hindered German inclusion, and made many German-born Americans become more withdrawn into their ethnic community after the Civil War, Carl Schurz and Francis Lieber notwithstanding. Keller, *Chancellorsville and the Germans*.

16. *Sixth National Congress of the Fenian Brotherhood...September, 1867*, 14. For examples of "whiteness studies," see Ignatiev, *How the Irish Became White*, and Roediger, *The Wages of Whiteness*.

17. For legislative histories of the Civil War amendments and other statutes, see work by William E. Nelson, Xi Wang, Earl M. Maltz, Michael Vorenberg, Herman Belz, Harold Hyman, and Michael Les Benedict. I am influenced by Michael Vorenberg's statement that "the fluid interaction between politics, law, and society in the Civil War era" defined the history of the Thirteenth Amendment, in which "political tactics, legal thought, and popular ideology were always intertwined, and, at every moment, unanticipated events interceded and led to unexpected consequences." Vorenberg, *Final Freedom*, 3, 4–7, 107–11, 130. Richards, *Conscience and the Constitution*, 14, 81, 98–99, 108–9, 113–14, 137, 144, 153. Maltz, *Civil Rights, The Constitution, and Congress*, 5, 7, 11, 29. Lloyd, "Revising the Republic," 71.

18. Wendell Phillips, "Under the Flag," in Phillips, *Speeches, Lectures, and Letters*, 396–414: 414. Francis Lieber denied that Americans in the 1860s held greater wisdom than the Founders, but he recognized the need for revision due to the Civil War and the country's territorial, economic, and technological expansion. Lieber, *Amendments of the Constitution*, 4, 8–9, 12. John M. Stearns honored founding documents which articulated "the radical rights of man," but he branded "toleration of slavery" as "a departure from principle" and argued for a corrective moment to bring Founding ideals into reality. Stearns, *The Rights of Man...An Address...July the Fourth 1866*, 11, 12, 13. See also Loring, *Oration...December 20, 1866*, 23. Vorenberg, *Final Freedom*, 4–7, 107–11. Lloyd, "Revising the Republic," 71. Kaczorowski, "To Begin the Nation Anew," 49. Richards, *Conscience and the Constitution*, 14, 98–99, 108–9, 113–14, 137, 144, 153.

19. Davis, *Speech...September 24, 1863*, 12, 13, 14, 19. Boutwell, *Reconstruction...July 4, 1865*, 5, 6, 8, 10. See also Kelley, *Safeguards of Personal Liberty...June 22, 1865*, 2, 9, 12–13. Dickson, *Address...October 3, 1865*, 5, 12 ("This solution introduces no new element, no new principle into our Government. It is but the complete application of the principles of our fathers, set forth in the declaration of independence."); 20 ("Our fathers, yielding to the embarrassments of the day permitted negro slavery to remain, with the expectation, it is true, that it would soon pass away," and it was thus the duty of the country to bring this "expectation" to fruition). Loring, *Safe and Honorable...July 4, 1866*, 5 ("Tell the signers of the Declaration of Independence, how the truths which they uttered were borne on to the glorious result, when emancipation was proclaimed, and the bondman went free; tell the founders of our Constitution, how that great instrument became, through fire and blood, the supreme law of the land, and the Union was preserved.").

20. Snay, *Fenians, Freedmen, and Southern Whites*.

21. Lawson, *Patriot Fires*, 2–3, 5, 7, 11.

22. Kaczorowski, "Revolutionary Constitutionalism," 903–5. John H. Schaar called the conscious embrace by groups of unifying principles "covenanted patriotism," and it intersects with Melinda Lawson's finding that organizations such as the Union League promoted the idea that "loyalty,

not race, defined a patriot." Schaar, *Legitimacy in the Modern State*, 287–96. Lawson, *Patriot Fires*, 112. Nativism tinged the Union League in the 1870s, as the elites who led the organization considered urban reform as well as Reconstruction issues. Gordon, *Orange Riots*, 14, 204, 209.

23. Lawson, *Patriot Fires*, 11, 19–20, 26, 29–32, 88–90, 110–11, 115, 117–18, 120. See Francis Lieber, *No Party Now; But All For Our Country;* and Joseph Fransioli, *Patriotism, A Christian Virtue: A Sermon Preached By The Rev. Joseph Fransioli, At St. Peter's (Catholic) Church, Brooklyn, July 26th, 1863* for two calls in 1863 for national patriotism and putting national interest above that of party.

Chapter 1. The Crisis of Citizenship in the 1850s

1. Kettner, *Citizenship*, 323–24. Kettner, "Revolutionary Era," 208–42.
2. Finkelman, "Prelude to the Fourteenth Amendment," 480. Kennedy, *Population…1860*, xii.
3. Kettner, *Citizenship*, 300, 311–12.
4. *Dred Scott v. Sandford*, 60 U.S. 393 (1857). Kettner, *Citizenship*, 312. Levine, *Politics of Representative Identity*, 62.
5. Oregon's 1859 state constitutional prohibition on black migration went unenforced, as did an 1851 Iowa law fining blacks who remained in the state after three days. Indiana enforced its 1851 prohibition against black migration, and the state's black population remained almost identical from 1850 to 1860. Illinois enforced, much less strictly than did Indiana, its 1853 legislation mandating the expulsion and fining of black immigrants, and its black population grew in the 1850s by almost 2,200. Paul Finkelman claims racist legislation in the North began to abate after the 1830s, despite continuing prejudice in practice. Finkelman sees the Civil War as an accelerant for a process of enlarging rights for Northern blacks that began before the 1860s, in contrast to Leon Litwack's view that "change did not seem imminent" for them. Finkelman, "Prelude to the Fourteenth Amendment," 417–21, 425–27, 437–41. Litwack, *Negro in the Free States, 1790–1860*, 279. Maltz, "Fourteenth Amendment Concepts," 306. Nieman, *Promises to Keep*, 28. *Roberts v. The City of Boston*, 59 Mass. 198 (1850).
6. Anbinder, *Nativism and Slavery*, 9–12. Clark, *Irish in Philadelphia*, 20–22. O'Connor, *Fitzpatrick's Boston*, 17–19. Pinheiro, "Anti-Catholicism, All Mexico, and the Treaty of Guadalupe Hidalgo," 72–73. O'Leary, *To Die For*, 17.
7. Handlin, *Boston's Immigrants*, 45, 51–52. Fanning, *Nineteenth Century Chicago Irish*, 2. Brown, *Irish American Nationalism*, 18. Miller, *Emigrants and Exiles*, 315. Clark, *Irish in Philadelphia*, 29, 36. Lawrence J. McCaffrey, "The Irish American Dimension," 3. Kennedy, *Population…1860*, 91–92. Anbinder, *Nativism and Slavery*, 25–29, 50–51.
8. Massachusetts removed 1,537 immigrant paupers in 1855 and 3,267 in 1858. Parker, "Legal Construction of Immigrants in Antebellum Massachusetts," 607, 622–24, 629, 631. Ryan, *Beyond the Ballot Box*, 85. O'Connor, *Boston Irish*, 65. Levine, *The Irish and Irish Politicians*, 58–59. Handlin, *Boston's Immigrants*, 60, 61, 63, 74, 76, 86, 91, 93–94, 99, 115, 121. O'Connor, *Fitzpatrick's Boston*, 83, 84. Miller, *Emigrants and Exiles*, 319–20. Lord, Sexton, and Harrington, *History of the Archdiocese of Boston*, 2:453–54. Clark, *Irish in Philadelphia*, 34, 41, 43.
9. Byron, *Irish America*, 55–56, 63–65, 169, 174 (discussing Albany). Wang, "Federal Enforcement Laws," 1035 n. 86. Holmes, *Irish in Wisconsin*, 27. Foreword by Lawrence J. McCaffrey in Fanning, *Nineteenth Century Chicago Irish*, viii. Miller, *Emigrants and Exiles*, 315. McCaffrey, "Irish American Dimension," 7. Skerrett, "Catholic Dimension," 22–60: 26.
10. Anbinder, *Nativism and Slavery*, ix, 29, 50–51, 104–7, 127–28, 145, 156.
11. Ibid., 135–41.
12. Anbinder, *Nativism and Slavery*, 137–41. Mulkern, *Know-Nothing Party in Massachusetts*, 211 n. 55. The margin of victory came from Massachusetts's more urban counties of Essex, Middlesex, Suffolk, and Norfolk. Banks, *Address of His Excellency Nathaniel P. Banks to the Two Branches of the Legislature of Massachusetts, January 6, 1860*, 11.
13. Anbinder, *Nativism and Slavery*, 145–57. An email exchange with Professor Anbinder provided insight into the subject of this paragraph.
14. Rev. Daniel W. Cahill, August 13, [1861] (*Pilot*, September 21, 1861).
15. *Pilot*, September 23, 1839; July 20, 1861; February 15, 1862; August 16, 1862. Handlin, *Boston's Immigrants*, 133. Hernon, *Celts, Catholics and Copperheads*, 65. Clark, *Irish in Philadelphia*, 73. McCaffrey, "Irish American Dimension," 5. *Citizen*, January 14, 1854 (Mitchel), in Truslow, "Peasants into Patriots," 53.

16. *Frederick Douglass' Paper,* January 12, 1855 (William J. Watkins to Frederick Douglass, Ellicottville, [New York?], January 3, 1855); January 19, 1855; August 17, 1855 (Julian); November 16, 1855. *National Era,* January 11, 1855.

17. Hall, "'Faithful Account of the Race,'" 157–58, 161, 165–66. Remond quoted in Lloyd, "Revising the Republic," 76, 78–79.

18. Nell, *Services of Colored Americans,* 6. Von Frank, *Anthony Burns,* 48. Hall, "'Faithful Account of the Race,'" 157–58, 161, 165–66. Lloyd, "Revising the Republic," 76, 78–79. *Proceedings of the State Convention of Colored Citizens of the State of Illinois, Held in the City of Alton, Nov. 13th, 14th and 15th, 1856* in Foner and Walker, *Proceedings of the Black State Conventions, 1840–1865:* 68–82, 68, 70, 75–77. For an example of a petition from blacks relying on the historical point raised by Nell, see the *Memorial of Thirty Thousand Disfranchised Citizens of Philadelphia to the Honorable Senate and House of Representatives* (1855).

19. Garrison, *The Loyalty and Devotion of Colored Americans in the Revolution and War of 1812.* Livermore, "An Historical Research Respecting the Opinions of the Founders of the Republic on Negroes as Slaves, as Citizens, and as Soldiers," in *Proceedings of the Massachusetts Historical Society,* 86–248. Hall, "'Faithful Account of the Race,'" 157–58, 161, 165–66, 170–72.

20. Joyce, *Editors and Ethnicity,* 11–12, 49, 75–76, 90–91, 101, 111, 124–25, 136–39; *The Nation,* March 31, 1849; *Irish American,* June 29, 1850; April 14, 1850, quoted on 4, 132–33. Brown, *Irish American Nationalism,* 28–31. Miller, *Emigrants and Exiles,* 338.

21. Brown, *Irish American Nationalism,* 20–23, 28–31, 41. Miller, *Emigrants and Exiles,* 8, 277, 279, 311, 337 (*Irish News* (New York), April 17, 1858, and *Phoenix* (New York), October 28, 1859, quotes), 340–43. Gleeson, *Irish in the South,* 7, 60, 73. Clark, *Irish in Philadelphia,* 35. McCaffrey, "Irish American Dimension," 11.

22. Levine, *Politics of Representative Identity,* 6, 8–11, 65–66, 183–85, 190, 197–98, 216. Rael, *Black Identity and Black Protest,* 238. Horton and Horton, *In Hope of Liberty,* xii. Moses, *Golden Age of Black Nationalism,* 11. Brown and Shaw, "Separate Nations," 26, 27. Bell, "Negro Nationalism in the 1850s," 100.

23. Horton and Horton, *In Hope of Liberty,* 247–48.

24. Watkins, *Our Rights As Men: An Address Delivered in Boston, before the Legislative Committee on the Militia, February 24, 1853,* 4–6, 10–19. Horton and Horton, *In Hope of Liberty,* 263.

25. Pinheiro, "Anti-Catholicism, All Mexico, and the Treaty of Guadalupe Hidalgo," 70–72, 81, 85–86.

26. *Pilot,* May 5, 1860. Ignatiev, *How the Irish Became White,* 162 (calling Irish Americans "the Swiss Guards of the slave power."). Von Frank, *Anthony Burns,* 72. Macnamara, *Ninth Massachusetts,* 2–4. Anbinder, *Nativism and Slavery,* 89 (*Liberator,* September 19, 1854), 136. *Dedham Gazette,* July 1, 1854 in Mulkern, *Know-Nothing Party in Massachusetts,* 65–66. Burton, *Melting Pot Soldiers,* 13. *Citizen,* July 8, 1854, in Joyce, *Editors and Ethnicity,* 132–33. O'Connor, *Fitzpatrick's Boston,* 153–54, 157–58.

27. For an 1860 critique of Banks's veto, see Bird, *Review of Gov. Banks' Veto.* John C. Tucker, *Pilot,* February 19, 1858, quoted in Bean, "Puritan versus Celt: 1850–1860," 88.

28. *New York Times,* November 17, 1860; January 9, 1861; March 16, 1861.

29. Ibid., March 16, 1861.

30. Anbinder, *Nativism and Slavery,* ix. *New York Times,* November 17, 1860; January 9, 1861; March 16, 1861. O'Gorman, *Speech of the Defendant's Counsel, Richard O'Gorman: State of New York vs. Col. M. Corcoran.*

Chapter 2. The Question of Armed Service

1. O'Connor, *Fitzpatrick's Boston,* 186, 187 (*Pilot,* November 3, 1860, quote). Gibson, *Attitudes of the New York Irish,* 105.

2. *First National Convention of the Fenian Brotherhood...November 1863,* 10. *Pilot,* February 2, 1861; May 4, 1861; June 8, 1861 (quotes); August 2, 1862. Burton, *Melting Pot Soldiers,* 23, 25.

3. Bruce, *Harp and the Eagle,* 70–71.

4. *Irish-American,* November 17, 1860; April 20, 1861. *Pilot,* November 2, 1861. "Marie," "Wake! Sons of Erin!" in *Pilot,* August 9, 1862 ("no thought"). Friendly Sons of St. Patrick resolutions quoted in Bruce, *Harp and the Eagle,* 73. *Irish News,* April 27, 1861, quoted in Joyce, *Editors and Ethnicity,* 134. Burton, *Melting Pot Soldiers,* 36. Truslow, "Peasants into Patriots," 69,

73. See also *Pilot*, June 14, 1862; *Irish-American*, April 27, 1861, and May 4, 1861; and Maguire, *The Irish in America*, 550.

5. O'Connor, *Fitzpatrick's Boston*, 192–93, 195. Michael A. Finnerty, Minor's Hill, Va., October 2, 1861 (*Pilot*, November 2, 1861).

6. *Pilot*, June 8, 1861; see also October 19, 1861; August 2, 1862. Peter Welsh to Margaret Welsh, c. February 1863; to Margaret Welsh, near Falmouth, Va., February 3, 1863; to Patrick Prendergast, near Falmouth, Va., June 1, 1863, in Kohl, *Irish Green and Union Blue*, 62–63, 65, 100–104. Thomas F. Meagher to B. S. Treanor, New York, September 5, 1861 (*Pilot*, September 14, 1861). *Irish-American*, January 11, 1862.

7. "A Constitutional Unionist," Washington, June 26, 1861 (*Pilot*, July 13, 1861). "Spectator," St. Paul, Minn., July 21, 1861 (*Pilot*, August 10, 1861). Spectator's missive shared the page with unqualifiedly patriotic articles.

8. *Pilot*, August 24, 1861.

9. Gleeson, *Irish in the South*, 2, 141–43, 156, 158.

10. Burton, *Melting Pot Soldiers*, ix–x, 67, 207–8. See McPherson, *For Cause and Comrades*; and Frank, *With Ballot and Bayonet*, regarding ideology and Civil War soldiers.

11. Athearn, *Meagher*, 1–89.

12. Ibid., 92–101. Burton, *Melting Pot Soldiers*, 115.

13. *New York Times*, August 30, 1861.

14. Ibid.

15. Ibid. For a similar Meagher speech, see ibid., October 7, 1861. In another speech, Meagher cited historical examples of how war invigorated national power and predicted that war would solidify the U.S. global position. Ibid., October 26, 1861.

16. Ibid., September 16, 1861.

17. Ibid., September 21, 24, 1861. Quotes from *Boston Morning Journal*, September 24, 1861, in Truslow, "Peasants into Patriots," 75–76.

18. *New York Times*, July 26, 1862; see also July 30, 1862, for a similar Meagher speech emphasizing Ireland.

19. Thomas F. Meagher to William J. Onhan, Camp California, Va., March 7, 1862, in ibid., March 22, 1862.

20. Kohl, *Irish Green and Union Blue*, 3–4.

21. Peter Welsh to Margaret Welsh, c. February 1863, in ibid., 62–63.

22. Peter Welsh to Margaret Welsh, near Falmouth, Va., February 3, 1863, in ibid., 65.

23. Ibid., at 65–67.

24. Peter Welsh to Margaret Welsh, near Falmouth, Va., February 3, 1863; to Margaret Welsh, near Falmouth, Va., February 8, 1863, in ibid., 65–67, 69–70.

25. Peter Welsh to Patrick Prendergast, Falmouth, Va., June 1, 1863, in ibid., 100–104.

26. Ibid.

27. *New York Times*, August 19, 1862. Burton, *Melting Pot Soldiers*, 53.

28. Green, *Letters and Discussions*, 3, 3, 9. *Pittsburgh Gazette*, April 18, 1861, in McPherson, *Negro's Civil War*, 19–20. William A. Jones to Simon Cameron, Oberlin, Ohio, November 27, 1861, in Berlin, *Black Military Experience*, 80–81. Marrs, *Life and History*, 16.

29. *Liberator*, May 10, 1861; May 17, 1861, in McPherson, *Negro's Civil War*, 20–22. Clark, *Black Brigade of Cincinnati*, 3–5. Seraile, "Struggle," 215, 218–19. Berlin, *Black Military Experience*, 5–6. *The War of the Rebellion: A Compilation of the Official Records of the Union and Confederate Armies*, ser. 1 vol. 6:176; ser. 3, vol. 1:107, 133, 609–10, 626 (hereafter cited as OR).

30. O'Connor, *Civil War Boston*, 51, 53, 67 (Morris in *Liberator*, April 26, 1861). *Liberator*, May 17, 1861 in McPherson, *Negro's Civil War*, 20–22.

31. Congress passed a stronger Second Confiscation Act on July 17, 1862. Siddali, *From Property to Person*, 3, 75, 81, 92, 127.

32. *Pine and Palm*, May 25, 1861 (New York City); *Anglo-African*, October 19, 1861 (Troy); William H. Parham to Jacob C. White, October 12, 1861, all in McPherson, *Negro's Civil War*, 30, 34, 35.

33. Green, *Letters and Discussions*, 3–4, 6, 10–11, 13–16, 31.

34. Ibid., 18–21, 24, 25, 31, 32–33, 34–35.

35. *Cong. Globe*, 37th Cong. 2nd Sess., 408 (January 21, 1862), 488 (January 24, 1862), 1321 (March 21, 1862), 2684 (June 12, 1862), 2802 (June 19, 1862).

36. Siddali, *From Property to Person*, 167.

37. *Cong. Globe*, 37th Cong. 2nd Sess., 3198 (July 9, 1862).

38. Ibid., 3198–99, 3203–5 (July 9, 1862).

39. Ibid., 3227–37 (July 10, 1862); 3249–57 (July 11, 1862); 3320–22 (July 14, 1862); 3337–51 (July 15, 1862); 3397–98 (July 16, 1862); 3403 (July 17, 1862). The act as to aliens is at 12 Stat. 594, Sec. 21. The act as to blacks is at 12 Stat. 597.

40. Ibid., 37th Cong. 2nd Sess., 3382–83 (July 16, 1862).

41. Howard, "Civil War in Kentucky," 246, 250. Smith, "Recruitment of Negro Soldiers in Kentucky," 364–90. Yacovone, *Voice of Thunder,* 27–28. The *Pilot* quoted in *Liberator,* May 15, 1863; *Boston Daily Advertiser,* May 28, 1863 ("obedience," "servility," "music"), both quoted in Yacovone, *Voice of Thunder,* 27–28. Mitchell, *Civil War Soldiers,* 195–96 ("blowed of"). Glatthaar, *Forged in Battle,* 29–30.

42. O'Rielly, *First Organization of Colored Troops in the State of New York,* 1–3, 5, 6, 14–15. New York Union League Club, *Report of the Committee on Volunteering,* 3–10. *Addresses of the Hon. W.D. Kelley, Miss Anna E. Dickenson, and Mr. Frederick Douglass...July 6, 1863,* 1. Seraile, "Struggle," 229.

43. Joseph E. Williams, New Bern, N.C., June 23, 1863 (*Christian Recorder,* July 4, 1863), in Redkey, *Grand Army,* 90–91. James H. Gooding, [undated] (*Mercury,* March 3, 1863); Readville, Ma., April 18, 1863 (*Mercury,* April 21, 1863), in Adams, *Altar of Freedom,* 4, 13.

44. *Addresses of the Hon. W. D. Kelley, Miss Anna E. Dickenson, and Mr. Frederick Douglass...July 6, 1863,* 5–7.

45. Levine, *Politics of Representative Identity,* 218–23.

46. *Record of Action of the Convention Held at Poughkeepsie, N.Y., July 15th and 16th, 1863, for the Purpose of Facilitating the Introduction of Colored Troops into the Service of the United States,* 1, 3, 5–6, 7, 8.

47. Ibid., 9–12. Glatthaar, *Forged in Battle,* 71. Kennedy, *Population...in 1860,* ix, xii.

48. Davis added that blacks would comprise a "guarantee" against further trouble in the South. Davis, *Speech...September 24, 1863,* 10–11, 23. See H. Ford Douglas, Colliersville, Tenn., January 8, 1863, in Redkey, *Grand Army,* 24–25, for an African American's argument that arming blacks should end talk of colonization.

49. 12 Stat. 597 (Act of July 17, 1862). 13 Stat. 6 (Act of February 24, 1864). 13 Res. 571 (Resolution of March 3, 1865). Yacovone, *Freedom's Journey,* xxx.

50. James H. Gooding, Readville, Mass., April 18, 1863 (*Mercury,* April 21, 1863) in Adams, *Altar of Freedom,* 13. Milton M. Holland to the *Messenger* (Athens, Oh.), Norfolk, Va., January 19, 1864, in Levstik, "From Slavery to Freedom," 12. O'Rielly, *First Organization of Colored Troops in the State of New York,* 16.

51. Schaar, *Legitimacy in the Modern State,* 287–96. John Higham identified nativism as a "certain kind of nationalism." Higham, *Strangers in the Land,* 4–9.

Chapter 3. African Americans in Arms

1. Alexander T. Augusta, Washington, D.C., May 15, 1863 (*Christian Recorder,* May 30, 1863).

2. Ibid.

3. Wilson, *Campfires of Freedom,* xi–xiii, xv. Berlin, *Black Military Experience,* 1–2. Vorenberg, *Final Freedom,* 141.

4. Brown, *Negro in the American Rebellion,* 280–81.

5. The work of Joseph T. Glatthaar, Donald Yacovone, Keith P. Wilson, and the editors of *Freedom: A Documentary History of Emancipation, 1861–1867,* provides details on racism in the Union army.

6. Marrs, *Life and History,* 22. Cowden, *Fifty-Ninth Regiment of United States Colored Infantry,* 44–46. Glatthaar, *Forged in Battle,* 79.

7. Wilson, *Campfires of Freedom,* 61–62, 157–58, 215–26.

8. The 55th Massachusetts reveals the diversity present in some black regiments. Of the men who enlisted in that unit whose birthplace was recorded, 139 came from Pennsylvania, 222 from Ohio, 97 from Indiana, 68 from Kentucky, and 66 from Missouri, with Illinois providing 56 and New York, 23. Only 22 enlistees were born in Massachusetts. Two hundred forty seven enlistees had once been slaves, with 106 from Virginia, 30 from North Carolina, and 24 from Tennessee. One enlistee was born in Africa. Most of the volunteers—596 men—listed their job as farmer, while 76 identified themselves as laborers; 34 barbers, 50 waiters, 27 cooks, 27 teamsters, 20 sailors, 21 blacksmiths, 6 teachers, 3 engineers, a confectioner, clergyman, and a student filled the ranks. Four hundred seventy-seven of the men could read and 319 could read and write. The unit brigaded with the 35th USCI, composed of ex-slaves recruited in North Carolina. Smith, "History

and Archaeology," 21–70, 28, 30. Fox, *Fifty-fifth Regiment of Massachusetts Volunteer Infantry,* 110–12. Wilson, *Campfires of Freedom,* 42. Shaffer, *After the Glory,* 11, 16. Berlin, *Black Military Experience,* 12.

9. George E. Stephens, Readville, Ma., May 1, 1863 (*Weekly Anglo-African,* May 9, 1863), in Yacovone, *Voice of Thunder,* 235. James H. Gooding, Readville, Ma., May 18, 1863 (*Mercury,* May 20, 1863), in Adams, *Altar of Freedom,* 21–22. Emilio, *Brave Black Regiment,* 24–30. Fox, *Fifty-fifth Regiment of Massachusetts Volunteer Infantry,* 5 (civilians visit the 55th Massachusetts in training camp and prepare a festival on July 4, 1863).

10. Yacovone, *Voice of Thunder,* 36–37.

11. Ibid., 36–37. Garth W. James recalled "the alternate huzza and reproach which attempted to deafen each other on our march down State street," while Nathaniel P. Hallowell recounted that members of a "prominent club" hissed as the regiment marched past them. James, "Assault on Fort Wagner," 13. Hallowell, "Negro as a Soldier in the War of the Rebellion," 31.

12. Brown, *Negro in the American Rebellion,* 157–58.

13. Other flag presentations at Camp William Penn proved inspirational, e.g., the 25th USCI's flag displayed a freedman broken from chains while grasping a musket and uniform. Paradis, *6th United States Colored Infantry in the Civil War,* 22–23, 27–30. Wert, "Camp William Penn and the Black Soldier," 345.

14. New York Union League Club, *Report of the Committee on Volunteering,* 10, 21–27, 44. *New York Times,* March 6, 1864; March 26, 1864; March 28, 1864. O'Rielly, *First Organization of Colored Troops in the State of New York,* 20–21. Seraile, "Struggle," 231.

15. Thomas H. C. Hinton, New York City, March 5, 1864 (*Christian Recorder,* March 12, 1864). New York Union League Club, *Report of the Committee on Volunteering,* 39–40.

16. *New York Times,* March 6, 1864; March 26, 1864; March 28, 1864. Excerpts from the newspapers are from the cover of O'Rielly, *First Organization of Colored Troops in the State of New York.* Excerpts from the *New York Times* on page i of the booklet noted that eight months earlier, whites "hunted down like wild beasts" blacks in New York City, yet black soldiers now marched "through our gayest avenues and our busiest thoroughfares to the pealing strains of martial music, and are everywhere saluted with waving handkerchiefs, with descending flowers, and with the acclamations and plaudits of countless beholders." See also O'Rielly, *First Organization of Colored Troops in the State of New York,* 20–21. Seraile, "Struggle," 231. *Herald* quoted in Quigley, *Second Founding,* 13.

17. William McCoslin, near Petersburg, Va., July 26, 1864 (*Christian Recorder,* August 27, 1864). Glatthaar, *Forged in Battle,* 195–96.

18. New York Union League Club, *Report of the Committee on Volunteering,* 21–30 (see also ceremonies for the 20th USCI).

19. Frederickson, *Inner Civil War,* 30, 72–73, 154–55.

20. John C. Brock, Camp near Hanover, Va., June 5, 1864 (*Christian Recorder,* June 18, 1864); Brock, Camp near Petersburg, Va., October 30, 1864 (*Christian Recorder,* November 12, 1864), in Smith, "Brock," 152, 161. George W. Hatton, Hampton, Va., May 1, 1864 (*Christian Recorder,* May 7, 1864). Marrs, *Life and History,* 22. See also James H. Gooding, Readville, Ma., April 3, 1863 (*Mercury,* April 6, 1863) (Gooding's "heart pulsate[d] with pride" to look upon "stout and brawny [black] men, fully equipped with Uncle Sam's accoutrements."), in Adams, *Altar of Freedom,* 9–10, 14–15.

21. Milton M. Holland to the *Messenger* (Athens, Oh.), Norfolk, Va., January 19, 1864; to the *Messenger,* Near Petersburg, Va., July 24, 1864, in Levstik, "From Slavery to Freedom," 11, 15. Col. Thomas J. Morgan to Col. R. D. Mussey, Chattanooga, Tenn., October 8, 1864 ("boys"), in Berlin, *Black Military Experience,* 556. Califf, *Seventh Regiment,* 75. See also Henry Carpenter Hoyle, Brownsville, Tex., August 28, 1865 (*Christian Recorder,* September 25, 1865); "A Soldier of the 55th Mass.," Jacksonville, Fla., March 18, 1864 (*Weekly Anglo-African,* April 9, 1864) (recalling the "unflinching and dauntless manner" of blacks in combat) in Trudeau, *Voices of the 55th,* 78.

22. H.C.P., Newbern, N.C., July 27, 1863 (*Weekly Anglo-African,* August 22, 1863) in Trudeau, *Voices of the 55th,* 36–37. George E. Stephens, Camp Meigs, Readville, Ma., May 1, 1863 (*Weekly Anglo-African,* May 9, 1863) in Yacovone, *Voice of Thunder,* 236. Joseph E. Williams, New Bern, N.C., June 23, 1863 (*Christian Recorder,* July 4, 1863). Yacovone, *Voice of Thunder,* 294 n. 1. O'Leary, *To Die For,* 74.

23. J.H.W.N.C., Deveaux Neck, S.C., January 24, 1865 (*Christian Recorder,* February 25, 1865) ("give it all"). See also George E. Stephens, November 28, 1863 (*Weekly Anglo-African,* December 12, 1863) in Yacovone, *Voice of Thunder,* 289. Glatthaar, *Forged in Battle,* 201; Capt. Louis F. Green to Alexander Calhoun, February 14, 1864, on 70–71. Ann to husband, Paris, Mo., January 19, 1864 (slave implores her soldier-husband to send money so as to clothe their "almost

naked" child, but also encourages him, "do not fret too much for me for it wont be long before I will be free and then all we make will be ours."); Aaron Oates to Edwin M. Stanton, Hampton, Va., January 26, 1865, in Berlin, *Black Military Experience,* 686–87, 692–93. Wilson, *Campfires of Freedom,* 182.

24. Spotswood Rice to My Children, St. Louis, Mo., September 3, 1864; to Kittey Diggs, St. Louis, Mo., September 3, 1864, in Berlin, *Black Military Experience,* 689–90.

25. George W. Hatton, Wilson's Landing, Va., May 10, 1864 (*Christian Recorder,* May 28, 1864), in Redkey, *Grand Army,* 95–96. Clopton's whipping comprised specifications of certain charges when brigade commander Brig. Gen. Edward A. Wild faced a court-martial for other matters, but the court excluded the incident from its consideration. Reid, "General Edward A. Wild and Civil War Discrimination," 19–20.

26. John C. Brock, Manassas Junction, Va., July 3, 1864 (*Christian Recorder,* July 30, 1864), in Smith, "Brock," 153–54. Cowden, *Fifty-Ninth Regiment of United States Colored Infantry,* 51–52. J.H.W.N. Collins, Savannah, Ga., March 19, 1865 (*Christian Recorder,* April 15, 1865). Charles E. Briggs to mother, St. Andrew's Parish opposite Charleston, S.C., May 28, 1865, in Briggs, *Civil War Surgeon in a Colored Regiment,* 153–54. Davidson "'First United States Colored," 20. Glatthaar, *Forged in Battle,* 214.

27. Wilson, *Campfires of Freedom,* 3, 12.

28. Emilio, *Brave Black Regiment,* 125. Capt. Edmund R. Fowler to Lt. Col. A. G. Bennett, Seabrook, S.C. August 3, 1863 (reporting his detachment of the 21st USCI performed an exhausting amount of labor in coaling ships, and other officers sometimes called the men "Black sons of bitches" and threatened to shoot them); Col. James C. Beecher to Brig. Gen. Edward A. Wild, Folly Island, S.C., September 13, 1863; Capt. R. T. Auchmuty to Col. E. D. Townsend, Washington, D.C., December 20, 1863; General Orders No. 77, Dept. of the South, September 17, 1863; General Orders No. 105, Dept. of the South, November 25, 1863, all in Berlin, *Black Military Experience,* 491–96. Wilson, *Campfires of Freedom,* 42.

29. R.W.W., Camp near White House, Folly Island, S.C., January 27, 1864 (*Christian Recorder,* February 13, 1864). D.I.I., Morris Island, S.C., July 18, 1864 (*Christian Recorder,* August 6, 1864).

30. Wilson, *Campfires of Freedom,* 45. Siddali, *From Property to Person.* 216, 221. *OR,* Ser. 3 vol. 5:632–33. 12 Stat. 599 (Act of July 17, 1862).

31. George E. Stephens, Morris Island, S.C., August 7, 1863 (*Weekly Anglo-African,* August 22, 1863) (quotes); Morris Island, S.C., September 4, 1863 (*Weekly Anglo-African,* September 19, 1863); Morris Island, S.C., August 1, 1864 (*Weekly Anglo-African,* August 27, 1864), all in Yacovone, *Voice of Thunder,* 252–53, 259, 320–21. James H. Gooding, Morris Island, S.C., August 9, 1863 (*Mercury,* August 21, 1863) in Adams, *Altar of Freedom,* 48–49. Fox, *Fifty-fifth Regiment of Massachusetts Volunteer Infantry,* 17 ("breach").

32. E. N. Hallowell to John A. Andrew, Morris Island, S.C., November 23, 1863, in Berlin, *Black Military Experience,* 387. "A Soldier of the 55th Massachusetts Volunteers," Folly Island, S.C., January 12, 1864 (*Weekly Anglo-African,* January 30, 1864) in Trudeau, *Voices of the 55th,* 58 ("fabric"). See also James H. Gooding, Morris Island, S.C., November 21, 1863 (*Mercury,* December 4, 1863) in Adams, *Altar of Freedom,* 83; S.J.R., Folly Island, S.C., January 18, 1864 (*Liberator,* January 29, 1864) and "De Waltigo," Palatka, Fla., April 4, 1864 (*Weekly Anglo-African,* April 30, 1864), in Trudeau, *Voices of the 55th,* 61–62, 83.

33. George E. Stephens, Morris Island, S.C., August 7, 1863 (*Weekly Anglo-African,* August 22, 1863)(54th resolutions) in Yacovone, *Voice of Thunder,* 254. James H. Gooding, Morris Island, S.C., November 21, 1863 (*Mercury,* December 4, 1863) in Adams, *Altar of Freedom,* 83. "From a Soldier," Folly Island, S.C., April 23, 1864 (*Christian Recorder,* May 21, 1864); James M. Trotter to Edward W. Kinsley, Palatka, Fla., March 13, 1864; Joseph H. Walker, Yellow Bluff, Fla., March 26, 1864 (*Weekly Anglo-African,* April 16, 1864), in Trudeau, *Voices of the 55th,* 71, 81. Milton M. Holland to the Athens, Ohio *Messenger,* Norfolk, Va., January 19, 1864, in Levstik, "From Slavery to Freedom," 11–13.

34. "Wolverine," [Folly Island, S.C.] (*Christian Recorder,* January 2, 1864). John H. B. Payne, Morris Island, S.C., May 24, 1864 (*Christian Recorder,* June 11, 1864). E.D.W., Jacksonville, Fla., March 13th, 1864 (*Christian Recorder,* April 2, 1864). See also "Massachusetts Soldier," Morris Island, S.C., December 1863, in Redkey, *Grand Army,* 235; R.W.W., Folly Island, S.C., May 1, 1864 (*Weekly Anglo-African,* June 4, 1864) and "Bellafonte," Folly Island, S.C., August 19, 1864 (*Christian Recorder,* September 3, 1864), both in Trudeau, *Voices of the 55th,* 102, 144.

35. James H. Gooding to Abraham Lincoln, Morris Island, S.C., September 28, 1863, in Adams, *Altar of Freedom,* 118–20.

36. Warren Hamilton to E. M. Stanton, Fort Jefferson, Tortugas, Fla., May 1865, in Berlin, *Black Military Experience*, 384. Warren Hamilton court-martial, 73rd USCI (LL 3106). Some family members also petitioned governmental authorities, see Rachel Ann Wicker to Mr. President Andrew, Piqua, Oh., September 12, 1864; Aaron Peterson to Edwin M. Stanton, Scio, N.Y., October 29, 1863 (Peterson questioned the paradox of blacks performing the same service as whites for lesser pay, and enclosed a letter from his son in the 2nd USCI, who did not even have the funds to pay for the letter's stamp, wrote of his contentment with everything in the service but his pay, and vowed that he "never can bee, contented untill I get my rits."), in Berlin, *Black Military Experience*, 374–75, 402–3.

37. John Murray Forbes et al., to John A. Andrew, November 11, 1863, in Yacovone, *Voice of Thunder*, 59–60. John A. Andrew to Frederick Johnson, Boston, August 24, 1863, in George E. Stephens, Morris Island, S.C., September 4, 1863 (*Weekly Anglo-African*, September 19, 1863) in Yacovone, *Voice of Thunder*, 258–59. During recruitment, the governors of Massachusetts and Ohio assured black leaders that African American enlistees would be treated the same as other volunteers. John A. Andrew to George T. Downing, Boston, March 23, 1863; David Tod to John M. Langston, Columbus, Oh., May 16, 1863, in Berlin, *Black Military Experience*, 88–89, 92. John A. Andrew to James B. Congdon, Boston, December 20, 1863, in Adams, *Altar of Freedom*, 122–24.

38. Maj. Jonathan C. Chadwick, Port Hudson, La., October 3, 1863, in Berlin, *Black Military Experience*, 383. *OR*, ser. 1, vol. 35 pt 2:68–69 ("mutiny"). B.W., Morris Island, S.C., July 8, 1864 (*Christian Recorder*, July 30, 1864). Yacovone, *Voice of Thunder*, 73, 76–77.

39. Garland H. White, near Petersburg, Va., September 8, 1864 (*Christian Recorder*, September 17, 1864).

40. Brig. Gen. Alexander Schimmelfennig to Capt. W. L. M. Burger, Folly Island, S.C., June 2, 1864, in Berlin, *Black Military Experience*, 397–98. "Bought and Sold," Yorktown, Va., February 6, 1864 (*Christian Recorder*, February 20, 1864). B. W., Morris Island, S.C., July 8, 1864 (*Christian Recorder*, July 30, 1864) (Clemens). Davidson, "First United States Colored," 11.

41. "De Waltigo," Palatka, Fla., April 4, 1864 (*Weekly Anglo-African*, April 30, 1864) ("blush"); "Bay State," Palatka, Fla., April 10, 1864 (*Weekly Anglo-African*, April 30, 1864); "Mon," Folly Island, S.C., April 27, 1864 (*Weekly Anglo-African*, May 21, 1864) (even though "our friends and ourselves may perish for want of money, but never—no, by the Eternal! never will we take it."); "Wolverine," Folly Island, S.C., April 30, 1864 (*Weekly Anglo-African*, May 14, 1864), in Trudeau, *Voices of the 55th*, 83, 86–88, 98–99, 101. "Bellafonte," Folly Island, S.C., August 19, 1864 (*Christian Recorder*, September 3, 1864) ("manfully"), in Redkey, *Grand Army*, 240.

42. *U.S. House Journal*, 38th Cong., 1st Sess., 39 (December 14, 1863); 82 (December 21, 1863); 121 (January 14, 1864); 214 (February 21, 1864); 341 (March 4, 1864). *U.S. Senate Journal*, 38th Cong., 1st Sess., 30 (December 16, 1863); 102 (January 20, 1864); 119 (February 1, 1864); 165 (February 18, 1864); 177 (February 23, 1864); 187 (February 25, 1864); 220 (March 8, 1864); 304 (April 7, 1864). New York Union League Club, *Report of the Committee on Volunteering*, 31, 45. *Addresses of the Hon. W.D. Kelley, Miss Anna E. Dickenson, and Mr. Frederick Douglass...July 6, 1863*, 2–4.

43. *Cong. Globe*, 38th Cong. 1st Sess., 481–82 (February 5, 1864).

44. Ibid., 564–65 (February 10, 1864).

45. Ibid., 632–35 (February 13, 1864); 818–24 (February 25, 1862) (Wilkinson, 823).

46. Ibid., 1030 (March 10, 1864); 1805–6 (April 22, 1864). On May 3, 1864, the House passed its version of the Senate bill equalizing pay, S. 145, ibid., 2056–57 (May 3, 1864), by a vote of 135–0, prompting a joint committee to reconcile the Senate and House versions, see 2963 (June 15, 1864), 3040 (June 17, 1864), 3063 (June 18, 1864) and 3116 (June 21, 1864) (Lincoln signs June 20, 1864).

47. 13 Stat. 126 (Act of June 15, 1864). 13 Stat. 487 (Act of March 3, 1865). Discussions over distinction in bounties based on race were also carried out on a state level, see Cannon, *Special Message of Governor Cannon, to the Legislature of Delaware, July 28, 1864*.

48. Fox, *Fifty-fifth Regiment of Massachusetts Volunteer Infantry*, 33 ("disappointments"), 35, 37. "Fort Green," Folly Island, S.C., August 21, 1864 (*Christian Recorder*, September 24, 1864).

49. George E. Stephens, Folly Island, S.C., May 26, 1864 (*Weekly Anglo-African*, June 18, 1864); Morris Island, S.C., August 1, 1864 (*Weekly Anglo-African*, August 27, 1864), in Yacovone, *Voice of Thunder*, 304–7, 319–21.

50. Emilio, *Brave Black Regiment*, 227 ("carnival"). C. M. Duren to Mother, Jacksonville, Fla., April 2, 1864 in Duren, "Letters of Lt. C. M. Duren," 283. John C. Brock, Camp in front of

Petersburg, Va., August 13, 1864 (*Christian Recorder,* August 20, 1864) in Smith, "Brock," 157. James M. Trotter to Edward Kinsley, Folly Island, S.C., November 21, 1864, in Trudeau, *Voices of the 55th,* 155. Fox, *Fifty-fifth Regiment of Massachusetts Volunteer Infantry,* 37. For the October 10, 1864 service, see F. S., Folly Island, S.C., October 14, 1864 and G. P. Touson, Folly Island, S.C., October 14, 1864, both in *Christian Recorder,* November 12, 1864.

51. Glatthaar, *Forged in Battle,* 172–74. Wilson, *Campfires of Freedom,* 57.

52. C. W. Foster to Colonel [unnamed], December 13, 1864, in Berlin, *Black Military Experience,* 304.

53. J. B. McPherson et al. to Abraham Lincoln, Camp Stanton near Bryantown, Md. [Feb. 1864], in Berlin, *Black Military Experience,* 356–57. "Fort Green," Folly Island, S.C., August 21, 1864 (*Christian Recorder,* September 24, 1864). Lt. C. M. Duren of the 54th Massachusetts supported commissioning blacks, but disfavored mixing black and white officers in the same unit. C. M. Duren to Father, Baldwin Station, Fla., February 18, 1864; to Mother, Jacksonville, Fla., February 29, 1864; to Father, Jacksonville, Fla., March 29, 1864, in Duren, "Letters of Lt. C. M. Duren," 268, 272, 282.

54. *Addresses of the Hon. W.D. Kelley, Miss Anna E. Dickenson, and Mr. Frederick Douglass...July 6, 1863,* 7. *Liberator,* August 5, 1864, in McPherson, *Negro's Civil War,* 237–38. *Proceedings of the State Equal Rights' Convention of the Colored People of Pennsylvania...February 8th, 9th, and 10th, 1865,* 37. See also *Christian Recorder,* January 9, 1864 (whites "must give place and preferment to men of character, worth and influence, among colored people, just as you do among our Dutch or Irish, or American citizens, when requiring their aid.").

55. John A. Andrew to Charles Sumner, Boston, February 7, 1863 (Andrew seeks to commission black chaplains, surgeons, and some second lieutenants in his state's black units); William U. Saunders to Edwin M. Stanton, Camp "Stannton" [Md.], February 3, 1864; Louis H. Douglass et al. to Edwin M. Stanton, January 1865?, [Washington, D.C.?] ("hundreds"); in Berlin, *Black Military Experience,* 337, 339–41.

56. H.S.H., Jacksonville, Fla., April 3, 1865 (*Christian Recorder,* April 22, 1865). James H. Gooding, Morris Island, S.C., January 17, 1864 (*Mercury,* January 28, 1864) in Adams, *Altar of Freedom,* 104.

57. McPherson, *Negro's Civil War,* 238–39. J.H.W.N. Collins, Savannah, Ga., March 19, 1865 (*Christian Recorder,* April 15, 1865) ("bound"). Miller, "Garland H. White," 201.

58. Berlin, *Black Military Experience,* 611–12, 614 (Capt. J. W. Greene to Lt. W. D. Putnam, Napoleanville, La., April 7, 1865).

59. Taggart, *Free Military School for Applicants for Command of Colored Troops,* 13. Hollandsworth, *Pretense of Glory,* 211. Blassingame, "Educational Institution," 152–59, 155–56. Wert, "Camp William Penn and the Black Soldier," 335, 344.

60. George E. Stephens, Philadelphia, November 14, 1859 (*Weekly Anglo-African,* November 26, 1859) in Yacovone, *Voice of Thunder,* 120. Berlin, *Black Military Experience,* 611–12, 627 (Henry M. Turner to Adjutant General U.S. Army, Roanoke Island N.C., June 29, 1865, quote). Redkey, "Black Chaplains," 331–50, 347.

61. Civilians from Boston joined officers and educated soldiers as teachers at a school at the training camp of the 55th Massachusetts in Readville, Massachusetts. The regiment continued its school while in the field, and large numbers of former slaves attended evening classes. Fox, *Fifty-fifth Regiment of Massachusetts Volunteer Infantry,* 7. "Sergeant" [55th Massachusetts], Folly Island, S.C., July 26, 1864 (*Liberator,* October 4, 1864) in Redkey, *Grand Army,* 69. John C. Brock, Camp near Petersburg, Va., July 16, 1864 (*Christian Recorder,* August 6, 1864); Camp near Richmond, Va., March 9, 1865 (*Christian Recorder,* March 18, 1865), in Smith, "Brock," 156, 162. General Order No. 37, Head Quarters 11th Regt. USCA, New Orleans, La., October 17, 1864, in Berlin, *Black Military Experience,* 618. Cowden, *Fifty-Ninth Regiment of United States Colored Infantry,* 60–62 (after the 59th USCI made winter quarters near Memphis in 1863, the men built a schoolhouse where the unit's chaplain and his wife taught soldiers and local black civilians).

62. Thomas M. Chester, Bermuda Hundred, Va., January 20, 1865, in Blackett, *Chester,* 228. Berlin, *Black Military Experience,* 612. Blassingame, "Educational Institution," 156–57.

63. The educational initiative came second to the exigencies of war: several times a Pennsylvania regiment erected a schoolhouse only to be ordered to relocate before it could be used in earnest. General Orders No. 9, Head Quarters 10th USCI, Port Hudson, La., March 15, 1864 (all noncommissioned officers and 25 privates selected by each company commander could attend mandatory schooling); E. S. Wheeler to Brig. Gen. Ullmann, Port Hudson, La., April 8, 1864 (chaplain reporting he had "never witnessed greater eagerness for study," and that already five hundred men in the brigade had learned to read and many, to write); Chaplain J. M. Mickly to

Adjt. Genl. U.S.A., [near Richmond, Va.], January 31, 1865 (Pennsylvania regiment); C. W. Buckley to Lt. Austin R. Mills, Vicksburg, Miss., February 1, 1865; Col. T. H. Barrett to the Officers & Men of the 62nd USCI, Ringgold Barracks, Tex., January 4, 1866, all in Berlin, *Black Military Experience*, 616, 618–19, 621, 623, 783. James Shaw, Jr. to Augustus Woodbury, Camp Stanton [Md.], January 17, 1864, quoted in Califf, *Seventh Regiment*, 18–19; 87–88. See also Sherman, *Negro as a Soldier*, 16–17 (7th USCI); Miller, "Garland H. White," 214 (300 of the 28th USCI could read and write, and 474 could spell and read, by September 1865). Berlin, *Black Military Experience*, 613. Blassingame, "Educational Institution," 155–56 (identifying schools in the 33rd, 35th, 55th, 67th, 73rd, 76th, 78th, 83rd, 88th, 89th, and 128th USCI regiments).

64. William P. Woodlin, Petersburg, Va., April 28, 1865 (*Christian Recorder*, July 22, 1865). Steiner, *Disease in the Sixty-Fifth United States Colored Infantry*, xviii, 16. B. J. Butler, Orangeburg, S.C., July 29, 1865 (*Weekly Anglo-African*, August 12, 1865) ("ourselves") in Redkey, *Grand Army*, 185. James H. Gooding, Morris Island, S.C., October 3, 1863 (*Mercury*, October 15, 1863) in Adams, *Altar of Freedom*, 66–67. Yacovone, *Voice of Thunder*, 286 n. 13. Blassingame, "Educational Institution," 156.

65. Sherman, *Negro as a Soldier*, 18. Blassingame, "Educational Institution," 155, 157.

66. *Christian Recorder*, July 23, 1864.

67. Joseph H. Barquet, Morris Island, S.C. [October 1864] (*Weekly Anglo-African*, November 5, 1864) in Redkey, *Grand Army*, 215–16. George S. Massey, Richmond, Va., March 27, 1865 (*Christian Recorder*, April 8, 1865).

68. George E. Stephens, near Budd's Ferry, Doncaster, Md., November 11, 1861 (*Weekly Anglo-African*, November 23, 1861); Near Budd's Ferry, Md., January 10, 1862 (*Weekly Anglo-African*, January 18, 1862); Near Budd's Ferry, Md., February 13, 1862 (*Weekly Anglo-African*, February 22, 1862) all in Yacovone, *Voice of Thunder*, 139, 163–64, 182. Yacovone, *Voice of Thunder*, 166 n. 6. Siddali, *From Property to Person*, 67.

69. [Livermore], *General Washington and General Jackson on Negro Soldiers*, 3. See also *Opinions of the Early Presidents, and of the Fathers of the Republic, upon Slavery, and Upon Negroes as Men and Soldiers*.

70. Dunkelman, "Through White Eyes," 97–102, 105, 106; Andrew D. Blood to Brother Wesley, January 3, 1865, on 101. See Horowitz, "Ben Butler and the Negro," for one politician-officer's conversion from opposing the arming of blacks to becoming an ardent advocate of the policy. See Colyer, *Report of the Services Rendered by the Freed People to the United States Army, in North Carolina, in the Spring of 1862*, for an assessment of loyalty to the Union among blacks and p. 61 for the engraving, "Services of the Freed People on the Battlefield." See also Charlotte L. Forten, St Helena's Island, Beaufort, S.C., November 20, 1862 (*Liberator*, December 12, 1862) (black "hearts are full of gratitude to the Government and to the 'Yankees,'" and, "in return for the least kindness that is done them, they insist on giving you something—potatoes, eggs, peanuts, or something else from their little store."), in Silber and Sievens, *Yankee Correspondence*, 93–94.

71. Glatthaar, *Forged in Battle*, 30. Howard, "Civil War in Kentucky," 246–47. M. P. Larry to sister, February 16, 1863, in Silber and Sievens, *Yankee Correspondence*, 98.

72. "Picket," Folly Island, S.C., June 30, 1864 (*Weekly Anglo-African*, July 30, 1864) in Trudeau, *Voices of the 55th*, 113. Newton, *Out of the Briars*, 35. Morgan, *Reminiscences*, 21 (recalling that an acquaintance in an Ohio regiment treated him coldly after he joined the USCT and stated that he "did not recognize these nigger officers." The insulting officer was dismissed from service.).

73. George E. Stephens seethed about Montgomery's diatribe. George E. Stephens, Morris Island, S.C., October 3, 1863 (*Weekly Anglo-African*, October 24, 1863), in Yacovone, *Voice of Thunder*, 277–82. George E. Stephens to Luis F. Emilio, June 8, 1886, cited in Yacovone, *Voice of Thunder*, 286 n. 12. Glatthaar, *Forged in Battle*, 197.

74. *OR*, ser. 1, vol. 39 pt. 1:557. Thomas W. Higginson Journal, April 19, 1863, in Looby, *War Journal*, 133.

75. Lorenzo Thomas to Henry Wilson, Washington, D.C., May 30, 1864, in Berlin, *Black Military Experience*, 530–31.

76. R.W.W., Palatka, Fla., March 14, 1864 (*Christian Recorder*, April 2, 1864). Thomas M. Chester, before Richmond, October 23, 1864, in Blackett, *Chester*, 168–69. George E. Stephens, [August] 1864 (*Weekly Anglo-African*, September 3, 1864) in Yacovone, *Voice of Thunder*, 322. Emilio, *Brave Black Regiment*, 217. Glatthaar, *Forged in Battle*, 200.

77. George E. Stephens, Morris Island, S.C., September 4, 1863 (*Weekly Anglo-African*, September 19, 1863) in Yacovone, *Voice of Thunder*, 258. James H. Gooding, Morris Island, S.C., August 30, 1863 (*Mercury*, September 15, 1863); Gooding, Morris Island, S.C., November 28, 1863

(*Mercury*, December 15, 1863), in Adams, *Altar of Freedom*, 54, 85–86. *OR*, ser. 1, vol. 28 pt. 2: 33. Thomas M. Chester, before Richmond, Va., February 23, 1865, in Blackett, *Chester*, 268–70.

78. James H. Gooding, Morris Island, S.C., January 2, 1864 (*Mercury*, January 14, 1864), in Adams, *Altar of Freedom*, 97–101. George E. Stephens, Morris Island, S.C., January 5, 1864 (*Weekly Anglo-African*, January 23, 1864) in Yacovone, *Voice of Thunder*, 291–92.

79. Davidson, "First United States Colored," 8. Glatthaar, *Forged in Battle*, 90.

80. "Wolverine," [Folly Island, S.C.] (*Christian Recorder*, January 2, 1864).

81. Daniel W. Sawtelle to Sister, Beaufort, Port Royal Isle, S.C. April 2, 1863, in Buckingham, *All's for the Best*, 225–26. James H. Gooding, Morris Island, S.C., July 20, 1863 (*Mercury*, August 1, 1863); Morris Island, S.C., August 3, 1863 (*Mercury*, August 16, 1863), in Adams, *Altar of Freedom*, 38, 46. Emilio, *Brave Black Regiment*, 67. Morgan, *Service with Colored Troops*, 30. Summers, "Negro Soldiers in the Army of the Cumberland," 425. See also Brig. Gen. Rufus Sexton to Edwin M. Stanton, Beaufort, S.C., April 4, 1863; Capt. Elias D. Strunk to Brig. Gen. Daniel Ullman, Baton Rouge, La., May 29, 1863), both in Berlin, *Black Military Experience*, 527–29. See also Henry M. Turner, City Point, Va., June 18, 1864 (*Christian Recorder*, June 25, 1864), in Redkey, *Grand Army*, 97–98. For examples of biracial expeditions, see Fox, *Fifty-fifth Regiment of Massachusetts Volunteer Infantry*, 53–55, and Califf, *Seventh Regiment*, 25.

82. Thomas B. Wester, Bermuda Hundred, Va., December, 1864 (*Christian Recorder*, January 7, 1865). John C. Brock, Camp near Petersburg, Va., October 30, 1864 (*Christian Recorder*, November 12, 1864) in Smith, "Brock," 160. C. W. Buckley to Brig. Gen. Lorenzo Thomas, before Blakely, Al., April 1, 1865, in Berlin, *Black Military Experience*, 564–65. Fox, *Fifty-fifth Regiment of Massachusetts Volunteer Infantry*, 83 ("loud"). McMurray, *Recollections*, 22–23.

83. General Order No. 50, Headquarters 14th USCI, Chattanooga, Tenn., November 23, 1864, in Berlin, *Black Military Experience*, 559. Davidson, "First United States Colored," 11. Diary entry of Joseph J. Scroggs, September 29, 1864, in Synnestvedt, "The Earth Shook and Quivered," 37. General Orders of Maj. Gen. D. B. Birney, Headquarters Tenth Army Corps, Fuzzel's Mills, Va., August 19, 1864, in Califf, *Seventh Regiment*, 37 (congratulating the Corps).

84. William H. Hunter, Petersburg, Va., July 9, 1864 (*Christian Recorder*, July 16, 1864), in Redkey, *Grand Army*, 101–2.

85. *New York Times*, June 18, 1864 (complimenting black troops in action in Mississippi). Thomas M. Chester, ten miles from Richmond, August 18, 1864 ("eradicate"); before Richmond, October 23, 1864; before Richmond, October 31, 1864; before Richmond, February 23, 1865; in Blackett, *Chester*, 102–3, 108, 168, 180, 268–70. Blackett, *Chester*, xi.

86. Thomas M. Chester, north of the James River, Va., September 7, 1864; Deep Bottom, Va., September 9, 1864; Deep Bottom, Va., September 11, 1864; Chapin's Bluff, Va., October 5, 1864 (regarding September 29, 1864); 5 1/2 miles from Richmond, October 17, 1864 (regarding September 29, 1864); before Richmond, October 31, 1864 (casualty list); Richmond, May 13, 1865 (compliment), in Blackett, *Chester*, 123, 124–25, 136, 139–40, 149–53, 182–84, 341.

87. R.W.W., Folly Island, S.C., January 27, 1864 (*Christian Recorder*, February 4, 1864).

88. Maj. Gen. David Hunter to Jefferson Davis, Hilton Head, S.C., April 23, 1863, in Berlin, *Black Military Experience*, 573–74. *New York Times*, June 11, 1863. See a similar discussion on a local level in correspondence between Maj. T. R. Livingston, C.S.A., and Col. J. M. Williams, U.S.A., in the spring of 1863 on the Kansas-Missouri border, in Berlin, *Black Military Experience*, 574–78. Rufus S. Jones, Jacksonville, Fla., March 20, 1864 (*Christian Recorder*, April 16, 1864) in Redkey, *Grand Army*, 42 (surgeon at the battle of Olustee, Florida, on February 20, 1864, places priority on collecting wounded black troops for fear of Confederate reprisal on them). For more on Confederate atrocities against black soldiers, see Burkhardt, *Confederate Rage, Yankee Wrath*.

89. McPherson, *Negro's Civil War*, 278–79. Lincoln to Michael Hahn, Washington, D.C., March 13, 1864, in Basler, *Collected Works of Abraham Lincoln*, 7: 243. *L'Union*, June 21, 28, 1864, in McPherson, *Negro's Civil War*, 281–82.

90. Garnet, *A Memorial Discourse by Rev. Henry Highland Garnet…February 12, 1865*, 73, 75, 77, 79–80, 85–87. Quigley, *Second Founding*, 15.

Chapter 4. Equal Rights and the Experience of Military Justice for African American Soldiers

1. Wallace Baker court-martial, 55th Massachusetts Volunteer Infantry. The defendant's first name and unit is given at the first citation; other citation information is in the Works Cited. Fox, *Fifty-fifth Regiment of Massachusetts Volunteer Infantry*, 103, 139.

2. "Bay State," Palatka, Fla., April 10, 1864 (*Weekly Anglo-African,* April 30, 1864), in Trudeau, *Voices of the 55th,* 86–88.

3. Sampson Goliah court-martial, 55th Massachusetts Volunteer Infantry (NN 2479). "War Letters of C. P. Bowditch," 469, in McPherson, *Negro's Civil War,* 200–201. *OR,* ser. 1 vol. 35 pt. 2:68–69. See Yacovone, *Voice of Thunder,* 73, 76–77, 274–75, for similar trouble in the 54th Massachusetts.

4. Goliah court-martial. Baker court-martial. Emilio, *Brave Black Regiment,* 329.

5. A court-martial found Henry M. Way guilty of mutinous conduct for not helping quell Baker's mutiny and for telling a lieutenant, "I would have done the same thing as Baker did," and, "I tell you Lieut. if you or any other officer should strike me, or attempt to, I would strike you back and do the best I could to defend myself[.]" The War Department remitted the unexpired portion of Way's confinement sentence on September 26, 1865, and ordered his muster out of the service. Henry M. Way court-martial, 55th Massachusetts. Baker court-martial. Fox, *Fifty-fifth Regiment of Massachusetts Volunteer Infantry,* 102. A defendant or his counsel was to write questions by hand to the judge advocate and offer legal objections the same way. It is unclear how strictly this procedure was enforced, though it appears that in this case, Baker questioned witnesses directly but through the judge advocate. Walton then asked additional questions pursuant to his charge to assist an unrepresented defendant. This is evidenced by the use of different pronouns—"I" and "he"—during defense questioning. Benet, *Treatise on Military Law,* 65

6. Baker court-martial. George E. Stephens, Folly Island, S.C., June 18, 1864 (*Weekly Anglo-African,* July 9, 1864) in Yacovone, *Voice of Thunder,* 317–18. Fox, *Fifty-fifth Regiment of Massachusetts Volunteer Infantry,* 29.

7. John F. Shorter et al. to the President, Folly Island, S.C., July 16, 1864, in Berlin, *Black Military Experience,* 401–2.

8. Most of the 53 general courts-martial proceedings that tried 9th Massachusetts soldiers involved charges against privates for desertion, absence without leave, or conduct prejudicial, e.g., being noisy despite orders, drunkenness, refusing to carry something, or striking an officer. I do not say 53 soldiers tried because some proceedings involved repeat offenders. A number of courts-martial indicate tensions between Col. Cass and his officers. Tension between Cass's successor, Patrick R. Guiney, and some of his officers, based on Guiney's status as a lawyer and his Republican affiliation, played out in several courts-martial as well. According to a search done though the Civil War Justice database for various Irish American regiments, the 9th Massachusetts had soldiers tried in 53 general courts-martial proceedings, the 28th Massachusetts had 59, the 63rd New York had 68, the 88th New York had 44, the 116th Pennsylvania had 46, the 155th New York had 58, and the 164th New York had 22. The average number of general courts-martial proceedings trying soldiers in the 1st through 25th USCI is 29.04, with a high of 69 in the 20th USCI and zero in the 24th USCI. Patrick R. Guiney to Col. James McQuade, Camp near Falmouth, Va., April 5, 1863, in Samito, *Irish Ninth,* 175; for tensions among officers in the 9th Massachusetts, see xxvii–xxx, 193 n. 48; see also Guiney to wife, Camp, May 16, 1863, on 192–93.

9. Brisbin addressed an 1867 convention of Kentucky blacks that made him an honorary member. *Proceedings of the State Convention of Colored Men, Held at Lexington, Kentucky, in the A.M.E. Church, November 26th, 27th, and 28th, 1867* in Foner and Walker, *Black National and State Conventions, 1865–1900,* 309–17: 310, 314. John Lewis court-martial, 13th USCHA. *Roster and Record of Iowa Soldiers in the War of the Rebellion,* 2:11.

10. Military justice existed outside the judiciary created by Article 3. U.S. Const., Art. 1, § 8; Fifth Amendment. *Dynes v. Hoover,* 61 U.S. 65, 78–79, 82 (1858). Stansfield, "A History of the Judge Advocate General's Department United States Army," 219–22. Berlin, *Black Military Experience,* 433. The navy had separate regulations.

11. 12 Stat. 597, Sec. 7 (Act of July 17, 1862). 12 Stat. 731, Sec. 30 (Act of March 3, 1863) authorized military commissions to try soldiers in time of war or rebellion and mandated "the punishments for such offenses shall never be less than those inflicted by the laws of the State, Territory, or district in which they may have been committed." President Johnson declared the rebellion over on April 2, 1866. S. 511, 37th Cong. 3d Sess. *Revised United States Army Regulations of 1861,* 125–26, 491, 495–96, 497, 498–99. Winthrop, *Digest of Opinions of the Judge Advocate General of the Army,* 12, 15, 21–23, 26, 28, 33, 37, 49, 129, 173–78, 222–23, 232. Halleck, "Military Tribunals and Their Jurisdiction," 966. *OR,* ser. 3 vol. 5: 1007–1012. Benet, *Treatise on Military Law,* 17. Fitzharris, "Field Officer Courts," 58, 71.

12. Thomas W. Higginson Journal, September 5, 1863, December 28, 1863, in Looby, *War Journal,* 165, 182.

13. McMurray, *Recollections,* 18–20.

14. For example, in May 1864, Secretary of War Stanton authorized that more than a hundred unwounded "cowardly deserters" found in Washington, D.C., could be "tried by a drum-head court, and if guilty, executed without delay," though he allowed Lt. Gen. Ulysses S. Grant discretion as to how to handle the matter. *OR,* vol. 36, pt. 2: 652–53. The official record of soldiers executed during the Civil War lists drumhead courts-martial of but one white and six black soldiers that resulted in execution, though this number is certainly too low. Four black soldiers executed by drumhead trial were Alfred Catlett, Alexander Colwell, Washington Jackson, and Charles Turner from the 1st USCHA. They left their regiment while on the march to Asheville, North Carolina, and raped a young white woman after nearly killing her elderly aunt and uncle when they tried to prevent the sexual assault. *OR,* ser. 1 vol. 49 part 2: 669. Lawson Kemp of the 55th USCI and Henry Jay of the 57th USCI were the other blacks tried by drumhead trial, both charged with rape. The lone white soldier listed, Henry Miller of the 3rd New Hampshire Infantry, was shot for desertion. *List of U.S. Soldiers Executed by United States Military Authorities during the Late War,* 2–11.

15. *OR* ser. 1, vol. 26, pt. 1:262–73; vol. 34, pt. 1:171; vol. 41 pt. 2:743.

16. To curb arbitrary punishment by the naval equivalent of regimental courts-martial, the Navy Articles of War adopted in July 1862 imposed specific punishments for particular crimes. No such system regulated regimental courts-martial. Ship commanders were free to punish ship rules within their discretion. Ramold, *Slaves, Sailors, Citizens,* 145, 148, 164–65. Berlin, *Black Military Experience,* 437–38. Glatthaar, *Forged in Battle,* 119. Wilson, *Campfires of Freedom,* 3, 12.

17. The most common offense in the 65th USCI was desertion, though only seven deserters were apprehended. Seventy-four of the 1,707 enlistees in the 65th USCI deserted, not including 93 recruits who deserted before they physically joined the regiment; 30 were members of the unit as originally mustered and 44 were later substitutes or transfers. Steiner, *Disease in the Sixty-Fifth United States Colored Infantry,* 16, 39. Dennett, *History of the Ninth U.S.C.,* 32–146. Glatthaar, *Forged in Battle,* 120. Wilson, *Campfires of Freedom,* xii.

18. Berlin, *Black Military Experience,* 434–35. Glatthaar, *Forged in Battle,* 117–18. Yacovone, *Voice of Thunder,* 75. Ramold overstates that the army "frequently" failed to follow proper procedures. While finding that the navy went to "great lengths to preserve individual rights," Ramold cites many of the same procedural safeguards that army general courts-martial provided to defendants. Ramold's analysis supports my argument that the federal government tried to impose an equal justice system regarding blacks in the armed services. A sharp contrast between the disciplining of black soldiers and sailors comes in the navy's lack of executions. Lincoln commuted the few condemnations issued. For a partial explanation of why army officers could be more arbitrary than their naval counterparts, see note 16. Ramold, *Slaves, Sailors, Citizens,* 5, 149, 151–52, 165. For a more critical view of race relations in the navy, see Bennett, *Union Jacks: Yankee Sailors in the Civil War.* Contrast the treatment of black Civil War soldiers facing general courts-martial with a military commission that tried nearly 400 Dakota men for murder, rape, and robbery following a brief war in Minnesota in 1862, convicting all but 70 and sentencing 303 to death. Forty of the Dakotas were executed, almost the same number of blacks executed by sentence of a general court-martial during the Civil War. Chomsky, "The United States-Dakota War Trials," 13–96.

19. Ramold, *Slaves, Sailors, Citizens,* 81–83. Berlin, *Black Military Experience,* 434–35, 437–38, 441, 475. Wilson, *Campfires of Freedom,* 21–22, 24, 185. Glatthaar, *Forged in Battle,* 90, 108–15. Yacovone, "The Fifty-fourth Massachusetts Regiment, the Pay Crisis," 38–39, 41–43.

20. In Higginson's regiment, one soldier who drew a bayonet on an officer, and another soldier who struck one, each received only one month's hard labor and loss of a month's pay for their violations. Stone did recommend tying by the thumbs as it subdued the offender but did not afflict serious injury. Endorsement by Judge Advocate General Joseph Holt, March 6, 1866, on Peter Birts, et al. to General Lorenzo Thomas, December 4, 1865 (recognizing black sensitivity to insult and urging clemency for several men who disobeyed orders because they were "jealous of every act of their white superiors, which might be…interpreted as a slur upon their race"); Simon Prisby to Edwin M. Stanton, near Brownsville, Tex., July 20, 1865 (officers in his regiment frequently prescribed tying or struck the men); Prince Albert to Andrew Johnson, Fort Livingston, La., January 28, 1866 (punished by having to stand on a barrel for refusing to fish for oysters for an officer); General Orders No. 36, Hd. Qrs. 1st Division, USCT, August 28, 1864; General Orders No. 36, Hd Qrs. 62nd USCI, November 9, 1864; General Orders No. 3, Hd. Qrs. 100th USCI, January 30, 1865, all in Berlin, *Black Military Experience,* 424–25, 428–29, 440, 452, 454, 457–58. Baker court-martial. Berlin, *Black Military Experience,* 434–35, 437–38, 441, 475. Wilson, *Campfires of Freedom,* 21–22, 24, 185. Glatthaar, *Forged in Battle,* 90, 108–15. Thomas W. Higginson Journal, December 31, 1862, February 20, 1863, c. February 23–27, 1863 in Looby, *War Journal,* 79, 106.

21. Samuel Green court-martial 109th USCI. For other examples of black resentment, see Sgt. J. Hall, Sgt. Anderson Tolliver et al., court-martial, 2nd USCA (Light) and Sgt. William Walker court-martial, 3rd South Carolina Volunteer Infantry; for an example of additional charges, see Henry M. Way court-martial, and Doctor Moore and Sgt. William Kease courts-martial, 116th USCI. Wilson, *Campfires of Freedom*, 33, 35. Winthrop, *Digest of Opinions of the Judge Advocate General of the Army*, 333.

22. Lt. Charles Duren recounted stunning one black subordinate who tried to strike him as he attempted to arrest two fighting men by hitting him with the butt end of his revolver. Duren added, "If that had not been effectual I should have shot the man on the spot—for I always said if a man ever offered to strike me in this Reg't—I should shoot him." C. M. Duren to Father, Jacksonville, Fla., March 23, 1864, in Duren, "Letters of Lt. C. M. Duren," 280–81; for compliments see C. M. Duren to Father, Baldwin Station, Florida, February 18, 1864; to Mother, Jacksonville, Fla., February 29, 1864; to Father, Jacksonville, Fla., March 29, 1864, on 268, 272, 282. George E. Stephens, near Jacksonville, Fla., March 6, 1864 (*Weekly Anglo-African*, March 26, 1864) in Yacovone, *Voice of Thunder*, 298–99. Thomas W. Higginson Journal, July 7, 1863, in Looby, *War Journal*, 158–59. Emilio, *Brave Black Regiment*, 329. Fox, *Fifty-fifth Regiment of Massachusetts Volunteer Infantry*, 5. Thomas M. Chester, Deep Bottom, Va., September 1, 1864, in Blackett, *Chester*, 115.

23. *United States Army Regulations of 1861*, 496–97. Winthrop, *Digest of Opinions of the Judge Advocate General of the Army*, 29, 31, 37, 127, 135, 205. For a panel excusing a member after a challenge see Adam Smalz court-martial, 66th New York Infantry.

24. Winthrop, *Digest of Opinions of the Judge Advocate General of the Army*, 391. Simms court-martial; Baker court-martial; Goliah court-martial; Moore court-martial; Kease court-martial; Samuel Mapp court-martial, 10th USCI; Aaron Collins court-martial, 6th USCC; John Mitchell court-martial, 53rd USCI. Ramold, *Slaves, Sailors, Citizens*, 138. Donald, *Charles Sumner and the Rights of Man*, 161.

25. Cummins heard her "master" Matthew Current ask black soldiers who approached his house what they wanted, and heard gunfire as she ran in to get her "old Mistress." Cummins identified the accused and a witness outside the court as the two soldiers she saw flee afterward. Collins court-martial. Berlin, *Black Military Experience*, 436

26. William Henderson court-martial, 66th USCI.

27. One of the black witnesses assured on cross-examination that he could recognize Henderson because of five freckles on his face. Henderson court-martial. It is unlikely Henderson's counsel, William Getchel, was an attorney; he served only as a noncommissioned officer in his prior regiment. Howard, *History of the 124th Regiment Illinois Infantry*, 506.

28. For examples of confessions, see Simon Grant court-martial, 21st USCI; William H. Harrison court-martial, 69th USCI. Sixteen members of the 49th USCI stacked arms near Vicksburg on June 13, 1864, after their captain opened some of their storage boxes to find spoiled meat and filthy clothing; he burned everything and told his men that he would punish the owners of any more such boxes. Giles Simms court-martial, 49th USCI. Price Warefield et al. to Hon. E. M. Stanton, Military Prison Alton, Ill., February 20, 1865, in Berlin, *Black Military Experience*, 459–60. The judge advocate should have brought Humphreys's exculpatory information to the court's attention. For other examples of a court-martial considering mitigating factors, see the Sampson Goliah court-martial and the Sgt. J. Hall, Sgt. Anderson Tolliver, et al., court-martial.

29. Thomas Four court-martial, 52nd USCI. William Jackson court-martial, 14th USCI.

30. One of his comrades recollected that Green went into his regiment as a sergeant because he had a "good voice and a better education than most of the soldiers." Green mustered out as a private. For Green's postwar life, see note 20 in the Epilogue. Green court-martial. Samuel Green pension file, National Archives, Washington, D.C. Nine men received sentences related to this mutiny. One, Sheldon Penock, cast aspersion on the testimony of other blacks as his only defense and offered that one man testified against him so as to obtain his sergeant's stripes, after receiving five dollars to identify participants in the incident. Penock's former master wrote on behalf of his "old *servant*," citing a "strong affection, between master, and slave," and explained that Penock endeavored to free the prisoners for fear they would be killed by enemy fire. Judge Advocate General Holt noted that there was no evidence of exposure to such fire but urged clemency by explaining that "the impulse of humanity which led this soldier to the violation of the military law, may be received as a palliation of the offense." Less than seven months after promulgation of his sentence, the War Department ordered Penock's discharge. See also the case of Private Sandy Fenqua in this same file, in which one officer testified that Fenqua declared, "The damned white sons of bitches think they can do as they please with us," and that "they have lied to us long enough."

Sheldon Penock and Sandy Fenqua courts-martial, 109th USCI. B. W. Penick to Andrew Johnson, Greensburg, Ky., April 16, 1866; endorsement of Holt, June 3, 1866, in Berlin, *Black Military Experience,* 471-73.

31. George Douglas court-martial, 38th USCI.

32. The National Archives cannot find John Shaw's court-martial file, but some relevant papers are in his military service file. Although the death sentence on Benjamin McCloud, 37th USCI, was ultimately carried out, see his mutiny case for another example of procedural review. Winthrop, *Digest of Opinions of the Judge Advocate General of the Army,* 318-23, 370-71. Fox, *Fifty-fifth Regiment of Massachusetts Volunteer Infantry,* 77. Endorsement of Joseph Holt, May 10, 1864, in Emanuel Davis court-martial, 48th USCI ("pleasure"). 12 Stat. 731, Sec. 21 (Act of March 3, 1863).

33. Irving Charles court-martial, 9th United States Cavalry; see also Charles Wood court-martial, 9th United States Cavalry; Winthrop, *Digest of Opinions of the Judge Advocate General of the Army,* 243 (judge advocate's office advises mitigation of death and prison sentences in several cases where black mutineers had been "provoked" by "cruel" or unnecessarily violent actions of their officer).

34. African American soldier/correspondent George E. Stephens felt that prejudice permeated the army's administration of justice toward black troops; see cites in this chapter. On the other hand, black correspondent Thomas M. Chester rarely mentioned capital punishment or courts-martial, perhaps to avoid bringing attention to disciplinary problems among black troops. Blackett, *Chester.* See also Garland H. White, April 20, 1865, City Point, Va., in *Christian Recorder* (May 6, 1865). *New York Times,* November 26, 1865; December 25, 1865. Berlin, *Black Military Experience,* 441-42.

35. See remarks in this chapter by Massachusetts governor Andrew and senator Wilson concerning William Walker's execution.

36. *United States Army Regulations of 1861,* 486. Benet, *Treatise on Military Law,* 205-6.

37. Glatthaar, *Forged in Battle,* 115.

38. The number of black soldiers who faced mutiny charges is derived from a search run through The Index Project. *List of U.S. Soldiers Executed by United States Military Authorities during the Late War,* 2-11. David Washington court-martial, 3rd USCC. Washington sought clemency because he did not "know nothing at all abought law." David Washi[ng]ton to Abraham Lincoln, November 26, 1864, in Berlin, *Black Military Experience,* 455. Wilson, *Campfires of Freedom,* 51-52. Glatthaar, *Forged in Battle,* 115-17.

39. Pvt. John Higgins of the 5th USCHA similarly declared, "God damn any nigger that will stand by and see another tied up for nothing.... We have been run over by our officers long enough; if we don't take our own part, nobody else will take it for us. The niggers are all a set of damned cowards, or they would not be imposed upon so." General Court Martial Orders No. 12, Headquarters Dept. of Mississippi, November 11, 1865, in Berlin, *Black Military Experience,* 474-76. For other courts-martial proceedings involving protest about or rescue of a tied up soldier, see the Samuel Green and Sheldon Penock courts-martial; George Douglas court-martial; David Washington court-martial; Irving Charles and Charles Wood court-martials; the Fort Jackson mutiny; and, the mutiny of the 3rd USCI at Jacksonville, Florida, all discussed in this chapter, as well as a mutiny in the 11th USCHA. For other demands for the release of an arrested comrade, see the Henry Hamilton court-martial, 2nd USCI, and those of William Kease and Doctor Moore. Goliah court-martial.

40. The court found Browning guilty of mutiny and sentenced him to hard labor without pay for the rest of his enlistment and dishonorable discharge. Browning lived in Boston in 1868. Goliah court-martial. Nelson Browning court-martial, 55th Massachusetts. Fox, *Fifty-fifth Regiment of Massachusetts Volunteer Infantry,* 114.

41. See also the introduction to this chapter regarding a petition sent to Lincoln in July 1864 by seventy-four soldiers of the regiment. Goliah court-martial. Col. Alfred S. Hartwell to John A. Andrew, May 10, 1864, quoted in Yacovone, "The Fifty-fourth Massachusetts Regiment, the Pay Crisis," 47. Col. Alfred S. Hartwell to Edwin M. Stanton, Folly Island, S.C., June 13, 1864; Lt. Col. Charles B. Fox to Col. A. S. Hartwell, [Folly Island, S.C.], June 14, 1864; Circular of Col. A. S. Hartwell, Folly Island, S.C., June 14, 1864, all in Berlin, *Black Military Experience,* 398-401. Fox, *Fifty-fifth Regiment of Massachusetts Volunteer Infantry,* 33.

42. Goliah court-martial.

43. Sgt. J. Hall, Sgt. Anderson Tolliver, et al. court-martial, 2nd USCA (Light).

44. Ibid.

45. For example, defense counsel objected that Marion's presence in the court during the proceedings influenced the testimony of witnesses under his command. The court overruled the objection. Ibid.

46. Sterling Bradley and Charles Davis courts-martial, 9th Louisiana Infantry of African Descent.

47. Ibid. See also the Brisbin-Coyl debate discussed earlier.

48. Ibid. Troops asserted their role as the protector of other blacks in another mutiny at Fort Jackson, Louisiana, on December 9, 1863. Lt. Col. Augustus W. Benedict earned the enmity of his 4th Louisiana Native Guard (76th USCI) by striking troops, and he once tied a man spread eagle for two days to stakes driven in the ground, with molasses smeared on his feet and hands. Additionally, several of the regiment's officers committed inappropriate acts toward black civilian laundresses. When Benedict whipped two musicians aged in their late teens or early twenties, half the regiment gathered on the parade ground, firing their guns and vowing to kill Benedict. Only with extreme effort did the fort commander, Col. Charles W. Drew, and his other officers quell the riot, after he ordered Benedict to his quarters. Maj. Gen. Nathaniel P. Banks assured his superiors that the government could continue to have confidence in black troops, and that Benedict's whipping of the two drummers caused the mutiny. Moreover, Banks refused to accept Benedict's resignation and instead ordered a commission to investigate his conduct. Benedict did not face any tough questioning by the commission, probably because the disgusted members found him so reprehensible. Because the permanent disgrace attached to dismissal was generally considered adequate punishment for officers, even where they committed crimes that would have earned the death penalty if perpetrated by enlisted men, Benedict was dismissed from the service. A court-martial also tried thirteen enlisted men. The panel acquitted four and sentenced two to death, six to imprisonment at hard labor for terms of between one and twenty years, and one, convicted of insubordinate conduct, to hard labor for a month. Banks commuted the death sentences to imprisonment and rejected the one month's sentence for conflicting evidence. OR ser. 1 vol. 26 pt. 1:456, 458, 460–62, 467, 468, 473–79. Berlin, *Black Military Experience*, 438–40. Glatthaar, *Forged in Battle*, 91–92.

49. Charges of mutinous conduct prejudicial to good order and military discipline stemmed from allegations that Walker participated in a mutiny on August 23, 1863; threatened to shoot Lt. George W. Wood; refused to obey Capt. Edgar Abeel's order to go into his tent under arrest; on October 31, 1863, threatened to shoot Sgt. Sussex Brown when ordered to fall into drill; and, prevented acting drum major William Smith from arresting drummer Rauty Pope on November 19, 1863. Walker also led his company in releasing Private Jacob Swith from arrest for being absent from camp. A charge of breach of arrest alleged that Walker left his tent on November 20, 1863, to play cards. Sgt. William Walker court-martial, 3rd South Carolina Volunteer Infantry. Westwood, "Consequence," 222.

50. Walker court-martial. OR, ser. 1, vol. 44:667. Westwood, "Consequence," 224, 226.

51. Col. A. G. Bennett et al. to Brig. Gen. Lorenzo Thomas, Hilton Head, S.C., November 21, 1863; Col. A. G. Bennett to Capt. William L. M. Burger, Hilton Head, S.C., November 30, 1863, endorsement by Maj. Gen. Q. A. Gillmore by A. A. Gen. Edward W. Smith, Folly Island, S.C., December 2, 1863; Col. William B. Barton to Brig. Gen. Rufus Saxton, Hilton Head, S.C., December 5, 1863, endorsement by Brig. Gen. Rufus Saxton through A. A. Gen. Capt. E. W. Hooper, Beaufort, S.C., Dec. 11, 1863, all in Berlin, *Black Military Experience*, 388–91. John A. Andrew to Abraham Lincoln, Boston, May 13, 1864, at <http://memory.loc.gov/cgi-bin/query/P?mal:1:./temp/~ammem_Ls4j:>.

52. Col. M. S. Littlefield to Col. P. P. Brown, Jr., Hilton Head, S.C., June 3, 1864, in Berlin, *Black Military Experience*, 394–95. Westwood, "Consequence," 231.

53. Walker court-martial.

54. Walker vigorously addressed in his defense statement all the allegations against him. Ibid.

55. Military courts could take cognizance of accusations against an individual without regard to their connection as to time, place, or subject. Walker court-martial. Winthrop, *Digest of Opinions of the Judge Advocate General of the Army*, 81.

56. Walker court-martial. George E. Stephens, near Jacksonville, Fla., March 6, 1864 (*Weekly Anglo-African*, March 26, 1864) in Yacovone, *Voice of Thunder*, 298–99; see also 303 n. 23. Thomas W. Higginson to the Editor of the *New York Tribune*, August 12, 1864, in Higginson, *Army Life in a Black Regiment*, 226. *Cong. Globe*, 38th Cong., 1st Sess., 1805 (April 22, 1864). Hallowell, *An Address by N. P. Hallowell, '61. Delivered on Memorial Day, May 30, 1896*, 8–9.

57. Trial testimony went poorly for Hamilton, and his statement pled his ignorance and begged the mercy of the court, which sentenced him to be shot. After sentencing, the judge advocate and two members of the panel, both from Hamilton's regiment, petitioned for clemency on his behalf, citing his ignorance, arguing that his act was not commensurate with the sentence, and claiming that two members of the panel wished to reconsider their vote. The department commander ordered Hamilton to be shot as a deterrent. Henry Hamilton court-martial. For another

mutiny in which a soldier suggested that perceived grievances justified a threat against an officer, see that of Samuel Mapp. Kease court-martial. Moore court-martial.

58. Bennett, "Jacksonville Mutiny," 40–41. R.H.B. to the editor, *Christian Recorder,* August 6, 1864.

59. Brower claimed Green was about to shoot him. Joseph Grien (Green), Richard Lee, Joseph Nathaniel, James Thomas, Calvin Dowrey, and James Allen courts-martial, all from the 3rd USCI and all individual proceedings. Bennett, "Jacksonville Mutiny," 42–44.

60. Bennett, "Jacksonville Mutiny," 45, 47.

61. The proceedings for David Craig cannot be located. Grien, Nathaniel, Thomas, Dowrey, Allen, Richard Lee, Thomas Howard, Jacob Plowden, John Miller, Theodore Waters, and Alexander Lee courts-martial, all from the 3rd USCI and all individual proceedings. Bennett, "Jacksonville Mutiny," 42, 43, 48, 49.

62. Roger Johnson court-martial, 6th USCHA. The army did not turn a blind eye toward whites who murdered blacks. See Frederick Letz court martial, teamster (Lincoln approved sentence of hanging for a white teamster who, on September 22, 1862, shot an elderly black Pennsylvanian teamster after an argument the day before; testimony of a free black man helped prosecution); George W. Johnson court-martial, 4th Delaware Volunteer Infantry (Lincoln approves death sentence for a soldier convicted of stabbing a black civilian on April 22, 1863, at Gloucester Point, Virginia; thirty-nine men and women from Wilmington, Delaware, including Johnson's parents and sister, petitioned Lincoln for clemency on the grounds that Johnson was drunk).

63. Thomas Four court-martial. See also Collins court-martial (tension between black soldiers and local white civilians resulted in violence).

64. Richard Simmons, another member of the party who turned state's evidence, also testified. Four court-martial.

65. When asked during trial if he recognized any of the defendants, J. R. Cook pointed at Johnson and said, "That one I know, but I did not see him here that night." Neither Cook nor Johnson spoke in specifics during the trial about their relationship. Ibid.

66. Ibid. Waldrep, *Roots of Disorder,* 93–94.

Chapter 5. Irish Americans in Arms

1. *Pilot,* March 28, 1863. Macnamara, *Ninth Regiment,* 460, 470. In an October 1863 speech in Boston, Thomas F. Meagher linked emigration with free choice, as did many middle-class Irish Americans in public pronouncements: "Most of the foreign-born citizens who have come to these shores have come because in the old world they were the sincere and devoted friends of Republican Government." This "free choice" model contrasts with the "emigration as exile" model, which more fully acknowledged the harsh realities that forced much of the Irish immigration, e.g., the Famine, as well as the homesickness that ensued. The "adopted country" language is distinguishable from these two models insofar as it does not address why Irish migrated in the first place, it concerns how Irish American leaders presented their actions once in America. *New York Times,* October 29, 1863.

2. See McPherson, *For Cause and Comrades,* on the ideological nature of Civil War soldiers.

3. Burton, *Melting Pot Soldiers,* 176 ("rites of passage" phrase). Breuilly, *Nationalism and the State,* 64.

4. While noting that Irish American writer Charles Halpine poked fun at the bombastic speeches of some ethnic leaders at flag presentation ceremonies, historian William Burton also underestimates the power these ceremonies held for recipients and audiences. Burton, *Melting Pot Soldiers,* 147, 176–77, 187–89. McDermott, *69th Regiment Pennsylvania,* 28, 83. Conyngham, *Irish Brigade,* 55–65, 330–36.

5. Macnamara, *Ninth Massachusetts,* 22–2. *Pilot,* June 29, 1861.

6. *Pilot,* June 29, 1861. Macnamara, *Ninth Massachusetts,* 22–24. See also *Pilot,* May 25, 1861 (ceremonies in Salem, Massachusetts, before the departure of its company of the 9th Massachusetts); Ryan, *Campaigning with the Irish Brigade,* 29, 38 n.2 (28th Massachusetts send-off on January 10 and 11, 1862).

7. *Pilot,* June 29, 1861 ("rubbish"); July 6, 1861.

8. *Pilot,* July 27, 1861. Thomas Cass to Charles R. Train, March 2, 1862 (*Pilot,* March 22, 1862) (When Bostonians sent the 9th Massachusetts another state banner in March 1862, Cass

declared that "we can justly claim in common with all our brothers in arms from Massachusetts, that the honor of our State and Flag *can be justly confided to our keeping*, and that we can be justly allowed the proud privilege of defending its honor, as well as the glorious emblem of our common country—the Stars and Stripes.").

9. *Pilot*, June 29, 1861. Michael A. Finnerty, Minor's Hill, Va., November 12, 1861 (*Pilot*, November 30, 1861)("atoms"; the "'green flag' was the centre of general observation" during a review); Finnerty, Minor's Hill, Va., November 28, 1861 (*Pilot*, December 14, 1861) ("a smile of grateful acknowledgement" came over the face of "honest father Abraham" when he saw the emerald banner during another review). *OR*, ser. 1, vol. 11 pt. 1:720.

10. O'Connor, *Civil War Boston*, 76, 78–79.

11. *Pilot*, October 19, 1861.

12. *Pilot*, October 26, 1861; November 2, 1861; December 14, 1861; see also August 2, 1862 for an article reprinted from the *Chicago Post*.

13. *Pilot* published Finnerty's letter in the same edition in which it urged Irish Americans to "assert themselves" in the November 1861 state elections. Michael A. Finnerty, Camp near Fall's Church, Va., October 15, 1861 (*Pilot*, October 26, 1861). John W. Mahan, Minor's Hill, Va., February 26, 1862 (*Pilot*, March 8, 1862). See also Michael A. Finnerty, June 2, 1862 (*Pilot*, June 14, 1862) (Finnerty fumed when he felt a reporter for the *New York Herald* ignored the role his regiment played at the battle of Hanover Court House due to its Irish American composition, and he expected "even handed justice" based on Irish American service).

14. Unsigned letter to [Patrick] Donahoe from an officer of the 9th Massachusetts, Warrenton, Va., November 9, 1862 (*Pilot*, November 22, 1862). Patrick R. Guiney to John A. Andrew, camp near Sharpsburgh [*sic*], October 22, 1862, in Samito, *Irish Ninth*, 143–44. John A. Andrew to Patrick R. Guiney, Boston, October 31, 1862 in *Pilot*, November 22, 1862. Baum, *Civil War Party System*, 48.

15. Michael A. Finnerty, On Board Steamer Ben DeFord, June 29, 1861 (*Pilot*, July 13, 1861). Crotty, *Four Years*, 30–32, 60.

16. Michael A. Finnerty, Washington D.C., July 6, 1861 (*Pilot*, July 20, 1861). Crotty, *Four Years*, 18–19. McDermott, *69th Regiment Pennsylvania*, 7 (service near Washington, D.C.).

17. Michael A. Finnerty, Minor's Hill, Va., February 25, 1862 (*Pilot*, March 15, 1862). See Halpine, *Baked Meats*, 256–57, for a poem declaring that Irish Americans and the native-born came together during Gettysburg.

18. Michael A. Finnerty, Washington, D.C., July 6, 1861 (*Pilot*, July 20, 1861) (members of the 9th Massachusetts visit the 69th NYSM); Finnerty, Arlington, Va., July 25, 1861 (*Pilot*, August 10, 1861); Finnerty, Minor's Hill, Va., October 2, 1861 (*Pilot*, November 2, 1861) (Irish American officers of the 33rd Pennsylvania visit the 9th's camp). "Erin," Minor's Hill, Va., February 14, 1862 (*Irish-American*, February 22, 1862). See also *Pilot*, August 10, 1861 (Irish Americans in San Francisco send a flag to the 69th New York).

19. *Harper's Weekly*, June 1, 1861. See also Michael A. Finnerty, Washington D.C., July 6, 1861 (*Pilot*, July 20, 1861) (officers of the 31st New York invited counterparts from the 9th Massachusetts to supper).

20. Michael A. Finnerty, Minor's Hill, Va., January 2, 1862 (*Pilot*, January 11, 1862). Patrick R. Guiney to Jennie Guiney, Minor's Hill, Va., December 27, 1861, in Samito, *Irish Ninth*, 59–60.

21. Conyngham, *Irish Brigade*, 485. Corby, *Memoirs*, 265–68.

22. McDermott, *69th Regiment Pennsylvania*, 5. Burton, *Melting Pot Soldiers*, 147. Edward Kelly, Alexandria, Va., November 20, 1861 (*Pilot*, November 30, 1861). Miller, "Trouble with Brahmins," 40. Bennett, *O'Rorke*, 9–11, 69. Conyngham, *Irish Brigade*, 436.

23. *Pilot*, April 25, 1863; P. McD., Beaufort, S. C., April 2, 1863 (*Pilot*, April 25, 1863). Bruce, *Harp and the Eagle*, 176. Daniel W. Sawtelle to Sister, Bermuda Hundred, Va., Sept. 18, 1864, in Buckingham, *All's for the Best*, 302 (8th Maine in Jacksonville; see also page 46).

24. Burton, *Melting Pot Soldiers*, 134. Patrick R. Guiney to wife, May 7, 1863, in Samito, *Irish Ninth*, 187–88.

25. Macnamara, *Ninth Massachusetts*, 60, 284–85. Samito, *Irish Ninth*, 105. Charles William Folsom Diary, March 17, 1863; March 17, 1864, cited in Handlin, *Boston's Immigrants*, 210. John Ryan of the 28th Massachusetts recalled duty on James Island, South Carolina, alongside native-born, German, and Scotch troops. Ryan, *Campaigning with the Irish Brigade*, 44. J. P Sullivan, Forest, Wis., February 13, 1883, in Beaudot and Herdegen, *Irishman in the Iron Brigade*, 92–93. Burton, *Melting Pot Soldiers*, 208. *New York Times*, June 17, 1863. Mulholland, *116th Regiment, Pennsylvania*, 35, 267.

26. Michael A. Finnerty, Minor's Hill, Va., November 20, 1861 (*Pilot,* December 7, 1861) (9th Massachusetts sends over $7,000 home). Corby, *Memoirs,* 147 (the 63rd, 88th, and 94th New York regiments contribute $1,240.50 to a fund to assist the poor in Ireland). *New York Times,* October 22, 1861. O'Connor, *Fitzpatrick's Boston,* 83. O'Connor, *Civil War Boston,* 162–63, 204. Handlin, *Boston's Immigrants,* 61, 86. Lawson, *Patriot Fires,* 56, 58–59.

27. Henry W. Lord to William H. Seward, Manchester, England, July 26, 1862, in OR, ser. 3 vol. 2:358–59. Cullop, "Union Recruiting in Ireland," 101–3. Circular No. 19, Department of State, August 8, 1862, in OR, ser. 3 vol. 2:358–59. Newman, *American Naturalization Processes and Procedures 1790–1985,* 15. See Peterson and Hudson, "Foreign Recruitment for Union Forces," 178–84, regarding Confederate attempts to combat immigration to the United States; see pages 187–89 regarding British debates in Parliament about federal recruiting in Ireland, which ultimately led to no official protest to the U.S. government.

28. Hanchett, *Halpine,* 2–4, 25–26, 33, 78, 98 (Horace Greeley to Abraham Lincoln, January 18, 1864), 131–32, 134–35. Timothy Walch, "Charles Graham Halpine," in Glazier, *Irish in America,* 374.

29. Halpine, *Miles O'Reilly,* viii. Hanchett, *Halpine,* 85–86, 94.

30. Halpine, *Miles O'Reilly,* ix–x.

31. Halpine, *Baked Meats,* 59–60, 206–7. Gannon, "The Won Cause," 179. Hanchett, *Halpine,* 113–14.

32. Halpine, *Miles O'Reilly,* 159–60. Hanchett, *Halpine,* 91. Irish Brigade historian David P. Conyngham described after the war, "On they marched, dark Puritans from the New England States; stalwart Yankees, of bone and muscle; men from the West and Northwest; exiles of Erin, from Munster's sunny plains, from Connaught's heights, and Leinster's vales; peasants from the Rhine: all march along through the glorious woods, through forest paths, as if of one race and nation." Conyngham neglected to mention blacks. Conyngham, *Irish Brigade,* 106.

33. Burton, *Melting Pot Soldiers,* 10–11, 112–15.

34. *New York Times,* August 19, 1862. See Chicago's similar reception of James A. Mulligan after his release from Confederate captivity. Burton, *Melting Pot Soldiers,* 113–15, 136.

35. *New York Times,* August 19, 1862.

36. Ibid. August 22, 23, 1862.

37. Ibid.

38. Burton, *Melting Pot Soldiers,* 116. Corcoran, *Captivity,* 21–22, 35.

39. Corcoran, *Captivity,* 22, 27–28, 30, 40, 44.

40. Ibid., 100. Burton, *Melting Pot Soldiers,* 119.

41. Samito, *Irish Ninth,* xi–xiv, 113–15. Attorney Guiney's election to the Roxbury town council in 1859, merchant Thomas Cass's position on the Boston school committee by 1860, and the election of Thomas W. Cahill, partner in a masonry firm, in 1859, 1860, and 1861 as New Haven alderman, all contrast sharply with the nativist impulse in Massachusetts and Connecticut at the time. On the other hand, both Cass and Cahill captained Irish American militia companies disbanded by Know Nothing governors prior to the Civil War. Burton, *Melting Pot Soldiers,* 13. Murray, *History of the Ninth Regiment, Connecticut Volunteer Infantry,* 322.

42. Guiney to wife, Arlington Heights near Washington, D.C., July 31, 1861; to Governor John A. Andrew, camp near Sharpsburgh, Md., October 22, 1862, in Samito, *Irish Ninth,* 29–30, 143–44. *Pilot,* September 13, 1862.

43. Guiney to wife, Camp Wightman, June 4, 1861; to wife, Washington, D.C., July 2, 1861; to wife, Arlington Heights near Washington, D.C., July 31, 1861, in Samito, *Irish Ninth,* 5–6, 11, 28–29.

44. Guiney to wife, Arlington Heights, Va., August 20, 1861; to wife, Arlington Heights, Va., September 1, 1861, in ibid. 47.

45. Guiney to wife, Camp, 9th Mass., January 6, 1863; to wife, Head Quarters 2nd Brigade, February 11, 1863; Guiney to Mrs. Shaw, Roxbury, Ma., June 2, 1864, in ibid. 162, 163, 246.

46. *Pilot,* April 26, 1862. Guiney to wife, near Bottom's Bridge, Va., May 22, 1862; to wife, Head Quarters 2nd Brigade, February 26, 1863, in Samito, *Irish Ninth,* 103, 167. Patrick R. Guiney to Editor of the *Boston Journal,* September 27, 1864 in Patrick R. Guiney's scrapbook, Patrick R. Guiney papers, College of the Holy Cross, Worcester, Ma. (hereafter cited as Guiney scrapbook), 3. Guiney scrapbook, 10, 13.

47. Some historians, such as William L. Burton and Marion Archer Truslow, argue that the Civil War accelerated Americanization of Irish Americans. Susannah Ural Bruce on the other hand contends that Civil War service did not aid Irish American assimilation to the United States and

that the level of prejudice against Irish Americans remained largely unchanged as a result of the war. Burton, *Melting Pot Soldiers*, x–xi, 51, 56, 67, 121–22, 135, 138, 152–54. Truslow, "Peasants into Patriots," v–vi, 13. Bruce, *Harp and the Eagle*, 4, 189. *Pilot*, July 29, 1865.

48. Faust, "Christian Soldiers," 64, 82–83. Watson, "Religion and Combat Motivation in the Confederate Armies," 30, 35–36, 41–44.

49. George Tipping to Wife, Staten Island, N.Y., October 14, 1862; to Wife, Staten Island, N.Y., October 18, 1862; to Wife, Newport News, Va., November 22, 1862; to Catharine, Suffolk, Va., February 1, 1863; to Catharine, Camp near Suffolk, Va., February 12, 1863; February 15, 1863; to Catharine, Second Division Hospital In the field, June 27, 1864. When Daniel Crotty's 3rd Michigan passed near St. Mary's College during the Gettysburg campaign, he joined other Catholics of his regiment to attend Mass. Crotty, *Four Years*, 88–89. See *Pilot*, May 25, 1861, and August 24, 1861, for early reports of devotion in the 9th Massachusetts.

50. By May 1863, the 35th Indiana marched as a unit directly to chapel to hear Mass every morning before breakfast and reassembled every evening for a prayer service. On Sundays, members of other regiments attended the High Mass Cooney celebrated for the unit. Peter Paul Cooney to Brother, Indianapolis, Ind., October 14, 1861; to Brother, Louisville, Ky., October 2, 1862; to Brother, Murfreesboro, Tn., January 12, 1863; to Brother, Murfreesboro, Tn., May 13, 1863; June 17, 1863, in McElroy, "War Letters of Father Peter Paul Cooney," 52, 68, 152, 157, 158. McDermott, *69th Regiment Pennsylvania*, 9. Corby, *Memoirs*, 181, 184–86, 218–19, 320–21.

51. Peter Paul Cooney to Brother, Indianapolis, Ind., October 14, 1861; to Brother, Murfreesboro, Tn., June 17, 1863; to Very Rev. Dear Father [Sorin], McMinnville, Tn., July 17, 1863 ("power"); to Brother, Blue Springs, Tn., April 26, 1864, in McElroy, "War Letters of Father Peter Paul Cooney," 53, 158, 165–65, 223. Also see a letter from a Protestant soldier in the Army of the Potomac who expressed that "Catholics...are the best friend the soldier has got," adding that the "Sisters of Charity are doing a noble work here, and although every regiment has its chaplain, he won't speak to a private. *The priest is the only man that is among the men.*" *Boston Courier*, July 18, 1862 (*Pilot*, July 26, 1862).

52. Conyngham, *Irish Brigade*, 372–80. Mulholland, *116th Regiment, Pennsylvania*, 77–83. Ryan, *Campaigning with the Irish Brigade*, 89–91. Corby, *Memoirs*, 139–40.

53. Brown, *Irish-American Nationalism*, 20–23, 28–31, 38–41; Bruce, *Harp and the Eagle*, 200.

54. Historians have largely ignored how Fenianism affected citizenship. William D'Arcy's *The Fenian Movement in the United States: 1858–1886* remains the most detailed narrative of the Fenian movement's activities, while Brian Jenkins's *Fenians and Anglo-American Relations During Reconstruction* provides a thorough diplomatic history. Neither book appreciates the paradoxical level to which Fenianism reveals a high extent of Americanization among the Irish Americans, nor sufficiently links the organization's impact on the redefinition of American citizenship during the 1860s. Despite the fact that she could have cited some of Fenianism's rhetoric in support of her overall thesis, Susannah Ural Bruce largely ignores the Fenian movement in *The Harp and the Eagle: Irish-American Volunteers and the Union Army, 1861–1865*. Brown, *Irish-American Nationalism*, 38–41.

55. D'Arcy, *Fenian Movement*, 181, 241, 243.

56. By May 1865, Halpine claimed fifteen army and navy circles contained 14,620 members, although he also overestimated a total Brotherhood membership of 80,000 Fenians. *Second National Congress of the Fenian Brotherhood...January, 1865*, 6, 22. Macnamara, *Ninth Massachusetts*, 429. *First National Convention of the Fenian Brotherhood...November 1863*, 15 (T. R. Bourke to John O'Mahony, near Warrenton, Va. ["duties"]), 16. Halpine, *Baked Meats*, 223, 225–27, 228–29. D'Arcy *Fenian Movement*, 30–31, 40–43, 61, 79, 100 n.5, 101 n. 6, 107 n. 25, 131 n. 92.

57. *First National Convention of the Fenian Brotherhood...November 1863*, 3, 6, 11, 43–45. *Second National Congress of the Fenian Brotherhood...January, 1865*, 3, 27, 32. Halpine, *Baked Meats*, 225–26.

58. *First National Convention of the Fenian Brotherhood...November 1863*, 3, 6, 11, 41, 46–47. Jenkins, *Fenians*, 28, 29. During the Civil War, the Irish-born O'Mahoney served as colonel of the 99th NYSM, a unit that mustered into service from August 2—November 9, 1864, and lost one man to disease. Bishops in the United States and Ireland condemned the Fenian Brotherhood, and the church officially condemned it by early 1870. D'Arcy, *Fenian Movement*, 33–35, 39, 49, 330–31. Beale, *Diary of Edward Bates*, 504. Seamus Metress, "John O'Mahoney," in Glazier, *Irish in America*, 740–41.

59. *First National Convention of the Fenian Brotherhood…November 1863*, 6, 10, 17, 36–38.
60. Ibid. 31–35.
61. Ibid. 31–32.
62. *Second National Congress of the Fenian Brotherhood…January, 1865*, 5–8, 13, 23.
63. Ibid. 46–48. Miller, *Emigrants and Exiles*, 346.
64. *Second National Congress of the Fenian Brotherhood…January, 1865*, 49–51. Snay, *Fenians, Freedmen, and Southern Whites*, 127.
65. Irish-born Roberts left for New York City in 1849 at the age of nineteen. There, Roberts became a businessman and was a millionaire by 1869. Roberts served in Congress as a Democrat from 1871–1874. Seamus Metress, "John O'Mahoney"; Daniel J. Kuntz, "William Randall Roberts," in Glazier, *Irish in America*, 740–41, 809–10. Jenkins, *Fenians*, 31–32, 83.
66. Halpine, *Baked Meats*, vii, 209–13, 215. Hanchett, *Halpine*, 153.
67. Halpine, *Baked Meats*, 215–18, 234, 238–39, 249.
68. In another article, Halpine had James T. Brady, an Irish-born prowar Democrat, toast Fenian success with the caveat that a war with Britain would enroll "every able-bodied true Irishman, both here and in Canada, under the banner of the Union!" Ibid. 23, 54, 78–79, 85, 236–37. Hanchett, *Halpine*, 85.
69. *Stephens' Fenian Songster*, 8, 18–20, 24, 25–26, 35, 47, 51–54.
70. Rev. Bernard O'Reilly, S.J. to Charles P. Daly, Maison Saint Joseph, Quimper [France], January 30, 1864 (Daly Papers, Rare Books and Manuscripts Division, New York Public Library).
71. Bruce, *Harp and the Eagle*, 4, 189 (quote).
72. *Pilot*, July 26, 1862 (funeral of 9th Massachusetts's Col. Cass); August 9, 1862 (funeral of 9th Massachusetts's Lt. John H. Rafferty). Blake McKelvey, who studied Rochester, contended that O'Rorke's death "made a union out of Rochester." Bennett, *O'Rorke*, 134, 136–37, 140.
73. For Irish American criticism of Copperheads and the Draft Riots, see Peter Welsh to Margaret Welsh, Pleasant Valley Maryland, July 18, 1863; Bloomfield, Va., July 22, 1863; In camp near Kelly's Ford, Va., August 2, 1863, in Kohl, *Irish Green and Union Blue*, 110, 113–15; Patrick R. Guiney to Jennie Guiney, Berlin, Md., July 16, 1863, in Samito, *Irish Ninth*, 203; Thomas F. Meagher's speech to the Irish Brigade in *New York Times*, January 17, 1864; Macnamara, *Irish Ninth in Bivouac and Battle*, 217–18.
74. McClintock, "Civil War Pensions," 460–61. O'Connor, *Civil War Boston*, 185.
75. Bruce cites reports in the *Waterloo Advocate*, August 1; September 12, 1862, and *Dubuque Herald*, August 10, 29, 1862, in Iowa, the *Milwaukee Daily News*, November 25, 1862, in Wisconsin, and the *Quincy Herald*, August 4, 1862, in Illinois, of Irish Americans trying to avoid state-level drafts to show that Irish American draft dodging generated a nativist backlash. Bruce, *Harp and the Eagle*, 143, 275–76 nn. 34, 35.
76. *Pilot*, June 8, 1861; August 9, 1862 ("fundamental"); August 16, 1862 (rest of the quotes); December 13, 1862 (calling slavery a "great vice"). Bruce, *Harp and the Eagle*, 137–38.
77. *Pilot*, December 13, 1862; January 17, 1863.
78. Bruce, *Harp and the Eagle*, 136–37 (*Pilot*, January 10, 1863, quoted on 136). *Pilot*, August 9, 1862; January 24, 1863; April 4, 1863; April 11, 1863; May 30, 1863; June 25, 1864.
79. Rev. Bernard O'Reilly, S.J. to Charles P. Daly, Maison Saint Joseph, Quimper [France], January 30, 1864 (Daly Papers, Rare Books and Manuscripts Division, New York Public Library).
80. Bruce, *Harp and the Eagle*, 188, 228. Quigley, *Second Founding*, 11.
81. Lawson, *Patriot Fires*, 68, 77, 79–84. Smith, *Gerrit Smith On M'Clellan's Nomination and Acceptance*, 14. The Loyal Publication Society's *The Two Ways of Treason: Or, The Open Traitor Of The South Face To Face With His Skulking Abettor At The North* (1863) equated Peace Democrats with traitors, and *Sherman vs. Hood—"A Low Tart, Inclined To Be Very Sweet"— Something For Douglas Democrats To Remember—An Appeal To History—Where Governor Seymour Got His "Lessons"—On the Chicago Surrender* (1864), compared New York's Democratic governor Horatio Seymour with Benedict Arnold on page 3.
82. Guiney scrapbook, 13–14. Draft of one of Guiney's speeches in support of Ulysses S. Grant, located in the Patrick R. Guiney papers, College of the Holy Cross, Worcester, Ma.
83. *Pilot*, August 9, 1862; January 24, 1863; April 4, 1863; April 11, 1863; June 25, 1864; November 5, 1864. See also *New York Times*, October 9, 1862 (speech by Richard O'Gorman). *Irish-American*, November 12, 1864; see also *Irish-American*, September 17, 1864 (McClellan as the Union's only hope, in contrast with the "prospect of unceasing, aimless bloodshed, the disruption of our national ties, overwhelming debt, insolvency and anarchy" represented by a Lincoln victory). *Pilot*, September 3, 1864, in Bruce, *Harp and the Eagle*, 227. Waugh, *Reelecting Lincoln*. Siddali, *From Property to Person*, 181–82. Lawson, *Patriot Fires*, 91–94.

84. Halpine, *Miles O'Reilly*, 87–95. *The Great Mass Meeting of Loyal Citizens at Cooper Institute, Friday Evening, March 6, 1863*, 3, 9. Siddali, *From Property to Person*, 2. *Pilot*, November 12, 1864, quoted in O'Connor, *Civil War Boston*, 216.

85. William Jones to Maggie Jones, Ft. Pulaski, Ga., January 10, 1863; Thomas Jones to Maggie Jones, Ft. Pulaski, Ga., February 18, 1863, in Trimble, *Brothers 'til Death*, ix, 42–33. George Tipping to Catharine, Suffolk, Va., June 6, 1863.

86. Frank, *With Ballot and Bayonet*, 67–70 (confronting the "harsh reality" of slavery hardened feelings against it among Northern troops). Michael A. Finnerty, Washington D.C., July 6, 1861 (*Pilot*, July 20, 1861). Guiney to wife, July 14, 1861; September 1, 1861; May 22, 1862, in Samito, *Irish Ninth*, 15–17, 46–48, 103. *Pilot*, April 26, 1862; September 13, 1862. Macnamara, *Ninth Regiment*, 78–79. See also draft of one of Guiney's speeches in support of Ulysses S. Grant, located in the Guiney Papers, College of the Holy Cross, Worcester, Ma.

87. Macnamara, *Irish Ninth in Bivouac and Battle*, 58, 59, 133, 152, 219–21.

88. Halpine, *Miles O'Reilly*, 55–57. Halpine, *Baked Meats*, 205 (poem "won over the Irish" to support the measure).

89. Meagher's October 1863 letter reveals that he embraced the Republican Party and did not merely promote it for personal gain as William L. Burton argued. The *Irish-American* lamented, "Between him and the people who loved and trusted him once he has opened a gulf he never can bridge over," and another edition declared, "Our indignation at his unprovoked attack upon our people has long since subsided into contempt." Thomas F. Meagher to Patrick R. Guiney, New York, October 7, 1863, in Samito, *Irish Ninth*, 225–27. Thomas F. Meagher to the Union Committee of Ohio, New York, September 23, 1863 (*Irish-American*, October 3, 1863). *Irish-American*, October 3, 1863; October 13, 1864; October 15, 1864; November 12, 1864. Athearn, *Meagher*, 139. Burton, *Melting Pot Soldiers*, 125, 210.

90. Bruce, *Harp and the Eagle*, 214–15.

91. John Higham contrasted the Irish Brigade's December 1863 charge at Fredericksburg with the last recorded meeting of the Grand Executive Committee of the Order of United Americans. Higham, *Strangers in the Land*, 12–13. Thomas N. Brown also thought that American prejudice against Irish Americans eased but did not vanish after the Civil War. Brown, *Irish-American Nationalism*, 44–45. Susannah Ural Bruce on the other hand contends that the level of prejudice against Irish Americans remained unchanged as a result of the war. Bruce, *Harp and the Eagle*, 189.

Chapter 6. African Americans and the Call for Rights

1. Runkle, *Address Delivered by Bvt. Col. Ben. P. Runkle*, 7–8.

2. Ibid., 10–14, 16–17, 19–21.

3. *Christian Recorder*, February 11, 1865, in McPherson, *Negro's Civil War*, 311.

4. J.H.W.N. Collins, Savannah, Geo., March 19, 1865 (*Christian Recorder*, April 15, 1865). "Arnold," Wilmington, N.C., March 29, 1865 (*Christian Recorder*, April 15, 1865). McMurray, *Recollections*, 12 (proud black men and women line the streets to watch the 6th USCI march through Williamsburg, Virginia, at least half a dozen times).

5. Garland H. White, Richmond, Va., April 12, 1865 (*Christian Recorder*, April 22, 1865) (describing the reaction of blacks during a visit by Lincoln to Richmond after its fall, as well as his own unexpected reunion with his mother following their twenty-year separation). Miller, "Garland H. White," 203. Thomas M. Chester, Richmond, April 9, 1865, in Blackett, *Chester*, 299 (Chester congratulates ex-slaves convened at the African Church in Richmond). Alexander Whyte, Jr., Memorandum of Extracts from Speech by Major Delaney, African, at the Brick Church, St. Helena Island, S.C. Sunday July 23rd 1865; Col. Charles H. Howard to Rufus Saxton, Beaufort, S.C., July 28, 1865, in Berlin, *Black Military Experience*, 739–41.

6. William A. Warfield, Camp Nelson, Ky., July 7, 1865 (*Weekly Anglo-African*, July 22, 1865), in Redkey, *Grand Army*, 187–88.

7. H. S. Harmon, Gainesville, Fla. (*Christian Recorder*, October 21, 1865).

8. George M. Turner to Cousin, Hilton Head, S.C., December 15, 1861; to Father, Hilton Head, S.C., June 19, 1862; to Cousin Ursula, Beaufort, S.C., July 28, 1863; and, to Aunt Susan, Jacksonville, Fla., May 2, 1864, in Silber and Sievens, *Yankee Correspondence*, 84–87. Brockway, *Speech of Capt. Charles B. Brockway...August 30, 1865*, 4, 9, 13.

9. Zalimas, "Disturbance," 354–69. Yacovone, *Voice of Thunder*, 87–89.

10. Zalimas, "Disturbance," 374–77. Yacovone, *Voice of Thunder*, 87–89.

11. Lt. Col. A. J. Willard to Capt. George W. Hooker, Georgetown, S.C., November 19, 1865; H. M. Turner to Edwin M. Stanton, Columbus, Ga., February 14, 1866, in Berlin, *Black Military Experience,* 754, 756–57. Williams, "Christmas Insurrection Scare of 1865," 40, 42–43, 48.

12. F. G. Wilkins, et al. to Governor Charles J. Jenkins, Columbus, Ga., February 13, 1866; H. M. Turner to Edwin M. Stanton, Columbus, Ga., February 14, 1866; Capt. Frederick Mosebach to Capt. W. W. Deane, Columbus, Ga., March 8, 1866, in Berlin, *Black Military Experience,* 756–57, 759–61.

13. William B. Johnson, Jacksonville, Fl., June 22, 1865 (*Christian Recorder,* July 8, 1865). N. B. Sterrett, Kinston, N.C., July 2, 1865 (*Christian Recorder,* July 8, 1865). Sgt. E. S. Robison to Maj. Gen. Q. A. Gillmore, Columbia, S.C., August 7, 1865, in Berlin, *Black Military Experience,* 742. No report can be found from the investigation Gillmore ordered.

14. Brown, *Negro in the American Rebellion,* 379–80. Glatthaar, *Forged in Battle,* 234. Shaffer, *After the Glory,* 29. As of September 1865, blacks comprised 83,079 (36.7 percent) of 226,611 U.S. soldiers. Williams, "Insurrection Scare," 41. Not all units enjoyed pride-inspiring military experiences. The 65th USCI, recruited in Missouri and serving from March 1864 until January 1867, saw no combat but suffered 742 deaths due to disease among 1,707 total enlisted men. The 65th USCI performed hard labor, had no chaplain, and frequently received bad inspection reports for unsanitary camp conditions and lax discipline; its muster out and discharge seem to have involved little fanfare. Yet 103 members of the regiment found military life satisfactory enough that they obtained discharge in September and October 1866 so as to be able to enlist in the 9th U.S. Cavalry regiment. Steiner, *Disease in the Sixty-Fifth United States Colored Infantry,* xiv, xv, xvii, xviii, 10–13, 16, 127.

15. Col. T. H. Barrett, Ringgold Barracks, Tex., January 4, 1866, in Berlin, *Black Military Experience,* 782–85. James S. Brisbin advised his 6th USCC, recruited out of Kentucky, to "save your money, buy property, and educate your children," strive to "become orderly, sober and industrious citizens," and remember that the "flag that now floats over us is as much yours, as it is mine." Lt. Col. C. T. Trowbridge of South Carolina's 33rd USCI advised his command to seek "paths of honesty, virtue, sobriety and industry," and to know that the "church, the school house and the right forever to be free, are now secured to you," along with a national guarantee of "full protection and justice." Trowbridge praised his "comrades" who "in the face of floods of prejudice, that well nigh deluged every avenue to manhood and true liberty…came forth to do battle for your country and your kindred," and who, united with whites, conquered the rebellion, freed the slaves, and altered "the fundamental law of the land." General Orders No. 1, Head Quarters, 33rd USCI, February 9, 1866; Order No. 43, Head Qrs. 6th USCC, April 16, 1866, in Berlin, *Black Military Experience,* 786–88.

16. "Hannibal," Western Theological Seminary, October 27, 1865 (*Christian Recorder,* November 4, 1865).

17. I. N. Triplett, Davenport, Ia., October 31, 1865 (*Muscatine* (Iowa) *Journal,* November 6, 1865) in Redkey, *Grand Army,* 293–96. W. A. Freeman (*Christian Recorder,* May 27, 1865). N. B. Sterrett, Caroline City, N.C., August 19, 1865 (*Christian Recorder,* August 26, 1865). See also William Gibson, City Point, Va., May 18, 1865 (*Christian Recorder,* May 27, 1865) (exasperation because Indiana hesitated to repeal its black laws). See Garland H. White, Corpus Christi, Tex., September 19, 1865 (*Christian Recorder,* October 21, 1865), for a more passive view.

18. A. H. Newton, Hartford, Ct., November 25, 1865 (*Weekly Anglo-African,* December 16, 1865) in Redkey, *Grand Army,* 286–87. Davidson, "First United States Colored," 21 (men of the 1st USCI reunite with families on the present site of Howard University). Fox, *Fifty-fifth Regiment of Massachusetts Volunteer Infantry,* 84 (55th Massachusetts returns to Boston).

19. The night before, police arrested two black soldiers guarding an arch that whites threatened to tear down. The mayor released them the following morning. The planning committee later charged that the police were "prowling around in colored localities to trump up charges or imagine offences" to humiliate the black community. *Ceremonies at the Reception of Welcome to the Colored Soldiers of Pennsylvania, in the City of Harrisburg, Nov. 14th, 1865, by the Garnet League,* 3–6, 7, 12, 21–22.

20. Ibid., 8–11.

21. 14 Stat. 332 (Act of July 28, 1866).

22. Cullen, "'I's a Man Now,'" 85, 86, 89 (Long quote), 91 (South Carolina soldier quote). Glatthaar, *Forged in Battle,* 248. Shaffer, *After the Glory,* 32, 59.

23. Foner and Walker, *Black National and State Conventions, 1865–1900,* xix. *Proceedings and Address of the Colored Citizens of N.J. Convened at Trenton, August 21st and 22d, 1849,*

in Foner and Walker, *Black State Conventions, 1840–1865*, 3–6. *Connecticut State Convention, of Colored Men…September 12th and 13th, 1849*, in ibid., 25–26, 29. *State Convention of Colored Citizens of the State of Illinois…Nov. 13th, 14th and 15th, 1856*, in ibid., 68, 70, 75–77. Blacks convened nine prewar state conventions each in New York and Ohio, three in California, two in Pennsylvania, Connecticut, Illinois, Massachusetts, and Indiana, and one each in Michigan, New Jersey, and Maryland, as well as a New England regional convention held in Boston in August 1859.

24. *State Council of Colored People of Massachusetts, Convention, January 2, 1854*, in Foner and Walker, *Black State Conventions, 1840–1865*, 89. *Convention of the Colored Citizens of Massachusetts, August 1, 1858*, in ibid., 97–100. *New England Colored Citizens' Convention August 1, 1859*, in ibid., 208, 211–14, 218, 219, 222–23. Rael, *Black Identity and Black Protest*, 27, 37, 114, 133, 176–77, 186, 205. Horton and Horton, *In Hope of Liberty*, 201, 223. Cheek and Cheek, *Langston*, 425. *Baltimore Sun*, July 28, July 29, 1852, in Foner and Walker, *Black State Conventions, 1840–1865*, 42–48.

25. *Preamble and Constitution of the Pennsylvania State Equal Rights' League, Acting Under the Jurisdiction of the National Equal Rights League of the United States of America*, in Foner and Walker, *Black National and State Conventions, 1865–1900*, 166–67, 169, 170, 171. *California State Convention of the Colored Citizens…on the 25th, 26th, 27th and 28th of October, 1865*, in Foner and Walker, *Black State Conventions, 1840–1865*, 197 (use of the "Battle Hymn of the Republic").

26. *Illinois State Convention of Colored Men…October 16th, 17th, and 18th* [1866], in Foner and Walker, *Black National and State Conventions, 1865–1900*, 259.

27. *Convention of the Colored People of Pennsylvania…February 8th, 9th, and 10th, 1865*, 22. *National Convention of Colored Men…1864*, 27, 38. *Annual Meeting of the Pennsylvania State Equal Rights' League…August 9th and 10th, 1865*, in Foner and Walker, *Black National and State Conventions, 1865–1900*, 150. *First Annual Meeting of the National Equal Rights League…October 19, 20, and 21, 1865*, 35, 47. *Illinois State Convention…October 16th, 17th, and 18th* [1866], 251. *National Convention of the Colored Men of America, Held in Washington, D.C., on January, 13, 14, 15, and 16, 1869*, in Foner and Walker, *Black National and State Conventions, 1865–1900*, 356–57.

28. For examples, see *National Convention of Colored Men…1864*, 6–12, 32; *Pennsylvania State Equal Rights' League…August 9th and 10th, 1865*, 135–36; *Preamble and Constitution of the Pennsylvania State Equal Rights' League, Acting under the Jurisdiction of the National Equal Rights' League of the United States of America and Constitution for Subordinate Leagues* (1866), in Foner and Walker, *Black National and State Conventions, 1865–1900*, 161–64 (proposed constitution for auxiliary leagues of the Pennsylvania chapter); *State Convention of the Coloured Men of the State of New Jersey…July 13th and 14th, 1865*, in Foner and Walker, *Black State Conventions, 1840–1865*, 7–14; *First Annual Meeting of the National Equal Rights League*, 7–12, 22, 36; "Convention of Colored Citizens in Boston," *Boston Daily Advertiser*, quoted in the *National Anti-Slavery Standard*, December 9, 1865, in Foner and Walker, *Black National and State Conventions, 1865–1900*, 203; *Proceedings of the Iowa State Colored Convention…February 12th and 13th, 1868*, in Foner and Walker, *Black National and State Conventions, 1865–1900*, 330.

29. Frederick Douglass, "The Douglass Institute: An Address Delivered in Baltimore, Maryland, on 29 September 1865," in Blassingame and McKivigan, *Frederick Douglass Papers Series One*, vol. 4:86–96, 93–95. Levine, *Politics of Representative Identity*, 8–11, 65–66, 183–85, 190, 197–98, 216. Moses, *Golden Age of Black Nationalism*, 11. Brown and Shaw, "Separate Nations," 26, 27. Bell, "Negro Nationalism in the 1850s," 100. Davis, "Pennsylvania State Equal Rights League," 612–13. Marable, *W.E.B. DuBois*, 38. William Nesbit, Joseph C. Bustill, William D. Forten, on behalf of the Pennsylvania State Equal Rights League, *To the Honorable The Senate and House of Representatives of the United States, in Congress Assembled* ([1866?]), 1. George A. Rue to Editor, March 31, 1865 (*Christian Recorder*, April 8, 1865). See *First Annual Meeting of the National Equal Rights League*, 52, for a resolution discouraging anyone from trying to "revive in this land, the dead carcass of Liberian Emigration."

30. *National Convention of Colored Men…1864*, 3–9. Vorenberg, *Final Freedom*, 152–59.

31. *National Convention of Colored Men…1864*, 12–15.

32. Ibid., 16–19, 36–39 (National Equal Rights League's constitution). Cheek and Cheek, *Langston*, 426–27.

33. The marginalization of blacks advocating colonization is apparent in Garnet's case. Garnet could not even win election as a delegate to the National Convention he had called, and

he attended as a representative of his African Civilization Society. Later nominated to serve as president of the National Equal Rights League, in the end, he was not even selected as one of its twenty-four other officers, although he did address the convention. While some speakers at the convention reiterated a belief in a separate black nation, most eschewed colonization; while that issue still simmered, the power of those advocating emigration had declined. *National Convention of Colored Men...1864*, 19, 20–24, 26–28, 29–30. Cheek and Cheek, *Langston*, 427.

34. *National Convention of Colored Men...1864*, 33–34, 41–42, 56.

35. Ibid., 44–51, 53, 55–56, 59.

36. Ibid., 44–46, 53, 56–61.

37. *First Annual Meeting of the National Equal Rights League...October 19, 20, and 21, 1865*, 4, 5–6, 8–9, 33. *National Convention of Colored Men...1864*, 36.

38. *First Annual Meeting of the National Equal Rights League...October 19, 20, and 21, 1865*, 29, 38.

39. Ibid., 38–39.

40. Ibid., 38–40.

41. *Cong. Globe*, 39th Cong. 1st Sess., 127–28 (January 5, 1866). *National Convention of Colored Men...1864*, 38. *Colored Men's Convention of the State of Michigan...Sept. 12th and 13th, '65*, 12, 17, 18, 21–23. *State Convention of the Coloured Men of the State of New Jersey...July 13th and 14th, 1865*, 7, 12–14.

42. *Convention of the Colored People of Pennsylvania...February 8, 9, and 10, 1865*, 4–7, 10, 14–15, 22, 27, 34, 40.

43. Ibid., 19–21, 26–27, 31–32. *Pennsylvania State Equal Rights' League...August 9th and 10th, 1865*, 133. The state league revisited some intraracial concerns considered at the earlier statewide meeting. Some black barbers refused to serve black patrons because they feared doing so negatively impacted their business with white customers. Delegate John Price offered a resolution that state league or auxiliary members who refused "to accommodate and treat colored men under all circumstances, in his place of business, as he treats white men, is guilty of the grossest dereliction of duty." Price noted that blacks could not ask "white men to extend equal rights to black men, while we refuse to do so." Other delegates believed that individuals should be able to regulate their businesses as they saw fit. Price and other attendees countered that sacrifices needed to be made and that blacks had to show Pennsylvania that they were willing to "accord each other the same rights we ask of them." The resolution carried. *Pennsylvania State Equal Rights' League...August 9th and 10th, 1865*, 147–48.

44. *Constitution of the Pennsylvania State Equal Rights' League*, 160. Rael, *Black Identity and Black Protest*, 205. Davis, "Pennsylvania State Equal Rights League," 614–16. 622. Nesbit, et al. *To the Honorable The Senate and House of Representatives of the United States*, 1. *Constitution of the Pennsylvania State Equal Rights' League*, 160–65.

45. See *Laws in Relation to Freedmen*, 39th Cong., 2nd Sess., Senate Executive Document No. 6 (1867) for a compendium of postwar Black Codes.

46. *Equal Suffrage. Address from the Colored Citizens of Norfolk, Va., to the People of the United States. Also an Account of the Agitation Among the Colored People of Virginia for Equal Rights. With an Appendix Concerning the Rights of Colored Witnesses Before the State Courts, June 5, 1865*, in Foner and Walker, *Black State Conventions, 1840–1865*, 83–88.

47. *Convention of the Colored People of Va., Held in the City of Alexandria Aug. 2, 3, 4, 5, 1865*, in Foner and Walker, *Black State Conventions, 1840–1865*, 258–60, 262–64.

48. Ibid., 264–65, 268, 271.

49. *State Convention of the Colored Men of Tennessee, Nashville, August 7, 1865*, in Foner and Walker, *Black State Conventions, 1840–1865*, 114–19. *An Address of the Colored People of Missouri to the Friends of Equal Rights, October 12, 1865*, in Foner and Walker, *Black State Conventions, 1840–1865*, 279–81.

50. *Colored People's Convention of the State of South Carolina...November, 1865*, in Foner and Walker, *Black State Conventions, 1840–1865*, 287–88, 289–90, 292, 298–302.

51. *Convention of Colored Citizens of the State of Arkansas...Nov. 30, Dec. 1 and 2, 1865*, in Foner and Walker, *Black State Conventions, 1840–1865*, 191, 192. Foner, *Freedom's Lawmakers*, 92.

52. *State Convention of the Colored People of Georgia, August, January 10, 1866*, in Foner and Walker, *Black State Conventions, 1840–1865*, 233–35.

53. O'Leary, *To Die For*, 113.

54. *Illinois State Convention of Colored Men...October 16th, 17th, and 18th* [1866], 251, 270–74. *California State Convention...October, 1865*, 174, 175, 178–79, 195–96, 198–99. *New*

Orleans Tribune, September 23, 1866, quoted in Snay, *Fenians, Freedmen, and Southern Whites,* 14. ("We said several times that having devoted our energies to the cause of general liberty, our wishes were for the independence of all nationalities, and the liberal progress of all nations. We, therefore, desire the success of the Fenians in the great work of regenerating old Ireland, and extending to that country the benefit of a Republican or popular government, according to the form of true democratic institutions.")

55. *Christian Recorder,* July 1, 1865. See also *National Convention of Colored Men...1864,* 59–60; J.H.B.P. [John H. B. Payne], Morris Island, S.C., May 24, 1864 (*Christian Recorder,* June 11, 1864). (A member of the 55th Massachusetts supports his claim to equal rights during the unequal pay crisis by denouncing foreigners and "ignorant Irish.")

56. Langston, *A Speech on "Equality Before the Law," Delivered by J. Mercer Langston, in the Hall of Representatives, in the Capitol of Missouri, on the Evening of the 9th Day of January, 1866,* 27. John Mercer Langston, "Daniel O'Connell," given in Washington, D.C., December 28, 1874 in Langston, *Freedom and Citizenship: Selected Lectures and Addresses of Hon. John Mercer Langston, LL.D., U.S. Minister Resident at Haiti,* 69–98: 72, 90. *Southern States Convention of Colored Men...October 18, Ending October 25, 1871,* 93. Giles, "Narrative Reversals," 780. Betts, "Negro and the New England Conscience," 251.

57. *Christian Recorder,* June 16, 1866; January 12, 1867; May 25, 1867 (reprinting a "soul-touching passage" in which a "NOBLE FENIAN" expressed his willingness to die "in defense of the rights of men to a free government, and of the rights of an oppressed people to throw off the yoke of the oppressor"); October 26, 1867.

58. R.B.H., "Fenianism," *Christian Recorder,* February 1, 1868. *Christian Recorder,* April 25, 1868. For another hostile reference, see *Christian Recorder,* March 23, 1867 (quoting the bishop of Kerry's condemnation of Fenians that "eternity is not long enough, nor hell hot enough to punish such miscreants").

59. Giles, "Narrative Reversals," 793–94, 796, 800, 802; Douglass quoted on 797, 798. Douglass quoted in McFeely, *Frederick Douglass,* 280 ("something of an Irishman"). Douglass in Foner, *Life and Writings,* 2:249 ("The Present Condition and Future Prospects of the Negro People"); 3:134–35; 5:365 ("Colored Americans, and Aliens T. F. Meagher").

60. Frederick Douglass, "What the Black Man Wants: An Address Delivered in Boston, Massachusetts, on 26 January 1865," in Blassingame and McKivigan, *Frederick Douglass Papers Series One,* vol. 4: 59–69: 65–66. See also Douglass, "Black Freedom is the Prerequisite of Victory: An Address Delivered in New York, New York, on 13 January 1865," in ibid., 51–59: 59 (depicting drunk Irishman at the polls). Douglass quoted Daniel O'Connell's remark that "the history of Ireland might be traced like a wounded man through a crowd by his tracks of blood" and declared that the statement applied to blacks as well. Douglass, "We Are Here and Want the Ballot-Box: An Address Delivered in Philadelphia, Pennsylvania, on 4 September 1866," in ibid., 123–33, 130.

61. Frederick Douglass, "Our Composite Nationality: An Address Delivered in Boston, Massachusetts, on 7 December 1869," in Blassingame and McKivigan, *Frederick Douglass Papers Series One,* vol. 4: 240–59: 250, 252, 256, 257, 259. *Christian Recorder,* January 30, 1869.

62. Frederick Douglass, "Santo Domingo: An Address Delivered in St. Louis, Missouri, on 13 January 1873," in Blassingame and McKivigan, *Frederick Douglass Papers Series One,* vol. 4:342–55: 344–45.

63. Blassingame and McKivigan, *Frederick Douglass Papers Series One,* vol. 4: 69–70. Shankman, "Afro-American Editors on Irish Independence," 284, 285, 287, 290, 293. Betts, "Negro and the New England Conscience," 246–47, 251–52.

64. See also Sumner's presentation, on January 11, 1866, of a petition of a convention of black Baptist churches calling for equal rights and suffrage. *Cong. Globe,* 39th Cong. 1st Sess., 107–8 (December 21, 1865), 127–28 (January 5, 1866), 184 (January 11, 1866). See also 43d Cong., 1st Sess., H.R. Misc. Doc. No. 44, *Memorial of National Convention of Colored Persons, Praying to be protected in their civil rights,* issued from the December 1873 National Civil Rights Convention and referred to the Committee on the Judiciary. Xi Wang agrees that black arguments "undoubtedly influenced Republican lawmakers." Xi Wang, "Black Suffrage," 2171.

65. 14 Stat. 27.

66. Rodrigue, "Freedmen's Bureau and Wage Labor in the Louisiana Sugar Region," 193–218.

67. *Cong. Globe,* 39th Cong., 1st Sess., 474, 476 (January 29, 1866).

68. Ibid., 477, 479 (January 29, 1866) (Saulsbury); 528 (January 31, 1866) (Davis).

69. Ibid., 504 (January 30, 1866) (Howard); 562 (January 31, 1866) (Davis); 570 (February 1, 1866) (Morrill); 599 (February 2, 1866) (Trumbull).

70. Ibid., 603 (Wilson), 606–7 (February 2, 1866), 1367 (March 13, 1866).

71. Richardson, *Compilation of the Messages and Papers of the Presidents 1789–1897,* 6:405–13.

72. Frederick Douglass, "Our Work is Not Done," December 4, 1863, in Foner, *Life and Writings* 3:383–84.

73. Thomas R. Hawkins et al., October 28, 1866, in *Christian Recorder* (November 3, 1866), in Foner and Walker, *Black National and State Conventions, 1865–1900,* 289–90. *Christian Recorder,* January 12, 1867, in ibid., 293–95: 293–94. *Christian Recorder,* October 28, 1866; January 5, 1867.

74. Dickson and Lincoln were related by marriage. Dickson, *Address...October 3, 1865,* 12, 14, 18 ("We need his labor in the South and we need the protection of his ballot against the ballot of his former traitorous master"), 19 (quote in text). Loring, *Safe and Honorable...July 4, 1866,* 19, 21–22. From the pulpit, Rev. Samuel T. Spear contrasted white Southern treason with black loyalty: "As now reconstructed, infamous traitors are in power at the South...and Union men...are persecuted, and in many instances...murdered for their loyalty." Thus, the Presbyterian preacher thundered, he would rather "*fight* again," if necessary, "to make treason odious and loyalty honorable." As to blacks, Spear continued, "They fought for us and they fought with us; they were our friends when we wanted friends and were very glad to welcome their services; and now to remit them to the tender mercies of our former enemies and their former oppressors, with no legal care for their interests, with no guaranteed equality before the law, with the liability to be virtually reenslaved by State laws regulating labor, would be an act of treachery and ingratitude well worthy of the curse of Heaven." Spear, *Citizen's Duty in the Present Crisis,* 10, 11. See also 11th USCHA veteran John Cajay's contrast of "true and loyal" blacks deprived of their rights with Southern white traitors ascendant under President Johnson. John Cajay to the Editor, Hollidaysburg, Pa., *Christian Recorder,* March 3, 1866.

75. Boutwell, *Reconstruction...July 4, 1865,* 30–31, 34, 42. See also Dickson, *Address...October 3, 1865,* 16. ("Again, it is objected, that the Southern negro is ignorant and unfit to vote. He seems to have been intelligent enough to be loyal, which was more than his master was. But I do not deny the ignorance; their condition of slavery forbids that it could be otherwise. Yet they share this ignorance in common with the poor whites; and I would be willing to apply to both these classes an educational test. Still I would not recommend this. Freedom is the school in which freemen are to be taught, and the ballot-box is a wonderful educator.")

76. Kelley, *Safeguards of Personal Liberty...June 22, 1865,* 13–14, 16. Union Judge Advocate General Joseph Holt similarly warned that failure to eliminate all vestiges of slavery equaled a failure to destroy treason. Holt, *Treason and its Treatment...14th of April, 1865,* 6–8.

77. U.S. Const., Art. 1, Sec. 3. Lieber, *Amendments of the Constitution,* 31, 38. Wang, "Black Suffrage," 2169–75, 2184.

78. 14 Stat. 428 (March 2, 1867), 15 Stat. 2 (March 23, 1867); 15 Stat. 14 (July 19, 1867). Foner, *Freedom's Lawmakers,* xiii–xxxi, 13, 171, 216, 236.

79. Foner, *Freedom's Lawmakers,* xiii, 222. Shaffer, *After the Glory,* 73–74.

80. Wang, "Black Suffrage," 2186, 2213–15. Pennsylvania blacks in February 1865, for example, expressed "sorrow" at "the attitude assumed by our long tried friend, Wm. Lloyd Garrison, on the subject of the colored man's franchise." *Convention of the Colored People of Pennsylvania...February 8th, 9th, and 10th, 1865,* 32. For examples of Republicans embracing the point articulated by Douglass on December 4, 1863, and other black conventions, see Boutwell, *Reconstruction...July 4, 1865,* 30–31, 34, 42; Dickson, *Address...October 3, 1865,* 16, 18–19; Loring, *Safe and Honorable...July 4, 1866,* 21–22; and Spear, *The Citizen's Duty in the Present Crisis,* 10, 11.

81. *National Convention...1869,* 345–56.

82. Ibid., 381–84.

83. Ibid., 384–85.

84. Voters in Connecticut, Wisconsin, Minnesota, and the Colorado Territory in 1865 rejected state constitutional amendments for black suffrage, though the vote in the three states was close, with 45 percent of the voters in Connecticut and Minnesota and 46 percent of the voters in Wisconsin supporting the proposal. Black suffrage went down in defeat in Kansas and Minnesota in 1867, and Michigan rejected a suffrage amendment to its state constitution in 1868. Wang, "Black Suffrage," 2186, 2213–15. Kaczorowski, "Revolutionary Constitutionalism," 878–79. Kaczorowski, "To Begin the Nation Anew," 53.

85. O'Leary, *To Die For,* 113. Wang, "Federal Enforcement Laws," 1014–21, 1029. Frederick Douglass, "At Last, At Last, the Black Man Has a Future: An Address Delivered in Albany, New

York, on 22 April, 1870," in Blassingame and McKivigan, *Frederick Douglass Papers Series One,* vol. 4:265–72: 266–67, 270–71.

86. Blight, *Race and Reunion,* 113, 119. Harcourt, "Whipping of Richard Moore," 261, 266–67, 271, 274, 276.

87. *Southern States Convention of Colored…October 18, Ending October 25, 1871,* 3, 39, 47, 97–100, 102–3. *State Convention of The Colored Citizens of Tennessee…Feb. 22d, 23d, 24th and 25th 1871,* 14–15.

88. 16 Stat. 140 (Act of May 31, 1870); 16 Stat. 254 (Act of July 14, 1870); 16 Stat. 443 (Act of Feb. 28, 1871); 17 Stat 13 (Act of April 20, 1871); and, 17 Stat. 347 (Act of June 10, 1872). Wang, "Federal Enforcement Laws," 1031–33, 1056.

89. Kaczorowski, "Revolutionary Constitutionalism," 920–21. Kaczorowski, *Politics of Judicial Interpretation.*

90. 18 Stat. part 3, 335. *Cong. Record,* 43rd Cong. 2nd Sess., 4782 (June 9, 1874).

91. James H. Hall, Morris Island, S.C., August 3, 1864 (*Christian Recorder,* August 27, 1864).

92. *Addresses of the Hon. W.D. Kelley, Miss Anna E. Dickenson, and Mr. Frederick Douglass…July 6, 1863,* 7. Broadside, "We fight for our rights, liberty, justice and union," [Louisiana?: n.p., 1866], in the Abraham Lincoln Presidential Library, Springfield, Illinois. I am grateful to the library for sending me a photocopy of this broadside, which also depicts America's agrarian tradition as well as a locomotive and ships to indicate its commercial power.

Chapter 7. The Affirmation of Naturalized Citizenship in America

1. *Pilot,* June 25, 1864.

2. Lawson, *Patriot Fires,* 179–80. Truslow, "Peasants into Patriots" 143. *New York Tribune,* July 6, 1865. McDermott, *69th Regiment Pennsylvania,* 51.

3. *Pilot,* July 15, 1865, in Bruce, *Harp and the Eagle,* 59. *Pilot,* March 21, 1866 in Joyce, *Editors and Ethnicity,* 152. Guiney scrapbook, 14.

4. Hanchett, *Hapine,* 158–59. Mulholland, *116th Regiment, Pennsylvania,* xv. Samito, *Irish Ninth,* 252–53, 256. Clark, *Irish in Philadelphia,* 123. Byron, *Irish America,* 67.

5. Gordon, *Orange Riots,* 15–16. Clark, *Irish in Philadelphia,* 127 (Philadelphia's less grand 1872 parade).

6. *Pilot,* April 15, 1865. *New York Times,* September 30, 1868.

7. Kettner, *Citizenship,* 17–18, 50. Tucker, *Blackstone's Commentaries,* 2: 366, 368, 369–70. Kettner, "Subjects or Citizens," 958 n. 41.

8. Kettner, *Citizenship,* 74–77, 78, 80, 83, 106–7, 194, 202, 206, 208, 213. Kettner, "Revolutionary Era," 225–26, 228, 238–41. Tucker, *Blackstone's Commentaries,* 2: 370 n. 4. Kettner, "Subjects or Citizens," 945–46. Regarding colonial diversity, see Butler, *Becoming America,* chapter 1.

9. British courts resolved in 1824, and the Supreme Court agreed in 1830, that the Treaty of 1783, which acknowledged American independence, released British subjects who lived in the United States at that time from their allegiance to the crown. *Inglis v. Trustees of Sailor's Snug Harbor,* 3 Pet. 99 (U.S. 1830); *Shanks v. Dupont,* 3 Pet. 242 (U.S. 1830). Kettner, *Citizenship,* 74–77, 78, 80, 83, 106–7, 194, 202, 206, 208, 213. Kettner, "Revolutionary Era," 225–26, 228, 238–41. Tucker, *Blackstone's Commentaries,* 2:370 n. 4. Kettner, "Subjects or Citizens," 945–46.

10. Pennsylvania's 1776 Constitution held that "all men have a natural inherent right to emigrate from one state to another that will receive them" so as to "promote their own happiness," and Vermont's 1777 Constitution incorporated this language. Virginia's Law of May 1779 applied this principle on a national level and Kentucky later passed similar legislation. Hening, *Statutes at Large: Being a Collection of All of the Laws of Virginia, from the First Session of the Legislature, in the Year 1619,* 10:129. Kettner, *Citizenship,* 268, 268 n. 67.

11. The 1790 Naturalization Act, which did not preempt state naturalization acts, mandated that naturalization must occur in federal or state courts of record that had a seal and a clerk, and it liberally allowed to become a citizen any free white of good character who resided for two years in the United States and one year in the state in which he sought naturalization, and swore to support the Constitution. In 1795, Congress increased the residency period from two to five years and mandated that applicants must declare intent to naturalize three years prior to taking the oath, renounce any title of nobility, and foreswear their previous allegiance. The Naturalization Act of June 18, 1798, increased the residency requirement to fourteen years in the United States and

a five-year period after declaring intent to become a citizen, and it prohibited naturalization for aliens born in a country at war with the United States. The 1802 legislation largely restored the timeframe implemented in 1795, though it maintained the 1798 act's prohibition against naturalization for aliens born in countries at war with the United States. Legislation in 1804, 1813, 1816, 1824, and 1828 adjusted certain procedures and timelines. From 1790 to 1922, wives whose husbands naturalized also became naturalized without the need for any further action. Newman, *American Naturalization*, 5–7, 14. Kettner, *Citizenship*, 232, 236–47.

12. For a summary of how the judiciary produced a muddled body of law concerning expatriation rights, see Kettner, *Citizenship*, 271–83. For a contemporary criticism of how this issue remained unsettled, see Tucker, *Commentaries on the Laws of Virginia*, 1:70–71. In *Ainslie v. Martin*, 9 Mass. 454 (1813), Massachusetts's Supreme Judicial Court affirmed that allegiance attached at birth and remained unimpaired by naturalization. Virginia, however, held in *Murray v. McCarty*, 16 Va. 393 (1811), that, while the government could regulate the manner and proof of its exercise, expatriation stood as an unassailable right. In 1839, Kentucky's court of appeals concurred with the *Murray* court: "Expatriation may be considered a practical and fundamental doctrine of America. American history, American institutions, and American legislation, all recognize it. It has grown with our growth and strengthened with our strength." *Alsberry v. Hawkins*, 39 Ky. 177, 178 (1839). Morrow, "Expatriation," 552–55. Thomas Jefferson to Gouverneur Morris, August 16, 1793, at <http://memory.loc.gov/cgi-bin/query/r?ammem/mtj:@field(DOCID+@lit(tj070203))>.

13. Morrow, "Naturalized Americans Abroad," 648–55. Hickey, *War of 1812*, 17.

14. Morrow, "Naturalized Americans Abroad," 655–56. Henry Wheaton to Johann P. Knocke, Berlin, July 24, 1840, in U.S. Dept. of State, *Opinions of the Principal Officers of the Executive Departments, and Other Papers Relating to Expatriation, Naturalization and Change of Allegiance*, 125. Hereafter cited as *Opinions...Expatriation*.

15. Daniel Webster to J. B. Nines, Washington, D.C., June 1, 1852; Edward Everett to Daniel D. Barnard, January 14, 1853, in *Opinions...Expatriation*, 126, 132–33. Morrow, "Naturalized Americans Abroad," 658–60.

16. William L. Marcy to John George Chevalier de Hulsemann, September 26, 1853, in *Opinions...Expatriation*, 22–23, 130–31. William L. Marcy to John M. Daniel, November 10, 1855, in Moore, *Digest of International Law*, 3: 569. 8 Op. Attorney Gen. 139 (October 31, 1856): 139–69. Attorney General Jeremiah S. Black affirmed Cushing's opinion at 9 Op. Attorney Gen. 63 (August 17, 1857).

17. Lewis Cass to Rudolph Schledien, April 9, 1859, in *Opinions...Expatriation*, 130. Lewis Cass to Felix LeClerc, May 17, 1859, in Beale, *Diary of Edward Bates*, 24. Bates diary, June 8; June 20, 1859; October 29, 1863; see also July 30, 1859, and a letter dated March 17, 1860, for Bates's belief that naturalization absolved one of all allegiance or duties to one's native land, all in Beale, *Diary of Edward Bates*, 23, 25, 39, 113, 313.

18. Cass based this letter on Attorney General Jeremiah S. Black's analysis days earlier that identified the "natural right" of expatriation as "incontestable" and held that a naturalized citizen who returned to his native land could be arrested for a crime, such as actual desertion or for debt, but he could not be punished for nonperformance that grew from an allegiance since renounced. Cass to Joseph A. Wright, July 8, 1859, in *Opinions...Expatriation*, 127. 9 Op. Attorney Gen. 356 (July 4, 1859): 357–60, 362.

19. *Appendix To the Cong. Globe*, 36th Cong. 2nd Sess., 4 (December 3, 1860). Lord Palmerston to M. Droney, October 16, 1859, in *Opinions...Expatriation*, 189.

20. Seward to Norman B. Judd, March 1863, in *Opinions...Expatriation*, 128. Morrow, "Naturalized Americans Abroad," 662–63.

21. Occasional attempts to appoint Fenians as American consuls also exacerbated Anglo-American tension. D'Arcy, *Fenian Movement*, 67–69, 86, 226–27. Bruce to Seward, December 26, 1865, quoted in Jenkins, *Fenians*, 33, see also 110–11. McDonough and Jones, *War So Terrible*, 246. *New York Times*, January 10, 1866.

22. William B. West to Seward, Dublin, September 16, 1865; West to Seward, Dublin, September 20, 1865; West to Seward, Dublin, September 30, 1865; West to Seward, Dublin, October 7, 1865; Michael O'Boyle to William West [undated]; West to Seward, Dublin, October 14, 1865; E. G. Eastman to Seward, Queenstown, October 18, 1865; Joseph H. Lawlor to Seward, Dublin, November 13, 1865, all in House Ex. Doc. 157, pt. 2, 40th Cong. 2d Sess., 7, 8, 11–15. Benjamin Moran diary, September 20, 1865, quoted in D'Arcy, *Fenian Movement*, 119 n. 37.

23. West to Seward, Dublin, February 17, 1866; *Evening Mail and Packet*, February 17, 1866; West to Charles F. Adams, Dublin, February 18, 1866; West to Adams, Dublin, February 19, 1866;

West to Seward, Dublin, February 24, 1866; West to Adams, Dublin, March 6, 1866; West to Michael McLoughlin, Dublin, April 19, 1866; West to Sir T. A. Larcom, Dublin, April 20, 1866, all in House Ex. Doc. 157, pt. 2, 40th Cong. 2d Sess., 37–41, 140, 143, 168, 216, 219. Jenkins, *Fenians*, 86–87, 96.

24. Adams to Seward, [February 22, 1866?], in Morrow, "Treaty of 1870," 663. Adams, *What Makes Slavery a Question of National Concern?* 31–41. Adams likely recognized that the situation in 1866 echoed Britain's response after reports arose that veterans from the Mexican War were en route to assist a revolt of the Young Irelanders in August 1848. Jenkins, *Fenians*, 14–19, 75–77, 80.

25. *New York Times*, March 5, 1866. Jenkins, *Fenians*, 75–77, 80. Adams to West, September 20, 1865; Adams to Seward, December 28, 1865 ("subjected"), in Jenkins, *Fenians*, 76, 80. Adams to Seward, March 8, 1866, cited in D'Arcy, *Fenian Movement*, 130.

26. Sir Thomas A. Larcom to William B. West, Dublin Castle, February 28, 1866; Larcom to West, March 10, 1866; Larcom to West, Dublin Castle, April 24, 1866; West to Seward, Dublin, March 10, 1866; West to Seward, Dublin, March 24, 1866, all in House Ex. Doc. 157, pt. 2, 40th Cong. 2d Sess., 45, 46, 49, 49, 50, 225. Lord Clarendon to Sir Frederick Bruce, March 10, 1866, in D'Arcy, *Fenian Movement*, 123, 130. Ó Broin, *Fenian Fever*, 63–64. Law Officers to Clarendon, March 9, 1866, in Jenkins, *Fenians*, 93–94; see also 90–91.

27. Jenkins, *Fenians*, 49, 50, 57, 98–99, 130.

28. Seward to Adams, March 22, 1866, in D'Arcy, *Fenian Movement*, 131–32. Jenkins, *Fenians*, 103.

29. Jenkins, *Fenians*, 102–4. D'Arcy, *Fenian Movement*, 132.

30. Jenkins, *Fenians*, 41–42. Brian Jenkins recognizes the Fenian movement played a "vital role" in fostering the Anglo-American resolution to the allegiance issue, although the negotiated peace ran contrary to Fenian hopes for war between both countries. Jenkins, *Fenians*, 280. Adams to Seward, [February 22, 1866?], quoted in Morrow, "Treaty of 1870," 663.

31. George Archdeacon to Andrew Johnson, Philadelphia, [c. September 29, 1866]; in House Ex. Doc. 157, pt. 1, 40th Cong. 2d Sess., 9–11.

32. *New York Times*, March 5, 1866. D'Arcy, *Fenian Movement*, 124 n. 68, 112, 112–13 n. 42. *Pilot*, March 10, 1866, in D'Arcy, *Fenian Movement*, 127.

33. *New York Times*, March 10, 1866.

34. D'Arcy, *Fenian Movement*, 163–65, 167, 356. Jenkins, *Fenians*, 124–26, 128–29, 149–50.

35. *U.S House Journal*, 39 Cong., 1st Sess., 790 (June 4, 1866), 816–19 (June 11, 1866), 860 (June 18, 1866). *Cong. Globe*, 39th Cong., 1st Sess., 2946 (June 4, 1866), 3085–86 (June 11, 1866), 3241 (June 18, 1866). Jenkins, *Fenians*, 158, 159.

36. *Cong. Globe*, 39th Cong. 1st Sess., 2545 (May 10, 1866), 3040 (June 8, 1866), 3148 (June 13, 1866). 14 Stat. 27 (Act of April 9, 1866). Michael Les Benedict's *A Compromise of Principle: Congressional Republicans and Reconstruction, 1863–1869*, William E. Nelson's *The Fourteenth Amendment: From Political Principle to Judicial Doctrine*, and Earl M. Maltz's *Civil Rights, The Constitution, and Congress, 1863–1869* do not mention this moment in the drafting of the Fourteenth Amendment.

37. Jenkins, *Fenians*, 159–60, 178, 188–89. D'Arcy, *Fenian Movement*, 187.

38. Fortune Wright court-martial, 96th USCI.

39. Jenkins, *Fenians*, 160 (*New York Tribune*, August 25, 1866), 188–89. Higham, *Strangers in the Land*, 20–21.

40. *Speeches of Hon. Schuyler Colfax and General J. O'Neill*, 1–3. D'Arcy, *Fenian Movement*, 178 n. 106. Christian G. Samito, "John O'Neill," in Glazier, *Irish in America*, 746. Clark, *Irish in Philadelphia*, 121. Holmes, *Irish in Wisconsin*, 45. Henry Wilson quoted in *Boston Daily Journal*, August 27, 1866, quoted in Baum, *Civil War Party System*, 111.

41. Roberts, *Message of President William R. Roberts to the Senators and Representatives of the Fenian Brotherhood in Congress Assembled*, 15–17. By the time of this 1867 Senate-wing convention, the Brotherhood's internal focus turned to negotiations for reunification with O'Mahoney's wing and trying to regain the movement's momentum as a whole. The convention thus urged local chapters to purchase no more green flags except if needed by military companies, and to forego "the large sums usually expended" on social celebrations, so that money could instead be "applied for revolutionary purposes." Roberts also reassured delegates that his wing practiced sound fiscal policy. *Sixth National Congress of the Fenian Brotherhood...September, 1867*, 4, 12, 14–15, 22–25.

42. *Sixth National Congress of the Fenian Brotherhood...September, 1867*, 4, 29.

43. Snay, *Fenians, Freedmen, and Southern Whites,* 44–46.

44. R.B.H., "Fenianism," *Christian Recorder,* February 1, 1868. *Christian Recorder,* November 21, 1868.

45. Baum, *Civil War Party System,* 112. Snay, *Fenians, Freedmen, and Southern Whites,* 44–45.

46. Dublin-born Thomas Antisell immigrated to New York in 1848 and worked as a government geologist before joining the Patent Office. The Department of Agriculture employed him after the war. [Antisell], *Address,* 3–4, 7–8. <www.library.georgetown.edu/dept/speccoll/cl137. htm>. Baum, *Civil War Party System,* 112.

47. [Antisell], *Address,* 3–6.

48. Ibid., 4, 7–8.

49. *U.S. House Journal,* 39th Cong., 1st sess., 1140 (July 26, 1866). *New York Times,* July 4, 1866. D'Arcy, *Fenian Movement,* 182–84, 185. Jenkins, *Fenians,* 181–83.

50. D'Arcy, *Fenian Movement,* 183–84, 185. C. C. Woodman to Nathaniel P. Banks, July 2, 1866; William R. Roberts to Nathaniel P. Banks, December 20, 1866, both in D'Arcy, *Fenian Movement,* 184, 217. Jenkins, *Fenians,* 181–84.

51. In Massachusetts in 1868, Irish Americans voted for Democratic presidential candidate Seymour two to one, while native-born voters supported Grant at a rate of six to one. Baum, "The 'Irish Vote,'" 133. Jenkins, *Fenians,* 205–14. Baum, *Civil War Party System,* 112. Sanford E. Church to Samuel J. Tilden, November 10, 1866, in D'Arcy, *Fenian Movement,* 211. John T. Hoffman to Tilden, November 7, 1866, in Jenkins, *Fenians,* 208. John T. Hoffman to John Sheedy and Jeremiah Donovan, New York, March 12, 1867, in Hoffman, *The Cause of Ireland and Adopted Citizens: The Record of John T. Hoffman, His Views on Fenianism Letter of March 12, 1867, His Message to the Common Council Relative to the Rights of Adopted Citizens Dated Nov. 30, 1867,* 3–4. Hoffman, *The Great Speech of Hon. John T. Hoffman at Buffalo, September 8th, 1868,* 2.

52. Brown, *Irish-American Nationalism,* 39.

Chapter 8. The Affirmation of Naturalized Citizenship Abroad

1. William J. Nagle to D. M. Nagle, County Cork Jail, June 14, 1867; Seward to Adams, Washington, D.C. August 7, 1867, both in House Ex. Doc. 157, pt. 1, 40th Cong. 2d Sess., 56–57, 60. D'Arcy, *Fenian Movement,* 245, 247, 266.

2. Adams to Seward, London, September 21, 1867; London *Times,* September 20, 1867; *Manchester Examiner and Times,* [undated], all in House Ex. Doc. 157, pt. 1, 40th Cong. 2d Sess., 76–83; for a transcript of the trial of the "Manchester Martyrs," see 100–183. Devoy, *Recollections of an Irish Rebel,* 239–43. Ò Broin, *Fenian Fever,* 193–94, 196. Walker, *Fenian Movement,* 154–55. Macnamara, *Ninth Massachusetts,* 361. D'Arcy, *Fenian Movement,* 269–71. *New York Times,* November 25, 26, 1867.

3. Savage, *Fenian Heroes and Martyrs,* 452–53.

4. Adams to Seward, London, December 7, 1866; Adams to Seward, London, February 6, 1867, in House Ex. Doc. 157, pt. 1, 40th Cong. 2d Sess., 24, 28. As noted by Brian Jenkins, the "liberation of emigrated Irishmen from the legal tentacles of British suzerainty" proved to be one of the few measures of success generated by the Brotherhood. Jenkins, *Fenians,* 211, 214–17, 220–21, 224.

5. *U.S. House Journal,* 40th Cong., 1st sess., 37 (March 11, 1867). *New York Times,* March 14, 15, 1867. *New York Herald,* March 14, 1867, in D'Arcy, *Fenian Movement,* 235–36.

6. Bruce to Stanley, in Ò Broin, *Fenian Fever,* 177–78.

7. London *Times,* November 5, 1867; Adams to Seward, London, December 24, 1867, in House Ex. Doc. 157, pt. 1, 40th Cong. 2d Sess., 150–51, 294. London *Times,* November 4, 1867, in Jenkins, *Fenians,* 245; see also 242, 243.

8. William J. Nagle to D. M. Nagle, Mount Joy Prison, Dublin, September 30, 1867; William J. Nagle to Congress, Dublin, Ireland, November 25, 1867, in House Ex. Doc. 157, pt. 1, 40th Cong. 2d Sess., 331–32, 350–51. D'Arcy, *Fenian Movement,* 272–73. Jenkins, *Fenians,* 244, 247, 268.

9. John Warren to the Irishmen in the United States, Dublin, Ireland, August 1867; John Warren to Andrew Johnson, Dublin, Ireland, August 3, 1867, in House Ex. Doc. 157, pt. 1, 40th Cong. 2d Sess., 69–72.

10. "Chief Baron Pigott's refusal of a mixed jury in Warren's case," in *Opinions...Expatriation,* 213–15. 12 Op. Attorney Gen. 319, 321 (November 26, 1867). For the transcript of Warren's trial, see House Ex. Doc. 157, pt. 1, 40th Cong. 2d Sess., 217–92.

11. House Ex. Doc. 157, pt. 1, 40th Cong. 2d Sess., 289–90.

12. 12 Op. Attorney Gen. 319, 322 (November 26, 1867). Seward to Stanbery, Washington, November 18, 1867, in House Ex. Doc. 157, pt. 1, 40th Cong. 2d Sess., 186–87. *Appendix to the Cong. Globe,* 40th Cong. 2nd Sess., 7 (December 3, 1867). D'Arcy, *Fenian Movement,* 274–75. Adams to Seward, November 5, 1867; London *Times,* November 5, 1867, both in Jenkins, *Fenians,* 250–51.

13. John Warren to Congress, Kilmainham Jail, November 28, 1867, in House Ex. Doc. 157, pt. 1, 40th Cong. 2d Sess., 196–97.

14. Miles J. O'Reilly (not Halpine's fictional character) to Seward, Detroit, June 16, 1867; Marcus L. Ward to Andrew Johnson, Trenton, N.J., July 12, 1867; *New York Sun,* July 16, 1867; Henry Liebenau to William H. Seward, New York, July 23, 1867; James J. Rogers to Seward, July 31, 1867; John Warren to Andrew Johnson, Kilmainham Prison, Dublin, Ireland, August 2, 1867; William J. McClure to Col. J. R. O'Beirne, New York, August 10, 1867; Seward to Adams, Washington, D.C., September 14, 1867; P. M. Devitt to Johnson, Cincinnati, Oh., September 23, 1867, all in House Ex. Doc. 157, pt. 1, 40th Cong. 2d Sess., 60–63, 74, 317–19, 325–26; see also 321–22.

15. John Savage to Seward, New York, November 11, 1867; Savage to Seward, New York, November 26, 1867, in House Ex. Doc. 157, pt. 1, 40th Cong. 2d Sess., 334, 342. Savage to Banks, November 27, 1867; William H. Grace to Banks, December 11, 1867, in D'Arcy, *Fenian Movement,* 272, 281. London *Times,* November 4, 1867, in Jenkins, *Fenians,* 245. Johnson appointed Savage to a consular vacancy at Leeds in late 1868 in an attempt to cultivate relations with Irish Americans. Britain protested and the Senate, not inclined to approve any of Johnson's nominees for any position anyway, rejected the Fenian. Jenkins, *Fenians,* 242, 243, 286–88.

16. U.S. Const., Fourteenth Amend.

17. *Irish-American,* November 9, 1867, in House Ex. Doc. 157, pt. 1, 40th Cong. 2d Sess., 339–40.

18. Patrick R. Guiney to Benjamin Butler, November 25, 1867, Boston, Ma., in Butler Papers, Manuscript Division, Library of Congress, Washington, D.C.

19. Endorsement, Benjamin Butler to Patrick R. Guiney, December 3, 1867, in ibid.

20. *Resolutions introduced by General Denis F. Burke . . . on the evening of Saturday, 23d day of November, 1867* in House Ex. Doc. 157, pt. 1, 40th Cong. 2d Sess., 359. *New York Times,* November 24, 1867. *Cong. Globe,* 40th Cong. 2nd Sess., 5–6 (December 2, 1867).

21. *Resolutions Introduced and Adopted at a Mass Meeting of the Citizens of New York, Held at the Cooper Institute, in the City of New York, on Tuesday, the 26th day of November, 1867,* in House Ex. Doc. 157, pt. 1, 40th Cong. 2d Sess., 360. John T. Hoffman to the Common Council of the City of New York, New York, November 30, 1867, in Hoffman, *Cause of Ireland and Adopted Citizens,* 5–7.

22. Josiah G. Abbott, Thomas Russell, William Schuler, C. Levi Woodbury, A. B. Underwood, G. Washington Warren, N. B. Shurtless, William L. Burt, and Peter Harvey served as the other vice presidents of the meeting. P. A. Collins to Andrew Johnson, Boston, December 7, 1867, in House Ex. Doc. 157, pt. 1, 40th Cong. 2d Sess., 343–44.

23. Guiney scrapbook, 15.

24. George S. Boutwell to Seward, Washington, D.C., January 7, 1868; Edward O'Neill to Seward, Milwaukee, January 7, 1868; W. F. Lyons to Seward, New York, January 8, 1868, all in House Ex. Doc. 157, pt. 1, 40th Cong. 2d Sess., 355–57.

25. L. Myron Slade to Seward, Bridgeport, Ct., January 20, 1868; James Lyon to Seward, Auburn, N.Y., February 13, 1868, both in House Ex. Doc. 157, pt. 2, 40th Cong. 2d Sess., 361–62. Resolves from Franklin county, N.Y., received by Seward January 23, 1868, in House Ex. Doc. 157, pt. 2, 40th Cong. 2d Sess., 111.

26. *Joint Resolutions of the Wisconsin Legislature, approved January 22, 1868,* in House. Ex. Doc. 157, pt. 1, 40th Cong. 2d Sess., 362–63; *Joint Resolutions of the Wisconsin Legislature, Approved February 22, 1868,* in House Ex. Doc. 157, pt. 2, 40th Cong. 2d Sess., 112–13. *Resolutions of the Legislature of Pennsylvania,* House Mis. Doc. No. 76, 40th Cong. 2d Sess. *Resolutions of the Legislature of Minnesota Relative to Protection to American Citizens in Foreign Countries,* Sen. Mis. Doc. No. 28, 40th Cong. 2d Sess. *Resolutions of the Legislature of California Asking Congress to Demand of Foreign Governments Full and Ample Protection to our Foreign-born Citizens while Temporarily Residing under Those Governments,* House Mis. Doc. No. 149, 40th Cong. 2d Sess. *Resolutions of the Legislature of Ohio in Relation to American citizens,* House Mis. Doc. No. 112, 40th Cong. 2d Sess.

27. *Resolutions of the Legislature of Maine, Relative to Naturalized Citizens of the United States,* House Mis. Doc. No. 59, 40th Cong. 2d Sess. *Resolution of the Legislature of Maryland,*

Relative to the Rights of Naturalized Citizens of the United States, House Mis. Doc. No. 75, 40th Cong. 2d Sess. *Resolutions of the Legislature of Kansas, in Relation to the Rights of American Citizens in Foreign Countries,* Sen. Mis. Doc. No. 25, 40th Cong. 2d Sess.

28. Seward to Adams, Washington, D.C., January 13, 1868, in House Ex. Doc. 157, pt. 1, 40th Cong. 2d Sess., 298–99. See petitions from (all citations are to the 40th Cong., 2nd Sess.): a meeting at Vincennes, Indiana (U.S. *House Journal,* December 17, 1867, 108); the city council of and a meeting in Cincinnati, Ohio (U.S. *House Journal,* December 18, 1867, 116); the city council of St. Louis, Missouri (U.S. *House Journal,* December 19, 1867, 121); the selectmen and four hundred others in Marlborough, Massachusetts; a meeting at Toledo, Ohio; and the citizens of Kearney City, Nebraska, and Goodhue County, Minnesota (*Cong. Globe,* January 8, 1868, 372); the 17th congressional district of Pennsylvania (U.S. *House Journal,* January 9, 1868, 162); a meeting in Worcester, Massachusetts; two hundred citizens of the 16th congressional district; 162 citizens of the 17th congressional district of New York; citizens in Illinois; and 278 citizens of Wooster, Ohio (*Cong. Globe,* January 10, 1868, 433, 452); citizens of Parkersburg, West Virginia (*Cong. Globe,* January 11, 1868, 453); a meeting in Milwaukee, Wisconsin; all the voters except one in Beacon Falls, Connecticut; the 2nd congressional district of Iowa; the 10th congressional district of New York; a meeting at Hamilton, Ohio; citizens in Iowa and Ohio; the St. Patrick's Society of Brooklyn, New York; a meeting at Kansas City, Missouri; and several petitions from New York (*Cong. Globe,* January 14, 1868, 490; U.S. *House Journal,* January 14, 1868, 183); a meeting at North Andover, Massachusetts; a meeting in Alleghany, New York, on January 2, 1868; citizens in Connecticut, Pennsylvania, and Franklin City, New York; a meeting in Elmira, New York; and three hundred citizens of the 27th congressional district of New York (*Cong. Globe,* January 20, 1868, 624, 638, 719); citizens of Minnesota; a meeting in St. Paul, Minnesota; and a meeting in Hampden County, Massachusetts (*Cong. Globe,* January 21, 1868, 649); 2,500 citizens of Lowell, Massachusetts (*Cong. Globe,* January 23, 1868, 699); 150 residents of Stamford, Connecticut; the city council of Rock Island, Illinois; the supervisors of Polk County, Iowa; the 3rd congressional district of Illinois; and citizens of Vermont (*Cong. Globe,* January 29, 1868, 815); the Rochester, New York, common council (*Cong. Globe,* January 31, 1868, 880); the Maine and Wisconsin legislatures (*Cong. Globe,* February 3, 1868, 920–21); citizens of Pennsylvania (*Cong. Globe,* February 3, 1868, 921); a meeting of naturalized citizens at Nashua, New Hampshire; citizens in St. Louis, Missouri; and GAR Post 159 in the Dept. of Ohio (*Cong. Globe,* February 4, 1868, 950, 967); twenty petitions from citizens in Maryland, Ohio, New York, Pennsylvania, Illinois, Massachusetts, Wisconsin, Kansas, Maine, Idaho Territory, Minnesota, and New Hampshire, as well as the Kansas legislature (U.S. *House Journal,* February 5, 1868, 300; *Cong. Globe,* February 5, 1868, 980); residents of Omaha, Nebraska (*Cong. Globe,* February 6, 1868, 998); 454 residents of Cattaraugus County, New York (U.S. *House Journal,* February 10, 1868, 322); a meeting of the Friendly Sons of Ireland in Jersey City, New Jersey (*Cong. Globe,* February 13, 1868, 1141–42); residents of St. Lawrence County, New York and Brush's Mills, New York (U.S. *House Journal,* February 18, 1868, 319–20; *Cong. Globe,* February 18, 1868, 1068); three hundred citizens of the 27th congressional district of New York (U.S. *House Journal,* February 19, 1868, 364); citizens of Nevada and the Minnesota legislature (U.S. *House Journal,* March 2, 1868, 434); the Wisconsin legislature (U.S. *House Journal,* March 9, 1868, 489); citizens of Montana Territory (U.S. *House Journal,* March 17, 1868, 535); the Ohio legislature (*Cong. Globe,* March 28, 1868, 2176); and citizens of Hennepin County, Minnesota; Fitchburg, Massachusetts; Troy, New York; Bridgeport, Connecticut; Syracuse, New York; Toledo, Ohio; the District of Columbia; Utica, New York; the California and Kansas legislatures; and the Knights of St. Patrick of New York; (U.S. *Senate Journal,* June 23, 1868, 534–35).

29. Seward to Charles F. Adams, Washington, D.C., March 28, 1867, in House Ex. Doc. 157, pt. 1, 40th Cong. 2d Sess., 34–35. Maltz, *Civil Rights, The Constitution, and Congress,* 135–36. Foner, *Reconstruction,* 315.

30. Impeachment provides the mechanism for removal of federal civil officers found to have engaged in "treason, bribery, or other high crimes and misdemeanors." Irish-born Robinson settled in New York City in 1836. He graduated from Yale College in 1841, became a newspaper correspondent, and gained admission to the New York bar in 1854. Lincoln appointed him an assessor of internal revenue in New York in 1862, and he served as a Democratic congressman from 1867 to 1869 and 1881 to 1885. *Cong. Globe,* 40th Cong. 1st Sess. 778 (November 21, 1867); 786–91 (November 25, 1867)

31. *Cong. Globe,* 40th Cong. 1st Sess., 791 (November 25, 1867).

32. *Cong. Globe,* 40th Cong. 2nd Sess., 4–5 (December 2, 1867)

33. Robinson proposed that the United States purchase Ireland, annex it, and let it be represented in Congress. Ibid., 6.

34. Ibid., 309 (December 20, 1867).

35. U.S. *House Journal,* 40th Cong. 2nd Sess., 162–63 (January 9, 1868). *Cong. Globe,* 40th Cong. 2nd Sess., 636 (January 20, 1868); 650 (January 21, 1868).

36. U.S. *House Journal,* 40th Cong. 2nd Sess., 258 (January 27, 1868); *Cong. Globe,* 40th Cong. 2nd Sess., 783 (January 27, 1868); 865 (January 30, 1868).

37. *Cong. Globe,* 40th Cong. 2nd Sess., 865–67 (January 30, 1868); 866 (Donnelly: "Only true remedy for this injustice which is practiced upon our citizens is...to declare that such an act shall be 'just ground for war.'"); 867 (Woodward: "It would be wise if the friends of this bill would incorporate in it a declaration that the American citizen may expatriate himself. If he chooses to go to Great Britain, or to Germany, or to France, or to any other foreign country, let him go.").

38. Ibid. (January 30, 1868); 986–87 (February 5, 1868).

39. Ibid., 1012–17 (February 6, 1868). Quigley, *Second Founding,* 48–50.

40. *Cong. Globe,* 40th Cong. 2nd Sess., 1294 (February 20, 1868). H.R. No. 768, 40th Cong. 2nd Sess.

41. London *Times,* December 11, 1867; January 8, 1868, January 10, 1868; *Dublin Freeman,* January 16, 1868; all in House Ex. Doc. 157, pt. 1, 40th Cong. 2d Sess., 94–95, 97–100, 206–11, 297–98. Adams Diary, December 11, 1867, quoted in Jenkins, 258–59.

42. Stanley also noted that Parliament's desire to adjourn left it unlikely to take up discussion on the issue even were the commission's report available. Lord Stanley to Thornton, February 15, 1868; Lord Stanley to Thornton, March 14, 1868; Lord Stanley to Thornton March 21, 1868; Lord Stanley to Thornton, March 31, 1868; Thornton to Lord Stanley, Washington, D.C., March 30, 1868; Thornton to Lord Stanley, Washington, D.C., April 13, 1868; Lord Stanley to Thornton, June 16, 1868, in Great Britain Foreign Office, *Correspondence...the "Alabama" and British Claims, Naturalization, and San Juan Water Boundary,* 1–6. Morrow, "Treaty of 1870," 671. D'Arcy, *Fenian Movement,* 291–92, 294–95. Seward to Adams, March 7, 1868, in D'Arcy, *Fenian Movement,* 288–89.

43. Seward to Thornton, May 28, 1868; Seward to Moran, June 22, 1868, in Jenkins, *Fenians,* 271, 274; see also 267–68, 272–73. Morrow, "Treaty of 1870," 670. *Cong. Globe,* 40th Cong. 2nd Sess., 2317–18 (April 20, 2868).

44. Both platforms can be found at www.presidency.ucsb.edu/platforms.php. Foner, *Reconstruction,* 343.

45. *Cong. Globe,* 40th Cong. 2nd Sess., 4445–46, 4474 (July 25, 1868). Morrow, "Treaty of 1870," 673–74.

46. 15 Stat. 223 (Act of July 27, 1868). *Cong. Globe,* 40th Cong. 2nd Sess., 4498.

47. Attorney General George H. Williams affirmed that expatriation rights applied to American citizens wishing to naturalize abroad. 14 Op. Attorney Gen. 296 (August 20, 1873).

48. Seward to Johnson, July 20, 1868; August 27, 1868, in D'Arcy, *Fenian Movement,* 305. Lord Stanley to Thornton, September 19, 1868; Lord Stanley to Thornton, October 9, 1868, in Great Britain Foreign Office, *Correspondence...the "Alabama" and British Claims, Naturalization, and San Juan Water Boundary,* 6, 7.

49. Great Britain Foreign Office, *Correspondence...the "Alabama" and British Claims, Naturalization, and San Juan Water Boundary,* 7–8 (Protocol). *Arrest of American Citizens in Great Britain,* 40th Cong. 3d Sess. House Rep. No. 44, 5–6.

50. Grant retorted in response to a recommendation that Fenian supplies be seized, "The British did not seize or stop the Alabama," and in discharging some detectives who investigated Fenian designs against Canada, he grumbled, "The British did not employ detectives to prevent raids from Canada during our war." *Report of the Royal Commissioners for Inquiring into the Laws of Naturalization and Allegiance,* iv, v. Jenkins, *Fenians,* 284, 293, 295–96, 303 (Grant quotes in Hamilton Fish diary, April 15; April 25, 1870).

51. *Opinions...Expatriation,* 82–83 (May 12, 1870, act). Bevans, *Treaties,* 12:158–60 (Treaty). On February 23, 1871, a supplemental convention, ratified by the Senate, President, and United Kingdom and entered into force on May 4, 1871, articulated the renunciation procedure contemplated by the May 13, 1870, treaty. Bevans, *Treaties,* 12: 167–69.

52. Page, *The Naturalization Question.* Quigley, *Second Founding,* 74–75, 80–81. This act is at 16 Stat. 254.

53. American forces captured O'Neill again after he led a small band in seizing a Canadian post on the Hudson Bay in October 1870. O'Neill avoided lengthy punishment and ended his days

settling Irish in Nebraska. He died in 1878. Samito, "John O'Neill," in Glazier, *Irish in America*, 746. Jenkins, *Fenians*, 305–6, 313–14.

54. For an example of this consciousness of American strength, see Davis, *Speech...September 24, 1863*, 27–29 ("Every despot in Europe curled his lips when the rebellion broke out, at the feeble, wretched, vacillating, dilapidated government that undertook to restore its authority," but on reunion, Davis looked forward "to the day when the black regiments shall stream to the capital of the Montezumas while the Army of the Potomac becoming the army of the St. Lawrence, shall march to Quebec and Montreal," and the American navy could match that of Britain so that he could "hear of the explosion of the bombshells over the dome of St. Paul's, and of the arches of London bridge sent into the air."). See also Boutwell, *Reconstruction...July 4, 1865*, 10. Higham, *Strangers in the Land*, 19.

55. Kerby Miller identified Fenianism as "the most popular and powerful ethnic organization in Irish-American history." Miller, *Emigrants and Exiles*, 336.

56. *Arrest of American Citizens in Great Britain*, 40th Cong. 3d Sess. House Rep. No. 44, 3. *New York Times*, May 24, 1870.

57. *New York Times*, May 24, 1870.

Epilogue

1. The number of Irish Americans who fought for the Union is much more difficult to pinpoint than the number of African Americans. Shaffer, *After the Glory*, 11. Miller, *Emigrants and Exiles*, 336.

2. Boutwell, *Reconstruction...July 4, 1865*, 15. *Elk v. Wilkins*, 112 U.S. 94 (1884) (Native Americans).

3. McClintock, "Civil War Pensions," 458, 460. O'Leary, *To Die For*, 6, 19. 10 Op. Attorney Gen. 382 (Nov. 29, 1862). Lieber, *Amendments of the Constitution*, 15–16, 27–28.

4. Basler, *Collected Works of Lincoln*, 2: 499–500. Lawson, *Patriot Fires*, 7. America's newfound security from outside attack helped this process to occur. Higham, *Strangers in the Land*, 19–21. Lloyd, "Revising the Republic," 23.

5. Wilson, *Black Phalanx*, 504. Foner, *Reconstruction*, 144–48. Blum, *Reforging the White Republic*, 51–86.

6. Higham, *Strangers in the Land*, 14–19, 28–30. O'Connor, *Civil War Boston*, 238–39. Frederick Douglass, "The Negro Exodus from the Gulf States: A Paper Read in Saratoga, New York, on 12 September 1879," in Blassingame and McKivigan, *Frederick Douglass Papers Series One*, vol. 4:510–33, 523.

7. Miller, *Emigrants and Exiles*, 493, 495, 500, 523, 533–34. Bhroiméil, "The Gaelic Movement, 1870–1915," 88–89, 99 100. Erie, *Rainbow's End*, 27, 76.

8. Miller, *Emigrants and Exiles*, 497, 498. *Harper's Weekly*, April 6, 1867; November 20, 1869; July 29, 1871.

9. Williams, "Irish-American Lace-Curtain Satire," 9–10, 12, 20, 22, 24.

10. Irish Americans comprised only 7.5 percent of the labor force but constituted one-sixth of the teamsters, metalworkers, and masons, and almost a third of the plumbers, steamfitters, and boilermakers. Nelson, "Irish Americans, Irish Nationalism, and the 'Social' Question," 147. Finley Peter Dunne used his fictional Mr. Dooley character to issue biting criticism of conditions in Bridgeport in the mid-1890s. Fanning, *Finley Peter Dunne and Mr. Dooley*, 85–100. Miller, *Emigrants and Exiles*, 500, 502–5, 508–9, 512, 516.

11. O'Donnell, "Henry George," 409, 410. Foner, "Land League and Irish-America," 150–51, 156–57, 171–73. Miller, *Emigrants and Exiles*, 524.

12. O'Donnell, "Henry George," 407–19: 409, 410. Foner, "Land League and Irish-America," 150–51, 156–57, 173, 179, 181, 183, 195–96.

13. Patrick Ford to Patrick R. Guiney, New York, July 19, 1873 in Guiney Papers, College of the Holy Cross, Worcester, Massachusetts. Rodechko, "Ford," 524–25, 527, 530, 532–33, 536. Macnamara, *Ninth Massachusetts*, 425, 436. Foner, "Land League and Irish-America," 157–61 (calling the *Irish World* the "voice of the politically conscious Irish-American working class" on 161), 178, 190–91. Nelson, "Irish Americans, Irish Nationalism, and the 'Social' Question," 154–57. O'Donnell, "Henry George," 410.

14. Gordon, *Orange Riots*, 189–90; *Irish World*, April 22 and June 24, 1871; March 2, 1872, quoted on 53, 190–91.

15. Guiney Scrapbook, 8–10.

16. Higham, *Strangers in the Land,* 41, 52–64. Rodechko, "Ford," 531. Nelson, "Irish Americans, Irish Nationalism, and the 'Social' Question," 156–57. Gordon, *Orange Riots,* 203, 212.

17. Gordon, *Orange Riots,* 1–2, 4, 5, 26, 52–53, 56, 70 (D. P. Conyngham to *Herald,* July 11, 1871), 151, 166, 188.

18. The American government's response to arrests under the 1881 Coercion Act was much cooler than its response in the 1860s. Sewell, "Irish-American Nationalism and American Diplomacy, 1865–1885," 723, 724, 727, 728–31, 733. Jenkins, *Fenians,* 321. Foner, "Land League and Irish-America," 154, 169, 173. O'Donnell, "Henry George," 410. Miller, *Emigrants and Exiles,* 538–39, 548–49.

19. Gannon, "The Won Cause," iii, 10, 24 (quote), 92, 94–95, 97–101, 105, 106, 115, 117–19, 124, 132–77, 226–27, 242, 270–72. Shaffer, *After the Glory,* 7, 165–67, 169, 173–74.

20. Shaffer, *After the Glory,* 7, 165–67, 169, 173–74. Reid, "USCT Veterans in Post-Civil War North Carolina," 403–8. See Samuel Green Pension File, No. 357631, for an example of postwar comradeship as well as the financial struggle of black veterans and their families. After the war, Green worked in a tannery, joined a GAR post, and remained friends with several comrades. After his first wife died in May 1874, leaving him with five children, Green married an ex-slave and had eight children with her (one was stillborn, six were under the age of sixteen when Samuel died, and one was born after his death). Green also raised his second wife's prior child until his stepdaughter died. Green died in Kentucky in 1892.

21. Shaffer, *After the Glory,* 52–56, 134, 195. Foreign-born troops did not experience disparity in being awarded monthly pension awards or pension increases, although foreign-born soldiers were less likely to apply for pensions in the first instance—German-, British- and Canadian-born 19 percent less likely, and Irish immigrants about 27 percent less likely. Blanck and Song, "Civil War Pensions for Native and Foreign-Born Union Army Veterans," 70, 72.

22. Shaffer, *After the Glory,* 122–23, 128–29.

23. *United States v. Rhodes,* 27 F. Cas. 785, 787, 788, 793–94 (C.C. Ky. 1866).

24. *Coger v. The North West. Union Packet Co.,* 37 Iowa 145, 148–51, 154–58 (1873).

25. O'Leary, *To Die For,* 26, 30–31, 33, 112. Higginson, *Army Life,* 30–31.

26. Lemann, *Redemption,* 49, 110–17. U.S. Congress, 43rd Cong., 2nd Sess., H.R. Rep. No. 265, *Vicksburgh Troubles.*

27. Lemann, *Redemption,* 11, 22, 77.

28. Gleeson, *Irish in the South,* 176–81, 185, 190. Waldrep, *Roots of Disorder,* 146–69.

29. O'Leary, *To Die For,* 113. Lemann, *Redemption,* 150, 154, 171.

30. *Slaughter-House Cases,* 83 U.S. 36 (1873). *United States v. Cruikshank,* 92 U.S. 542 (1875). *United States v. Harris,* 106 U.S. 629 (1883). *United States v. Reese,* 92 U.S. 214 (1875)

31. 18 Stat. 335 (Civil Rights Act of 1875). *Civil Rights Cases,* 109 U.S. 3 (1883).

32. Kaczorowski, "To Begin the Nation Anew," 67–68. Blight, *Race and Reunion.* Richardson, *The Death of Reconstruction,* 32–34, 40, 124, 134–37, and chap. 6.

33. Simpson, "Land and the Ballot." 176. Shaffer, *After the Glory,* 4–5. Fleetwood, *The Negro as a Soldier,* 18.

34. Faehtz, *The National Memorial Day: A Record of Ceremonies over the Graves of the Union Soldiers, May 29 and 30, 1869,* 5, 97–98, 101–2, 938, 940.

35. Flood, *Lee: The Last Years,* 65–66.

36. Blight, "'For Something beyond the Battlefield': Frederick Douglass and the Struggle for the Memory of the Civil War," 1160, 1162, 1165, 1169. Frederick Douglass, "Address delivered on the Twenty-sixth Anniversary of Abolition in the District of Columbia, April 16, 1888, quoted in ibid., 1161. Frederick Douglass, "Speech at the Thirty-Third Anniversary of the Jerry Rescue," 1884, quoted in ibid., 1177. *Plessy v. Ferguson,* 163 U.S. 337 (1896).

Works Cited

Archival

Benjamin Butler Papers, Manuscript Division, Library of Congress, Washington, D.C.

Charles P. Daly Papers, Rare Books and Manuscripts Division, New York Public Library, New York, New York

Patrick R. Guiney Papers, Rare Book Room, Dinand Library, College of the Holy Cross, Worcester, Massachusetts

Pension Records of Michael H. Macnamara, Daniel G. Macnamara, James Macnamara, and Samuel Green, National Archives, Washington, D.C.

John Shaw, Military Service Record, National Archives, Washington, D.C.

George Tipping letters (typescript copies courtesy of Ben Maryniak of Lancaster, New York).

10th USCHA, Broadside, "We fight for our rights, liberty, justice and union," [Louisiana?: n.p., 1866], Abraham Lincoln Presidential Library, Springfield, Illinois

Courts-Martial

Court-martial files cited here are located in Record Group 153 in the National Archives, Washington, D.C. After the name and unit of the defendant, the proceeding's file number is provided in parentheses.

James Allen, 3rd USCI (OO 1477)

Wallace Baker, 55th Massachusetts Volunteer Infantry (LL 2112)

Sterling Bradley and Charles Davis, 9th Louisiana Infantry of African Descent (MM 1442)

Nelson Browning, 55th Massachusetts Volunteer Infantry (NN 2479)

Irving Charles, 9th United States Cavalry (OO 2301)

Aaron Collins, 6th USCC (MM 2571)

Emanuel Davis, 48th USCI (NN 1707)

George Douglas, 38th USCI (MM 3064)
Calvin Dowrey, 3rd USCI (OO 1477)
Sandy Fenqua, 109th USCI (MM 3244)
Thomas Four, 52nd USCI (MM 2079)
Sampson Goliah, 55th Massachusetts Volunteer Infantry (NN 2479)
Simon Grant, 21st USCI (MM 2139)
Samuel Green 109th USCI (MM 3244)
Joseph Grien (Green), 3rd USCI (OO 1477)
J. Hall, Anderson Tolliver, et al., 2nd USCA (Light) (MM 1279)
Henry Hamilton, 2nd USCI (LL 2628)
Warren Hamilton, 73rd USCI (LL 3106)
William H. Harrison, 69th USCI (OO 911)
William Henderson, 66th USCI (NN 3192)
Thomas Howard, 3rd USCI (OO 1477)
William Jackson, 14th USCI (OO 786)
George W. Johnson, 4th Delaware Volunteer Infantry (MM 394)
Roger Johnson, 6th USCHA (LL 2577)
William Kease, 116th USCI (MM 2394)
Alexander Lee, 3rd USCI (OO 1477)
Richard Lee, 3rd USCI (OO 1477)
Frederick Letz, teamster (KK 435)
John Lewis, 13th USCHA (OO 933)
Samuel Mapp, 10th USCI (MM 1847)
Benjamin McCloud, 37th USCI (MM 3243)
John Miller, 3rd USCI (OO 1477)
John Mitchell, 53rd USCI (LL 2350)
Doctor Moore, 116th USCI (MM 2394)
Joseph Nathaniel, 3rd USCI (OO 1477)
Sheldon Penock, 109th USCI (MM 3244)
Jacob Plowden, 3rd USCI (OO 1477)
Giles Simms, 49th USCI (LL 2492)
Adam Smalz, 66th New York Volunteer Infantry (LL 861)
James Thomas, 3rd USCI (OO 1477)
William Walker, 3rd South Carolina Volunteer Infantry (African Descent) (MM 1320)
David Washington, 3rd USCC (LL 2783)
Theodore Waters, 3rd USCI (OO 1477)
Henry M. Way, 55th Massachusetts Volunteer Infantry (NN 2479)
Charles Wood, 9th United States Cavalry (OO 2488)
Fortune Wright, 96th USCI (No. OO 1494)

Attorney General Opinions, Legal Cases

8 Op. Attorney Gen. 139 (October 31, 1856)
9 Op. Attorney Gen. 63 (August 17, 1857)
9 Op. Attorney Gen. 356 (July 4, 1859)
10 Op. Attorney Gen. 382 (November 29, 1862)
14 Op. Attorney Gen. 296 (August 20, 1873)
Ainslie v. Martin, 9 Mass. 454 (1813)
Alsberry v. Hawkins, 39 Ky. 177 (1839)
Barron v. Baltimore, 32 U.S. 243 (1833)
Civil Rights Cases, 109 U.S. 3 (1883)
Coger v. The North Western Union Packet Co., 37 Iowa 145 (1873)
Dred Scott v. Sandford, 60 U.S. 393 (1856)

Dynes v. Hoover, 61 U.S. 65 (1858)
Elk v. Wilkins, 112 U.S. 94 (1884)
Inglis v. Trustees of Sailor's Snug Harbor, 3 Pet. 99 (U.S. 1830)
Murray v. McCarty, 16 Va. 393 (1811)
Plessy v. Ferguson, 163 U.S. 337 (1896)
Roberts v. The City of Boston, 59 Mass. 198 (1850)
Shanks v. Dupont, 3 Pet. 242 (U.S. 1830)
Slaughter-House Cases, 83 U.S. 36 (1873)
United States v. Cruikshank, 92 U.S. 542 (1875)
United States v. Harris, 106 U.S. 629 (1883)
United States v. Reese, 92 U.S. 214 (1875)
United States v. Rhodes, 27 F. Cas. 785 (C.C. Ky. 1866)

Newspapers

Boston Pilot
Christian Recorder
Congressional Globe
Congressional Record
Frederick Douglass' Paper
Harper's Weekly
New York Irish-American
National Era
New York Times
New York Tribune

Conventions and Related Documents (in chronological order)

African American Conventions

Foner, Philip S., and George E. Walker, eds., *Proceedings of the Black State Conventions, 1840–1865.* Vol. 2, Philadelphia: Temple University Press, 1980. Cited as Foner and Walker I.
———, eds., *Proceedings of the Black National and State Conventions, 1865–1900.* Vol. 1, Philadelphia: Temple University Press, 1986. Cited as Foner and Walker II.
Proceedings and Address of the Colored Citizens of N.J. Convened at Trenton, August 21st and 22d, 1849 For the Purpose of Taking the Initiatory Measures for Obtaining the Right of Suffrage in This Our Native State, in Foner and Walker I: 3–6.
Proceedings of the Connecticut State Convention, of Colored Men, Held at New Haven on the September 12th and 13th, 1849, in Foner and Walker I: 20–33.
State Council of Colored People of Massachusetts, Convention, January 2, 1854, reported in *The Liberator, February 24, 1854,* in Foner and Walker I: 88–94.
Memorial of Thirty Thousand Disfranchised Citizens of Philadelphia to the Honorable Senate and House of Representatives. Philadelphia: Printed for the Memorialists, 1855.
Proceedings of the State Convention of Colored Citizens of the State of Illinois, Held in the City of Alton, Nov. 13th, 14th and 15th, 1856, in Foner and Walker I: 68–82.
Convention of the Colored Citizens of Massachusetts, August 1, 1858, reported in *The Liberator,* August 13, 1858, in Foner and Walker I: 96–105.
New England Colored Citizens' Convention August 1, 1859, reported in *The Liberator,* August 19, 26, 1859, in Foner and Walker I: 207–25.
Record of Action of the Convention Held at Poughkeepsie, N.Y., July 15th and 16th, 1863, for the Purpose of Facilitating the Introduction of Colored Troops into the Service of the United States. New York: Francis and Loutrel, 1863.

Proceedings of the National Convention of Colored Men, Held in the City of Syracuse, N.Y. October 4, 5, 6, and 7, 1864; with the Bill of Wrongs and Rights and the Address to the American People. Boston: Geo. C. Rand and Avery, 1864.

Proceedings of the State Equal Rights' Convention of the Colored People of Pennsylvania Held in the City of Harrisburg February 8th, 9th, and 10th, 1865 Together with a Few of the Arguments Presented Suggesting the Necessity for Holding the Convention and an Address of the Colored State Convention to the People of Pennsylvania. Printed for and by order of the Convention, 1865.

Equal Suffrage. Address from the Colored Citizens of Norfolk, Va., to the People of the United States. Also an Account of the Agitation among the Colored People of Virginia for Equal Rights. With an Appendix Concerning the Rights of Colored Witnesses before the State Courts, June 5, 1865, in Foner and Walker I: 83–103.

Proceedings of the State Convention of the Coloured Men of the State of New Jersey, Held in the City of Trenton, N.J., July 13th and 14th, 1865 with a Short Address to the Loyal people of New Jersey, Together with the Constitution of the Equal Rights League of the State of New Jersey, in Foner and Walker I: 7–15.

Proceedings of the Convention of the Colored People of Va., Held in the City of Alexandria Aug. 2, 3, 4, 5, 1865, in Foner and Walker I: 258–74.

Proceedings of the Annual Meeting of the Pennsylvania State Equal Rights' League, held in the city of Harrisburg, August 9th and 10th, 1865. Philadelphia, 1865. In Foner and Walker II: 133–51.

State Convention of the Colored Men of Tennessee, Nashville, August 7, 1865, in *The Colored Tennessean, August 12, 1865,* in Foner and Walker I: 119–27.

Proceedings of the Colored Men's Convention of the State of Michigan Held in the City of Detroit, Tuesday and Wednesday, Sept. 12th and 13th, '65, with Accompanying Documents. Adrian, Mich.: Adrian Times Office, 1865.

An Address of the Colored People of Missouri to the Friends of Equal Rights, October 12, 1865, in Foner and Walker I: 279–82.

Proceedings of the First Annual Meeting of the National Equal Rights League, Held in Cleveland Ohio, October 19, 20, and 21, 1865. Philadelphia: E. C. Markley, 1865.

Proceedings of the California State Convention of the Colored Citizens, Held in Sacramento on the 25th, 26th, 27th and 28th of October, 1865, in Foner and Walker I: 168–201.

Proceedings of the Colored People's Convention of the State of South Carolina, held in Zion Church, Charlestown, November, 1865. Together with the Declaration of Rights and Wrongs; An Address to the People; A Petition to the Legislature, and a Memorial to Congress, in Foner and Walker I: 286–302.

State Convention of the Colored People of Indianapolis, Indiana, October 24, 1865, in *National Anti-Slavery Standard,* November 4, 1865, in Foner and Walker II: 184–85.

Proceedings of the Convention of Colored Citizens of the State of Arkansas, held in Little Rock, Thursday, Friday, and Saturday, Nov. 30, Dec. 1 and 2, 1865, in Foner and Walker I: 189–94.

"Convention of Colored Citizens in Boston," *The Boston Daily Advertiser,* quoted in the *National Anti-Slavery Standard,* December 9, 1865, in Foner and Walker I: 201–4.

Preamble and Constitution of the Pennsylvania State Equal Rights' League, Acting under the Jurisdiction of the National Equal Rights' League of the United States of America and Constitution for Subordinate Leagues. Philadelphia, 1866. In Foner and Walker II: 156–71.

State Convention of the Colored People of Georgia, August, January 10, 1866, in *the American Freedman,* April 1866, in Foner and Walker I: 232–36.

Proceedings of the Illinois State Convention of Colored Men, Assembled at Galesberg, October 16th, 17th, and 18th [1866]. Chicago, 1867. In Foner and Walker II: 249–75.

Proceedings of the State Convention of Colored Men, Held at Lexington, Kentucky, in the A.M.E. Church, November 26th, 27th, and 28th, 1867, in Foner and Walker II: 309–17.

Proceedings of the Iowa State Colored Convention, held in the City of Des Moines, February 12th and 13th, 1868. Muscatine, Iowa, 1868. In Foner and Walker II: 328–33.

Proceedings of the National Convention of the Colored Men of America, Held in Washington, D.C., on January, 13, 14, 15, and 16, 1869. Washington, D.C., 1869. In Foner and Walker II: 344–91.

Proceedings of the State Convention of The Colored Citizens of Tennessee, Held in Nashville, Feb. 22d, 23d, 24th and 25th 1871. Nashville: C. LeRoi, 1871.

Proceedings of the Southern States Convention of Colored Men, Held in Columbia, S.C., Commencing October 18, Ending October 25, 1871. Columbia, S.C.: Carolina Printing Company, 1871.

Fenian Conventions

Proceedings of the First National Convention of the Fenian Brotherhood Held in Chicago, Illinois, November 1863. Philadelphia: James Gibbons, 1863.

Proceedings of the Second National Congress of the Fenian Brotherhood Held in Cincinnati, Ohio, January, 1865. Philadelphia: James Gibbons, 1865.

Proceedings of the Sixth National Congress of the Fenian Brotherhood, at Cleveland, Ohio, September, 1867. New York: J. Craft, 1867.

Published Primary Sources

Adams, Charles Francis. *What Makes Slavery a Question of National Concern? A Lecture Delivered, by Invitation, at New York, January 20, and at Syracuse, February 1, 1855.* Boston: Little, Brown, 1855.

Adams, Virginia M., ed. (James Henry Gooding), *On the Altar of Freedom: A Black Soldier's Civil War Letters from the Front.* Amherst: The University of Massachusetts Press, 1991.

[Andrew, John A.], *Answers of the Governor of Massachusetts to Inquiries Respecting Certain Emigrants Who Have Arrived in This Country from Europe and Who Are Alleged to be Illegally Enlisted in the Army of the United States, and Other Papers on the Same Subject.* Washington, D.C.: Government Printing Office, 1864.

[Andrew, John A., et al.], *Addresses by His Excellency Governor John A. Andrew, Hon, Edward Everett, Hon, B. F. Thomas, and Hon. Robert C. Winthrop, Delivered at the Mass Meeting in Aid of Recruiting, Held on the Common Under the Auspices of the Committee of One Hundred and Fifty, on Wednesday, August 27, 1862.* Boston: J.E. Farwell and Company, 1862.

[Antisell, Thomas], *Address of the Central Executive Committee of Irish Citizens, at Washington, D.C., to Their Countrymen throughout the United States.* Washington, D.C.: McGill and Witherow, 1866.

Banks, Nathaniel P. *Address of His Excellency Nathaniel P. Banks to the Two Branches of the Legislature of Massachusetts, January 6, 1860.* Boston: William White, 1860.

Basler, Roy P., ed. *The Collected Works of Abraham Lincoln.* 9 vols. New Brunswick, N.J.: Rutgers University Press, 1953.

Beale, Howard K., ed. *The Diary of Edward Bates: 1859–1866.* Washington, D.C.: Government Printing Office, 1933.

Beaudot, William J. K., and Lance J. Herdegen, eds. *An Irishman in the Iron Brigade: The Civil War Memoirs of James P. Sullivan, Sergt., Company K, 6th Wisconsin Volunteers.* New York: Fordham University Press, 1993.

Benedict, E. C., *The Constitutional Amendment.* n.p., 1866.

Benet, Stephen V. *A Treatise on Military Law and the Practice of Courts-Martial.* New York: D. Van Nostrand, 1864.

Berlin, Ira, et al., eds. *Freedom: A Documentary History of Emancipation 1861–1867.* Series 2. *The Black Military Experience.* Cambridge: Cambridge University Press, 1982.

Bevans, Charles I., ed. *Treaties and Other International Agreements of the United States of America 1776–1949.* 13 vols. Washington, D.C.: Government Printing Office, 1968.

Bird, F. W., *Review of Gov. Banks' Veto of the Revised Code, on Account of its Authorizing the Enrolment of Colored Citizens in the Militia.* Boston: John P. Jewett, 1860.

Blackett, R.J.M., ed. *Thomas Morris Chester: Black Civil War Correspondent.* New York: De Capo Press, 1989.

Blassingame, John W., and John R. McKivigan, eds. *The Frederick Douglass Papers. Series One Speeches, Debates and Interviews.* 5 vols. New Haven, Ct.: Yale University Press, 1979–1992.

Boutwell, George S., *Reconstruction: Its True Basis: Speech of Hon, George S. Boutwell, at Weymouth, Mass., July 4, 1865.* Boston: Wright and Potter, 1865.

Briggs, Walter DeBlois, ed. (Charles E. Briggs diary). *Civil War Surgeon in a Colored Regiment.* Berkeley: University of California Press, 1960.

Brockway, Charles B., *A Soldier's Sentiments: Speech of Capt. Charles B. Brockway, At the Great Knob Mountain Meeting, Columbia County, Pa., on Wednesday, August 30, 1865.* Penn. [?]: n.p., [1865?].

Brown, William Wells, *The Negro in the American Rebellion: His Heroism and His Fidelity.* Boston: Lee and Shepard, 1867.

Buckingham, Peter H., ed. *All's for the Best: The Civil War Reminiscences and Letters of Daniel W. Sawtelle Eighth Maine Volunteer Infantry.* Knoxville: University of Tennessee Press, 2001.

Califf, Joseph Mark. *Record of the Service of the Seventh Regiment, U.S. Colored Troops: from September, 1863 to November, 1866.* Providence: E. L. Freeman, 1878.

Cannon, William. *Special Message of Governor Cannon, to the Legislature of Delaware, July 28, 1864.* Wilmington, Del.: Henry Eckel, 1864.

Ceremonies at the Reception of Welcome to the Colored Soldiers of Pennsylvania, in the City of Harrisburg, Nov. 14th, 1865, by the Garnet League. Harrisburg, Penn.: Telegraph Steam Book and Job Office, 1866.

Clark, Peter H. *The Black Brigade of Cincinnati.* Cincinnati: Joseph B. Boyd, 1864.

Colfax, Schuyler, et al. *Speeches of Hon. Schuyler Colfax and General J. O'Neill.* n.p., 1866.

Colyer, Vincent. *Report of the Services Rendered by the Freed People to the United States Army, in North Carolina, in the Spring of 1862, after the Battle of Newbern.* N.Y.: Vincent Colyer, 1864.

Conyngham, David P. *The Irish Brigade and Its Campaigns.* New York: William McSorley, 1867.

Corby, William. *Memoirs of Chaplain Life: Three Years with the Irish Brigade in the Army of the Potomac.* Edited by Lawrence F. Kohl. 1893; repr. New York: Fordham University Press, 1992.

Corcoran, Michael. *The Captivity of General Corcoran: The Only Authentic and Reliable Narrative of the Trials and Sufferings Endured During His Twelve Months' Imprisonment in Richmond and Other Southern Cities.* Philadelphia: Barclay, 1865.

Cowden, Robert. *A Brief Sketch of the Organization and Services of the Fifty-Ninth Regiment of United States Colored Infantry and Biographical Sketches.* Dayton, Ohio: United Brethren, 1883.

Crotty, D. G. *Four Years Campaigning in the Army of the Potomac, by Color Sergeant, D.G. Crotty, Third Michigan Volunteer Infantry.* Grand Rapids, Mich.: Dygert Bros, 1874.

Davis, Henry Winter. *Speech of Hon. Henry Winter Davis at Concert Hall, Philadelphia, September 24, 1863.* Philadelphia, 1863.

Dennett, George M. *History of the Ninth U.S.C. Troops.* Philadelphia: King and Baird, 1866.

Devoy, John. *Recollections of an Irish Rebel.* New York: Chas. D. Young, 1929.

Dickson, William M. *An Address by William M. Dickson, Delivered at Oberlin, Ohio, October 3, 1865.* Cincinnati: Robert Clarke, 1865.

Duren, C. M. "The Occupation of Jacksonville, February 1864 and the Battle of Olustee: Letters of Lt. C. M. Duren, 54th Massachusetts Regiment, U.S.A." *The Florida Historical Quarterly* 32 (1954): 262–87.

Emilio, Luis F. *A Brave Black Regiment: The History of the Fifty-Fourth Regiment of Massachusetts Volunteer Infantry, 1863–1865.* 2d ed. Boston: Boston Book, 1894.

Faehtz, E. F. M. ed., *The National Memorial Day: A Record of Ceremonies over the Graves of the Union Soldiers, May 29 and 30, 1869.* Washington, D.C.: Headquarters Grand Army of the Republic by M'Gill and Witherow, 1870.

Foner, Philip S., ed. *The Life and Writings of Frederick Douglass.* 5 vols. New York: International, 1950.

Fox, Charles B. *Record of the Service of the Fifty-fifth Regiment of Massachusetts Volunteer Infantry.* Cambridge, Mass.: Press of John Wilson and Son, 1868.

Fransioli, Joseph. *Patriotism, A Christian Virtue: A Sermon Preached By The Rev. Joseph Fransioli, at St. Peter's (Catholic) Church, Brooklyn, July 26th, 1863.* New York: Loyal Publication Society, 1863.

Garnet, Henry Highland. *A Memorial Discourse by Rev. Henry Highland Garnet, Delivered in the Hall of the House of Representatives, Washington City, D.C. on Sabbath, February 12, 1865.* Philadelphia, Joseph M. Wilson, 1865.

Garrison, William Lloyd. *The Loyalty and Devotion of Colored Americans in the Revolution and War of 1812.* Boston: R. F. Wallcut, 1861.

Great Britain Foreign Office. *Correspondence Respecting the Negotiations with the United States' Government on the Questions of the "Alabama" and British Claims, Naturalization, and San Juan Water Boundary.* London: Harrison and Sons, 1869.

[Great Britain]. *Correspondence Respecting Recruitment in Ireland for the Military Service of the United States Presented to both Houses of Parliament by Command of Her Majesty.* London: Harrison and Sons, 1864.

[————]. *Report of the Royal Commissioners for Inquiring into the Laws of Naturalization and Allegiance.* London: George Edward Eyre and William Spottiswoode, 1869.

Green, Alfred M. *Letters and Discussions on the Formation of Colored Regiments and the Duty of the Colored People in Regard to the Great Slaveholders' Rebellion, in the United States of America.* Philadelphia: Ringwalt and Brown, 1862.

Halleck, Henry W. "Military Tribunals and Their Jurisdiction." *American Journal of International Law* 5 (1911): 958–67.

Hallowell, Norwood P. *An Address by N. P. Hallowell, '61. Delivered on Memorial Day, May 30, 1896, at a Meeting Called by the Graduating Class of Harvard University.* Boston: Little, Brown, 1896.

————. "The Negro as a Soldier in the War of the Rebellion." In *Selected Letters and Papers of N.P. Hallowell.* 1896–97; repr. Peterborough, N.H.: Richard R. Smith, 1963.

Halpine, Charles G. *The Life and Adventures, Songs, Services, and Speeches of Private Miles O'Reilly.* New York: Carleton, 1864.

————. *Baked Meats of the Funeral: A Collection of Essays, Poems, Speeches, Histories, and Banquets.* New York: Carleton, 1866.

Hening, William W., ed. *The Statutes at Large: Being a Collection of All of the Laws of Virginia, from the First Session of the Legislature, in the Year 1619.* [n.p., 1809–23].

Higginson, Thomas Wentworth. *Army Life in a Black Regiment.* repr.; Lansing: Michigan State University Press, 1960.

Holt, Joseph. *Treason and Its Treatment: Remarks of Hon. Joseph Holt, at a Dinner in Charleston, S.C., on the Evening of the 14th of April, 1865, After the Flag Raising at Fort Sumter.* New York: New York Young Men's Republican Union, 1865.

Hoffman, John T. *The Great Speech of Hon. John T. Hoffman at Buffalo, September 8th, 1868.* Buffalo: Joseph Warren, 1868.

———. *The Cause of Ireland and Adopted Citizens: The Record of John T. Hoffman, His Views on Fenianism Letter of March 12, 1867, His Message to the Common Council Relative to the Rights of Adopted Citizens Dated Nov. 30, 1867*. New York: n.p., 1868[?].

Howard, R. L. *History of the 124th Regiment Illinois Infantry Volunteers*. Springfield, Ill.: H. W. Rokker, 1880.

Iowa Adjutant General's Office. *Roster and Record of Iowa Soldiers in the War of the Rebellion*. 6 vols. Des Moines: Emory H. English, 1908.

James, Garth W. "The Assault on Fort Wagner." In *War Papers Read before the Commandery of the State of Wisconsin, Military Order of the Loyal Legion of the United States*, vol. 1: 9–30. Milwaukee: Burdick, Armitage and Allen, 1891.

Jenkins, Howard M. *Our Democratic Republic: Its Form—Its Faults—Its Strength—Its Need. Three Articles on the Suffrage Question*. Wilmington, Del.: Jenkins and Atkinson, 1868.

Johnson, William Henry. *Autobiography of Dr. William Henry Johnson*. Albany, N.Y.: Argus, 1900.

Kelley, William D. *The Safeguards of Personal Liberty: An Address Hon. Wm. D. Kelley, Delivered at Concert Hall, Thursday Evening, June 22, 1865*. Philadelphia: Social, Civil and Statistical Association of Colored People of Pennsylvania, 1865.

Kelley, William D., et al. *Addresses of the Hon. W.D. Kelley, Miss Anna E. Dickenson, and Mr. Frederick Douglass, at a Mass Meeting, Held at National Hall, Philadelphia, July 6, 1863, for the Promotion of Colored Enlistments*. n.p., 1863.

Kennedy, Joseph C. G. *Population of the United States in 1860; Compiled From the Original Returns of the Eight Census, Under the Direction of the Secretary of the Interior*. Washington, D.C.: Government Printing Office, 1864.

Kohl, Lawrence F., ed. *Irish Green and Union Blue: The Civil War Letters of Peter Welsh*. New York: Fordham University Press, 1986.

Langston, John Mercer. *A Speech on "Equality before the Law," Delivered by J. Mercer Langston, in the Hall of Representatives, in the Capitol of Missouri, on the Evening of the 9th Day of January, 1866*. St. Louis: Democrat Book and Job Printing, 1866.

———. "Daniel O'Connell," given in Washington, D.C., December 28, 1874. In John Mercer Langston, *Freedom and Citizenship: Selected Lectures and Addresses of Hon. John Mercer Langston, LL.D., U.S. Minister Resident at Haiti*. 1883 repr., 69–98. Miami, Fla.: Mnemosyne, 1969.

Levstik, Frank R., ed. (Milton M. Holland). "From Slavery to Freedom: Two Wartime Letters by One of the Conflict's Few Black Medal Winners." *Civil War Times Illustrated* 1, no. 11 (November 1972): 10–15.

Lieber, Francis. *No Party Now; But All for Our Country*. New York: C. S. Westcott, 1863.

———. *Amendments of the Constitution, Submitted to the Consideration of The American People*. New York: Loyal Publication Society, 1865.

Livermore, George. "An Historical Research Respecting the Opinions of the Founders of the Republic on Negroes as Slaves, as Citizens, and as Soldiers." In *Proceedings of the Massachusetts Historical Society*, 86–248. Boston: Massachusetts Historical Society, 1863.

[———]. *General Washington and General Jackson on Negro Soldiers*. Philadelphia: Henry Carey Baird, 1863.

Looby, Christopher, ed. *The Complete Civil War Journal and Selected Letters of Thomas Wentworth Higginson*. Chicago: University of Chicago Press, 2000.

Loring, George B. *Safe and Honorable Reconstruction. An Oration, Delivered at Newburyport, July 4, 1866, by George B. Loring, of Salem*. South Danvers, Mass.: Charles D. Howard, 1866.

———. *An Oration, Delivered at Bolton, Mass., December 20, 1866, at the Dedication of the Tablets, Erected in the Town Hall, to Commemorate the Deceased Volunteers of the Town in the War of the Great Rebellion*. Clinton, Mass.: Clinton Courant, 1867.

Loyal Publication Society. *The Two Ways of Treason: Or, The Open Traitor Of The South Face To Face With His Skulking Abettor At The North*. New York: Wm. C. Bryant, 1863.

———. *The Great Mass Meeting of Loyal Citizens at Cooper Institute, Friday Evening, March 6, 1863*. New York: Loyal Publication Society, 1863.

———. *Sherman Vs. Hood—"A Low Tart, Inclined To Be Very Sweet"—Something For Douglas Democrats To Remember—An Appeal To History—Where Governor Seymour Got His "Lessons"—On the Chicago Surrender.* New York: Loyal Publication Society, 1864.

Macnamara, Daniel G. *History of the Ninth Massachusetts Volunteer Infantry.* Christian G. Samito, ed. 1899; repr. New York: Fordham University Press, 2000.

Macnamara, Michael. *The Irish Ninth in Bivouac and Battle.* Boston: Lee and Shepard, 1867.

Maguire, John Francis. *The Irish in America.* London: Longmans, Green, 1868.

Marrs, Elijah P. *Life and History of The Rev. Elijah P. Marrs.* Louisville, Ky.: Bradley and Gilbert, 1885.

McDermott, Anthony W. *A Brief History of the 69th Regiment Pennsylvania Veteran Volunteers, from its Formation Until Final Muster Out of the United States Service.* Philadelphia: D. J. Gallagher, 1889.

McElroy, Rev. Thomas, C.S.C., ed. "The War Letters of Father Peter Paul Cooney of the Congregation of Holy Cross." *Records of the American Catholic Historical Society* 44 (1933): 47–69; 151–69; 220–37.

McMurray, John. *Recollections of a Colored Troop.* Brookville, Penn.: privately published, 1916.

McPherson, James M. *The Negro's Civil War.* New York: Pantheon Books, 1965.

Mickley, Jeremiah M. *Forty-third Regiment United States Colored Troops.* Gettysburg, Penn.: J. H. Wible, 1866.

Moore, John Bassett, ed. *Digest of International Law.* 8 vols. Washington, D.C.: Government Printing Office, 1906.

Morgan, Thomas J. *Reminiscences of Service with Colored Troops in the Army of the Cumberland, 1863–65.* Providence, R.I.: Providence Press Company, 1885.

Mulholland, St. Clair A. *The Story of the 116th Regiment, Pennsylvania Volunteers in the War of the Rebellion,* ed. Lawrence Frederick Kohl. 1903; repr. New York: Fordham University Press, 1996.

Murray, Thomas Hamilton. *History of the Ninth Regiment, Connecticut Volunteer Infantry, "The Irish Regiment," in the War of the Rebellion, 1861–65.* New Haven: Price, Lee and Adkins, 1903.

Nell, William C. *Services of Colored Americans, in the Wars of 1776 and 1811.* 2d ed. Boston: Robert F. Wallcut, 1852.

Nesbit, William, Joseph C. Bustill, William D. Forten, on behalf of the Pennsylvania State Equal Rights League. *To the Honorable The Senate and House of Representatives of the United States, in Congress Assembled.* Pennsylvania[?]: n.p., 1866[?].

Newton, A. H. *Out of the Briars: An Autobiography and Sketch of the Twenty-ninth Regiment Connecticut Volunteers.* Philadelphia: A.M.E. Book Concern: 1910.

New York Union League Club. *Report of the Committee on Volunteering.* New York: Club House, 1864.

O'Gorman, Richard. *Speech of the Defendant's Counsel, Richard O'Gorman: State of New York vs. Col. M. Corcoran.* New York: n.p., 1860.

Opinions of the Early Presidents, and of the Fathers of the Republic, upon Slavery, and Upon Negroes as Men and Soldiers. New York: Wm C. Bryant, 1863.

O'Rielly, Henry. *First Organization of Colored Troops in the State of New York, to Aid in Suppressing the Slaveholders' Rebellion.* New York: Baker and Godwin, 1864.

Osborne, William H. *The History of the Twenty-Ninth Regiment of Massachusetts Volunteer Infantry in the Late War of the Rebellion.* Boston: Albert J. Wright, 1877.

Page, Charles A. *The Naturalization Question: From the Stand-Point of a United States Consul in Europe.* Washington, D.C.: Philp and Solomons, 1869.

Phillips, Wendell. "Under the Flag." In Wendell Phillips, *Speeches, Lectures, and Letters,* 396–414. Boston: James Redpath, 1863.

Pinkerton, Allan. *Spy in the Rebellion.* New York: G. W. Carleton, 1883.

Redkey, Edwin S. *A Grand Army of Black Men: Letters from African-American Soldiers in the Union Army, 1861–1865.* Cambridge: Cambridge University Press, 1992.

Richardson, James D., ed. *A Compilation of the Messages and Papers of the Presidents 1789–1897*. 11 vols. Washington, D.C.: Government Printing Office.

Roberts, William R. *Message of President William R. Roberts to the Senators and Representatives of the Fenian Brotherhood in Congress Assembled*. Cleveland, Ohio: n.p., 1867[?].

Runkle, Benjamin P. *Address Delivered by Bvt. Col. Ben. P. Runkle, U.S.A. Chief Supt. Freedmen's Affairs, State of Kentucky, to the Freedman of Louisville, October, 1868*. Louisville, Ky.: Calvert, Tippett, 1868.

Ryan, John. *Campaigning with the Irish Brigade: Pvt. John Ryan, 28th Massachusetts*. Edited by Sandy Barnard. Terre Haute, Ind.: AST Press, 2001.

Samito, Christian G., ed. *Commanding Boston's Irish Ninth: The Civil War Letters of Colonel Patrick R. Guiney, Ninth Massachusetts Volunteer Infantry*. New York: Fordham University Press, 1998.

Savage, John. *Fenian Heroes and Martyrs*. Boston: Patrick Donahoe, 1868.

Sherman, George R. *The Negro as a Soldier*. Providence: Snow and Farnham, 1913.

Silber, Nina, and Mary Beth Sievens, eds. *Yankee Correspondence: Civil War Letters between New England Soldiers and the Home Front*. Charlottesville, Va.: University Press of Virginia 1996.

Smith, Eric Ledell, ed. "The Civil War Letters of Quartermaster Sergeant John C. Brock, 43rd Regiment, United States Colored Troops." In *Making and Remaking Pennsylvania's Civil War*, ed. William Blair and William Pencak, 141–64. University Park: The Pennsylvania State University Press, 2001.

Smith, Gerrit. *Gerrit Smith on M'Clellan's Nomination and Acceptance*. New York: Loyal Publication Society, 1864.

Spear, Samuel T. *The Citizen's Duty in the Present Crisis: A Sermon Preached in the South Presbyterian Church of Brooklyn, by the Pastor, Rev. Samuel T. Spear, D.D., October 7th, 1866*. New York: N. Tibbals, 1866.

Stearns, John M. *The Rights of Man The True Basis of Reconstruction: An Address Delivered at North Springfield, Vermont, July the Fourth 1866*. Williamsburgh, N.Y.: L. Darbee and Son, 1866.

Stephens' Fenian Songster, Containing all the Heart-Stirring and Patriotic Ballads and Songs, as Sung at the Meetings of the Fenian Brotherhood. New York: Wm. H. Murphy, 1866.

Summers, O. "The Negro Soldiers in the Army of the Cumberland." In George Washington Herr, *Episodes of the Civil War*, 424–32. San Francisco: Bancroft, 1890.

Taggart, John H. *Free Military School for Applicants for Command of Colored Troops, No. 1210 Chestnut Street, Philadelphia, Established by the Supervisory Committee for Recruiting Colored Regiments*. Philadelphia: King and Baird, 1864.

Trimble, Richard, ed. *Brothers 'til Death: The Civil War Letters of William, Thomas, and Maggie Jones 1861–1865*. Macon, Ga.: Mercer University Press, 2000.

Trudeau, Noah Andre, ed. *Voices of the 55th: Letters from the 55th Massachusetts Volunteers 1861–1865*. Dayton, Ohio: Morningside House, 1996.

Tucker, St. George, ed. *Blackstone's Commentaries: with Notes of Reference, to the Constitution and Laws, of the Federal Government of the United States; and of the Commonwealth of Virginia*. 5 vols. Philadelphia: William Young Birch, 1803.

———. *Commentaries on the Laws of Virginia, Comprising the Substance of a Course of Lectures Delivered to the Winchester Law School*. 3d ed. 2 vols. Richmond: Shepherd and Colin, 1846.

U.S Congress. 39th Cong., 2d Sess., Senate Ex. Doc. No. 6 (*Laws in Relation to Freedmen*).

———. 40th Cong. 2d Sess., House Ex. Doc. 157, pt. 1 (*Message from the President of the United States, in Answer to A Resolution of the House of November 25, 1867, Relative to Trial and Conviction of American Citizens in England for Fenianism*).

———. 40th Cong. 2d Sess., House Misc. Doc. No. 59 (*Resolutions of the Legislature of Maine, Relative to Naturalized citizens of the United States*).

———. 40th Cong. 2d Sess., House Misc. Doc. No. 75 (*Resolution of the Legislature of Maryland, Relative to The Rights of Naturalized citizens of the United States*).

———. 40th Cong. 2d Sess., House Mis. Doc. No. 76 (*Resolutions of the Legislature of Pennsylvania*).

———. 40th Cong. 2d Sess., House Mis. Doc. No. 112 (*Resolutions of the Legislature of Ohio in Relation to American citizens*).

———. 40th Cong. 2d Sess., House Mis. Doc. No. 149 (*Resolutions of the Legislature of California Asking Congress to Demand of Foreign Governments Full and Ample Protection to Our Foreign-born Citizens while Temporarily Residing under Those Governments*).

———. 40th Cong. 2d Sess., Sen. Misc. Doc. No. 25 (*Resolutions of the Legislature of Kansas, in Relation to the Rights of American Citizens in Foreign Countries*).

———. 40th Cong. 2d Sess., Sen. Mis. Doc. No. 28 (*Resolutions of the Legislature of Minnesota Relative to Protection to American citizens in Foreign Countries*).

———. 40th Cong. 3d Sess. House Rep. No. 44 (*Arrest of American Citizens in Great Britain*).

———. 43d Cong., 1st Sess., H.R. Misc. Doc. No. 44 (*Memorial of National Convention of Colored Persons, Praying to Be Protected in Their Civil Rights*).

———. 43rd Cong., 2d Sess., H.R. Rep. No. 265 (*Vicksburgh Troubles*).

———. *Journal of the House of Representatives.* 38th Cong., 1863–65; 39th Cong., 1865–67; and 40th Cong., 1867–69.

———. *Journal of the Senate.* 38th Cong., 1863–65; 39th Cong., 1865–67; and 40th Cong., 1867–69.

U.S. Dept. of State. *Opinions of the Principal Officers of the Executive Departments, and Other Papers Relating to Expatriation, Naturalization, and Change of Allegiance.* Washington, D.C.: Government Printing Office, 1873.

U.S. Dept. of War. *Revised United States Army Regulations of 1861, with an Appendix Containing the Changes and Laws Affecting Army Regulations and Articles of War to June 25, 1863.* Washington, D.C.: Government Printing Office, 1863.

———. *List of U.S. Soldiers Executed by United States Military Authorities during the Late War.* Washington, D.C.: Government Printing Office, 1885.

United States. *Statutes at Large of the United States of America, 1780–1783.* 17 vols. Washington, D.C.: Government Printing Office, 1850–1873.

———. *The War of the Rebellion: A Compilation of the Official Records of the Union and Confederate Armies.* 128 vols. Washington, D.C.: Government Printing Office, 1880–1901.

Watkins, William J. *Our Rights As Men: An Address Delivered in Boston, Before the Legislative Committee on the Militia, February 24, 1853, by William J. Watkins.* Boston: Benjamin F. Roberts, 1853.

Wilson, Joseph T. *Black Phalanx: A History of the Negro Soldiers of the United States in the Wars of 1775–1812, 1861–65.* Hartford: American Publishing, 1890.

Winthrop, W., ed. *Digest of Opinions of the Judge Advocate General of the Army: Containing A Selection of Official Opinions Furnished to the President, the Secretary of War, the Adjutant General, Heads of Bureaus of the War Department, Commanding Officers, Judge Advocates and Members of Military Courts, and Other Officers of the Army, and Soldiers—Between September 1862 and July 1868.* Washington, D.C.: Government Printing Office, 1868.

Yacovone, Donald, ed. *A Voice of Thunder: The Civil War Letters of George E. Stephens.* Chicago: University of Chicago Press, 1997.

———, ed. *Freedom's Journey: African-American Voices of the Civil War.* Chicago: Lawrence Hill Books, 2004.

Secondary Sources

Ackerman, Bruce. *We the People: Transformations.* Cambridge, Mass.: Harvard University Press, 2000.

Anbinder, Tyler. *Nativism and Slavery: The Northern Know Nothings and the Politics of the 1850s.* New York: Oxford University Press, 1992.

Athearn, Robert G. *Thomas Francis Meagher: An Irish Revolutionary in America*. Boulder, Colo.: University of Colorado Press, 1949.

Baum, Dale. "The 'Irish Vote' and Party Politics in Massachusetts, 1860–1871." *Civil War History* 26 (1980): 117–41.

———. *The Civil War Party System: The Case of Massachusetts, 1848–1867*. Chapel Hill: University of North Carolina Press, 1984.

Bean, William G. "Puritan versus Celt: 1850–1860." *New England Quarterly* 7 (1934): 70–89.

Bell, Howard H. "Negro Nationalism in the 1850s." *Journal of Negro Education* 35 (1966): 100–104.

Benedict, Michael Les. *A Compromise of Principle: Congressional Republicans and Reconstruction, 1863–1869*. New York: Norton, 1974.

Bennett, B. Kevin. "The Jacksonville Mutiny." *Civil War History* 38 (1992): 39–50.

Bennett, Brian A. *The Beau Ideal of a Soldier and a Gentleman: The Life of Col. Patrick Henry O'Rorke from Ireland to Gettysburg*. Wheatland, N.Y.: Triphammer, 1996.

Bennett, Michael J. *Union Jacks: Yankee Sailors in the Civil War*. Chapel Hill: The University of North Carolina Press, 2004.

Betts, John R. "The Negro and the New England Conscience in the Days of John Boyle O'Reilly." *Journal of Negro History* 51 (1966): 246–61.

Bhroiméil, Úna Ní. "The Creation of an Irish Culture in the United States: The Gaelic Movement, 1870–1915." *New Hibernia Review* 5 (2001): 87–100.

Blanck, Peter, and Chen Song. "'With Malice toward None; With Charity toward All': Civil War Pensions for Native and Foreign-Born Union Army Veterans." *Transnational Law and Contemporary Problems* 11 (2001): 1–73.

Blassingame, John W. "The Union Army as an Educational Institution for Negroes, 1862–1865." *Journal of Negro Education* 43 (1965): 152–59.

Blight, David W. "'For Something beyond the Battlefield': Frederick Douglass and the Struggle for the Memory of the Civil War." *Journal of American History* 75 (1989): 1156–78.

———. *Race and Reunion: The Civil War in American Memory*. Cambridge, Mass.: Harvard University Press, 2001.

Blum, Edward J. *Reforging the White Republic: Race, Religion, and American Nationalism 1865–1898*. Baton Rouge: Louisiana State University Press, 2005.

Breuilly, John. *Nationalism and the State*. 2d ed. Chicago: University of Chicago Press, 1994.

Brown, Robert A., and Todd C. Shaw. "Separate Nations: Two Attitudinal Dimensions of Black Nationalism." *Journal of Politics* 64 (2002): 22–44.

Brown, Thomas N. *Irish-American Nationalism*. New York: J. B. Lippincott, 1966.

Bruce, Susannah Ural. *The Harp and the Eagle: Irish-American Volunteers and the Union Army, 1861–1865*. New York: New York University Press, 2006.

Burkhardt, George S. *Confederate Rage, Yankee Wrath: No Quarter in the Civil War*. Carbondale, Ill.: Southern Illinois University Press, 2007.

Burton, William L. *Melting Pot Soldiers: The Union's Ethnic Regiments*. 2d ed. 1988; repr. New York: Fordham University Press, 1998.

Butler, Jon. *Becoming America: The Revolution before 1776*. Cambridge, Mass.: Harvard University Press, 2000.

Byron, Reginald. *Irish America*. New York: Oxford University Press, 1999.

Cheek, William, and Aimee Lee Cheek. *John Mercer Langston and the Fight for Black Freedom*. Urbana: University of Illinois Press, 1996.

Chomsky, Carol. "The United States-Dakota War Trials: A Study in Military Injustice," *Stanford Law Review* 43 (1990): 13–96.

Clark, Dennis. *The Irish in Philadelphia: Ten Generations of Urban Experience*. Philadelphia: Temple University Press, 1973.

Cullen, Jim. "'I's a Man Now': Gender and African American Men." In *Divided Houses: Gender and the Civil War*, ed. Catherine Clinton and Nina Silber, 76–91. New York: Oxford University Press, 1992.

Cullop, Charles P. "An Unequal Duel: Union Recruiting in Ireland, 1863–1864." *Civil War History* 13 (1967): 101–13.

D'Arcy, William. *The Fenian Movement in the United States: 1858–1886.* Washington, D.C.: Catholic University of American Press, 1947.

Davidson, Roger A., Jr. "'They Have Never Been Known to Falter': The First United States Colored Infantry in Virginia and North Carolina." *Civil War Regiments* 6 (1996): 1–26.

Davis, Hugh. "The Pennsylvania State Equal Rights League and the Northern Black Struggle for Legal Equality, 1864–1877." *The Pennsylvania Magazine of History and Biography* 126 (2002): 611–34.

Donald, David. *Charles Sumner and the Rights of Man.* New York: Knopf, 1970.

Dunkelman, Mark H. "Through White Eyes: The 154th New York Volunteers and African-Americans in the Civil War." *Journal of Negro History* 85 (2000): 96–111.

Erie, Steven P. *Rainbow's End: Irish-Americans and the Dilemmas of Urban Machine Politics, 1840–1985.* Berkeley: University of California Press, 1988.

Faust, Drew Gilpin. "Christian Soldiers: The Meaning of Revivalism in the Confederate Army." *Journal of Southern History* 53 (1987): 63–90.

Fanning, Charles. *Finley Peter Dunne and Mr. Dooley: The Chicago Years.* Lexington: University Press of Kentucky, 1978.

Fanning, Charles, et al. *Nineteenth Century Chicago Irish: A Social and Political Portrait.* Chicago: Center for Urban Policy Loyola University of Chicago, 1980.

Finkelman, Paul. "Prelude to the Fourteenth Amendment: Black Legal Rights in the Antebellum North." *Rutgers Law Journal* 17 (1986): 415–82.

Fitzharris, Joseph C. "Field Officer Courts and U.S Civil War Military Justice." *Journal of Military History* 68 (2004): 47–72.

Flood, Charles Bracelen. *Lee: The Last Years.* Boston: Houghton Mifflin, 1981.

Foner, Eric. "Class, Ethnicity, and Radicalism in the Gilded Age: The Land League and Irish-America." In *Politics and Ideology in the Age of the Civil War,* 150–200. New York: Oxford University Press, 1980.

———. *Reconstruction: America's Unfinished Revolution 1863–1877.* New York: Harper and Row, 1988.

———. *Freedom's Lawmakers: A Directory of Black Officeholders during Reconstruction.* Rev. end. Baton Rouge: Louisiana State University Press, 1996.

———. *Story of American Freedom.* New York: Norton, 1998.

Frank, Joseph Allan. *With Ballot and Bayonet: The Political Socialization of American Civil War Soldiers.* Athens: University of Georgia Press, 1998.

Frederickson, George M. *The Inner Civil War: Northern Intellectuals and the Crisis of the Union.* 1965; repr. Chicago: University of Illinois Press, 1993.

Gannon, Barbara A. "The Won Cause: Black and White Comradeship in the Grand Army of the Republic." Ph.D. diss., Pennsylvania State University, 2005.

Gibson, Florence E. *The Attitudes of the New York Irish toward State and National Affairs 1848–1892.* New York: Columbia University Press, 1951.

Giles, Paul. "Narrative Reversals and Power Exchanges: Frederick Douglass and British Culture." *American Literature* 73 (2001): 779–810.

Glatthaar, Joseph T. *Forged in Battle: The Civil War Alliance of Black Soldiers and White Officers.* New York: Free Press, 1990.

Glazier, Michael, ed. *The Encyclopedia of the Irish in America.* Notre Dame, Ind.: University of Notre Dame Press, 1999.

Gleeson, David T. *The Irish in the South, 1815–1877.* Chapel Hill: The University of North Carolina Press, 2001.

Gordon, Michael A. *The Orange Riots: Irish Political Violence in New York City, 1870 and 1871.* Ithaca: Cornell University Press, 1993.

Grant, Susan-Mary. *North over South: Northern Nationalism and American Identity in the Antebellum Era.* Lawrence: University Press of Kansas, 2000.

Hall, Stephen Gilroy. "'To Give a Faithful Account of the Race': History and Historical Consciousness in the African-American Community, 1827–1915." Ph.D. diss., Ohio State University, 1999.

Hanchett, William. *Irish / Charles G. Hapine in Civil War America.* Syracuse, N.Y.: Syracuse University Press, 1970.

Handlin, Oscar. *Boston's Immigrants 1790–1880: A Study in Acculturation.* Cambridge, Mass.: Belknap Press of Harvard University, rev. and enl. ed. 1979.

Harcourt, Edward John. "The Whipping of Richard Moore: Reading Emotion in Reconstruction America." *Journal of Social History* 36 (2002): 261–82.

Hernon, Joseph M., Jr. *Celts, Catholics, and Copperheads.* Columbus: Ohio State University Press, 1967.

Hickey, Donald R. *The War of 1812: A Forgotten Conflict.* Chicago: University of Chicago Press, 1989.

Higham, John. *Strangers in the Land: Patterns of American Nativism, 1860–1925.* 2d ed. New Brunswick, N.J.: Rutgers University Press, 1988.

Hollandsworth, James G. Jr. *Pretense of Glory: The Life of General Nathaniel P. Banks.* Baton Rouge: Louisiana State University Press, 1998.

Holmes, David G. *Irish in Wisconsin.* Madison: The Wisconsin Historical Society Press, 2004.

Horowitz, Murray M. "Ben Butler and the Negro: 'Miracles Are Occurring.'" *Louisiana History* 17 (1976): 159–86.

Horton, James Oliver, and Lois E. Horton. *In Hope of Liberty: Culture, Community and Protest among Northern Free Blacks, 1700–1860.* New York: Oxford University Press, 1997.

Howard, Victor B. "The Civil War in Kentucky: The Slave Claims His Freedom." *Journal of Negro History* 67 (1982): 245–56.

———. *Black Liberation in Kentucky: Emancipation and Freedom, 1862–1884.* Lexington: University Press of Kentucky, 1983.

Ignatiev, Noel. *How the Irish Became White.* New York: Routledge, 1995.

Jenkins, Brian. *Fenians and Anglo-American Relations during Reconstruction.* Ithaca, N.Y.: Cornell University Press, 1969.

Joyce, William Leonard. *Editors and Ethnicity: A History of the Irish-American Press, 1848–1883.* New York: Arno Press, 1976.

Kaczorowski, Robert J. *The Politics of Judicial Interpretation: The Federal Courts, Department of Justice, and Civil Rights, 1866–1876.* 2d ed. 1985; New York: Fordham University Press, 2005.

———. "Revolutionary Constitutionalism in the Era of the Civil War and Reconstruction." *New York University Law Review* 61 (1986): 863–940.

———. "To Begin the Nation Anew: Congress, Citizenship, and Civil Rights after the Civil War." *American Historical Review* 92 (1987): 45–68.

Keller, Christian B. *Chancellorsville and the Germans: Nativism, Ethnicity, and Civil War Memory.* New York: Fordham University Press, 2007.

Kettner, James H. "The Development of American Citizenship in the Revolutionary Era: The Idea of Volitional Allegiance." *American Journal of Legal History* 18 (1974): 208–42.

———. "Subjects or Citizens? A Note on British Views Respecting the Legal Effects of American Independence." *Virginia Law Review* 62 (1976): 945–67.

———. *The Development of American Citizenship, 1608–1870.* Chapel Hill: University of North Carolina Press, 1978.

Koerting, Gayla. "For Law and Order: Joseph Holt, the Civil War, and the Judge Advocate General's Department." *Kentucky Historical Society Register* 97 (1999): 1–25.

Lawson, Melinda. *Patriot Fires: Forging a New American Nationalism in the Civil War North.* Lawrence: University Press of Kansas, 2002.

Lemann, Nicholas. *Redemption: The Last Battle of the Civil War.* New York: Farrar, Straus and Giroux, 2006.

Levine, Edward M. *The Irish and Irish Politicians.* Notre Dame, Ind.: University of Notre Dame Press, 1966.

Levine, Robert S. *Martin Delany, Frederick Douglass, and the Politics of Representative Identity.* Chapel Hill: University of North Carolina Press, 1997.

Litwack, Leon. *North of Slavery: The Negro in the Free States, 1790–1860.* Chicago: University of Chicago Press, 1961.

Lloyd, John P. "Revising the Republic: Popular Perceptions of Constitutional Change during the Civil War and Reconstruction." Ph.D. diss., Claremont Graduate University, 2000.

Lord, Robert H., John E. Sexton, and Edward T. Harrington. *History of the Archdiocese of Boston.* 3 vols. New York: Sheed and Ward, 1944.

Maltz, Earl M. "Fourteenth Amendment Concepts in the Antebellum Era." *American Journal of Legal History* 32 (1988): 305–46.

———. *Civil Rights, the Constitution, and Congress, 1863–1869.* Lawrence: University Press of Kansas, 1990.

Marable, Manning. *W.E.B. DuBois: Black Radical Democrat.* 2d ed. 1986; Boulder, Colo.: Paradigm, 2005.

Marshall, T. H. *Citizenship and Social Class.* 1950; repr. Concord, Mass.: Pluto Press, 1992.

McCaffrey, Lawrence J. "The Irish-American Dimension." In *The Irish in Chicago,* ed. Lawrence J. McCaffrey et al., 1–21. Urbana: University of Illinois Press, 1987.

McClintock, Megan J. "Civil War Pensions and the Reconstruction of Union Families." *Journal of American History* 83 (1996): 456–80.

McDonough, James Lee, and James Pickett Jones. *War So Terrible: Sherman and Atlanta.* New York: Norton, 1987.

McFeely, William S. *Frederick Douglass.* New York: Norton, 1991.

McPherson, James M. *Battle Cry of Freedom.* New York: Oxford University Press, 1988.

———. *Abraham Lincoln and the Second American Revolution.* New York: Oxford University Press, 1990.

———. *For Cause and Comrades: Why Men Fought in the Civil War.* New York: Oxford University Press, 1997.

Miller, Edward A., Jr. "Garland H. White, Black Army Chaplain." *Civil War History* 43 (1997): 201–18.

Miller, Kerby. *Emigrants and Exiles: Ireland and the Irish Exodus to North America.* New York: Oxford University Press, 1985.

Miller, Richard F. "The Trouble with Brahmins: Class and Ethnic Tensions in Massachusetts' 'Harvard Regiment.'" *New England Quarterly* 76 (2003): 38–72.

Mitchell, Reid. *Civil War Soldiers: Their Expectations and Their Experiences.* New York: Simon and Schuster, 1988.

Moore, Wayne D. *Constitutional Rights and Powers of the People.* Princeton, N.J.: Princeton University Press, 1996.

Morrow, Rising Lake. "The Early American Attitude toward the Doctrine of Expatriation." *American Journal of International Law* 26 (1932): 552–64.

———. "The Negotiation of the Anglo-American Treaty of 1870." *American Historical Review* 39 (1934): 663–81.

———. "Early American Attitude toward Naturalized Americans Abroad." *American Journal of International Law* 30 (1936): 647–63.

Moses, Wilson Jeremiah. *The Golden Age of Black Nationalism, 1850–1925.* 2d ed. 1978; New York: Oxford University Press, 1988.

Mulkern, John R. *The Know-Nothing Party in Massachusetts: The Rise and Fall of a People's Movement.* Boston: Northeastern University Press, 1990.

Nelson, Bruce. "Irish Americans, Irish Nationalism, and the 'Social' Question, 1916–1923." *boundary 2* 31 (2004) 147–78.

Nelson, William E. *The Fourteenth Amendment: From Political Principle to Judicial Doctrine.* Cambridge, Mass.: Harvard University Press, 1988.

Newman, John J. *American Naturalization Processes and Procedures 1790–1985*. Indianapolis: Indiana Historical Society, 1985.

Nieman, Donald G. *Promises to Keep: African-Americans and the Constitutional Order, 1776 to the Present*. New York: Oxford University Press, 1991.

Novak, William J. "The Legal Transformation of Citizenship in Nineteenth-Century America." In *The Democratic Experiment*, ed. Meg Jacobs et al., 84–119. Princeton, N.J.: Princeton University Press, 2003.

Ò Broin, Leon. *Fenian Fever: An Anglo-American Dilemma*. London: Chatto and Windus, 1971.

O'Connor, Thomas H. *Fitzpatrick's Boston 1846–1866: John Bernard Fitzpatrick, Third Bishop of Boston*. Boston: Northeastern University Press, 1984.

———. *The Boston Irish: A Political History*. Boston: Northeastern University Press, 1995.

———. *Civil War Boston: Home Front and Battlefield*. Boston: Northeastern University Press, 1997.

O'Donnell, Edward T. "'Though Not an Irishman': Henry George and the American Irish." *American Journal of Economics and Sociology* 56 (1997), 407–19.

O'Leary, Cecilia Elizabeth. *To Die For: The Paradox of American Patriotism*. Princeton, N.J.: Princeton University Press, 1999.

Paradis, James M. *Strike the Blow For Freedom: The 6th United States Colored Infantry in the Civil War*. Shippensburg, Penn.: White Mane Books, 1998.

Parker, Kunal M. "State, Citizenship, and Territory: The Legal Construction of Immigrants in Antebellum Massachusetts." *Law and History Review* 19 (2001): 583–643.

Peterson, Robert L., and John A. Hudson. "Foreign Recruitment for Union Forces." *Civil War History* 7 (1961): 176–89.

Pinheiro, John C. "'Religion without Restriction': Anti-Catholicism, All Mexico, and the Treaty of Guadalupe Hidalgo." *Journal of the Early Republic* 23 (2003): 69–96.

Quigley, David. *Second Founding: New York City, Reconstruction, and the Making of American Democracy*. New York: Hill and Wang, 2004.

Rael, Patrick. *Black Identity and Black Protest in the Antebellum North*. Chapel Hill: The University of North Carolina Press, 2002.

Ramold, Steven J. *Slaves, Sailors, Citizens: African Americans in the Union Navy*. DeKalb: Northern Illinois University Press, 2002.

Redkey, Edwin S. "Black Chaplains in the Union Army." *Civil War History* 33 (1987): 331–50.

Reid, Richard. "General Edward A. Wild and Civil War Discrimination." *Historical Journal of Massachusetts* 13 (1985): 14–29.

———. "USCT Veterans in Post-Civil War North Carolina." In *Black Soldiers in Blue: African American Troops in the Civil War Era*, ed. John David Smith, 391–421. Chapel Hill: University of North Carolina Press, 2002.

Richards, David A. J. *Conscience and the Constitution: History, Theory, and Law of the Reconstruction Amendments*. Princeton, N.J.: Princeton University Press, 1993.

Richardson, Heather Cox. *The Death of Reconstruction: Race, Labor, and Politics in the Post-Civil War North, 1865–1901*. Cambridge, Mass.: Harvard University Press, 2001.

Rodechko, James P. "An Irish-American Journalist and Catholicism: Patrick Ford of the Irish World." *Church History* 39 (1970): 524–40.

Rodrigue, John C. "The Freedmen's Bureau and Wage Labor in the Louisiana Sugar Region." In *The Freedmen's Bureau: Reconsiderations*, ed. Paul A. Cimbala and Randall M. Miller, 193–218. New York: Fordham University Press, 1999.

Roediger, David R. *The Wages of Whiteness*. Rev. ed. New York: Verso, 1999.

Ryan, Dennis P. *Beyond the Ballot Box: A Social History of the Boston Irish, 1845–1917*. Rutherford, N.J.: Fairleigh Dickinson University Press, 1983.

Schaar, John H. *Legitimacy in the Modern State*. New Brunswick, N.J.: Transaction Books, 1981.

Seraile, William. "The Struggle to Raise Regiments in New York State, 1861–1864." *New York Historical Society Quarterly* 58 (1974): 215–33.

Şewell, M. J. "Rebels or Revolutionaries? Irish-American Nationalism and American Diplomacy, 1865–1885." *Historical Journal* 29 (1986): 723–33.

Shaffer, Donald R. *After the Glory: The Struggles of Black Civil War Veterans*. Lawrence: University Press of Kansas, 2004.

Shankman, Arnold. "Black on Green: Afro-American Editors on Irish Independence, 1840–1921." *Phylon* 41 (1980): 284–99.

Shklar, Judith N. *American Citizenship: The Quest for Inclusion*. Cambridge, Mass.: Harvard University Press, 1991.

Siddali, Silvana R. *From Property to Person: Slavery and the Confiscation Acts, 1861–1862*. Baton Rouge: Louisiana State University Press, 2005.

Silbey, Joel H. *A Respectable Minority: The Democratic Party in the Civil War Era, 1860–1868*. New York: Norton, 1977.

Simpson, Brooks D. "Land and the Ballot: Securing the Fruits of Emancipation?" *Pennsylvania History* 60 (1993): 176–88.

Skerrett, Ellen. "The Catholic Dimension." In *The Irish in Chicago*, ed. Lawrence J. McCaffrey et al., 22–60. Urbana: University of Illinois Press, 1987.

Smith, John David. "The Recruitment of Negro Soldiers in Kentucky, 1863–1865." *Register of the Kentucky Historical Society* 72 (1974): 364–90.

Smith, Rogers M. *Civic Ideals: Conflicting Visions of Citizenship in U.S. History*. New Haven: Yale University Press, 1997.

Smith, Steven D. "History and Archaeology: General Edward Wild's African Brigade in the Siege of Charleston, South Carolina." *Civil War Regiments* 5 (1997): 21–70.

Snay, Mitchell. *Fenians, Freedmen, and Southern Whites: Race and Nationality in the Era of Reconstruction*. Baton Rouge: Louisiana State University Press, 2007.

Stansfield, George James. "A History of the Judge Advocate General's Department United States Army." *Military Affairs* 9 (1945): 219–37.

Steiner, Paul E. *Medical History of a Civil War Regiment: Disease in the Sixty-Fifth United States Colored Infantry*. Clayton, Miss.: Institute of Civil War Studies, 1977.

Sullivan, Barry. "Historical Reconstruction, Reconstruction History, and the Proper Scope of Section 1981." *Yale Law Journal* 98 (1989): 541–64.

Synnestvedt, Sig, ed. "The Earth Shook and Quivered." *Civil War Times Illustrated* 11, no. 12 (December 1972): 30–37.

Truslow, Marion Archer. "Peasants into Patriots: The New York Irish Brigade Recruits and Their Families in the Civil War Era, 1850–1890." Ph.D diss., New York University, 1994.

Von Frank, Albert J. *The Trials of Anthony Burns: Freedom and Slavery in Emerson's Boston*. Cambridge, Mass.: Harvard University Press, 1998.

Vorenberg, Michael. *Final Freedom: The Civil War, the Abolition of Slavery, and the Thirteenth Amendment*. New York: Cambridge University Press, 2001.

Waldrep, Christopher. *Roots of Disorder: Race and Criminal Justice in the American South, 1817–80*. Urbana: University of Illinois Press, 1998.

Walker, Mabel Gregory. *The Fenian Movement*. Colorado Springs, Colo.: Ralph Myles, 1969.

Wang, Xi. "The Making of Federal Enforcement Laws, 1870–1872." *Chicago-Kent Law Review* 70 (1995): 1013–58.

———. "Black Suffrage and the Redefinition of American Freedom, 1860–1870." *Cardoza Law Review* 17 (1996): 2153–2223.

Watson, Samuel J. "Religion and Combat Motivation in the Confederate Armies." *Journal of Military History* 58 (1994): 29–55.

Waugh, John C. *Reelecting Lincoln: The Battle for the 1864 Presidency*. New York: Crown, 1997.

Wert, Jeffrey D. "Camp William Penn and the Black Soldier." *Pennsylvania History* 46 (1979): 335–46.

Westwood, Howard C. "The Cause and Consequence of a Union Black Soldier's Mutiny and Execution." *Civil War History* 31 (1985): 222–36.

Williams, Chad. "Symbols of Freedom and Defeat: African-American Soldiers, White Southerners, and the Christmas Insurrection Scare of 1865." *Southern Historian* 21 (2000): 40–55.

Williams, William H. A. "Green Again: Irish-American Lace-Curtain Satire." *New Hibernia Review* 6 (2002): 9–24.

Wilson, Keith P. *Campfires of Freedom: The Camp Life of Black Soldiers during the Civil War.* Kent, Ohio: Kent State University Press, 2002.

Yacovone, Donald. "The Fifty-fourth Massachusetts Regiment, the Pay Crisis, and the 'Lincoln Despotism.'" In *Hope and Glory: Essays on the Legacy of the Fifty-Fourth Massachusetts Regiment,* ed. Martin H. Blatt, Thomas J. Brown, and Donald Yacovone, 35–51. Amherst: University of Massachusetts Press, 2001.

Zalimas, Robert J., Jr. "A Disturbance in the City: Black and White Soldiers in Postwar Charleston." In *Black Soldiers in Blue: African American Troops in the Civil War Era,* ed. John David Smith, 361–90. Chapel Hill: University of North Carolina Press, 2002.

Index

Page numbers in italics refer to illustrations